Conformity and Deviation

Conformity and Deviation

Edited by
IRWIN A. BERG and BERNARD M. BASS
Louisiana State University

Harper & Brothers

Publishers, New York

Contents

Preface

Back about 1700, William Penn wrote in "Some Fruits of Solitude": "It is reasonable to concur where conscience does not forbid a compliance; for conformity is at least a civil virtue. But we should only press it in necessaries, the rest may prove a snare and a temptation to break society. But above all, it is a weakness in Religion and Government, where it is carried to things of an indifferent nature. . . . Liberty is always the price of it. Such conformists have little to boast of, and therefore the less reason to reproach others that have more latitude."

Thus concern with conformity is not new on the American scene. What is new is the ever-growing body of experimental evidence on the subject, a direct result of the pioneering work of Solomon Asch and Muzafer Sherif. Accordingly, a symposium on conformity and deviation was organized with the aim of presenting the latest theoretical and experimental contributions of leaders in this area of research, including pioneers Asch and Sherif. The symposium was held at Louisiana State University in March, 1960, and the present book is the result. This collection of hitherto unpublished papers includes the most recent research developments in the social psychological facets of conformity and deviation as a matter of course and, as a matter of increasing significance, certain clinical-experimental investigations as well.

In large part, this assembly of social scientists was made possible by the financial support of the Louisiana State Department of Hospitals. It is a pleasure, therefore, to thank Mr. Charles Rosenblum, Director of the Department of Hospitals, Mr. E. Roy Rogillio, Assistant Director of the Department, and Mr. Winborn E. Davis, Director of Training and Research in the Department. The present symposium is but one product of their concern with quality in professional training.

In preparing the final manuscript copy, a great deal of typing and even retyping was necessary. The unfailing good humor of Mrs. Vera M. Foil and Mrs. Floy E. Brown, who completed the typescript, made this task far less onerous than it ordinarily would have been. Also to be thanked heartily are Mrs. Sylvia T. Berg, who organized the Author Index, and Mrs. Jacqueline Nacewski, for the Subject Index.

IRWIN A. BERG

BERNARD M. BASS

Baton Rouge, Louisiana

Conformity and Deviation

CHAPTER 1

Conformity, Resistance, and Conversion

ROBERT R. BLAKE and JANE SRYGLEY MOUTON

The University of Texas

Conformity is one of the significient issues of social psychology. By comparison with other problem areas, results are striking, partly because they *are* consistent, with findings from one study dovetailing with those from others. What better place to begin than with a review of these investigations, delineating aspects which have been investigated and suggesting problems that merit further investigation.

Conformity, resistance, and conversion share basic psychological processes in common, based on the fact that an individual requires a stable framework, including salient and firm reference points, in order to orient himself and to regulate his interactions with others (Helson, 1955; Sherif, 1936). This framework consists of external and internal anchorages available to the individual whether he is aware of them or not. With an acceptable framework he can *resist* giving or accepting information that is inconsistent with that framework or that requires him to relinquish it. In the absence of a stable framework he actively seeks to establish one through his own strivings by making use of significant and relevant information provided within the context of interaction. By controlling the amount and kind of information available as framework for orientation, he can be led

1

to embrace *conforming* attitudes which are entirely foreign to earlier ways of thinking. Conversion can be produced by demonstrating the inadequacy of a presently accepted frame of reference and then introducing another which is more satisfactory. Under optimal conditions such shifts in attitudes, opinions, understandings, and convictions can be brought about without a person even recognizing that his behavior has been subjected to subtle influences. Techniques of persuasion and other forms of exerting influence are based on the use of such strategies and tactics.

RESTRICTIONS.   Conformity, resistance, and conversion have been evaluated in a number of disciplines. Since the studies are not always acceptable in terms of systematic formulation or experimental design, some have been omitted. It is desirable to specify the kinds of investigations summarized here. Studies employed are those where a measurable discrepancy is possible between the opinions, actions, or judgments that a person would give when he is alone and the opinions, actions, or judgments he gives when others present in the situation react in a different manner. An example is an individual who comes into a social situation and finds his actions, judgments, or opinions to be different from those of others. Then he is confronted by a dilemma. He can either conform by shifting his behavior so that it corresponds more closely with that of others, or he can resist by maintaining his personal position which is to some degree deviant from that of the others. The average or typical behavior of others in the situation constitutes the framework within which the critical subject is required to adjust. Whether he conforms, deviates, or resists can then be determined. Also included are studies in which the aftereffects of conformity pressures are measured in another later situation, when the pressures intended to produce conformity have been relieved. Influence, in the direction of the conformity pressures which remain, constitutes evidence of *conversion*.

Excluded are anthropological reports in which conformity, resistance, or conversion aspects of behavior have been noted but have not been subjected to experimental analysis. Also excluded are investigations of audiences or meetings of larger assemblages where acceptance of or resistance to influence is not from direct interaction among those composing the situation. Investigations dealing with shifts in reaction from knowledge or awareness of norms *attributed* by the experimenter to groups whose members are not psychologically present also are not reported. Influence aspects of reference group behavior contain variables different from those where the influence is exerted under face-to-face conditions, and inclusion of such studies would unduly increase the complexity of this report. Programmatic research reports and theoretical discussions of various aspects of the problem are available in a number of other sources (Asch, 1952; Blake, 1958; Blake & Helson, 1956; Cohen, 1958; Festinger, 1953; French, 1956; Hoffman, 1953; Hollander, 1958; Luchins & Luchins, 1955a; Luchins & Luchins, 1955b; Mausner, 1955; Sherif, 1935; Steiner & Peters, 1958).

The present chapter is divided into four main parts. The first part presents a description of the experimental situations used to study conformity, resistance, and conversion. A review of studies in which factors associated with conformity behavior are evaluated is presented in the second section. Next, studies are reviewed which are concerned with factors associated with conversion behavior. In the final part, suggestions are offered concerning future research possibilities and problems which if undertaken could make substantial contributions to the understanding of conformity and conversion behavior.

Experimental Situations Used to Study Conformity, Resistance, and Conversion

Conditions employed to study conformity, resistance, and conversion include stimulus materials, the context or background condition in which pressures are exerted on the critical subject, and personal dimensions used to assess the contribution of individual differences to conformity and conversion behavior. Study of these conditions requires an examination also of the methods of measuring the impact of conformity pressures on the critical subject.

MATERIALS AND INSTRUCTIONS. One of the conditions for evaluating conformity, resistance, or conversion is that there be materials which constitute the task to which the responses of individuals constitute adjustments. In the autokinetic situation investigated by Sherif (1935), for example, the task was to judge the amount of movement of a pinpoint of light exposed in the darkened room. Straight lines on a white background constitute the materials in the Asch (1951) problem with instructions to the subject to select from among the several lines, each of different length, the one which matches the standard. Another kind of stimulus material is the case study (Festinger & Thibaut, 1951). A brief description of a problem is given with instructions indicating that the task is to choose the most desirable alternative for the achievement of some designated results, from among the several given. Other examples of materials with instructions that identify for the subject the manner in which he should react to them are counting metronome clicks, solving arithmetic problems, or judging attitude statements (Blake, Helson, & Mouton, 1956). Instructions in the first two cases require identifying the correct answer. In the latter case the subject indicates his own opinion with respect to the statement. Behavior in prohibition situations also contains important implications for conformity, resistance, and conversion. An example is a pedestrian approaching a stop light (Lefkowitz, Blake, & Mouton, 1955) or a person moving toward the entrance of a building where he finds a sign forbidding further progress (Freed, Chandler, Mouton, & Blake, 1955). One of the necessary conditions for studying conformity, resistance, or conversion, therefore, is that of identifying the specific materials and the orientation of a subject regarding an appropriate adjustment to them.

In over half of the studies reviewed, tasks requiring either judgments of a perceptual character or expressions of opinions were employed as stimulus materials in investigating shifting of personal behavior. Attitudes or preferences were asked for in the majority of the other studies. These studies also included responses given to factual or logical materials or responses where the act investigated was designated by a direct request or an explicit prohibition.

Emphasis has been placed on the selection of materials with certain common characteristics. One is that the responses elicited are relatively simple and easily measured. Most frequently used are simple judgments of physical measurements or attitude preferences given in terms of a numerical scale. They are not tasks which arouse the kind of behavior that is ordinarily subject to conformity or conversion pressures. Another characteristic of stimulus materials is that they frequently provoke little intrinsic interest. The situations often have a quality of artificiality which makes difficult the generalizing of conclusions for interpreting reactions in more vital and lifelike situations. The value of research in the conformity-resistance-conversion area can be increased through the use of situations that elicit more personally significant and important dimensions of behavior.

FRAMEWORK OR SOCIAL BACKGROUND. Beyond stimulus materials and instructions for reacting to them, other properties of the situation contribute to determining the particular adjustment which occurs. The effect of context or framework in modifying the response that designated stimulus materials produce is well known in sensory and perceptual work. The analogue of context or framework in the social situation is provided through the social background which consists of reactions to the same or comparable stimulus materials by others. Reactions by group members or by a single other individual, therefore, constitute a significant component of context or framework for the critical subject. The importance of social context in shifting adjustment is most clearly evident when the response dictated by the stimulus material itself would produce a discrepancy between the individual's own adjustments and the adjustments of others.

Social backgrounds may vary from simple awareness of the reactions by others to direct efforts by others to exert influence on the critical subject. An example of the latter is the judging situation where others present give uniformly incorrect reports prior to the responses of the critical subject. If he then gives the response which constitutes the correct adjustment to the stimulus material, his adjustment is different from that of others. Resolution of the contradiction by conforming to the social background provides an index to conformity, whereas resolution through a response which is consistent with the stimulus material provides an index of deviation from or resistance to the influence exerted by others. In some few studies the discrepancy between the subjects' private response and those by others in the situation is "spontaneous" or "natural." Over half of the experiments utilize a social background in which the reports of instructed subjects, who actually are in the situation, are controlled by the experimenter. Other reports employ various methods of background simulation which allows the experimenter to control unwanted variations in the behavior of persons used to produce conformity pressures. The simulated group where the responses of others are "heard" by means of tape recordings is one such procedure. The panel-of-lights technique where the reactions of others are indicated on a board of lights is another. Still another version of inducing influence involves individual responses being given in private and collected by the experimenter. He then reports to subjects either the actual or a fictitious norm representing the responses of others or instructs the subject how to shift his behavior in line with others' performance.

An example of direct influence which is more "real" to the subjects, but which lacks experimenter control, is the situation where group members are expected to agree on a single option from among a set of alternatives. Those who hold divergent views may be recipients of direct influence from others. Influence exerted usually is in the direction of converting the deviant member's point of view. Interaction occurs by means of actual discussion, or through the use of notes, ballots, or votes passed among members.

Influences exerted are not of an extreme emergency or life and death character. The interaction often is no more than the fact that the subject simply hears how others are adjusting to the situation. Relatively little involvement is aroused. The experience is frequently of a laboratory nature in which the fact of being in an experimental situation can serve to distort responses. In order to more closely approximate the life conditions of conformity, resistance, and conversion it will be necessary to design experimental situations where the maintenance of resistance to conformity pressures places an individual in jeopardy of relinquishing valued status, prestige, or membership, or where conversion is a means toward the attainment of important utilitarian objectives.

PROPERTIES OF THE PERSON. Another set of factors associated with conformity, resistance, and conversion is associated with the "state of the person" at a particular time. Such factors can be identified through reference to individual differences in previous experience, personality characteristics, or physiological states. For example, ascendant, dominant, or aggressive persons are more resistant to conformity pressures or conversion influences than are submissive, compliant, or docile individuals. As contrasted with a novice, a specialist in dealing with a certain type of materials is more resistant to shifting his reactions toward those who are attempting to influence him. The contribution of physiological factors in determining adjustment can be seen in reactions to a prohibition against drinking while the individual is experiencing intense thirst as contrasted with his behavior when satiated. Under the former condition he violates a prohibition against drinking more frequently than under conditions of satiation. The preceding examples, then, are indications of the manner in which properties of the person at a particular time contribute in determining adjustment in a situation designed to extract conformity or conversion. Investigations of experimentally induced individual differences in acceptance of conformity pressures related to properties of the person include experimentally created prior experiences such as those of success or failure on a prior task, and measures of induced physiological states such as anxiety, sleep deprivation, or thirst. Indices of psychological experiences subsequent to behavior in the pressure situation constitute the most popular method of assessing individual differences. Measures range from specially constructed scales to the better known indices. Most tests have been used only once or twice with the result that relatively little direct comparison between experimental findings is possible. Frequently the scales have no known validity. In addition, results from the better known tests, such as the MMPI, are contradictory.

Thus, demonstrating a relationship between personal characteristics and conformity behavior is made difficult because of measuring-scale imperfections.

INDICES USED TO EVALUATE CONFORMITY, RESISTANCE, AND CONVERSION. Measures of conformity, resistance, and conversion have included indices based on progressive changes with trials within the group situations, with shifts in response evaluated as a function of differences between trials; change scores between pregroup and group conditions; deviation from correct or modal responses; discrepancy between others' and subject's responses; differences between groups in terms of average scores and magnitude of variability; and action criteria. However, assessing the impact of the pressure situation on behavior at a later time under "alone" conditions has been found in only a few studies.

Psychological Dimensions of Conformity and Resistance

Many factors related to conformity and resistance can be delineated by examining what happens when conformity pressures created by others in the situation have been demonstrated to shift a person's reaction away from what he would do alone or privately.

CONFORMITY BEHAVIOR AND THE NATURE OF THE MATERIALS EMPLOYED. Increasing or decreasing a person's readiness to conform in the presence of others who give reactions different from his own due to the nature of the task and the conditions of presentation has been shown to be related to four considerations. One is the nature of the task itself (Crutchfield, 1955; Festinger & Thibaut, 1951; Helson, Blake, & Mouton, 1958a). Materials that have been studied range from questions that have literal answers, through social attitudes, to personal preferences for which the existence of "correct" responses cannot be presumed. Factually anchored materials, such as items of information and clear-cut perceptual judgments, which have a "correct" or objective answer, appear to be most resistant to change from conformity pressures. For these types of items individuals find it relatively easier to repudiate the false reports of others than to shift away from subjectively certain "truth." By comparison, reactions that appear more subject to influence are those which are based on materials that derive validity from a social frame of reference, such as attitudes toward social problems. The propriety of this type of reaction is more likely to be judged in terms of what other people say or think. Also, it would seem that those materials which evoke personal preferences are least influenced by social pressures. These materials appear to be anchored in neither factual nor social frames of reference, but rather, derive their meaningfulness from subjective and private considerations.

For a given task, however, increases in susceptibility to conformity presures have been demonstrated to be related to increases in the difficulty of the materials presented (Asch, 1956; Berenda, 1950; Blake, Helson & Mouton, 1956; Caylor, 1957; Coleman, Blake, & Mouton, 1958; Fisher, Williams, & Lubin, 1957; Goldberg & Lubin, 1957; Kelley & Lamb, 1957; Weiner, 1956; Weiner, Carpenter, & Carpenter, 1956). Difficulty has been assessed under alone or private conditions in terms of number of correct responses to an item, degree of stimulus ambiguity or similarity to responses obtained from other naive subjects, and from the degree of certainty expressed by subjects when giving a judgment. These results indicate that if an individual is certain of the correct answer, he is more able to resist conformity pressures. Conformity is more frequent when the person is unfamiliar with the correct answer.

A related aspect to difficulty of judging an item is one in which the ease of discrimination has been varied by changing the conditions of presentation (Deutsch & Gerard, 1955; Luchins, 1944; Raven & Rietsema, 1957). Increased conformity occurs as the subject is prevented from employing an objective frame of reference in giving his judgments.

The orientation of an individual to the task is important in determining whether he will succumb to conformity pressures (Blake, Mouton, & Hain, 1956; Freed *et al.*, 1955; Rosenbaum, 1956). The greater the strength of command the greater the susceptibility to conformity pressures created by others in the situation who comply. A decrease in susceptibility as a function of compellingness of request strength occurs when conformity pressures are created by a person who refuses to comply.

In summary, conformity behavior increases when it is necessary for an individual to rely more heavily on the responses of others in making his own adjustment. Attitudes are more easily shifted than are reactions to factual or logical items, probably because attitudes are more social in character. Increasing the degree of difficulty of items, reducing external cues which provide objective information, and increasing the strength of the command in the direction of the compliant behavior all serve to increase the effectiveness of conformity pressures in shifting a person's response.

BACKGROUND CONDITIONS RELATED TO THE EXERTION OF CONFORMITY PRESSURES. Knowledge of reactions of others can influence behavior in the conformity direction. Susceptibility exerted in this manner is not limited to any particular kind of task, but is found for a wide variety of tasks including the expression of opinions and attitudes (Duncker, 1938; Gordon, 1952; Helson, Blake, Mouton, & Olmstead, 1956; Horwitz, Piana, Goldman, & Lee, 1955; Wheeler & Jordan, 1929), violation of prohibitions and acceptance of requests (Barch, Trumbo, & Nangle, 1957; Blake, Berkowitz, Bellamy, & Mouton, 1956; Blake, Helson, & Mouton, 1956; Freed *et al.,* 1955; Grosser, Polansky, & Lippitt, 1951; Rosenbaum, 1956; Rosenbaum & Blake, 1955; Schachter & Hall, 1952) and reactions to perceptual, judgmental and factual materials (Asch, 1951; Blake & Brehm, 1954; Clark, 1916; McConnell & Blake, 1953; Musterberg, 1950; Olmstead & Blake, 1955; Schonbar, 1945; Sherif, 1935).

Various additional features of the social context have been demonstrated to increase or decrease susceptibility to conformity pressures. The size of the group, for example, is a critical factor (Asch, 1951; Goldberg, 1954; Hare, 1952; Helson, 1948; Kidd, 1958; Luchins & Luchins, 1955a; Schroder & Hunt, 1958; Ziller & Behringer, 1958). Progressive increases in shifting occur for objective type tasks when the others who are present increase in number from one, to two, to three, in addition to the subject. There is little or no evidence that an additional number of participants beyond three contributes further influence in the direction of shifting the critical subject's response. For other types of materials such as attitude items and ambiguous perceptual judgments, the addition of more than one person to the background appears to produce little increased effect.

Findings are clear with respect to degree of unanimity among others present (Asch, 1956; Hardy, 1957; Mouton, Blake, & Olmstead, 1956). Conformity influences are decreased significantly when other members are not in unanimous agreement. The presence of a single ally giving the correct answer seems to be sufficient to remove, or at least significantly reduce, the pressure effects from the majority without regard for its absolute size, particularly for objective task material.

Degree of discrepancy between the reports by others and the position the subject would take if he were not exposed to pressures is related to conformity, from at least two points of view (Asch, 1956; Blake, Helson, & Mouton, 1956; Festinger, Gerard, Hymovitch, Kelley, & Raven, 1952; Goldberg, 1954; Harvey, Kelley, & Shapiro, 1957; Harvey & Rutherford, 1958; Helson *et al.*, 1958a; Jenness, 1932, Mouton *et al.*, 1956; Olmstead & Blake, 1955; Whittaker, 1958; Weiner, 1956). On one hand subjects are influenced more toward agreement when the discrepancy is small than when it is large. On the other hand, for socially anchored materials, more subjects are influenced to shift *away* from their alone positions, though not necessarily into full agreement with others, when the magnitude of discrepancy is *large* than when it is *small*.

Other studies have related differences in susceptibility to conformity pressures to differences in characteristics of the persons creating the influence relative to the same characteristics of the naive subject. Age differences between the critical subject and others present in the situation are found to be important to conformity behavior (Berenda, 1950; Duncker, 1938; Jackson & Saltzstein, 1958). Among children, greater influence is exerted on children by other children than by adults, and greater influence is exerted on younger children by older children than on older children by younger ones. When acquaintance based on prior social interaction is the variable, the susceptibility to conformity pressures created by such acquaintances is greater than conformity pressures created by strangers (Harvey *et al.*, 1957; Kidd, 1958; Lambert & Lowy, 1957).

Greater conformity influences are exerted when the other person in the situation has a status higher than that of the subject (Cole, 1955; Lefkowitz *et al.*, 1955; Mausner, 1953; Mausner, 1954a; Mausner, 1954b; Mausner & Bloch, 1957; Raven & French, 1958). This is found true regardless of the manner in which status is created, whether by the attribution through experimenter's remarks of differences in status between the critical subject and others, by varying the perceived characteristics of the other person present in the situation, or by varying the relative success or failure of the accomplice on the same task performed by the critical subject.

Experiments designed to evaluate the role of homogeneity among members regarding their degree of equality in ability, skill, and knowledge generally have failed to demonstrate a relationship between this factor and susceptibility to conformity pressure (Festinger *et al.*, 1952; Festinger & Thibaut, 1951; Gerard, 1954). Inability to link the homogeneity factor to conformity pressures in all probability is related to the superficial manner in which homogeneity has been varied. For the most part variations in homogeneity have not involved actual differences among participants but have been based on similarities and differences attributed to strangers by the experimenter.

Differences have also been found related to both sex of the subject relative to others in the situation (Luchins & Luchins, 1955a) and religious affiliation of others in the situation relative to the subject (Bray, 1950). Anonymity of the subject and commitment by the subject concerning his response are factors which have opposite effects on individual reactions in a situation designed to exert conformity pressures. Individuals are less influenced to accept group influences when acting under conditions of personal anonymity than when the situation requires them to reveal personal identity (Asch, 1956; Deutsch & Gerard, 1955; Mouton *et al.*, 1956). In addition, when an individual makes a definite commitment to a position prior to receiving conformity pressures to change, he maintains his position more strongly than when the conditions do not require a prior commitment. Furthermore, the degree of publicness in the commitment is found to be related positively to the degree of resistance to influence (Deutsch & Gerard, 1955; Fisher, Rubenstein, & Freeman, 1956).

Variations in experiences prior to social interaction have been related to susceptibility to influence. Where prior experience with other members results in feelings of success on a group task, the same participants judging together in a later situation, in which conformity pressures are exerted, are found to be more susceptible than are participants whose initial experience together produces feelings of failure (Kidd & Campbell, 1955). Conformity pressures exerted on members who are interacting under the participatory style of leadership or group-centered approach to teaching produce a greater shifting of opinion than conformity pressures exerted on persons who participate under either the supervisory style of leadership, where the leader's effort is limited to that of keeping the group on the task, or the leader-centered classroom behavior of a teacher (Bovard, 1951; Hare, 1953; McKeachie, 1954; Maier & Solem, 1952; Preston & Heintz, 1959).

Studies of the influence of differences in attractiveness of the group for members are in agreement (Back, 1951; Berkowitz, 1957b; Dittes & Kelley, 1956; Festinger *et al.*, 1952; Gerard, 1954; Grosser *et al.*, 1951; Jackson & Saltzstein, 1958; Kelley & Shapiro, 1954; Schachter, Ellertson, McBride, & Gregory, 1951; Thibaut & Strickland, 1956). They show that participants in high cohesion groups are more susceptible to conformity pressures than are subjects whose membership is in groups characterized by low cohesion. The conditions of group organization in which members are attractive to one another, in other words, creates a situation where members are more prepared to accept influence from one another. There also is some evidence that perceived dependency on another for attaining a goal is a significant factor increasing susceptibility to influence in a designated direction (Berkowitz, 1957a).

Variations in pressures toward uniformity, created through differences in experimenter's remarks or instructions, tend to be related to differences in shifting of response under conformity producing conditions (Blake, Mouton, & Olmstead, 1956; Brehm & Festinger, 1957; Deutsch & Gerard, 1955; Festinger *et al.*, 1952; Festinger & Thibaut, 1951; Gerard, 1953; Jones, Wells, & Torrey, 1958). One aspect of the situation that has been varied includes the experimenter's giving instructions regarding the degree of unanimity desired. A request for a unanimous decision or indications that there is a "correct" answer to the problem also increases conformity. Instructions which indicate that a second discussion with experts present will follow the first experimental situation are associated with increased conformity. Finally, emphasis on rewards for good performance and emphasis on the importance of accuracy, or penalties for mistakes, also have been found to be related to increased susceptibility.

Numerous aspects of the social context in which conformity pressures have been created, then, are related to the degree of susceptibility to such pressures. By varying such features as characteristics of other members relative to the individual, the size, degree of unanimity, degree of discrepancy and degree of attractiveness of others in the situation, conformity pressures can be increased or decreased. In *addition,* conditions of response such as whether acting in public or in private, with or without prior commitment, and under instructions which emphasize rewards and penalties also are features of the social context which have been demonstrated to be significant in producing variations in conformity behavior.

PSYCHOLOGICAL AND PHYSIOLOGICAL PROPERTIES OF THE PERSON. Important in determining adjustment in a conformity producing situation are personal characteristics of the subject. Personal characteristics may be described by either of several kinds of measures. One way in which personal differences have been characterized is in terms of amount or type of prior experience. Other ways involve measuring psychological characteristics and physiological states.

Amount of prior experience with the task without the experience being evaluated as good, poor, or indifferent, does not appear to be related to susceptibility to conformity of failure on the task, which later is subjected to conformity pressures (Goldberg, 1954). A prior individual experience of failure on the task, which later is subjected to conformity pressures, on the other hand, consistently is found to render an individual less resistant to such pressures, and prior experience of success renders individuals more able to resist such pressures (Blake, Helson, & Mouton, 1956; Harvey & Rutherford, 1958; Keisler, 1956; Kelman, 1950; Mausner & Bloch, 1957; Schroder & Hunt, 1958). A direct correlation also is reported between the degree of experimentally produced anxiety experienced prior to the pressure situation and susceptibility to social pressure, with subjects experiencing the greatest degree of anxiety being least resistant to effects from conformity pressures (Sherif & Harvey, 1952).

Properties of a prior task on which an accomplice gives a false response are found to be related to the degree of susceptibility of the individual to conformity pressures exerted by the same confederate on a later different task. When the preliminary series consists of unclear stimulus materials and responses by the confederate are consistent with features in the stimulus materials, greater conformity in the later series occurs than when the materials are clear and the response by the confederate is experienced as inconsistent with features in the preliminary task (Luchins, 1944; Luchins, 1945; Luchins & Luchins, 1955b). Pretraining with reward for incorrect responses is shown to render a person more susceptible to social pressure in the conformity producing situation (Crutchfield, 1955; Luchins, 1944; Luchins & Luchins, 1955b; McQueen, 1957; Scott, 1957).

The effect of personality differences related to prior experiences has been approached in a number of studies through evaluating the effects of childhood experiences on differences in susceptibility to conformity pressures. Persons who conform more in a pressure situation can be characterized as perceiving their parents as harsh, punitive, restricting, and rejecting and are classified as late in independence training (Krebs, 1958; Mussen & Kagan, 1958). Greater susceptibility to conform with ethical standards under social influence conditions is found for students classified in the dominant life style (McQueen, 1957).

Five ways of describing physiological characteristics of the person have been related to susceptibility to conformity pressures. They include the sex of the subjects, age differences, sleep deprivation, food preferences, and degree of anxiety. While sex and age are classified here as physiological indices, the interpretation that differences are due to the physiological factor may not be appropriate since results obtained may be due to other variables such as role expectancy or amount of experience which are related to but not "caused by" the physiological factor varied. There is some evidence that men may be more resistant to social pressures than women (Burtt, 1920; Crutchfield, 1955; Jenness, 1932; Kirkpatrick, 1936). The most appropriate conclusion with respect to differential susceptibility to conformity effects by men and women would seem to be that differences if present are not of an extreme character. With respect to age, it is consistently found that younger people are more responsive to social pressures than are older individuals (Berenda, 1950; Duncker, 1938; Luchins & Luchins, 1955a). In one study it is reported that loss of sleep renders a person more susceptible to social pressures (Fisher & Rubenstein, 1956), while another demonstrates that under conditions of moderate thirst violation of a sign prohibiting drinking is significantly influenced by a confederate (Kimbrell & Blake, 1958). Several studies report that shifts toward conformity pressures are accompanied by decrements in the amount of anxiety shown by the subject in the pressure situation (Hoffman, 1957; Lawson & Stagner, 1957). With respect to food preferences, it is found that when preferences are definite the individual is more resistant to change as a function of social pressures (Marinho, 1942).

Numerous psychological characteristics of subjects differing in susceptibility to conformity pressures have been investigated. Individual differences on standard personality measures have been related to frequency of shifting under social influence conditions. Results show that those who are more susceptible to conformity pressures are more likely to be submissive (Beloff, 1958; Berenda, 1950; Bray, 1950; Helson et al., 1956; Jenness, 1932; Kelman, 1950; Mouton et al., 1956), low in self-confidence (Bray, 1950; Kelman, 1950), show less nervous tension (Beloff, 1958; Bray 1950; Kelman, 1950), score higher on authoritarian scales (Beloff, 1958; Crutchfield, 1955; Hardy, 1957; Millon & Simkins, 1957; Wells, Weinert, & Rubel, 1956), be less intelligent (Berenda, 1950; Crutchfield, 1951; Crutchfield, 1953; Fisher, Rubinstein, & Freeman, 1956; Jenness, 1932; Nakamura, 1958), less original (Barron, 1955; Crutchfield, 1951), and to score on the simplicity end of the dimension of the complexity-simplicity scale (Barron, 1953; Crutchfield, 1951). They are more likely to be characterized as low in need achievement(Krebs, 1958; Samelson, 1957), high in need for social approval (Moeller & Applezweig, 1957), conventional in values (Beloff, 1958) and to have greater inner conformity needs (Hoffman, 1957). In addition, they show greater dependence on the perceptual field and are more compliant in social situations (Helson et al., 1958; Jacubczak & Walters, 1958; Linton, 1955; Rosner, 1957; Weiner, Carpenter, & Carpenter, 1956). By comparison with subjects classified as neurotic, those described as normal show more conforming tendencies in the pressure situation (Cervin, 1955; Crutchfield, 1953; Didato, 1955; Goldberg, Hunt, Cohen, & Meadow, 1954; Levine, Laffal, Berkowitz, Lindemann, & Drevdahl, 1954; Spohn, 1956). Differences in scores on projective measures and differences in self-ratings on adjective check lists are found for groups selected to represent extremes in susceptibility to social influence, but results obtained are not subject to brief summary (Barron, 1952; Crutchfield, 1951; Crutchfield, 1953; Crutchfield 1955; Hardy, 1957; Hoffman, 1953; Linton, 1954). Finally, in several investigations it has been reported that on an individual-by-individual basis conformity tendencies are *general* across several tasks administered under conditions of social contradiction, thus showing personal consistency to conformity behavior (Asch, 1956; Blake, Helson, & Mouton, 1956; Crutchfield, 1955; Helson *et al.*, 1956; Luchins, 1955a; Rosner, 1957).

The nature of the task, the social situation in which a critical subject's adjustment is evaluated, and individual personality characteristics all are of demonstrated importance in determining whether or not conformity pressures will be accepted or resisted. These three factors do not act in isolation of one another, however, but rather the final outcome is a function of interactions among factors.

Psychological Dimensions of Conversion Behavior

Conversion has received far less attention in research studies than has conformity behavior. The result is that only a limited picture can be drawn with respect to the psychological factors associated with conversion behavior. A simple operational way of identifying conversion is in terms of the aftereffects remaining from conformity pressures when the conformity pressures have been relieved. An example of the research design through which degree of conversion can be assessed follows. First, individual performance is evaluated under alone conditions. Next, conformity pressures are exerted to shift responses away from those under alone conditions. Then, the subject's behavior under alone, postpressure conditions is measured at some later time. Conversion is evident when performance in the postpressure situation is different from performance in the prepressure situation in the direction of the divergent reports others gave in the conformity situation.

Results are generally consistent in showing that responses altered due to social pressures persist into the future and are reflected in the person's behavior under alone or private conditions (Bovard, 1948; Rohrer, Baron, Hoffman, & Swander, 1954; Schachter & Hall, 1952; Schonbar, 1945; Sherif, 1937). This conclusion is limited, however, by the intensity of one's initial position or preference (Duncker, 1938; Gerard, 1954; Marinho, 1942). The general rule is that the more indefinite one's initial position, the greater the impact of the social situation and the greater the conversion effect. Also suggestive is the finding that the longer one is resistant to altering his position under conditions of social pressure, the longer is the altered position retained in the postpressure situation (Schonbar, 1945).

Although increased susceptibility to pressure in the conformity situation is shown to be related to higher inner conformity needs of subjects, it appears that those lower in inner conformity needs are more likely to show increased conversion effects at a later time (Hoffman, 1957). Properties of the social context that have been varied and related to conversion behavior include the unanimity of responses by others and whether or not naive subjects had a prior history of interaction in a leader-centered as contrasted with a group-centered atmosphere. Persons exposed to unanimous in contrast to near unanimous divergent responses of others in the conformity situation are more likely to demonstrate conversion behavior (Bennett, 1952; Hardy, 1957). In addition, if the prior interaction of the group in which conformity pressures are exerted is characterized by leader-centered behavior, rather than group-centered interaction, then greater conversion is to be expected (McKeachie, 1954).

Implications of Research

Individuals appear to be more susceptible to conformity pressures when expressing social opinions and ideological attitudes and when dealing with abstractions that are not rooted in concrete experience than when they are dealing with factual materials with which they are well acquainted or with personal preferences. Regardless of the materials being dealt with, however, increases in susceptibility appear when an individual is uncertain as to his own beliefs, uninformed with respect to the facts of the situation, or when objective cues that could aid him in maintaining his orientation to the situation are reduced or eliminated. Then he distrusts himself and he can be influenced by others or by "leading" questions. Available experimental evidence can be interpreted as demonstrating the key importance in susceptibility and conversion of inadequate individual knowledge and understanding. An important inference is that *resistance* to conformity pressures can be heightened by insuring that an individual is well informed, educated with respect to facts and their implications, opinions, etc.

Tendencies toward conformity and conversion are heightened when an individual is with others, at least three in number, where the others are in uniform agreement and where their reactions represent only small departures from the position believed by the individual to represent his own convictions. If the others present are personally acquainted with the individual, and are persons whom he respects, additional conformity pressures are created. Furthermore, if the individual is required to act in his own name and the situation is such that he is not required to commit himself to a position prior to the period when the conformity pressure is applied, greater influence in the conformity direction can be exercised. If the group is led according to a permissive group-centered approach, if members are dependent on one another to obtain significant goals, if the situation calls for unanimous agreement among members, and if the group is cohesive, then the situation is favorable for arousing conformity attitudes.

To create these conditions in a life, as contrasted with a laboratory situation, it would be necessary to compose groups by careful selection in order to insure friendliness and responsibility among members, with those other than the person on whom pressures are to be applied to be in unanimous agreement and supporting a position not greatly divergent from the position held by the critical person himself.

It would appear that the best single prescription for enabling an individual to resist conformity pressures is intimate acquaintance with and thorough understanding of the issues involved. Though it is yet to be demonstrated experimentally, it also is probable that an individual would be aided in maintaining independence through acquaintance with an understanding of the psychological forces of the kind characterized here. If not understood, they can operate "silently" to render an individual uncertain of himself and therefore ready to follow others or to capitulate to an interrogator.

From a personality angle, the kind of individual who is the least able to resist conformity pressures, and probably interrogation pressures as well, is: submissive, lacking in self-confidence, less intelligent, lacking in originality, authoritarian-minded, lacking in achievement motivation, conventional, and searching for social approval.

As with conformity, conversion is highest for individuals whose initial position of response, whether with regard to factual matters, or to the expression of attitudes, is indefinite, vague, and uncertain. Furthermore, conversion appears to be more complete for individuals who resist conformity pressures for a longer time before they capitulate. Unlike conformity, however, conversion effects are heightened when capitulation occurs under leader-centered group pressure conditions. Here again it would seem that one of the most powerful factors determining conversion is limited understanding of the problem or minimum insight into one's own attitudes or convictions. Resistance to conversion in all probability can be increased througlh insuring that the individual is well informed with respect to factual matters and clear-minded with respect to his own opinions and attitudes.

Future Research Directions

Research to date undoubtedly has identified many of the variables and conditions which are of importance in understanding problems of conformity, resistance, and conversion. A number of limiting factors make generalizations from laboratory situations to real life circumstances difficult, however. For future research to be of maximum use it is important that the following limitations be eliminated insofar as possible.

LABORATORY SETTINGS VS. REAL LIFE SITUATIONS. Laboratory situations are relatively bland, as far as involvement is concerned, at least in comparison with real life settings where the personal stakes connected with conformity, resistance, or conversion are high. Because of the limited investment that an individual can bring to a laboratory situation, direct comparisons between results obtained in it and the actual life settings are likely to be treacherous, and in some cases wrong. Needed are opportunities for research which provide the experimenter the opportunity of controlling and manipulating variables under realistic operating circumstances. Only then can generalizations be made with high probability of accuracy regarding the factors responsible for conformity, resistance, and conversion. With the knowledge of the variables responsible for conformity, resistance, and conversion which currently is available, it should be possible to design experiments in actual life settings with a minimum of trial and error and exploratory work. The yield of insights regarding basic psychological processes of social adjustment, therefore, should be high.

ARTIFICIAL TASKS VS. SIGNIFICANT ISSUES.   Many of the experiments reported in this study have employed tasks requiring adjustments of individuals under conformity or conversion conditions which are artificial in the extreme. A result is that conformity may occur or resistance may develop under conditions that bear little resemblance to actual situations. Future laboratory investigations can benefit from employing tasks which arouse individual feelings of personal commitment and group loyalties.

THEORY VS. EMPIRICISM AND INTUITION.   Even a cursory examination of the principal reports summarized here shows that much of the work in this area is designed according to empirical understanding, intuition, and hunch. Much needed are experiments designed to test systematic and theoretical issues. Helson's adaptation-level theory (Helson, 1955) and Sherif's general formulations concerned with frames of reference (Sherif, 1936) applied in analyzing the conditions of social adjustment constitute examples of theories which have already been demonstrated to be useful in the design of experiments. These theoretical statements can serve to bring order to an otherwise quasichaotic field of endeavor.

SIMULTANEOUS VARIATION OF FACTORS VS. SINGLE VARIABLE DESIGNS.   Results from more recent experiments give substantial support to the view that conformity, resistance, and conversion are complex matters of adjustment which occur when a host of circumstances are favorable, rather than under the influence of a single consideration. Critical sources of influence are referable to the nature of the task, the circumstances of the situation within which the behavior occurs, and properties and characteristics of the individual on whom pressures are exerted. Factors from each source of influence need to be varied simultaneously within the design of single experiments in order to present a realistic picture of the dynamics of conformity and conversion. In terms of present understanding, it can be stated that the interaction of influence is not additive in all cases, but that true interaction among variables occurs to determine the degree to which conformity, resistance, or conversion are aroused.

REPLICATIONS VS. ONE-SHOT STUDIES.   The literature is laden with "one-shot" studies which make acceptance of conclusions tenuous. Replication experiments are much needed to insure that the conclusions from studies are reproducible in a repetition of conditions.

CONFORMITY VS. CONVERSION.   Over 90 percent of work in this area has been concerned with conformity, yet of critical concern are those conditions under which changes in behavior induced by conformity pressures extend into future behavior. Such experiments are not difficult to design. For the most part they represent an extension of the conditions already used in studying conformity in order to measure the aftereffects that remain when conformity pressures have been relieved. Great progress in the understanding of both conformity and conversion phenomena is predicted from investigations designed to measure the *conversion* aspects of the problem.

INDIVIDUAL DIGNITY VS. DISREGARD OF CONSEQUENCES OF EXPERIMENTATION. The design of experiments intended to extract conformity or to create conversion effects easily can infringe on the basic rights of individuals for dignity and respect. Needed to insure freedom to experiment in this vital area is a well designed set of rules to guide investigators. Such rules should provide the opportunity to experiment with significant variables and yet they also should protect individuals who serve as subjects from psychological injury.

Summary

Individuals appear to be more susceptible to conformity pressures when expressing social opinions and ideological attitudes and when dealing with abstractions that are not rooted in concrete experience than when they are dealing with factual materials with which they are well acquainted or with personal preferences. Regardless of the materials being dealt with, however, increases in susceptibility appear when an individual is uncertain as to his own beliefs, uninformed with respect to the facts of the situation, or when objective cues that could aid him in maintaining his orientation to the situation are reduced or eliminated. Then he distrusts himself and he can be influenced by others.

Tendencies toward conformity and conversion are heightened when an individual is with others, at least three in number, where the others are in uniform agreement and where their reactions represent only small departures from the position believed by the individual to represent his own convictions. If the others present are personally acquainted with the individual, and are persons whom he respects, additional conformity pressures are created. Furthermore, if the individual is required to act in his own name and the situation is such that he is not required to commit himself to a position prior to the period when the conformity pressure is applied, greater influence in the conformity direction can be exercised. If the group is led according to a permissive group-centered approach, if members are dependent on one another to obtain significant goals, if the situation calls for unanimous agreement among members, and if the group is cohesive, then the situation is favorable for arousing conformity attitudes.

From a personality angle, the kind of individual who is least able to resist conformity pressures, and probably interrogation pressures as well, is: submissive, lacking in self-confidence, less intelligent, lacking in orginality, authoritarian-minded, lacking in achievement motivation, conventional, and searching for social approval.

REFERENCES

Asch, S. E.   Effects of group pressure upon the modification and distortion of judgments. In H. Guetzkow (Ed.), *Groups, leadership and men.* Pittsburgh: Carnegie Press, 1951.

Asch, S. E.   *Social psychology.* New York: Prentice-Hall, 1952.

Asch, S. E.   Studies of independence and conformity. A minority of one against a unanimous majority. *Psychol. Monogr.,* 1956, **70**, No. 9 (Whole No. 416).

Back, K. W.   Influence through social communication. *J. abnorm. soc. Psychol.,* 1951, **46**, 9–23.

Barch, A. M., Trumbo, D., & Nangle, J.   Society setting and conformity to a legal requirement. *J. abnorm. soc. Psychol.,* 1957, **55**, 396-398.

Barron, F.   Some personality correlates of independence of judgment. *J. Pers.,* 1952, **21**, 287–297.

Barron, F.   Complexity-simplicity as a personality dimension. *J. abnorm. soc. Psychol.,* 1953, **48**, 163–172.

Barron, F.   The disposition toward originality. *J. abnorm. soc. Psychol.,* 1955, **51**, 478–485.

Beloff, H.   Two forms of social conformity: acquiescence and conventionality. *J. abnorm. soc. Psychol.,* 1958, **56**, 99–104.

Bennett, Edith B. Group discussion, decision, public commitment, and perceived unanimity as factors in the effectiveness of "group design." *Amer. Psychologist,* 1952, **7**, 315. (Abstract)

Berenda, Ruth W. *The influence of the group on the judgments of children.* New York: King's Crown Press, 1950.

Berkowitz, L. Effects of perceived dependency relationships upon conformity to group expectations. *J. abnorm. soc. Psychol.,* 1957a, **55**, 350–354.

Berkowitz, L. Liking for the group and the perceived merit of the group's behavior. *J. abnorm. soc. Psychol.,* 1957b, **54**, 353–357.

Blake, R. R. The other person in the situation. In R. Tagiuri and L. Petrullo (Eds.), *Person perception and interpersonal behavior.* Stanford, Calif.: Stanford Univer. Press, 1958, 229–242.

Blake, R. R., Berkowitz, A., Bellamy, R. Q., & Mouton, Jane S. Volunteering as an avoidance act. *J. abnorm. soc. Psychol.,* 1956, **53**, 154–156.

Blake, R. R., & Brehm, J. W. The use of tape recording to simulate a group atmosphere. *J. abnorm. soc. Psychol.,* 1954, **49**, 311–313.

Blake, R. R., & Helson, H. (Eds.), *Adaptability screening of flying personnel. Situational and personal factors in conforming behavior.* School of Aviation Medicine, USAF, 1956.

Blake, R. R., Helson, H., & Mouton, Jane S. The generality of conformity behavior as a function of factual anchorage, difficulty of task, and amount of social pressure. *J. Pers.,* 1956, **25**, 294–305.

Blake, R. R., Mouton, Jane S., & Hain, J. D. Social forces in petition signing. *Southwestern soc. Sci. quart.,* 1956, **36**, 385–390.

Blake R. R., Mouton, Jane S., & Olmstead, J. A. Susceptibility to counternorm attitude expressions in a small group situation. In R. R. Blake & H. Helson (Eds.), *Adaptability screening of flying personnel. Situational and personal factors in conforming behavior.* School of Aviation Medicine, USAF, 1956. Pp. 49–55.

Bovard, E. W., Jr. Social norms and the individual, *J. abnorm. soc. Psychol.,* 1948, **43**, 62–69.

Bovard, E. W., Jr.   Group structure and perception. *J. abnorm. soc. Psychol.*, 1951, **46**, 398–405.

Bray, D. W.   The prediction of behavior from two attitude scales. *J. abnorm. soc. Psychol.*, 1950, **45**, 64–84.

Brehm, J., & Festinger, L.   Pressures toward uniformity of performance in groups. *Hum. Relat.*, 1957, **10**, 85–91.

Burtt, H. E.   Sex differences in the effect of discussion. *J. exp. Psychol.*, 1920, **3**, 390–395.

Caylor, J. S.   Stimulus factors in confromity. *Amer. Psychologist*, 1957, **12**, 388. (Abstract)

Cervin, V.   Experimental investigation of behavior in social situations. I. Behavior under opposition. *Canad. J. Psychol.*, 1955, **9**, 107–116.

Clark, Helen.   The crowd. *Psychol. Monogr.*, 1916, **21**, 26–36.

Cohen, B. P.   A probability model for conformity. *Sociometry*, 1958, **21**, 69–81.

Cole, D. L.   The influence of task perception and leader variation on autokinetic responses. *Amer. Psychologist*, 1955, **10**, 343. (Abstract)

Coleman, Janet F., Blake, R. R., & Mouton, Jane S.   Task difficulty and conformity pressures. *J. abnorm. soc. Psychol.*, 1958, **57**, 120–122.

Crutchfield, R. S.   Assessment of persons through a quasi-group-interaction technique. *J. abnorm. soc. Psychol.*, 1951, **46**, 577–588.

Crutchfield, R. S.   Correlates of individual behavior in a controlled group situation. *Amer. Psychologist*, 1953, **8**, 338. (Abstract)

Crutchfield, R. S.   Conformity and character. *Amer. Psychologist*, 1955, **10**, 191–198.

Deutsch, M., & Gerard, H. B.   A study of normative and informational social influences upon individual judgment. *J. abnorm. soc. Psychol.*, 1955, **51**, 629–636.

Didato, S. V.   The influence of social factors on group conformity in normal and abnormal personalities: a study of perception of untable stimuli and norm formation. *Amer. Psychologist*, 1955, **10**, 366–369. (Abstract)

Dittes, J. E., & Kelley, H. H.   Effect of different conditions of acceptance upon conformity to group norms. *J. abnorm. soc. Psychol.*, 1956, **53**, 100–107.

Duncker, K. Experimental modifications of children's food preferences through social suggestion. *J. abnorm. soc. Psychol.*, 1938, **33**, 489–507.

Festinger, L. An analysis of compliant behavior. In M. Sherif and M. O. Wilson (Eds.), *Group relations at the crossroads.* New York: Harper, 1953.

Festinger, L., Gerard, H. B., Hymovitch, B., Kelley, H. B., & Raven B. The influence process in the presence of extreme deviates. *Hum. Relat.*, 1952, **5**, 327–346.

Festinger, L., & Thibaut, J. Interpersonal communication in small groups. *J. abnorm. soc. Psychol.*, 1951, **46**, 92–99.

Fisher, S., & Rubenstein, I. The effects of moderate sleep deprivation on social influence in the autokinetic situation. *Amer. Psychologist*, 1956, **11**, 411. (Abstract)

Fisher, S., Rubinstein, I., & Freeman, R. W. Intertrial effects of immediate self-committal in a continuous social influence situation. *J. abnorm. soc. Psychol.*, 1956, **52**, 200–207.

Fisher, S., Williams, H. L., & Lubin, A. Personal predictors of susceptibility to social influence. *Amer. Psychologist*, 1957, **12**, 360. (Abstract)

Freed, A., Chandler, P. J., Mouton, Jane S., & Blake, R. R. Stimulus and background factors in sign violation. *J. Pers.*, 1955, **23**, 499.

French, J. R. P., Jr. A formal theory of social power. *Psychol. Rev.*, 1956, **63**, 181–194.

Gerard, H. B. The effect of different dimensions of disagreement on the communication process in small groups. *Hum. Relat.*, 1953, **6**, 249–272.

Gerard, H. B. The anchorage of opinions in face-to-face groups. *Hum. Relat.*, 1954, **7**, 313–326.

Goldberg, S. C. Three situational determinants of conformity to social norms. *J. abnorm. soc. Psychol.*, 1954, **49**, 325–329. (Abstract)

Goldberg, S. C., Hunt, R. G., Cohen, W., & Meadow, A. Some personality correlates of perceptual distortion in the direction of group conformity. *Amer. Psychologist*, 1954, **9**, 378. (Abstract)

Goldberg, S. C., & Lubin, A. Influence as a function of prior judgment error. *Amer. Psychologist,* 1957, **12**, 360. (Abstract)

Gordon, R. L. Interaction between attitude and the definition of the situation in the expression of opinion. *Amer. sociol. Rev.,* 1952, **17**, 50–58.

Grosser, D., Polansky, N., & Lippitt, R. A laboratory study of behavioral contagion. *Hum. Relat.,* 1951, 4, 115–142.

Hardy, K. R. Determinants of conformity and attitude change. *J. abnorm. soc. Psychol.,* 1957, **54**, 289–294.

Hare, P. A. Interaction and consensus in different sized groups. *Amer. sociol. Rev.,* 1952, **17**, 261–267.

Hare, P. A. Small group discussion with participatory and supervisory leadership. *J. abnorm. soc. Psychol.,* 1953, **48**, 273–275.

Harvey, O. J., Kelley, H. H., & Shapiro, M. M. Reactions to unfavorable evaluations of self made by other persons. *J. Pers.,* 1957, **25**, 393–411.

Harvey, O. J., & Rutherford, Jeanne. Gradual and absolute approaches to attitude change. *Sociometry,* 1958, **21**, 61–68.

Helson, H. Adaptation-level as a basis for a quantitative theory of frames of reference. *Psychol. Rev.,* 1948, **55**, 297–313.

Helson, H. An experimental approach to personality. *Psychiat. Res. Rep.,* 1955, **2**, 89–99.

Helson, H., Blake, R. R., & Mouton, Jane S. An experimental investigation of the effectiveness of the "big lie" in shifting attitudes. *J. soc. Psychol.,* 1958a, **48**, 51–60.

Helson, H., Blake, R. R., & Mouton, Jane S. Petition signing as adjustment to situational and personal factors. *J. soc. Psychol.,* 1958b, **48**, 3–10.

Helson, H., Blake, R. R., Mouton, Jane S., & Olmstead, J. A. Attitudes as adjustments to stimulus background and residual factors. *J. abnorm. soc. Psychol.,* 1956, **52**, 314–322.

Hoffman, M. L. Some psychodynamic factors in compulsive conformity. *J. abnorm. soc. Psychol.,* 1953, **48**, 383–393.

Hoffman, M. L. Conformity as a defense mechanism and a form of resistance to genuine group influence. *J. Pers.,* 1957, **25**, 412–424.

Hollander, E. P. Conformity, status and idiosyncrasy credit. *Psychol. Rev.,* 1958, **65**, 117–127.

Horwitz, M., Piana, Gabriel M., Goldman, Della M., & Lee, F. J. Veridicality of attitudes toward authority and effects on learning. *Amer. Psychologist,* 1955, **10**, 336. (Abstract)

Jackson, J. M., & Saltzstein, H. D. The effect of person-group relationships on conformity processes. *J. abnorm. soc. Psychol.,* 1958, **57**, 17–24.

Jacubczak, L., & Walters, R. H. An experimental investigation of suggestibility in terms of dependency behavior. *Amer. Psychologist,* 1958, **13**, 328. (Abstract)

Jenness, A. The role of discussion in changing opinions regarding a matter of fact. *J. abnorm. soc. Psychol.,* 1932, **27**, 279–296.

Jones, E. E., Wells, H. H., & Torrey, R. Some effects of feedback from the experimenter on conformity behavior. *J. abnorm. soc. Psychol.,* 1958, **57**, 207–213.

Keislar, E. R. The differential effect of success and failure upon imitative behavior. *Amer. Psychologist,* 1956, **11**, 369. (Abstract)

Kelley, H. H., & Lamb, T. W. Certainty of judgment and resistance to social influence. *J. abnorm. soc. Psychol.,* 1957, **55**, 137–139.

Kelley, H. H., & Shapiro, M. M. An experiment on conformity to group norms where conformity is detrimental to group achievement. *Amer. sociol. Rev.,* 1954, **19**, 667–677.

Kelman, H. C. Effects of success and failure on "suggestibility" in the autokinetic situation. *J. abnorm. soc. Psychol.,* 1950, **45**, 267–285.

Kidd, J. S. Social influence phenomena in a task oriented group situation. *J. abnorm. soc. Psychol.,* 1958, **56**, 13–17.

Kidd, J. S., & Campbell, D. T. Conformity to groups as a function of group success. *J. abnorm. soc. Psychol.,* 1955, **51**, 390–393.

Kimbrell, D. L., & Blake, R. R. Motivational factors in the violation of a prohibition. *J. abnorm. soc. Psychol.,* 1958, **56**, 132–133.

Kirkpatrick, C. An experimental study of the modification of social attitudes. *Amer. J. Sociol.,* 1936, **41**, 649–656.

Krebs, A. M. Two determinants of conformity, age of independence training and *n* achievement. *J. abnorm. soc. Psychol.*, 1958, **56**, 130–131.

Lambert, W. E., & Lowy, F. H.   Effects of the presence and discussion of others on expressed attitudes. *Canad. J. Psychol.*, 1957, **11**, 151–156.

Lawson, E. D., & Stagner, R.   Group pressure, attitude change, and autonomic involvement. *J. soc. Psychol.*, 1957, **45**, 299–312.

Lefkowitz, M., Blake, R. R., & Mouton, Jane S.   Status factors in pedestrian violation of traffic signals. *J. abnorm. soc. Psychol.*, 1955, **51**, 704–706.

Levine J., Laffal, J., Berkowitz, M., Lindemann, J., & Drevdahl, J.   Conforming behavior of psychatric and medical patients. *J. abnorm. soc. Psychol.*, 1954, **49**, 251–255.

Linton, Harriet B.   Rorschach correlates of response to suggestion. *J. abnorm. soc. Psychol.*, 1954, **49**, 75–83.

Linton, Harriet B.   Dependence on external influence: correlates in perception, attitudes, and adjustment. *J. abnorm. soc. Psychol.*, 1955, **51**, 502–507.

Luchins, A. S.   On agreement with another's judgments. *J. abnorm. soc. Psychol.*, 1944, **39**, 97–111.

Luchins, A. S.   Social influences on perception of complex drawings. *J. soc. Psychol.*, 1945, **21**, 257–274.

Luchins, A. S., & Luchins, Edith H.   On conformity with true and false communications, *J. soc. Psychol.*, 1955a, **42**, 283–304.

Luchins, A. S., & Luchins, Edith H.   Previous experience with ambiguous and non-ambiguous perceptual stimuli under various social influences. *J. soc. Psychol.*, 1955b, **42**, 249–270.

McConnell, J. V., & Blake, R. R.   A methodological study of tape-recorded synthetic group atmospheres. *Amer. Psychologist,* 1953, **8**, 395. (Abstract)

McKeachie, W. J.   Individual conformity to attitudes of classroom groups. *J. abnorm. soc. Psychol.*, 1954, **49**, 282–289.

McQueen, R.   Examination deception as a function of residual, background, and immediate stimulus factors. *J. Pers.*, 1957, **25**, 643–650.

Maier, N. R. F., & Solem, A. R.   The contribution of a discussion leader to the quality of group thinking: the effective use of minority opinions. *Hum. Relat.*, 1952, **5**, 277–288.

Marinho, Heloisa. Social influence in the formation of enduring preferences. *J. abnorm. soc. Psychol.*, 1942, **37**, 448–468.

Mausner, B. Studies in social interaction: III. Effect of variation in one partner's prestige on the interaction of observer pairs. *J. appl. Psychol.*, 1953, **37**, 391–393.

Mausner, B. The effect of one partner's success in a relevant task on the interaction of observer pairs. *J. abnorm. soc. Psychol.*, 1954a, **49**, 557–560.

Mausner, B. The effect of prior reinforcement on the interaction of observer pairs. *J. abnorm. soc. Psychol.*, 1954b, **49**, 65–68.

Mausner, B. Studies in social interaction: I. A conceptual scheme. *J. soc. Psychol.*, 1955, **41**, 259–270.

Mausner, B., & Bloch, Barbara L. A study of the additivity of variables affecting social interaction. *J. abnorm. soc. Psychol.*, 1957, **54**, 250–256.

Millon, T., & Simkins, L. C. Suggestibility of authoritarians and equalitarians to prestige influence. *Amer. Psychologist*, 1957, **12**, 404. (Abstract)

Moeller, G., & Applezweig, M. H. A motivational factor in conformity. *J. abnorm. soc. Psychol.*, 1957, **55**, 114–120.

Mouton, Jane S., Blake, R. R., & Olmstead, J. A. The relationship between frequency of yielding and the disclosure of personal identity. *J. Pers.*, 1956, **24**, 339–347.

Munsterberg, H. Beiträgezur experimentellen psychologie. In Ruth W. Berenda, (Ed.), *The influence of the group on the judgments of children.* New York: King's Crown Press, 1950.

Mussen, P. H., & Kagan, J. Group conformity and perceptions of parents. *Child Develpm.*, 1958, **29**, 57–60.

Nakamura, C. Y. Conformity and problem-solving. *J. abnorm. soc. Psychol.*, 1958, **56**, 315–320.

Olmstead, J. A., & Blake, R. R. The use of simulated groups to produce modifications in judgment. *J. Pers.*, 1955, **23**, 335–345.

Preston, M. G., & Heintz, R. K. Effects of participatory vs. supervisory leadership on group judgment. *J. abnorm. soc. Psychol.*, 1949, **44**, 345–355.

Raven, B. H., & French, J. R. P., Jr. Group support, legitimate power, and social influence. *J. Pers.*, 1958, **26**, 400–409.

Raven, B. H., & Rietsema, J. The effects of varied clarity of group goal and group path upon the individual and his relation to his group. *Hum. Relat.,* 1957, **10,** 29–45.

Rohrer, J. H., Baron, S. H., Hoffman, E. L., & Swander, D. V. The stability of autokinetic judgments. *J. abnorm. soc. Psychol.,* 1954, **49,** 595–597.

Rosenbaum, M. E. The effect of stimulus and background factors on the volunteering response. *J. abnorm. soc. Psychol.,* 1956, **53,** 118–121.

Rosenbaum, M. E., & Blake, R. R. Volunteering as a function of field structure. *J. abnorm. soc. Psychol.,* 1955, **50,** 193–196.

Rosner, S. Consistency in response to group pressures. *J. abnorm. soc. Psychol.,* 1957, **55,** 145–146.

Samelson, F. Conforming behavior under two conditions of conflict in the cognitive field. *J. abnorm. soc. Psychol.,* 1957, **55,** 181–187.

Schachter, S. Ellertson, N., McBride, Dorothy, & Gregory, Doris. An experimental study of cohesiveness and productivity. *Hum. Relat.,* 1951, **4,** 229–238.

Schachter, S., & Hall, R. Group-derived restraints and audience persuasion. *Hum. Relat.,* 1952, **5,** 397–406.

Schonbar, Rosealea A. The interaction of observer-pairs in judging visual extent and movement. *Arch. Psychol., N.Y.,* 1945, **41,** No. 299.

Schroder, H. M., & Hunt, D. E. Dispositional effects upon conformity at different levels of discrepancy. *J. Pers.,* 1958, **26,** 248–258.

Scott, W. A. Attitude change through reward of verbal behavior. *J. abnorm. soc. Psychol.,* 1957, **55,** 72–75.

Sherif, M. A study of some social factors in perception. *Arch. Psychol., N.Y.,* 1935, **27,** No. 187.

Sherif, M. *The psychology of social norms.* New York: Harper, 1936.

Sherif, M. An experimental approach to the study of attitudes. *Sociometry,* 1937, **1,** 90–98.

Sherif, M., & Harvey, O. J. A study in ego functioning: Elimination of stable anchorages in individual and group situations. *Sociometry,* 1952, **15,** 272–305.

Spohn, H. E.   The effect of group norms upon perception in chronic schizophrenic patients. *Amer. Psychologist,* 1956, **11,** 366. (Abstract)

Steiner, I. D., & Peters, S. C.   Conformity and the A-B-X model. *J. Pers.,* 1958, **26,** 229–242.

Thibaut, J. W., & Strickland, L.   Psychological set and social conformity. *J. Pers.,* 1956, **25,** 115–129.

Weiner, M.   Uncertainty of judgment as a determinant of conformity behavior. *Amer. Psychologist,* 1956, **11,** 407. (Abstract)

Weiner, M., Carpenter, Janeth T., & Carpenter, B.   External validation of a measure of conformity behavior. *J. abnorm. soc. Psychol.,* 1956, **52,** 421–422.

Wells, W. D., Weinert, G., & Rubel, Marilyn.   Conformity pressures and authoritarian personality. *J. Psychol.,* 1956, **42,** 133–136.

Wheeler, D., & Jordan, H.   Change of individual opinion to accord with group opinion. *J. abnorm. soc. Psychol.,* 1929, **24,** 203–306.

Whittaker, J. O.   The effects of experimentally introduced anchorages upon judgments in the autokinetic situation. Unpublished doctoral dissertation, Univer. of Oklahoma, 1958.

Ziller, R. C., & Behringer, R.   Group persuasion under conditions of incubation and varying group size. *Amer. Psychologist,* 1958, **13,** 353. (Abstract)

CHAPTER 2

Conformity, Deviation, and a General Theory of Interpersonal Behavior[1]

BERNARD M. BASS

Louisiana State University

Why do we conform? The answer to this question is to be found in a multiplicity of causes. Conforming behavior is an aspect of the general phenomenon of interaction. The answer is as complex as if we were asking: why do we lead or why does prejudice develop? But despite its complexity, conforming behavior, like interpersonal behavior in general, can be understood in terms of a variety of simple effects and their interplay. We can do this by assuming that con- formity is a consequence of successful influence. If this is true generally, currently available theorems offered by Bass (1960) about interaction and influence describe quite well the facts about conformity.

DEFINITIONS.   Conforming behavior is regarded as behavior reflecting the *successful* influence of other persons. What we know about successful influence can be employed to promote our understanding of one of its possible reflections—the behavior of those accepting the successful influence. It is

[1] Aided by support of Contract N7 ONR 35609, Group Psychology Branch, Office of Naval Research.

not to be inferred that successful influence produces *only* conformity. As Rokeach notes in Chapter 7 successful influence may yield independence or what you will. But, except for chance, drugs, brain surgery, or parallelisms in behavior of unconnected individuals, it is difficult to see how the conforming of one individual to the ideas, values, and norms of others could be produced without the occurrence of successful influence, defined (p. 94)[2] as the behavior of one individual which results in changing the behavior of another. On the other hand, it probably would not be too profitable to restrict *independence,* by definition, to a reflection of successful influence, *although it is such a reflection.* For independent behavior, by its very nature, is much more often likely to result from nonpersonal stimuli and from idiosyncratic rather than shared needs (see Chapter 11), although it could arise as a consequence of successful influence. Thus, we know that leadership or influence will be successful if the leader is perceived as *more* able than those he leads. It is not surprising to learn that a member will conform to the suggestion of another, or a group of others, to the extent he perceives himself as *less* able than the others.

Since the leader cannot be too much more able (p. 177) it may be that correspondingly some minimum self-perception of one's own ability may be required for conforming behavior to occur. A member may withdraw from the group rather than try to conform to the group's standards if he perceives his ability is too far below the group's average. Abundant evidence is available to support the first theorem concerning ability and conformity. As far as we know, there has been no experiment on the second theorem concerning the *minimum* ability requirement for conforming behavior to occur. Herein lies the profitability of an exploration such as that presented in this chapter. We may be able to offer

[2] Unless otherwise specified, page citations refer to pages in Bass, B. M., *Leadership, Psychology, and Organizational Behavior,* New York: Harper, 1960.

generalizations for a collection of facts about conformity which have been already well established. The generalizations will be connected to a larger body of theory proposed by Bass (1960). In addition, we will be able to formulate a number of propositions subject to future experimental verification concerning conformity to expand our understanding of the phenomenon in a systematic way.

Just as conforming behavior is behavior reflecting the successful influence of other persons, *deviating* behavior can be defined as behavior reflecting the *rejected* influence of other persons. A Samoan's behavior may be different from an Australian's behavior. The Samoan only becomes a deviate with reference to the Australian scene when he moves to Australia, has an opportunity to accept the Australian way of life, but rejects it. At this point his behavior in Australia becomes deviant and can be understood in terms of conformity and deviation principles. With this definition in mind, several propositions about deviation can be derived in the same way as we derive theorems about conformity starting with the general theory of interpersonal behavior in Bass (1960).

Defining conformity and deviation as mirror images of successful and rejected influence means that mere statistical similarity or differences of persons from other persons will not necessarily imply conformity or deviation. By our definition, chance communalities or parallel behaviors of individuals in collections are not necessarily conforming behavior. For us, a monk becomes a deviant only when his withdrawal becomes an interpersonal matter. He becomes a deviant to be treated by others as such when his withdrawal implies an effort to avoid influence by most others of his social group. If becoming a monk is accepted procedure for the group, as among Buddhists, such behavior is not deviant. Indeed, if withdrawal by one member results in the mass withdrawal of many others to group around him such as occurred to the

Anchorite monks up through the middle of the fifth century A.D. in Egypt, conforming rather than deviating behavior may be involved by those who followed the leader into the desert.

PLAN.   When directly applicable, I shall present propositions, one-by-one, taken directly from the theory. When they are not immediately applicable to understanding conformity or deviation, I shall present both the original postulate or theorem, and the theorem derived by assuming that conformity is the reflection of successful leadership. Still other derivations will deal with deviation, accepting the assumption that deviation is a reflection of rejected influence. Derivations usually will involve stating the obverse of the original postulate or theorem; for where a theorem or postulate deals with successful leadership, its obverse will concern conformity, the consequence of successful leadership. Derivations about deviation usually will be obverse of original statements about rejected influence. Following each stated or derived proposition, I shall review some of the experimental literature supporting the validity of the statement.[3]

Conformity: Person vs. Situation

1.   **The importance of the group, the situation, and the individual members are relative matters. We can increase or decrease the significance of each at will (p. 17).**

The controversy in social psychology concerning the relative importance of personality, group, and situation is a pseudoproblem. In a particular study, situational effects can

[3] The propositions, per se, will appear in boldface type. The original postulate or theorem from which the proposition was derived will appear in italics followed by the page reference in *Leadership, Psychology, and Organizational Behavior* (Bass, 1960). When the original statement, itself, serves as a proposition about conformity without requiring further derivation, it will be presented in boldface type followed by its page reference also in boldface type.

be reduced by making the situations more similar. Personality effects can be increased by using individuals who vary more in selected personality characteristics affecting the social behavior under study. As was shown elsewhere (pp.15-20) concerning *leadership behavior,* considerable evidence is also available supporting the importance of personal effects, situational effects, and group effects as well as various combinations in determining whether or not *conforming behavior* will occur.

CONFORMITY EFFECTS DUE TO PERSONS REGARDLESS OF SITUATIONS. Two kinds of evidence point to the significance of personal effects: observations of consistencies in conformity and observed correlations of personal characteristics with conformity. Consistent individual difference have been reported by Blake, Helson, and Mouton (1957), Rosner (1957), Tuddenham (1957), MacBride (1958), Bass (1959b), and McDonald (1960), in the tendency of experimental subjects to conform to the group decision or to majority decisions. For 10 to 12 trials, Bass reported split-half reliabilities averaging .52 for subjects in groups of five trying to determine the correct rank ordering of the familiarity of words. McDonald attained similar consistencies for groups judging alternative solutions to human relations problems. When the tasks were systematically altered by Blake, Helson, and Mouton, consistent individual differences in tendency to conform still maintained themselves. Again, Rosner found phi correlation coefficients of .33 to .54 across situations in subjects' tendencies to conform to three accomplices making erroneous judgments about nonsense words, nonsense figures, and a simple paragraph. In the same way, Tuddenham obtained highly consistent individual differences across 74 trials concerning judging visual targets, information, and opinion. Using the same measuring procedures, MacBride was impressed by the high degree of individual consistency in conforming obtained even after he systematically had raised or lowered the self-confidence of his subjects. On the other hand, Goldberg (1954) was unable to find anything but low intercorrelations between conformity and different experimental conditions and was unable to observe any general personality characteristics of suggestibility or conformity. Goldberg's failure may be due to a restriction in the range in personality of the subject and/or the differences in the way he measured conformity in contrast to the preceding studies.

PERSONAL CHARACTERISTICS ASSOCIATED WITH CONFORMITY. Tuddenham (1957), Applezweig and Moeller (1958), and Beloff (1958) observed that women conformed much more than men when subjected to pressures to conform by their groups. This finding was corroborated by Coleman, Blake, and Mouton (1958), who obtained correlations between difficulty of general information items and the tendency to conform of .58 for men and .89 for women. Tuddenham (1957) found similar differences among college men and women although the sex difference was somewhat less among 35-year olds. Again, Tuddenham, MacBride, and Zahn (1958) showed women generally conforming more to men than vice versa.

These sex differences may be due to differences in motivational orientation by men and women. Unpublished studies at Louisiana State University suggest that college men tend to be much more task-oriented, more concerned about getting the job done, getting the correct answer, or doing the best job possible. On the contrary, women are much more interaction-oriented, concerned with obtaining harmonious relations with others, receiving social approval from others, being accepted as a member of their groups. Consistent with this is Tuddenham and MacBride's (1958) finding that women were more conforming if they were concerned about their answers not appearing peculiar to the other participants while men conformed more when they said they were concerned with doing the job faster. These results also fit in with what we know about cultural deviants. Men, for example, are much more prone to suicide or criminal activities than are women.

Other evidence of the contribution of personal effects to conforming behavior is to be found in the available correlations between various measures of attitudes and beliefs and the observed tendency to conform in small groups. Beloff (1958) obtained significant correlations between conformity to a laboratory group and political conventionality as measured by an attitude scale. Similarly, Frye and Bass (1958) obtained a correlation of .39 between the tendency to conform to group decisions in the laboratory and social acquiescence —the tendency to accept rather than reject any generalizations (proverbs) about human behavior. Again, Canning and Baker (1959) found that conformity to accomplices in the autokinetic situation was much greater among subjects with extreme religious authoritarian attitudes. In line with this evidence, Nadler (1959) noted that conformity in the Asch judging situation correlated .30 with ethnocentrism as measured by the E scale and .48 with authoritarianism as measured by the F scale. According to Tuddenham (1958b), yielders to simulated group pressure were much more likely to be conventional, nurturant, affiliative, conscientious, and sociable. It is probable that similar correlations will be found with a variety of other related measures such as dogmatism, conventionality, xenophobia, religiosity, militancy, and intolerance of ambiguity. At the roots of consistent individual differences in conforming behavior as well as related actions and attitudes such as conventionality, authoritarianism, and dogmatism may be correlated differences in the generalized tendency to acquiesce, the generalized need for certainty or assuredness, and perhaps generalized feelings of insecurity.

CONFORMITY EFFECTS DUE TO SITUATION REGARDLESS OF
PERSONS. Several lines of evidence demonstrate that under
certain conditions no matter who is put into a given circumstance, whether or not he conforms will depend on systematic
alterations in the situation rather than who the person is.
For example, Argyle (1957) showed that conformity to influence will be greater if one must respond publicly rather
than be permitted to respond in private only. Likewise, Mouton, Blake, and Olmstead (1956) noted that more yielding
to incorrect background reports occurred when responding
was public rather than private. Numerous studies at
Louisiana State University served to corroborate these findings. We have found fairly consistently that subjects in five-
man groups tend to conform to each others' opinions much
more publicly than privately.

Barch, Tromboe, and Nangle (1957) found that conformity may depend on whether or not we are cued to conform. They reported that auto drivers were slightly more
likely to signal that they were turning if the car 100 feet or
less in front of them signaled before them. The suggestion, then, is that some conformity occurs if there is a cue
in the situation to prime its occurrence, regardless of who
it is who is being cued.

Blake, Helson, and Mouton (1957) showed that conformity
increases systematically with increases in the difficulty of the
problem facing the group. Coleman, Blake, and Mouton
(1958) obtained the same results with another experimental
setting. Likewise, Chapman and Volkman (1939) showed that
once subjects have established their own standards of judgment in an originally ambiguous situation, the experimenter
cannot make them shift towards him as easily as when the
subjects have not had an opportunity to establish their own
base of judgment. Numerous other studies as will be noted
later report the generalization that as the situation becomes

more ambiguous, conformity of most or all subjects is likely to increase.

PRIMITIVE SOCIETIES. Anthropology provides still further evidence of the significance of situational effects on conformity. Cultural anthropologists such as Kluckhohn (1951) have observed that cultures vary in their response to the relation of man to nature, the forces of nature to be accepted versus the forces of nature which must be overcome. Cultures vary regarding man as good or regarding man as evil. Cultures vary in whether the past, the present, or the future is to be most important. Cultures vary in which interactions are most valued: lineal, collateral, or individualistic. Cultures provide the learned values for goals of behavior. A limited number of problems exist for humans everywhere requiring some solution. When the solution has already been obtained by the group into which we have been born our subsequent responses are limited, as long as we remain a member of that group. We will be observed conforming in numerous ways as a consequence of what we have learned from membership in that cultural setting.

As Mead *et al.* (1939) were able to show, it is possible to order primitive societies according to how much members of the society, as a whole, regardless of who they may be personally, conform to group norms, to standard ways of behaving. At one extreme are the Zuni, the Samoans, the Bathonga, and the Manus, whose behavior can be described as highly conforming to group standards, whatever the standards happen to be. Thus, among the Zuni, deviant behavior results in public reproof and deliberate efforts to inhibit individuality. Humility and self-abasement are highly valued. The Samoan's behavior must conform to his rank. With whom he competes or whom he obeys depends on his position in society not his own personal idiosyncrasies. The Bathonga have a highly cooperative economic order with little opportunity for individual originality or rivalry in technology or social affairs. Obedience and respect for the elders, the chiefs, and the gods are indoctrinated early. Among the Manus, personal tendencies and needs for affection, loyalty, or love are banned. The only valid motivation is to succeed in one's efforts relative to the group's standards of success. Recently dead ghosts visit sickness and death on those who fail. Retirement is without honor. To remain in this society, one must "play the game to win." Those who do not, or cannot, withdraw to live apart.

At the other extreme may be listed the Eskimo, the Obijiwa, and the Bachiga. Among the Obijiwa, everyone in the family owns his own individual property which he can transfer at his pleasure to another owner. Individuality is paramount in the only institutionalized activities—playing games. There are opportunities for success for the Bachiga but no stigma is attached to failure. There is no standard way of competing with others. Families and clans tend to break up. The nonconforming Eskimo has no social sanction against murder—widely deviating behavior is tolerated.

INTERACTIONAL EFFECTS OF PERSONS AND SITUATIONS.   The interacting effects of persons and situations on conformity or deviation have been noted often. For example, Stogdill (1959) suggests that as threat increases in a situation, persons with high self-esteem tend to undergo perceptual closure rejecting the existence of discrepancies between themselves and others. On the contrary, as threat increases in a situation, persons of low self-esteem become more cognizant and sensitive to discrepancies between themselves and others, demanding more situational structure conforming to their own value systems.

Previously cited studies by Blake and Mouton in Chapter 1 reveal how the combination of personality and situational effects combine to produce conforming behavior. Again,

Bass (1959b) showed that conformity to the decisions of one's group was a complex function of the motivational level of all concerned. In a different vein, but supporting the same contention, are the delinquency studies of the Glueck's (1950) who found that adolescents with a particular athletic body-build coupled with a poor under-the-roof environment, are most susceptible to juvenile delinquency. With the same environment, but a slender body-build, the adolescent is more likely to deviate revealing neurotic tendencies rather than overt aggression against society.

Group Effectiveness and Individual Conformity

2.   Group goals modify subsequent behavior to the extent they are relevant to the members of the group (p. 51).

Many studies followed Lewin's (1939) initial suggestion that conformity to the group's aims and the group's standards is much greater where the members have an opportunity, as a group, to select those aims and standards; thereby presumably insuring that the group's goals will be more relevant to the members (e.g., Coch & French, 1948; Levine & Butler, 1952; Radke & Klisurich, 1947). Several other illustrations can be cited which are more specifically related to the proposition. Stagner (1958) noted that conformity in the industrial group is likely to increase when a member's goals are identical with those of his group. Since our own goals are likely to be highly relevant, identical group goals should have the same relevancy to us.

The effects of relevancy are seen also in Lieberman's (1954) finding that workers promoted to foremen subsequently shared their management's attitudes and values much more than workers who were elected as union shop stewards, even when both sets of workers started out, prior to promotion or election, with the same attitudes. On the other hand, those workers who became shop stewards tended to develop more favorable union attitudes. In both cases, workers shifted their attitudes, and presumably their behavioral tendencies, in a direction in line with what was becoming more relevant for them. The goals of management were more relevant to foremen than to workers before they became foremen; union goals were more relevant to shop stewards than to workers before they became shop stewards. The third bit of evidence about the significance of the relevance of group goals comes from Schachter's (1951) study of deviancy. Deviants were found more likely to be rejected, and more conformity was demanded of group members, when the issue under consideration was more relevant to the group.

It is not difficult to observe the effect of goal relevancy on conformity in work groups, committees, and meetings. Consider the differential expectations and demands for conformity among a committee of executives discussing a stand their company should take in forthcoming negotiations with a union in contrast to these gentlemen discussing whether people should stop smoking because of the health hazard. The implication for laboratory studies is that the conformity of subjects will depend on how much they see the decisions requested of them have relevancy for them in maintaining their own self-esteem, their esteem among their colleagues, or their expectations about winning or losing or about being right.

3. Immediate rather than ultimate effectiveness is more significant for understanding interaction among individuals (p. 54).

No evidence from laboratory studies is specifically available on this version of the goal gradient hypothesis but it would seem to be a simple matter to study the effects of delay in reinforcement, or the effects of long range versus short range goals on the tendency of subjects to conform. Particularly among less mature, less intelligent, and less interested subjects, the expectation is that conformity would be greater when rewards were immediate rather than delayed.

4. *Members will tend to behave in ways to maintain or increase a group's effectiveness to the extent the group rewards its members (p. 75).* Assuming that absence of conflict in interaction is rewarding, **members will conform to each other rather than disagree in the expectation of maintaining secure, harmonious, and satisfying relationships.**

Considerable evidence supports the fact that conflict is dissatisfying and its absence is preferred. For example, French (1941) found that attractiveness of members for each other in a group was reduced considerably when they disagreed over the way to solve the group's problems. Again, Peterman (1951) found that among 72 conference groups, congruence of goals was correlated .51 with satisfaction.

In an unpublished study I conducted in a management training laboratory, each of 36 participants spent a half hour discussing alternative solutions to a human relations problem with two other participants with whom he had agreed initially. He also spent another half-hour with two other participants with whom he disagreed initially. In contrast to trios of men in initial disagreement, trios composed of men initially in agreement were more satisfied with their team's final decision, experienced much less difficulty in getting their ideas across, had less difficulty in understanding each other, felt more comfortable during the discussion, felt more free to participate in their team's decision and preferred being again with members who agreed with rather than disagreed initially with them. In contrast to those initially disagreeing trios who eventually reached agreement, trios still deadlocked when the period of discussion was over were least satisfied with the trio and experienced the most difficulty in understanding.

The desire to avoid conflict with one's associates is probably one of the main reasons for the restriction of output in industry (Mathewson, 1931). Conformity by all workers in a department to a common standard eliminates the possibilities of invidious comparison and disproportionate sharing of rewards for greater or lesser effort. Piece rate incentive plans are often rejected by worker groups and by unions because of the increased conflict they are likely to engender within the work group; even though the total take-home pay for all concerned is likely to be greater.

In the desire to avoid conflict, Festinger (1957) notes, persons tend to interpret events around them consonant with their own opinions, filtering out only what is in disagreement with them and their needs and accepting what is in agreement with them. Experimental evidence of this is supplied by Brodbeck (1956) who showed that subjects in discussion groups tend to hear only those who agree with them ignoring arguments of their opponents. In the same way, Blake and Mouton (1959) have demonstrated that groups in competition with other groups are much more knowledgable about their own product than the product prepared by the other groups. The desire for agreement is reflected in the greater tension observed when disagreement occurs. Hoffman (1956) found that psychogalvanic skin responses of subjects were higher in those confronted with the realization that they were in disagreement with their group than in those who found themselves in agreement with their group. Similarly, Horwitz (1954) found tension among subjects greater, as measured by the Zeigarnik effect, when the subjects personally voted one way while the group voted another.

Attractiveness and Conformity

5. **Conformity is greater in more attractive groups (p. 244).**

Substantial evidence has accumulated in the past two decades supporting this proposition. Newcomb (1943) showed that Bennington College students became more liberal in social attitudes as a consequence of the desire to "belong" to campus society—a liberal one. In the same way, Rasmussen and Zander (1954) found that the more a teacher was attracted to his group, the more his level of aspiration approximated the ideal of his group.

One of the basic tenets of informal social communication advanced by Festinger (1950) was that subjects would conform to the extent they were attracted to a group. This was corroborated in experimental studies by Gerard (1954), Scott (1956), and Jackson and Saltzstein (1958), all of whom found conformity greater in more attractive groups. Consistent with these findings is Schachter's (1951) report that the deviant is more likely to be rejected in attractive in comparison to unattractive groups, i.e., pressure to conform is greater in more attractive groups.

6. If the group's source of attraction to members is its control of what is wanted by the members, the group has the power to coerce motivated members, resulting in increases in public but not necessarily private conformity (coercion) with increases in attraction. The greater the group's control, the more conformity is likely to occur (p. 241).

7. If the group's source of attraction is its perceived greater ability to cope with problems than can be done by the lone individual, members can be persuaded by the group's decisions—resulting in increases in both public and private conformity with increases in the group's attractiveness (p. 240).

The argument for Propositions 6 and 7 is that we may conform simply because we see conformity as the way to gain reward and avoid punishment *or* as the way to achieve the correct decision or the right answer. One person can influence the behavior of another in at least two ways: (1) he can grant or deny rewards and punishments or arbitrarily control the delivery of these rewards or punishment; (2) he can serve as the cue, the bearer of information concerning how to reach goals which are rewarding or avoid goals which are punishing to the other person (p. 221). Particularly in groups where consensus, majority opinion, or other democratic decision-making techniques distribute power and control among the members rather than center it on one member, many or all of the members are seen as the purveyors of rewards and punishments to each other as well as the sources of information concerning the correct answer. We allow ourselves to be influenced by the "others"; we conform to majority opinion, or consensus, or what we believe is the group point of view for two reasons: (1) The "others" have the power to deny us what we want if we reject their influence. If we remove this power, or if we do not want what is controlled by the "others," we will be less likely to conform. (2) We are searching for the best possible decision—the right answer. We are uncertain as to how personally accurate we are. We yield to influence by others since we are uncertain ourselves about the correct answer. In turn, we try less to influence others. Uncertain or indifferent about how right we are, we shift towards any offered opinion, particularly when it seems to have universal acceptance by others in the group, not because conformity itself is directly rewarding, but because we think this is the way to obtain the right answer. If we are not instructed to find the right answer but are merely instructed to discuss a problem, we will be less likely to conform.

EVIDENCE CONCERNING THE POWER OF A GROUP TO COERCE (PROPOSITION 6). Support for Proposition 6 is found in both experiment and in survey. Discussing stages in a doctor's medical career, Hall (1948) described how occupational success depends on integrating one's behavior with the group that controls the rewards within one's profession. As many as one-third of subjects confronted by Asch (1952) with the conflict between what their senses told them and what they found was the opinion of the remainder of their group, con- conformed to the erroneous judgments of the remainder of their group. The coerciveness of such circumstances can be inferred from numerous reports of investigators such as Raven (1959), Mouton, Blake, and Olmstead (1956) and Argyle (1957) that conformity to erroneous majority opinion is greater when one is forced to reveal his own decisions publicly rather than allowed to maintain privacy of response.

REACTIONS TO COERCION. Many individuals do not like to admit even to themselves that they have been coerced. They prefer pseudosolutions in the face of such conflict. Thus, Asch (1952) noted that some of his conforming sub- jects suffered actual distortion in what they perceived, mak- ing it possible for them to disclaim any deliberate falsifica- tion of their own results in order to avoid appearing different to others in their group. Again, Gorden (1952) found that the typical pattern of 24 members of a cooperative living project was for them to compromise between their private opinions and their conception of group opinion when ex- pressing their public opinions. Raven (1959) found similar results with laboratory subjects. Examining the dynamics more fully, he found that subjects' descriptions were distorted toward the group norm when opinion was to be made public and when there was a possibility of being rejected. At first, subjects distorted the arguments and contents of communica- tions from others to bring themselves in line with the group norms in order to avoid ostracism or rejection. But an even more complete pseudosolution was achieved by these sub- jects when they began to see more merit in what they had been sold and now were communicating than in the initial positions they had held.

There may be at least four levels of awareness concerning one's conforming reactions to coercion. The verbal illustrations below describe these levels:

Overt: "I tell you openly that I still think I am right, but I'll go along with the group to avoid further argument."

Concealed: "I agree with the group openly, but secretly I think I was right."

Hidden: "I agree with the group because I am a member of the group and I like to be thought of one in good standing. Being right is not as important as being accepted."

Buried: "I'm an inadequate person; I must be wrong about this; the others are much more adequate to judge. I actually do see what they see. They are right; I was wrong before."

EFFECTS OF INCREASED CONTROL. Fearing and Krise (1941) were able to demonstrate how conformity increased with increased control by the agent of conformity. It is obvious that a roadblock will stop more cars than a policeman; a policeman will stop more cars than a STOP sign because a roadblock represents maximum physical control and a policeman has more potential to punish than has a STOP sign. But data gathered by Fearing and Krise also showed that a STOP sign will stop more cars during the day than at night when it is easier to violate the rule without being caught. Moreover, a STOP sign will stop fewer drivers who are alone since less social disapproval is likely to occur when someone else is not watching.

Scott (1956) has shown that the greater the number of members in a group who hold a value and the more strongly they each hold it, the more important it becomes to all. It follows that conformity to a group demand is apt to be greatest when it has the maximum number of members supporting it, but the relation does not seem to be a simple linear cumulative one for as Asch (1952) and Hardy (1957) have shown, conformity by a subject to an erroneous majority opinion is markedly reduced, when even one other dissenting voice is raised against the announced majority. Hardy noted that public conformity may not be reduced much by the dissention, but private conformity is lowered considerably. The same result is seen in the management training laboratory group in which members try to feed back counsel to each other concerning their respective assets and weaknesses observed during the group's development:

> Whether or not feedback given to a member of a group carries the weight of the rest of the group makes quite a difference. For example, if Joe says that Bill talks too much, Bill is much more likely to accept as a fact that he talks too much if the rest of the group concurs with Joe about Bill than if only a few other members of the group make the same comment or agree with Joe about Bill. Even if there is only one other dissenter in the group to Joe's feedback to Bill, Bill is less likely to accept the criticism as true. For the one dissenter gives Bill an excuse to reject the feedback. If Bill really feels strongly that he does not talk too much, he may continue to maintain this position given the support of only a single other person in the group who shares the same opinion about himself as he does. If there is no consensus behind the feedback to Bill, Bill is much less likely to accept the feedback [Bass, 1959b, p. 28].

Conversely, in groups where each member supposedly has as much power as every other, when only one or two members try to make self-authorized or mutually supportive "handclasps" or render an opinion for the rest of the group, their efforts are likely to be rejected completely. Opposition rather than conformity to the decisions will result. It is probable that a group's control cumulates with increasing member support. Anything other than complete consensus is likely to be relatively inefficient in producing complete conformity to the group's norms.

EVIDENCE CONCERNING CONFORMING TO BE RIGHT (PROPO-SITION 7). Various sources of indirect evidence support the contention that conformity and deviation depend upon the subject's effort to find the right answer. Asch noted that subjects who remain independent of the group's pressure to conform in the erroneous direction, were more self-confident about their own judgments and had greater feelings of need for dealing adequately with the task at hand. Again, Flint (1960) showed that a member's knowledge of his ability carried much more weight than did knowledge of his deviation from the rest of the group in determining whether or not he would try to influence others in the group rather than remain passive. Moreover, whether or not he knew about his ability relative to others in the group was critical in determining how much he would stick to his original position. On the other hand, it made no difference in his tendency to shift his opinion following discussion with other members if a member knew how much he deviated initially or whether this was not revealed to him. Again, Samelson (1957) showed that the amount of conformity to erroneous majority opinion was reduced by further instructions implying that individual subjects might be more accurate than the majority opinion. In the same way, Tuddenham (1958a) found a marked reduction in conformity when subjects were told that the simulated group norm might be in error occasionally.

The significance of being correct was shown also by Jones, Wells, and Torrey (1958). When the experimenter fed back information to subjects supporting the correct answer and opposing the incorrect solution reached by a hypothetical majority, conformity to the incorrect hypothetical majority was greatly inhibited. The effect of the experimenter here was much greater than his effect when he added his weight to supporting the incorrect answer reached by the hypothetical majority. When the experimenter entered the scene with the correct solution, subjects were ready to reject majority opinion without too much concern. When the experimenter joined forces with the clearly erroneous majority, he gave it little extra weight.

Again, the importance of being correct was cited by Tuddenham (1957) to account for the tendency of both "yielders" and "independents" in Asch-type situations to try to compromise between reality and social demands. Thus, extreme "yielders" will still choose the more reasonable of two false norms.

8. *The clearer the group's rewards and goals, the more attractive will be the group (p. 65);* hence **the clearer its goals, the more members will conform to the group.**

Direct support for this proposition comes from the variety of previously mentioned studies on setting group goals. Presumably, when individuals participate in selecting their own goals they are much clearer about those goals than if the goals are set for them by higher authority or by outsiders. Conformity to new ways of operating, to new standards, or to new ways of behaving was found greater in numerous experiments when members of groups were able to select these new approaches rather than have them imposed by higher authority (Coch & French, 1948; Levine & Butler, 1952; Radke & Klisurich, 1947).

Suppose, for example, the goal is to find the correct answer. When such is the case, goal clarity strongly increases conformity. Thus, Marple (1933) found that high school and college students as well as adults shifted markedly toward both majority and "expert" opinion when they were revealed. Again, Wheeler and Jordan (1929) noted that 60 percent of their subjects shifted in the direction of majority opinion on matters of social, political, and economic opinion when it was revealed while only 4 percent shifted away from it. Similarly, Pennington, Haravey, and Bass (1958) observed that members of a discussion group conformed to each other's opinion much more when the group's decision was announced to them than when no such announcement was made after a private ballot.

9. *The more members share the same goals obtainable through cooperation, the more they will be attracted to each other (p.69);* hence **the more members share the same goals obtainable through cooperation, the more likely they are to conform to each other in their behavior.**

A variety of commentary and evidence supports Proposition 9, in whole or part. Stogdill (1959) noted that once members accept a common goal with expectations that can be mutually reinforced, they show concern for conformity by all members in the group to the norms of the group. Common goals were added by Jackson and Saltzstein (1958) to already operating laboratory groups. Some of the groups were attractive; others were unattractive. Members were either of high or low esteem. Conformity was increased with the addition of the common goals particularly among those members of high esteem in attractive groups.

Deutsch and Gerard (1955) showed the significance of the set to cooperate. They found that subjects working together to minimize errors were much more likely to conform than when each subject worked to minimize his own errors only. And Mausner and Bloch (1957) showed the same process as an aftereffect, finding that subjects who had worked cooperatively in the past currently tended to converge.

Getting different groups to conform to each other also is accomplished by the development of common goals. As long as groups remain in competition with each other so that if one wins the other loses, there seems to be no basis on which they can reach agreement (without resort to arbitration or force) on the basic issues dividing them, save perhaps on how to negotiate with each other. About the only known method of getting groups to agree after a struggle has developed between them, is to locate superordinate goals which both groups can share and for which both can work. Ultimately, with such goals, competing groups can develop means for joint-decision making and conformity to each others practices and standards without resort to force or arbitration by higher authority (Sherif, 1953).

10. *A group is more attractive, the greater the rewards which may be earned by membership and the greater the expectancy of earning them (p. 60);* hence **the greater the rewards and expectancies of reward for membership, more likely the conformity to group demands.**

In direct support of this proposition, Grossack (1954) found that members demanded much more uniformity in behavior from each other when they were rewarded as groups rather than when they competed with each other for rewards. Bryant, Dobbins, and Bass (1958) obtained greater conformity among 75 institutionalized delinquent boys in contrast to a matched sample of 75 high school boys. The results supported the hypothesis that the delinquent's peer group is much more significant to him than the corresponding peer group of the normal high school boy. For the delinquent, his peer group becomes a substitute family with much greater power to reward and punish him than is true for the normal adolescent.

11. *Current effectiveness promotes subsequent attractiveness (p. 79);* hence **conformity currently is likely to be greater in a group that experienced effectiveness earlier; more dissension and deviation is likely to occur in a group with a preceding history of failure.**

Evidence to support this proposition is to be found in the studies of intergroup competition by Blake and Mouton

(1959). Based on the experience of as many as 60 groups of 8 to 12 men each following victory or defeat after a day of competition with other similar groups, Blake and Mouton have noted characteristic differences in the perceptions and behavior of the victorious compared with the defeated groups. Victorious groups become more cohesive and attractive than before the competition and induce among members even greater conformity. Members cooperate with one another, avoiding any detailed critique of their own previous behavior which might lead to dissension and conflict in trying to deal with means for further improvement. On the other hand, defeated groups fall apart; members fight among themselves. They argue about their defeat and try to determine who led them astray.

Those popular writers (e.g., editors of *Life*) who view the past ten years in the United States as a period of unsurpassed material growth and splendor tend to focus on our need to accept all this bounty and to avoid any major modifications in our country's political and economic institutions. On the contrary, those commentators (e.g., Arthur Schlesinger) who view the past ten years as a series of defeats for American science, politics, and social development, see the coming decade as demanding radical change, need for facing up to problems realistically, and planning for the future more rather than conforming to the past.

Hamblin and Wiggins (1959) suggest that groups develop in cycles. When the group has achieved a high degree of success in coping with its problems, a high degree of conformity to prescribed ways is maintained because these ways ensure continued successful goal attainment. But this conformity to what was successful during the "equilibrium" or success phase, continues even after the problems have changed for the group and the previously successful techniques are no longer appropriate. During this period of inertia, ritualistic conformity abounds. Old norms and techniques are conformed to because of their earlier applicability. In the case of military ritualism and innovation, it often has taken a series of disasters to break conformity to rules and techniques appropriate to the past, but not the present. A generation elapsed between the time Billy Mitchell sank a battleship by air bombardment and the launching of our last battleship.

Influence, Interaction, and Conformity

12. *Members of groups are motivated by consideration or lack of it: promises of reward, support, affection, or threats of punishment, burdensome demands and deflation of self-esteem (p. 99).* Since conformity is defined as a reflection of influence, **conformity will depend upon how much consideration members receive for conforming.**

One must look to the sociological and anthropological literature for support for this and the next proposition. It is obvious that the man in the gray flannel suit acts as he does in response to support by his associates for doing so. Wearing a beret or loud ties or deviating in more critical areas of behavior is likely to bring ridicule, scorn, ostracism, and even loss of job opportunities. The Zuni child learns early that deviation is punished by scorn and shaming; as an adult he remains highly conforming (Mead *et al.*, 1939). Hemphill (1961) was able to increase systematically the amount members attempted leadership by providing social approval for doing so. In the same way, it should be possible in the laboratory to increase systematically conforming behavior by giving approval and support for it or increasing deviating behavior by the same means.

13. *Leadership is accomplished by initiating structure—making others more able to overcome the obstacles thwarting goal attainment (p. 101).* Assuming conformity is the obverse

of leadership, it follows **that conformity of an individual will depend on the extent others in his group instruct, supervise, inform, or decide for him.**

Again, no experimental evidence is yet available on this rather obvious proposition but anthropology supplies illustrations. For example, the absence of close supervision and the wide toleration of almost any behavior by the Eskimo child is cited by Mead (*et al.,* 1939) as a reason for the nonconformity of Eskimos as adults.

In any laboratory experiment, subjects usually begin by conforming to a whole series of limitations and boundaries established for them by the experimenter. Conformity of the subjects varies directly with the scope and detail of the instructions and the attention paid to them by the experimenter. Similar kinds of conforming at the overt and concealed levels; or even at more hidden or buried levels, to the demands of the experimenters, instructors, therapists, or supervisors occur in varying degrees during role taking, role playing, play acting, and hypnosis. Freedom to deviate is inversely related to the limitations and restrictions imposed on the individual member by the laboratory experimenter, by one's culture or society or by one's boss. Thus, Mead (1959) observed that opportunities for creativity are greatest among the Manus with few fixed cultural traditions of their own. This makes it possible for the Manus to seek out, to use and to manipulate the useful ideas they find among their neighbors. Only minor innovations occur in cultures richer in tradition such as the Samoan.

14.   *Influence occurs sooner, to a greater extent and brings more reinforcement as a consequence of interaction (p. 129).* Assuming that conformity reflects leadership, a function of interaction, **conformity to the demands of others is more likely to occur and to occur faster when interaction is possible.**

Several experiments support the validity of this deduction. Independent of whether or not a group decision was made or announced, Pennington, Haravey, and Bass (1958) found that members given opportunity to discuss with each other the solution to a series of problems were more likely to coalesce than when not permitted to interact in the same way. Again, Scott (1956) noted that values held in common by members of a group became more important to the members following intensive discussion about those values. Sherif, White, and Harvey (1955) observed that a member of a group who is deviant prior to experience with the group, will shift his responses to conform to the group norm or modal response. The member's shift toward the group then will persist even after he leaves it. If the member does not have an opportunity to interact with the group, as time goes on, he will maintain his deviant position, conforming increasingly to his own individual standard, actually reducing rather than increasing his shift away from his own position of deviancy (Sherif, 1935).

15. *As problems facing the group become more difficult or as the members become less able to cope with their problems, more leadership becomes possible (p. 134).* Since conformity is a reflection of leadership, **as problems of a group become more difficult or as the members become less able, conformity is likely to increase in that group.**

Both Mowrer (1942) and Festinger (1954) use this proposition about conformity and difficulty to explain why we show greater conformity in matters of social belief compared to matters of physical technique and fact. Matters of social belief are much more ambiguous, open to argument and disagreement, while matters of fact are more easily tested and less likely to remain ambiguous. Conformity is greater to social beliefs because the correct answers to the problems they concern are less easy to obtain with assuredness. Consistent with these comments, Luchins and Luchins (1955) found that when an ambiguous rather than clear stimulus was presented to subjects, they increased in conformity to distorting suggestions by others. Similarly, Chapman and Volkman (1939) reduced the conformity subjects displayed to the experimenter's suggestions by permitting the subjects to reduce the ambiguity of circumstances first by allowing them to establish their own standards of judgment originally before being faced with the suggestions.

Considerable evidence also exists to support more specifically the statement that conformity is a function of problem difficulty or the inability of members to cope with the problem. For example, Thorndike (1938) demonstrated that the closer a participant was to the right answer initially on matters of fact, the less he was affected by a subsequent majority vote. Flint (1960) reported similar results showing that subjects with greater initial accuracy, who knew of this accuracy, were much less prone to shift their opinion as a consequence of discussion. On the contrary they were more likely to try to change other participant's opinions.

With reference to problem difficulty, per se, Blake, Helson, and Mouton (1957) showed consistent increases in conforming behavior with increases in the difficulty of the problems faced by the participants. In a related analysis, Coleman, Blake, and Mouton (1958) established a correlation of .58 between the difficulty of general information items and the tendency to conform by men. For women, the correlation was .89 between the difficulty of general information items and their tendency to conform. In a series of unpublished studies, I obtained similar results showing that both public and private coalescence increased significantly with increases in the difficulty of the problems worked.

16. *If the difficulties facing a group are too great, members' expectations of failure may make the groups sufficiently* *unattractive to cause the members to withdraw rather than attempt to solve the problems or attempt to succeed as leaders (p. 137).* Assuming that conformity is the obverse of leadership, **if the group's difficulties are too great, members may deviate further from the norms of the group rather than increase in conformity.**

History is replete with examples of societal breakdown in the face of almost insurmountable problems in which the institutions of society became so ineffective that increased deviation from its norms rather than increased conformity resulted. Thus, Christian "deviancy" became the means for withdrawing from the disatisfying, disintegrating Roman world.

Mowrer (1942) describes various types of deviants in modern society whose behavior is an outgrowth of overwhelming personal difficulties of one kind or another. Thus, the victim of seasonal work, industrial inadequacy, feeble-mindedness, crises in his family, or racial discrimination may solve his problems by becoming a hobo, deviating from the traditional American custom that an able-bodied man should work or seek employment until retirement. Faced with somewhat less severe problems, the typical adolescent, the half-child-half-adult, like the marginal man at the edge of two cultures, is likely to overconform rather than deviate. What we are suggesting, therefore, is that up to a certain point, as problem difficulties increase, solutions to these problems by conforming to suggestions of others will increase. But beyond a certain point, difficulties may become so great, that conformity is no longer a possible solution. Answers can be achieved only through deviation from the group or society.

Personality, Ability, and Conformity

17. *The task-oriented leader will attempt leadership most often when the group is attractive to him because of its tasks*

and the rewards for task success (p. 155). Considering conformity as the obverse of leadership, **the task-oriented member will attempt to conform to his group to the extent it is
attractive to him because of its tasks and rewards for task effectiveness, and when he sees such conformity enables him to
achieve task success.**

A direct test of the proposition as stated would involve a
task such as judging opinion where the group or majority
opinion was always superior to any individual opinion and
where this fact was made known. In such circumstances,
task-oriented members would be expected to shift more to
the group decision possibly than interaction-oriented members, particularly if their shifts were never made public so
that the interaction-oriented members would not be under
as much pressure to conform for social reasons. While no
direct test has been discovered in the literature, experiments
on conformity such as those by Asch (1952) making use of
circumstances in which conforming is antithetical to true task
success, demonstrate the converse of the above proposition;
namely, that task-oriented members are *less* likely to conform when conformity will be *detrimental* to true task effectiveness. Thus, Asch reported that a subject was much
less likely to yield to group pressure to make an erroneous
judgment about the length of two lines when he maintained
a feeling of necessity for dealing adequately with the task
and avoiding an erroneous, defective solution. In the same
way, Thibaut and Strickland (1956) showed that in similar
circumstances conformity was decreased when members of a
group were given the set to do the best job possible—the "task
set." Again, McDavid (1959) showed that "message-oriented"
subjects concerned with the contents of communications
(task-oriented) differed from "source-oriented" members
more concerned with who sent the messages (interaction-
oriented). In contrast to source-oriented subjects, the message-

oriented participants were less susceptible to group influence, less concerned about discrepancies with others in the group and more likely to effect compromises with discrepancies between their own and group decisions rather than simply to conform to them.

18. *The interaction-oriented member will avoid attempting leadership likely to disrupt current patterns of interaction or likely to involve risks of making mistakes while interacting with others (p. 156).* Considering conformity as the reflection of leadership, **the interaction-oriented member will attempt to conform to avoid disrupting current patterns of interaction or to avoid risking mistakes while interacting with others.**

In the Asch-type experiments, conformity has been found greater among interaction-oriented rather than task-oriented subjects, but, as mentioned earlier, in all these experiments, accepting the group decision or the norm or the simulated influence of the group requires a subject to reject the truth of what actually impinges on his senses. In these analyses, conformity earns or maintains social approval at the expense of true task accomplishment and avoids the risks of ostracism or the possible rejection by the group for disagreeing with them. It also avoids risking showing oneself to be in error and thereby losing esteem among others. Those subjects most desirous of earning or maintaining social approval therefore are most likely to conform in such circumstances.

In addition to the just cited experiment by Thibaut and Strickland (1956) who showed that conformity could be increased by making the members more interaction-oriented imposing a "group set" on them rather than a "task set," several other studies have found conformity greater among interaction-oriented participants. Hardy (1957) found that conformity was least among those subjects with the least need for affiliation. But contrary to expectations, highest conformity was shown by those with medium needs rather than very strong needs for affiliation. McDavid's (1959) previously mentioned study likewise illustrated that source-oriented members concerned with who sent the message rather than what message was sent were more susceptible to group influence and were more likely to conform. The same result was obtained by Schroder and Hunt (1958). They found that subjects concerned more about the esteem of the source of a suggestion are more likely to conform when large discrepancies exist between the truth and the suggestion. Again, Raven (1959) found that subjects who do not feel rejected by others and presumably are less concerned about what others think of them, conform less than those that do feel such concern when the possibility of being rejected exists. In the same way, Moeller and Applezweig (1957) noted that subjects high in the need for social approval and low in the need for self-approval were most likely to conform in the Asch line-judging situation compared to those low in need for social approval and high in need for self-approval on the Behavior Interpretation Inventory. I too found (Bass, 1961) that interaction-oriented women showed more public acceptance of group decisions than task-oriented women, but less private acceptance. Results were inconclusive with men.

19. *The self-oriented member is more concerned with his success rather than effectiveness as a leader (p. 153).* Considering conformity as the obverse of leadership, it follows that **the self-oriented member conforms to the extent that doing so meets his own personal needs irrespective of whether it is conducive to the task or interaction effectiveness of the group.**

Again, as in the case of task-orientation, no specific experimental evidence is available although the significance of self-orientation has been mentioned by investigators. Asch (1952) noted that some of his nonconformists did so because of a stronger need to maintain their own individual integrity compared with the need to avoid appearing different and being ostracized by others. The circumstances under which typical representatives from different national or ethnic backgrounds conform may be seen as a function of their differential needs and orientations. Tureen and Palmer (1955) found that German prisoners-of-war exhibited much greater need to defend themselves from frustration and hostility on the Cornell Selectee Index while American soldiers were much more prone to openly demand love and approval. It follows that conformity by typical Americans would be more common in circumstances where the conforming behavior resulted in gaining for them love and approval which they seek. On the contrary, conformity by model Germans might be more likely to occur as a means of escaping from frustrating or hostile circumstances.

Benne and Sheats (1948) described a series of individual roles played in discussion groups which usually contribute little to group progress and serve mainly to meet the needs of the individuals playing those roles. Seldom can these needs be met through conforming behavior. On the contrary, deviancy of one form or another is most likely to be seen. For example, the "playboy" obtains his satisfactions through clowning, deflating the esteem of others, showing off, and diverting the group from its task activities. Conformity to the group's tasks or interaction needs has relatively little reward value for the "playboy." Similarly, the "dominator" gains his satisfactions through monopolizing the discussion, trying to impose his decisions on everyone else, trying to authorize his own agenda rather than by trying to conform to the wishes of his group as a whole.

Just when would the highly self-oriented individual conform? Plato recognized this occuring in the self-seeking politician before his power is established: "In the early days of his power, he is full of smiles, and he salutes everyone he meets" (*The Republic*). A good illustration is supplied by the New York gubernatorial candidates who eat pizza in Italian neighborhoods, speak Spanish in Puerto Rican neighborhoods, and generally conform in various ways to national customs of each of the ethnic groups to whom they are appealing for votes. They conform, not because of fear of ostracism or rejection, or as the way to get a job done best for themselves and their group, but rather to meet their own needs, namely to earn more votes. Of coures, this behavior is commonplace among political office seekers. And, as Merei (1949) showed, a newcomer to a group must first conform to the norms of the group before he gains acceptance from other members sufficient to influence them. If he enters the group and does not first show his willingness to conform to current standards and practices of the group, his subsequent efforts to influence others are likely to be rejected. Armed with such information, the would-be leader of a group first may exhibit conformity to further his own self-interests, to gain for himself the acceptance necessary for him to become more influential in the group subsequently. The overconformity of some northerners in the South, assimilated second-generation immigrants or middle-class Negroes or other marginal people may have at its roots personal needs not accounted for simply in terms of the need for social approval. For example, the middle-class Negro may overconform not only to gain approval and acceptance by his white associates, but also to demonstrate that he can outdo his white associates, measure for measure.

Ability and Conformity

20. *One member can persuade another if he has demonstrated his ability to solve the other member's problems (p. 162).* Considering conformity as the obverse of leadership, it follows that **one member will conform to the suggestions of another if the other has demonstrated his ability to solve the first member's problems.**

Mausner (1954) showed that judgments of subjects with a previous history of failure tended to converge towards partners who had experienced greater success in the past. Again, Mausner and Bloch (1957) showed that some subjects would converge less when positively reinforced for holding their position—when they had experienced success in holding to their position. Similarly, Thorndike (1938) found that those individuals closer to the right answers initially were much less affected by learning of the vote of the majority of their group, over which they personally had no great influence, one way or the other.

Yet, when the true norm developed freely by the group, subject to the greater influence of the more able members, is the standard for measuring conformity, the ability-conformity relationship is obscured. Among 350 subjects working in small groups on ten judgmental problems, I have found low but significant *positive* correlations between the initial accuracy of the subjects and their tendency to accept the group decision and be in agreement with other members following interaction with them (Bass, 1955). For 120 additional subjects, Flint (1960) removed the error in these correlations associated with practice and group effects and still obtained positive significant associations between ability and agreement with others following interaction. The reason for these findings is rather simple. In the judgmental situations involved, group judgment is almost always more accurate than the average initial judgment of the members and is more like the judgment of the more accurate of the members. Group opinion develops freely and is true group opinion rather than simulated. In this situation, the best possible group decision is strived for by the members of the group. Those members with more ability are likely to contribute more to the group decision finally reached and to accept this decision to a greater extent.

The group decision is more like the original opinion of the

most able members so that, in reality, other members have shifted more towards the more accurate member rather than vice versa. This can be seen in the correlation of .28 found between the initial accuracy of a subject and his relative successful leadership as measured by the greater tendency of other members to shift towards his initial judgment rather than vice versa (Bass, 1959d).

It has been fairly well established that deviants from the group opinion are most likely to be the targets of communication. Other members closer to the group norm are most prone to attempt to influence and persuade the deviant (Back, 1951). Yet, Flint (1960) showed that deviants, themselves, may become the ones who attempt to influence the rest of the group rather than vice versa, *when they learn through feedback that their opinions are more correct and more accurate than the average other member in their group*. What is implied by the Flint and Bass results is that Proposition 20 is an adequate statement for "rigged" laboratory studies, but must be qualified if applied to settings where true answers and true group opinions are involved.

21. *In a wide variety of situations, the more fluent, intelligent, original and adaptable member is more likely to succeed as the leader (p. 166).* Considering conformity as the obverse of leadership, it follows that **in a wide variety of situations, the less fluent, less intelligent, less original, and less adaptable member is more likely to conform to the suggestions of others.**

While Proposition 20 dealt with the actual ability of participants with the task at hand, Proposition 21 is concerned with how the tendency to conform to the suggestions of others is affected by generalized aptitudes conducive to success or failure with the tasks. Supporting Proposition 21 is a study of Nakamura (1958) who found that a low intelligence quotient contributed to conforming behavior in problem solving settings. Similarly, Toboski, Juliano, and Kerr (1956) found that conformity decreased among individual members to the extent to which they were rated higher in their chances for success as an actor, showed more ability to assume a character and to create an atmosphere in the field of dramatics.

22. *The would-be leader cannot be too much more able than those he leads to succeed maximally as a leader (p. 177).* Considering conformity as the obverse of leadership, it follows that **a member may be unable rather than unwilling to conform to the norms of his group, because of his very great lack of ability in comparison to the abilities of others in his group.**

What is implied in Proposition 22 is that deviation may stem from lack of ability rather than from motivational reasons (the unattractiveness of the group) as implied by Proposition 16. Similarly, deviation from a group may be due to inadequacy or inability relative to the average ability of the group rather than absolute inadequacy in the face of external challenge to the group.

The deviancy of the mental defective is obvious. The retarded child's deviation from the standards of his normal classmates obviously results initially from his lack of ability rather than his lack of need for social approval or his lack of other needs likely to be satisfied by means of conformity.

23. *The ability of the leader must be relevant to solving the problems of the groups he expects to lead (p. 174).* Considering conformity as the obverse of leadership, **conformity of the less able person will depend upon his inadequacies in solving the particular problems of the group in which he is a member.**

Proposition 23 suggests that the sporadic, unsophisticated playgoer who is also a golfing enthusiast is likely to be much more concerned about conforming to what is expected of spectators in a small playhouse than is the regular habitué of the theater who seldom ventures out on the golf course. But conforming behavior may be reversed for both on the golf course. No experimental evidence has been found on this matter.

Transfer of Conforming Behavior

24. *If he has been successful and effective earlier, a leader will succeed and be effective to a maximum in any situation the more it actually resembles the earlier one (p. 183);* as-suming that conformity is a reflection of leadership, **conformity to others will be maximum in a new situation the more the new situation resembles an earlier one in which conformity occurred in the same way for the same reasons.**

Supporting Proposition 24 is Shils' (1950) discussion of the effects on American servicemen of their primary groups. Shils suggests that the extent a soldier conforms to the norms of the group to which he belongs depends on whether he identifies with other reference groups whose norms are similar to this group.

Asch (1952) reported considerable consistency in the tendency for individuals to yield or remain nonconformists over successive replications of the same line-judging situation. These results were corroborated and extended by Rosner (1957). In addition to observing the same consistencies as Asch, he found that conforming behavior or nonconforming behavior was transferred to similar judgmental situations in simulated groups, where planted accomplices always gave erroneous judgments as in the Asch line-judging situation. Conformists in the line-judging situations also tended to conform when faced with judgments about nonsense syllables, about nonsense figures and about simple paragraphs.

25. *Successful leaders are more likely to have been the youngest child in their family; had facilitating, stimulating, approving, accepting parents; and come from harmonious, friendly, tolerant, family atmospheres (pp. 195–198).* Assuming conformity is the obverse of leadership, it follows that, **conformists are more likely to have been the oldest child in their family; had domineering, inconsistent, rejecting, parents; and come from discordant, unfriendly, intolerant family atmospheres.**

Anthropological evidence suggests that those primitive societies in which conforming behavior predominates maintain the pattern from one generation to the next by the child-raising procedures they tend to follow. For example, among the Bathonga, a highly conformist culture, there is little room for children to question the decisions of their elders, their chiefs, or their gods (Mead *et al.*, 1939).

Based on a review of many studies on the subject, Hurlock (1950) suggested that there is a slight tendency for the oldest child of the family to be more conservative and more easily influenced by suggestion. An explanation for this may lie in the lack of experience of the parents with their first child as compared to later children, their lesser financial and emotional security, as well as the need for the first child to adjust from being an only child to being one among many (Goodenough & Leahy, 1927).

The significance of parental attitudes and behavior on the subsequent conformity found in their children was dealt with by Champney (1941), who suggested that when parents tend to dominate their children, restraining the children's efforts to solve some of their own problems, demanding obedience before everything else, they are likely to create shy, docile, self-conscious, conforming children, overly sensitive to criticism. Again, parents who neglect rather than stimulate their children with new challenges are likely to develop strong feelings of rejection in such children, who in turn will be strongly motivated to seek praise. Since this strong motivation for approval is characteristic of the highly conforming person, it follows that parents who ignore their children with unconcern, nonchalance, or who openly reject their children, are likely to create future conformists. Mowrer (1939) suggested that children from autocratic homes or schools are either likely to become domineering and autocratic themselves or highly conforming and dependent on the suggestions of others.

A more specific test of Proposition 25 as stated is provided by Mussen and Kagan (1958) who found that extreme conformists in the Asch situation were more likely to perceive their parents on the Thematic Apperception Test as harsh, punitive, restrictive, and rejecting.

Status, Esteem, and Conformity

26. **Conformity to group standards and decisions is greater among more influential members and those closer initially to the majority or group decision (p. 247).**

Consistent with the qualification needed to interpret Proposition 20 concerning ability and conformity, the argument here is that the more a member contributes to a group decision and the more he influences others in the group or helps establish the norm of the group, the more he, himself, will conform to those norms or group decisions. This reasoning is supported by studies of the significance of participation in setting one's goals in determining whether one accepts those goals (e.g., Coch & French, 1948).

In determining how much we will conform to the group's goals, the importance of how much we influence those goals cannot be studied when the group norm is imposed on a single subject in a simulated group such as in the Asch experiment, for here, the subject has no control over what will be the group norm. In freer circumstances, successful leaders do tend to conform more than nonleaders. Thus, a correlation of .38

has been obtained between the tendency of the final group decision to be like one's initial opinion and the extent one accepts that final group decision for 350 subjects (Bass, 1955). Gurman (1959) extended these findings, showing that the participants of such experiments with true group decisions perceive the positive correlation in their own behavior, and see it in the behavior of the other members of their groups. In addition, outside observers of discussions among the members are likely to also report the same positive correlation.

In this free circumstance, however, the relationship is contaminated by a number of other variables and interrelationships. The relationship between influence, yielding, and conformity depends, therefore, on how we measure the three variables and what we mean by them as well as the extent we allow each of the variables to fluctuate freely. For example, as mentioned in discussing Proposition 20, the more influential member is likely to be more accurate originally. The final group decision is likewise more accurate. The more influential person, therefore, has to shift his own opinion less in order to be in more agreement with the group decision than does the originally highly deviant member. If conformity is measured by the amount of shift (viz., Goldberg, 1954) or the amount of yielding to an arbitrarily "rigged" group norm rather than acceptance of the group norm, per se, then the initially widely deviant person will show up as more conforming; for, as Festinger (1954) has noted, those originally closer to the mode of the group will have stronger tendencies to change or influence the positions of those who are at the extremes and will have less need to change their positions.

27. *The higher one's status, the more likely he is to succeed as a leader among those of lower status (p. 269).* Assuming conformity is the obverse of leadership, it follows that **the lower one's status the more likely he is to conform to those of higher status.**

The proverbial yes man who exhibits unswerving acceptance of decisions made for him by those of higher status than
himself symbolizes Proposition 22. Considerable experimental and survey evidence supports this proposition. Gorden
(1952) showed that the extent a person conformed to the
opinions of 24 others living with him in a cooperative project
depended on his conception of his own position in the group
compared to the others. Both Crutchfield (1955) and Jones,
Wells, and Torrey (1958) demonstrated that the experimenter can carry great weight (presumably because of his
status) in increasing the amount of conformity exhibited by
subjects to an erroneous majority decision.

Status differences associated with sex differences also result
in differential tendencies to inform. Just as Strodtbeck (1954)
had demonstrated that the differential status of men and
women led to the differential tendencies of husbands or wives
to lead in problem-solving discussions, so did Tuddenham,
MacBride, and Zahn (1958) demonstrate, as previously cited,
that women tended to conform in simulated mixed-sex groups
to a greater extent than did men, and that women tended to
conform more when more men were supposedly contained in
their simulated groups.

**28. Conformity to the person with status but without
power will continue until it becomes apparent that the figure-
head has only the symbols of status. Even then, others may
conform ritualistically to the powerless bearer of status symbols because the ritual is habitual and satisfying in its own
right, or is a custom approved by the group whose violation
would bring social disapproval (p. 267).**

A great deal of conforming ritual still surrounds the British
monarch who is almost completely powerless in contrast to
the prime minister and his cabinet or parliament. The Prot-
estant minister may wield little power compared to some of
his wealthy parishioners, yet he is treated in many ways with

deference and respect which stem from still-satisfying custom
and traditions of the past when his power was much greater.
Hamblin and Wiggins (1959) have developed procedures
which may lend themselves to the experimental study of these
ritualistic relations.

29. *The higher one's esteem, the more likely he is to succeed as a leader among those of lower esteem (p. 289).* Assuming conformity is the obverse of leadership, it follows that
**the less esteem a member has, the more likely he is to con-
form to the suggestions of others.**

Numerous early studies such as those by Moore (1921) and
Marple (1933) showed students both in high school and
college as well as adults tended to shift their opinions in the
direction of what they perceived to be expert opinion. Experimental and survey studies, to be described in more detail
to support Proposition 30 (Berkowitz, 1957; Dittes and
Kelley, 1956; Menzel, 1957; Schroder, 1958), all attest to the
effect of esteem on conformity and demonstrate that individuals tend to conform more to those they esteem.

30. *The more esteemed member can be more persuasive
if his esteem depends on his being perceived as being able to
solve the group's problems; he can be more coercive if his
esteem depends on his personal control of what is desired by
others in the group (p. 289).* Assuming that conformity is
the obverse of leadership, it follows that (a) **a member is
more likely to be persuaded, conforming both publicly and
privately, if his lack of esteem is due to lack of ability** and (b)
**he is more likely to be coerced, conforming publicly but not
privately, if his lack of esteem is due to his lack of personal
power.**

Berkowitz (1957) provided evidence supporting section (a)
of Proposition 30 showing that individuals may conform more

to preferred groups or better-liked partners because they attach more *merit* to the opinions of those they like and to whom they are attracted. Presumably, in such circumstances, they are likely to conform to the group to the extent they like the group and see merit in the group's opinions. Data by Dittes and Kelley (1956) strongly support section (b) of Proposition 30 for their results show that their highest public conformity occurred among experimental subjects whose fictitious acceptance (or esteem) as a group member was reputed to be very low. Yet, their private conformity was low. These subjects also reported feeling least free to deviate from the group opinion. In the same way, Menzel (1957) found that physicians of low esteem according to sociometric ratings by fellow physicians, showed the greatest tendency to state that they had prescribed new drugs prior to the actual date which they really prescribed those drugs according to pharmaceutical records. Contrarily, those physicians highly esteemed by their colleagues did not attempt to show themselves as conforming publicly to what Menzel inferred was a norm for physicians, namely to be up to date in prescribing new drugs as they came on the market. Physicians of lower esteem evidently felt the stronger need to be seen publicly conforming to the norms of their professional group.

More complicated evidence supporting section (b) of Proposition 30 on how those of lower esteem are likely to be coerced is provided by Schroder (1958). Schroder contrasted three samples of subjects: (1) those who would never yield or be coerced in the Asch-type experiment, (2) those who yielded only when the group norm and the truth were close together, and (3) those who yielded even when the truth and the simulated majority opinion were far apart. In describing themselves afterwards, subjects who never yielded seemed to attach somewhat less importance to the esteem of a supposed source of disapproval. On the other hand, those subjects who were most likely to be coerced into accepting a markedly erroneous majority opinion were more likely to also accept and be influenced by disapproval from supposedly esteemed sources, yet at the same time were more likely than the first group of subjects to reject similar disapproval from disliked sources. Evidently the source of disapproval is more important in influencing the behavior of those who are easily coerced, while the esteem of the source of disapproval is of less significance to those who cannot be coerced as readily. It goes without saying that all three samples of subjects were more likely to be influenced on the whole by esteemed sources of influence than disliked sources.

31.   Since *conformity is greater in more attractive groups and mutual esteem correlates highly with attractiveness (p. 297)*, it follows that **conformity to group decisions, modal opinion, or norms of behavior, should be greater among groups where mutal esteem is high.**

This proposition is consistent with Thelen's (1954) suggestion that the power of a group, and presumably the amount of conformity likely to occur within that group, depends on the extent that mutual influence is seen as helpful. Specific evidence is provided by DiVesta (1959), who showed that there was a systematic decrease in conformity in a group upon learning of the inadequency of other members in the group. Again, Gerard (1954) found more convergence of opinion in groups with high mutual liking for each other.

32.   **The person with high self-esteem appears more likely to change others, to lead others, rather than to be changed by others or to conform readily (p. 299).**

A great deal of evidence is available supporting this proposition. Thorndike's (1938) previously mentioned analysis showed that the vote of the majority exerted less influence among those subjects who had confidence in themselves.

Similarly, Hochbaum (1954) showed that the self-confident member was more likely to resist conforming to his group. Again, in the same way, Asch (1952), Kelley and Lamb (1957), and Wiener (1956), all demonstrated that subjects who were less confident or less certain about their own opinion, were more likely to conform to a simulated majority opinion. Similarly, when esteem differences are simulated, subjects tend to estimate their own ability and self-esteem in line with the esteem they believe they have, and this in turn influences whether or not they will conform to the group's norms (Dittes & Kelley, 1956).

The significance of self-confidence may have been the reason that DiVesta (1959) observed that conformity decreases among subjects as they gain experience with their task and presumably increase in self-confidence. A more confounded result is reported when the level of aspiration of subjects is examined. Sears (1940) noted that children with low levels of academic aspiration or low scholastic self-esteem were more likely to shift their levels toward the group mean. But if they were above the mean they were less likely to shift down towards it.

Some of the sex differences noted by Tuddenham, Mac-Bride, and Zahn (1958) may have been due to the differential self-confidence and self-esteem of men compared with women. For Tuddenham and MacBride (1958) reported that according to postexperimental survey reactions, men seemed much higher in self-esteem than women, more satisfied with their own performance, much more confident of their own answers, and more flattering to themselves in comparison to others.

Both Flint (1960) and MacBride (1958) have shown that a subject can be made less likely to conform either to simulated groups or in a freely participated group if he is given feedback concerning his own accuracy. MacBride (1958, p. 38) concluded: "A demonstration of ability to perform a task can prepare an individual better to withstand contradictory group pressure. At the same time, a demonstration of inaccuracy can weaken self-confidence and reduce ability to withstand pressure." Flint's subjects who were accurate and learned of their ability were much more likely to hold to their own positions and less likely to conform than correspondingly able subjects who did not receive information about their ability. Thus, Flint demonstrated the significance to conformity of self-awareness and self-confidence in distinction to actual ability.

The inverse relation between maturation and suggestibility or gullibility noted by Triplett (1900) manifests itself in increasing confidence with age with one's own opinion in contrast to majority or expert opinion. Thus, Berenda (1950) noted that older children were more cautious and less prone to conform than younger children in the Asch experiment. Similar results were obtained by Marple (1933) with high school students, college students, and adults. High school students were most prone to conform to majority or expert opinion while adults were least likely to do so on an original test of civic problems about which adolescents knew the least and adults the most, presumably.

33. *Increases in self-accorded status increase attempts to lead (p. 300).* Assuming conformity is the obverse of leadership, it follows that **increases in self-accorded status reduces the tendency to conform.**

No specific evidence is available testing this proposition. However, previously reported results concerning the greater tendency of women to conform rather than men may in part be due to the differential self-estimates of status by men and women in our society.

34. *Events preceding the attempted leadership, or taking place concurrently, may result in the failure of what would have been successful leadership (p. 302).* Assuming conformity is a function of leadership, **events preceding the conforming behavior or taking place concurrently may result in the failure of what would have been conforming behavior.**

In addition to MacBride's study showing how individuals can be prepared to withstand group pressure by earlier experience building up their self-confidence, studies by Kelley and Woodruff (1956), Mausner and Bloch (1957), and Samelson (1957) also support Proposition 34. Kelley and Woodruff imposed on subjects an environmental circumstance in which the subjects had to listen to arguments against their own group norms. The investigators found that some subjects would shift away from their own group norms if they perceived that any others in their own group were doing so when presented with such counter norms; other subjects rejected as impossible the idea that some members of their own group were shifting as was indicated; and still others maintained their conformity despite the imposition of the counter norm. These latter subjects distorted the counter norm arguments so as to infer that they were really consistent with group norms, conforming at what we referred to earlier as the "buried" level. Mausner and Bloch found that subjects will conform least to each other's suggestions when they have experienced success previously at holding their own individual positions or when they have not worked together before. In a study similar to that of Kelley and Woodruff, Samelson was able to reduce conformity to the majority erroneous opinion by implying that the majority might be in error. Similar results were obtained by Jones, Wells, and Torrey (1958) and Tuddenham (1958a).

35.   Conformity to attempted leadership may require excessive energy expenditure not commensurate with promised rewards for compliance; it may demand an unacceptable distribution of rewards; it may threaten loss of esteem or status. In all of these cases despite the power or ability behind the

promotion of the conformity, the attempted leadership may be rejected and the conformity may not occur (p. 304).

DiVesta's (1959) analysis of the effects of confidence and motivation on susceptibility to informational social influence lends support to one part of the above proposition. DiVesta found a systematic decrease in conformity when subjects were told that their performance was a reflection of their intelligence. Conforming brought with it some loss of self-esteem for it implied that one was less able and less intelligent if he conformed.

Conformity and Interaction Potential

36. *One member can influence others to the extent they can interact (p. 128); more influence is likely with increased interaction potential among members (p. 132);* hence, **more conformity is likely with increased interaction potential.**

Interaction potential, and therefore **conformity, is likely to be greater under the following circumstances: among members of small rather than large groups; geographically proximate rather than distant groups; connected and communicative groups; intimate, familiar, mutually esteemed, attractive groups; homogenous in abilities rather than heterogeneous; more in contact with reality and more mature than groups of young children (p. 342).**

Other factors likely to promote interaction potential, hence **conformity, include: alcohol, boredom, third parties, the importance of the communications of the members, the amount of stimulation, the time available to interact, and the amount of coordination required for completion of the task (p. 343).**

Available evidence is somewhat mixed concerning the overall validity of Proposition 36, perhaps because of the difficulty in isolating the various factors. For example, as members become more familiar with each other and interaction potential, hence conformity, increases, the members also become more familiar with the tasks and more self-confident about what they are doing, hence less conforming.

EFFECTS OF GROUP SIZE.   Asch (1952) reported no differences in the amount of conformity observed in groups varying in size from 3 to 16, counter to what would be expected if Proposition 36 was valid. On the other hand, as Blake and Mouton note in Chapter 1, progressive increases in shifting of judgments occur for objective tasks (but not attitudinal or ambiguous perceptual ones) when the number of associates in a group increases from one to three. Also, Frye and Stritch (1961) found coalescence maximum in dyads and groups of 5 or 6 when groups of every size up to 13 were tested.

EFFECTS OF HOMOGENEITY.   It is rather obvious that persons with a homogeneous history who have developed common expectations will tend to conform to each other's opinion when faced with a relevant stimulus. For example, if a sketch of an old lady is shown to one group of subjects asking them to consider how they would describe such a woman, then a picture of a young lady is shown to a second group asking them to do likewise, almost all the members of the first group when confronted with an ambiguous sketch containing both an old and a young lady will report seeing the old lady. But, the second group will conform highly to their common expectation for seeing a young lady when confronted with the same ambiguous sketch.

ATTRACTION AND ESTEEM EFFECTS.   The effects on conformity of attractiveness and mutual esteem have already been discussed.

EFFECTS OF PERSONAL IMMATURITY.   Supporting evidence comes from studies of neurotics and psychotics when placed in interaction with each other. Spohn (1956) reported the disappearance of group control among markedly regressed and withdrawn schizophrenics. In the same way Levine *et al.* (1954) found that hospitalized neurotics tend to converge less towards their group's autokinetic norms. Another facet of evidence supporting the need for maturity and contact with reality was supplied by Gunderson, Grant, and Ballard (1959) who showed that delinquency-prone attitudes (antisocietal deviancy) can be reduced among "high maturity" confinees convicted for naval offenses using a closed-living-group program. This program required close, continuing, interpersonal relationships among 20 men living, working, studying, and undergoing therapy together with three supervisors. Much less shift in a direction of increased conformity and acceptance of responsibility was shown by confinees of low maturity— confinees who feel that the world exists to take care of them.

Conformity consistently has been found greater among younger in contrast to older children (Berenda, 1950).

EFFECTS OF ALCOHOL. Compared to deviation or conformity when sober, alcoholic intoxication is likely to produce both an increase in deviancy and a susceptibility to new kinds of conformity. Intoxication reduces inhibition. This reduced inhibition brings with it increased deviancy and susceptibility to influence resulting in increased conformity to new demands.

37. *Interaction potential,* hence **conformity, can be increased by establishing formal organizations and increasing the differentiation of members and status; increasing the training of assigned leaders; increasing the educational level and the degree of understanding of the members; establishing and reinforcing reliable sources of information; increasing the rapidity and frequency of transmittal of information; and splintering the group. It also can be increased by increas-**

ing cross-training; restricting size arbitrarily; increasing familiarity; promoting feelings of homogeneity; increasing mutual esteem; and developing new communication procedures (p. 19).

Both Propositions 36 and 37 are statements of research needed, rather than a review of what has already been done. Some aspects of these two propositions seem almost self-evident; for example, that conformity increases in groups that are converted from informal into formal organizations. Other parts of the propositions require qualification. For example, conformity *is* a function of educational level when what is implied is education for particular activities, not education in general. Equally obvious is the impact of the rapid growth of mass media of communication on our increase in conformity in speech, dress, and attitudes. George Orwell's *1984* is a threat of what may come to pass as a consequence of a completely formally organized society coupled with rapid and frequent mass communication procedures.

38. *Attempts to lead are more likely to be accepted readily during crises than if no emergency was present (p. 437).* Assuming conformity is the obvious of leadership, **conformity is likely to be greater in situations of crisis or emergency.**

As was noted by a Spanish sage of the 13th Century, "Misfortune unites men when the same thing is harmful to both." The best evidence supporting Proposition 38 is to be found in the analyses by Blake and Mouton (1959) of what happens to a group suddenly threatened with competition by one or more other groups. The outcome of the competition will result in a clear victory or defeat for the group. Blake and Mouton note first the increased attraction of the members to their own group as a consequence of the external threat. Members close ranks, become more unified, and increase in their conformity to each other and to the norms of the group. Fighting between the members is reduced and play is eliminated. (Plato observed this phenomenon noting that dictators were prone to stir up a foreign war in order to bring unity at home.)

Under the effects of competition, group members conform highly in their universally higher evaluation of their own solutions in contrast to the quality they see in the other groups' solutions. They see their own solution particularly better than the quality of enemy groups, ignoring the performance of neutral groups who are not in competition with them.

When representatives from the different groups meet, they each must conform to their own group's appraisal of the situation. Seldom will any representative capitulate to agreeing that another competing group's product is better than his own. Failure to conform would mean ostracism and rejection by one's own group. Only twice in 33 groups did a spokesman ever acknowledge defeat. For spokesmen are committed people, individuals who would prefer to be loyal than to solve the problem.

These results in turn may be consistent with various studies of perception under stress. Generally, as Smock (1955) has found, under stress, subjects reach structure or closure earlier, developing less tolerance for uncertainty. In a group under threat, this need manifests itself with greater demands for conformity or closure in order to minimize risk and uncertainty in the situation with knowledge of what everyone else in the group is going to do.

Summary

Conformity has been conceived as the reflection of successful influence. This conception makes it possible to apply a general theory of interpersonal behavior in order to derive a series of theorems accounting for much of what is known about conformity and deviation as well as providing hypotheses about conforming behavior for which no experimental evidence yet exists.

REFERENCES

Anderson, H. H., & Brandt, H. F.   A study of motivation involving self-announced goals of fifth-grade children and the concept of level of aspiration. *J. soc. Psychol.*, 1939, **10**, 209–232.

Applezweig, M. H., & Moeller, G.   Conforming behavior and personality variables. *Tech. Rept. 8*, Contract NONR 996 (02), Connecticut College, 1958.

Argyle, M.   Social pressure in public and private situations. *J. abnorm. soc. Psychol.*, 1957, **54**, 172–175.

Asch, S. E.   *Social psychology.* New York: Prentice-Hall, 1952.

Back, K. W.   Influence through social communication. *J. abnorm. soc. Psychol.*, 1951, **46**, 9–23.

Barch, A. M., Trumbo, D. & Nangle, J. E.   Social setting and conformity to a legal requirement. *J. abnorm. soc. Psychol.*, 1957, **55**, 396–398.

Bass, B. M.   Interrelations among measurements of member and group performance. *Tech. Rept. 4*, Contract N7 ONR 35609, Louisiana State Univer., 1955.

Bass, B. M.   Development and evaluation of a social acquiescence scale. *J. abnorm. soc. Psychol.*, 1956, **53**, 296–299.

Bass, B. M.   Effects of motivation on consistency of performance in groups. *Educ. psychol. Measmt.*, 1959a, **19**, 247–252.

Bass, B. M.   Feedback. In *Action Research Training Laboratory Proceedings.* 10th Session, West Point, N.Y., December 8–17, 1959b.

Bass, B. M.   Decision-making in small groups. In *Action Research Training Laboratory Proceedings.* 10th Session, West Point, N.Y., December 8–17, 1959c.

Bass, B. M.   An approach to the objective assessment of leadership. In B. M. Bass and I. A. Berg (Eds.), *Objective approaches to personality assessment.* New York: Van Nostrand, 1959d.

Bass, B. M. *Leadership, psychology and organizational behavior.* New York: Harper, 1960.

Bass, B. M. Comparisons of the behavior in groups of self-oriented, interaction-oriented and task-oriented members. *Tech. Rept. 25,* Contract N7 ONR 35609, Louisiana State Univer., 1961.

Bechterew, W., & Lange, A. Die Ergebnisse des experiments auf dem Gebiete der Kollektiven Reflexologie. *Zsch. f. angew. Psychol.,* 1924, 24, 224–254 (original not seen).

Beloff, H. Two forms of social conformity: acquiescence and conventionality. *J. abnorm. soc. Psychol.,* 1958, 56, 99–104.

Benne, K. D., & Sheats, P. Functional roles of group members. *J. soc. Issues,* 1948, 4 (2), 41–49.

Berenda, R. W. *The influence of the group on the judgments of children.* New York: King's Crown Press, 1950.

Berkowitz, L. Liking for the group and the perceived merit of the group's behavior. *J. abnorm. soc. Psychol.,* 1957, 54, 353–357.

Blake, R. R., Helson, H., & Mouton, J. S. The generality of conformity behavior as a function of factual anchorage, difficulty of task, and amount of social pressure. *J. Pers.,* 1957, 25, 294–305.

Blake, R. R., & Mouton, J. S. Intergroup relations. In *Action Research Training Laboratory Proceedings.* 10th Session, West Point, N.Y., December 8–17, 1959.

Brodbeck, M. The role of small groups in mediating the effects of propaganda. *J. abnorm. soc. Psychol.,* 1956, 52, 166–70.

Bryant, H. A., Dobbins, D. A., & Bass, B. M. Group effectiveness, coercion, change and coalescence among delinquents compared to non-delinquents. *Tech. Rept. 15,* Contract N7 ONR 35609, Louisiana State Univer., 1958.

Canning, R. R., & Baker, J. M. Effect of the group on authoritarian and non-authoritarian persons. *Amer. J. Sociol.,* 1959, 64, 579–581.

Champney, H. The variables of parent behavior. *J. abnorm. soc. Psychol.,* 1941, 36, 525–542.

Chapman, D. W., & Volkman, J. A. A social determinant of

the level of aspiration. *J. abnorm. soc. Psychol.*, 1939, **34**, 225–238.

Clark, H.   The crowd. *Psychol. Monogr.*, 1916, **21**, 26–36.

Coch, L., & French, J. R. P., Jr.   Overcoming resistance to change. *Hum. Relat.*, 1948, **1**, 512–532.

Coffin, T. E.   Some conditions of suggestion and suggestability: a study of some attitudinal and situational factors influencing the process of suggestion. *Psychol. Monogr.*, 1941, No. 241.

Coleman, J. F., Blake, R. R., & Mouton, J. S.   Task difficulty and conformity pressures. *J. abnorm. soc. Psychol.*, 1958, **57**, 120–122.

Conradi, E.   Song and call-notes of English sparrows when reared by canaries. *Amer. J. Psychol.*, 1905, **16**, 190–199.

Crutchfield, R. S.   Conformity and character. *Amer. Psychologist*, 1955, **10**, 191–198.

Deutsch, M., & Gerard, H. B.   A study of normative and informational social influences upon individual judgment. *J. abnorm. soc. Psychol.*, 1955, **51**, 629–636.

Dittes, J. E., & Kelley, H. H.   Effects of different conditions of acceptance upon conformity to group norms. *J. abnorm. soc. Psychol.*, 1956, **53**, 100–107.

DiVesta, F. J.   Effects of confidence and motivation on susceptibility to informational sound influence. *J. abnorm. soc. Psychol.*, 1959, **59**, 204–209.

Fearing, F., & Krise, E. M.   Conforming behavior and the J-curve hypothesis. *J. soc. Psychol.*, 1941, **44**, 109–118.

Fensterheim, H., & Tresselt, M. E.   The influence of value systems on the perception of people. *J. abnorm. soc. Psychol.*, 1953, **48**, 93–98.

Festinger, L.   Informal social communication. *Psychol. Rev.*, 1950, **57**, 271–282.

Festinger, L.   A theory of social comparison processes. *Hum. Relat.*, 1954, **7**, 117–140.

Festinger, L.   *A theory of cognitive dissonance.* Evanston: Row, Peterson, 1957.

Festinger, L., Gerard, H. B., Hymovitch, G., Kelley, H. H., & Raven, B.   The influence process in the presence of extreme deviates. *Hum. Relat.*, 1952, **5**, 327–346.

Festinger, L., & Thibaut, J. Interpersonal communication in small groups. *J. abnorm. soc. Psychol.*, 1951, **46**, 92–99.

Flint, A. W. Conformity, deviation and leadership as a function of feedback in groups. Unpublished doctoral dissertation, Louisiana State Univer., 1960.

French, J. R. P., Jr. The disruption and cohesion of groups. *J. abnorm. soc. Psychol.*, 1941, **36**, 361–377.

Frye, R., & Bass, B. M. Social acquiescence and behavior in groups. Paper read at Midwest Psychol. Ass., Detroit, May 3, 1958.

Gerard, H. B. The effect of different dimensions of disagreement on the communication process in small groups. *Hum. Relat.*, 1953, **6**, 249–271.

Gerard, H. B. The anchorage of opinions in face-to-face groups. *Hum. Relat.*, 1954, **7**, 313–325.

Glueck, S., & Glueck, E. *Unraveling juvenile delinquency.* New York: Commonwealth, 1950.

Goldberg, S. C. Three situational determinants of conformity to social norms. *J. abnorm. soc. Psychol.*, 1954, **49**, 325–329.

Goodenough, F. L., & Leahy, A. M. The effect of certain family relationships upon the development of personality. *Ped. Sem.*, 1927, **34**, 45–71.

Gorden, R. L. Interaction between attitude and the definitions of the situation in the expression of opinion. *Amer. social. Rev.*, 1952, **17**, 50–58.

Grossack, M. M. Some effects of cooperation and competition upon small group behavior. *J. abnorm. soc. Psychol.*, 1954, **49**, 341–348.

Gunderson, E. K., Grant, J. D., & Ballad, K. B. Changes in non-conformist attitudes induced by closed living groups. *U.S. Naval Retraining Command Tech. Rept. 12*, Contract NONR 1535 (00), San Diego, 1959.

Gurman, E. Objective vs. rated measures of performance in groups. Unpublished master's thesis. Louisiana State Univer., 1959.

Hall, O. The stages of a medical career. *Amer. J. Sociol.*, 1948, **53**, 327-336.

Hamblin, R. L., & Wiggins, J. A. Ambiguity and the rate of social adaptation. *Tech. Rept. 1,* Contract NONR 811 (16), Washington Univer., 1959.

Hardy, K. R. Determinants of conformity and attitude change. *J. abnorm. soc. Psychol.,* 1957, **54,** 289–294.

Hemphill, J. K. Why people attempt to lead. In L. Petrullo & B. M. Bass (Eds.), *Leadership and interpersonal behavior,* New York: Holt, 1961.

Hochbaum, G. M. The relation between group members' self-confidence and their reactions to group pressures to uniformity. *Amer. sociol. Rev.,* 1954, **19,** 678–687.

Hoffman, M. L. Conformity to the group as a defense mechanism. *Amer. Psychologist,* 1956, **11,** 375. (Abstract)

Horwitz, M. The recall of interrupted group tasks: an experimental study of individual motivation in relation to group goals. *Hum. Relat.,* 1954, **7,** 3–38.

Hurlock, E. B. *Child development.* New York: McGraw-Hill, 1950.

Jackson, J. M., & Saltzstein, H. D. The effect of person-group relationships on conformity processes. *J. abnorm. soc. Psychol.,* 1958, **57,** 17–24.

Jones, E. E., Wells, H. H., & Torrey, R. Some effects of feedback from the experimenter on conformity behavior. *J. abnorm. soc. Psychol.,* 1958, **57,** 207–213.

Kelley, H. H., & Lamb, T. W. Certainty of judgment and resistance to social influence. *J. abnorm. soc. Psychol.,* 1957, **55,** 137–139.

Kelley, H. H., & Woodruff, C. L. Members' reactions to apparent group approval of a counternorm communication. *J. abnorm. soc. Psychol.,* 1956, **52,** 67–74.

Kidd, J. S., & Campbell, D. T. Conformity to groups as a function of group success. *J. abnorm. soc. Psychol.,* 1955, **51,** 390–393.

Kluckhohn, F. R. Dominant and variant culture value orientation. In *The Social welfare forum.* New York: Columbia Univer., 1951.

Levine, J., & Butler, J. Lecture vs. group decision in changing behavior. *J. appl. Psychol.,* 1952, **35,** 29–33.

Levine, J., Laffal, J., Birkowitz, M., Lindemann, J., & Drevdahl J. Conforming behavior of psychiatric and medical patients. *J. abnorm. soc. Psychol.*, 1954, **49**, 251–255.

Lewin, K. Field theory and experiment in social psychology: concepts and methods. *Amer. J. sociol.*, 1939, 44, 869–896.

Lewin, K. Forces behind food habits and methods of change. *Bull. Nat. Res. Council*, 1943, **108**, 35–65.

Lieberman, S. The relationship between attitudes and roles: a natural field experiment. *Amer. Psychologists*, 1954, **8**, 418–419. (Abstract)

Luchins, A. S., & Luchins, E. H. Previous experience with ambiguous and non-ambiguous stimuli under various social influences. *J. soc. Psychol.*, 1955, **42**, 249–270.

MacBride, P. D. The influence of confidence upon resistance to perceptual judgments to group pressure. *Tech. Rept. 10*, Contract NR 170–159, Univer. of California, 1958.

McDavid, J. Dispositional effects upon conformity at different levels of discrepancy and structure. *Tech. Rept. 4*, Contract NONR 171–055, Princeton Univer., 1958.

McDavid, J., Jr. Personality and situational determinants of conformity. *J. abnorm. soc. Psychol.*, 1959, **58**, 241–246.

McDonald, W. Consistency of objectively assessed performance in group evaluation of case histories. Unpublished master's thesis, Louisiana State Univer., 1960.

McKeachie, W. J. Individual conformity to attitudes of classroom groups. *J. abnorm. soc. Psychol.*, 1954, **49**, 282–289.

Marple, C. H. The comparative susceptibility of three age levels to the suggestion of group versus expert opinion. *J. soc. Psychol.*, 1933, **4**, 176–186.

Maslow, A. H. Dominance, personality and social behavior in women. *J. soc. Psychol.*, 1939, **10**, 3–40.

Mathewson, S. B. *Restriction of output among unorganized workers.* New York: Viking Press, 1931.

Mausner, B. The effect of one partner's success in a relevant task on the interaction of observer pairs. *J. abnorm. soc. Psychol.*, 1954, **49**, 557–560.

Mausner, B., & Bloch, B. L. A study of the additivity of variables affecting social interaction. *J. abnorm. soc. Psychol.,* 1957, **54,** 250–256.

Mead, M. Creativity in cross-cultural prospective. In H. H. Anderson (Ed.), *Creativity and its cultivation.* New York: Harper, 1959.

Mead, M. *et al. Cooperation and competition among primitive peoples.* New York: McGraw-Hill, 1939.

Menzel, H. Public and private conformity under different conditions of acceptance in the group. *J. abnorm. soc. Psychol.,* 1957, **55,** 398–402.

Merei, F. Group leadership and institutionalization. *Hum. Relat,* 1949, **2,** 23–39.

Moeller, G., & Applezweig, M. H. A motivational factor in conformity. *J. abnorm. soc. Psychol.,* 1957, **55,** 114–120.

Moore, H. T. The comparative influence of majority and expert opinion. *Amer. J. Psychol.,* 1921, **32,** 16–20.

Mouton, J. S., Blake, R. R., & Olmstead, J. A. The relationship between frequency of yielding and the disclosure of personal identity. *J. Pers.,* 1956, **24,** 339–396.

Mowrer, E. R. *Disorganization, personal and social.* New York: Lippincott, 1942.

Mowrer, O. H. Authoritarianism vs. "self-government" in the management of children's aggressive (anti-social) reactions as a preparation for citizenship in a democracy. *J. soc. Psychol.,* 1939, **10,** 121–126.

Munch, P. A. *Sociology of Tristan da Cunha: results of the Norwegian scientific expedition to Tristan da Cunha, 1937–1938,* No. 13. Oslo: I Kommisjon Hos Jacob Dybwad, 1945.

Mussen, P. H., & Kagan, J. Group conformity and perception of parents. *Child Development,* 1958, **29,** 57–60.

Nadler, E. B. Yielding, authoritarianism, and authoritarian ideology regarding groups. *J. abnorm. soc. Psychol.,* 1959, **58,** 408–410.

Nakamura, C. Y. Conformity and problem solving. *J. abnorm. soc. Psychol.,* 1958, **56,** 315–320.

Newcomb, T. M. *Personality and social change; attitude formation in a student community.* New York: Dryden, 1943.

Pennington, D. F., Haravey, F., & Bass, B. M. Some effects of decision and discussion on coalescence, change and effectiveness. *J. appl. Psychol.*, 1958, **42**, 404–408.

Peterman, J. N. Satisfaction with conference decision. Unpublished doctoral dissertation, Univer. of Michigan, 1951.

Radke, M., & Klisurich, D. Experiments in changing food habits. *J. Amer. dietetics Ass.*, 1947, **23**, 403–409.

Rasmussen, G., & Zander, A. Group membership and self-evaluation. *Hum. Relat.*, 1954, **7**, 239–251.

Raven, B. H. Social influence on opinions and the communication of content. *J. abnorm. soc. Psychol.*, 1959, **54**, 119–128.

Rosner, S. Consistency of response to group pressures. *J. abnorm. soc. Psychol.*, 1957, **55**, 145–146.

Samelson, F. Conforming behavior under two conditions of conflict in the cognitive field. *J. abnorm. soc. Psychol.*, 1957, **55**, 181–187.

Schachter, S. Deviation, rejection, and communication. *J. abnorm. soc. Psychol.*, 1951, **46**, 190–207.

Schroder, H. M. Dispositional effects upon conformity at different discrepancy levels. *Tech. Rept. 3*, Contract NONR 171–055, Princeton Univer., 1958.

Schroder, H. M., & Hunt, D. E. Dispositional effects upon conformity at different levels of discrepancy. *J. Pers.*, 1958, **26**, 244–258.

Scott, S. A. Factors affecting the learning of personal values through social reinforcement. *Amer. Psychologist*, 1956, **11**, 407–408. (Abstract)

Sears, P. S. Levels of aspiration in academically successful and unsuccessful children. *J. abnorm. soc. Psychol.*, 1940, **35**, 498–536.

Sherif, M. A study of some social factors in perception. *Arch. Psychol. N.Y.*, 1935, **27**, No. 187.

Sherif, M., & Sherif, C. W. *Groups in harmony and tension.* New York: Harper, 1953.

Sherif, M., White, B. J., & Harvey, O. J. Status in experimentally produced groups. *Amer. J. Sociol.*, 1955, **60**, 370–379.

Shils, E. A. Primary groups in the American army. In R. A. Merton and P. F. Larzarsfeld, *Studies in the scope and method* of *"The American Soldier."* Glencoe, Ill.: Free Press, 1950.

Smock, C. D.   The influence of stress on the perception of incongruity. *J. abnorm. soc. Psychol.,* 1955, **50**, 354–356.

Spohn, H. E.   The effect of group norms upon perception in chronic schizophrenic patients. *Amer. Psychologist,* 1956, **11**, 366. (Abstract)

Stagner, R.   Motivational aspects of industrial morale. *Personnel Psychol.,* 1958, **11**, 64–70.

Stogdill, R. M.   Individual behavior and group achievement. New York: Oxford Univer. Press, 1959.

Stone, P., & Kamiya, J.   Judgments of consensus during group discussion. *J. abnorm. soc. Psychol.,* 1957, **55**, 171–175.

Strodtbeck, F. L.   Husband-wife interaction over revealed differences. *Amer. J. Sociol.,* 1951, **16**, 468–473.

Thelen, H. A.   Dynamics of groups at work. Chicago: Chicago Univer. Press, 1954.

Thibaut, J. W., & Strickland, L. H.   Psychological set and social conformity. *J. Pers.,* 1956, **25**, 115-129.

Thorndike, R. L.   The effect of discussion upon the correctness of group decisions when the factor of majority influence is allowed for. *J. soc. Psychol.,* 1938, **9**, 343–362.

Toboski, F. P., Juliano, C. V., & Kerr, W. A.   Conformity and success in the field of dramatics. *J. soc. Psychol.,* 1956, **43**, 269–273.

Toch, H. H.   The psychology of heresy. *Etc. Rev. gen. Semant.,* 1957, **15**, 9-20.

Tresselt, M. E.   The influence of amount of practice upon the formation of a scale of judgment. *J. exp. Psychol.,* 1947, **37**, 251–260.

Triplett, N.   The psychology of conjuring perceptions. *Amer. J. Psychol.,* 1900, **11**, 439–510.

Tuddenham, R. D.   The influence upon judgment of a grossly distorted norm. *Tech. Rept. 2,* Contract NR 170–159, Univer. of California, 1957.

Tuddenham, R. D.   The influence upon judgment of an avowedly distorted norm. *Tech. Rept. 5,* Contract NR 170–159, Univer. of California, 1958a.

Tuddenham, R. D.   Some correlates of yielding to a distorted group norm. *Tech. Rept. 8,* Contract NR 170–159, Univer. of California, 1958b.

Tuddenham, R. D., & MacBride, P. D.   The yielding experiment from the point of view of the subject. *Tech. Rept. 9,* Contract NR 170–159, Univer. of California, 1958.

Tuddenham, R. D., MacBride, P. D., & Zahn, V.   The sex composition of the group as a determinant of yielding to a distorted norm. *Tech. Rept. 4,* Contract NR 170–159, Univer. of California, 1958.

Tureen, L. L., & Palmer, J. O.   Some group differences in personal values between American soldiers and German prisoners of war. *J. soc. Psychol.,* 1955, **42,** 305–313.

Wheeler, D., & Jordan, H.   Change of individual opinion to accord with group opinion. *J. abnorm. soc. Psychol.,* 1929, **24,** 203–206.

Wiener, M.   Uncertainty of judgment as a determinant of conformity behavior. *Amer. Psychologist,* 1956, **11,** 407. (Abstract)

Wyatt, D. F., & Campbell, D. T.   On the liability of stereotype or hypothesis. *J. abnorm. soc. Psychol.,* 1951, **46,** 496–500.

CHAPTER 3

Conformity in Psychology's Theories of Acquired Behavioral Dispositions[1]

DONALD T. CAMPBELL

Northwestern University

This chapter represents a second step in an effort by the present author to consolidate psychology's several dispositional theories. The first step (Campbell, 1960a) was concerned with reconciling those dispositional theories which express the residues of past experience as meanings, views of the world, definitions of the situation, social perceptions, etc., with those dispositional theories describing the elicitation of overt responses in the presence of external stimuli. The translation concepts developed utilized such hypotheses as Murphy's (1947) "unity of perception and action," Asch's (1952) "isomorphism of experience and action," and Sherif and Sherif's (1956) "unity of experience and behavior." The conscious, perceptual experience thus referred to contains within it both central nervous system projections of the current external objects plus residues of past experience with similar objects. The sensory neural input has been, so to speak, filtered through the brain's association areas, resulting in perceptions in which learned meanings are represented. Such awarenesses, phenomenal givens, or perceptions, are hypothesized to be "isomorphic" to behavior, action, or the

---

[1] This chapter draws freely from the manuscript of a book in preparation *Principles of Social Psychology,* to be published by John Wiley & Sons.

molar responses of current behaviorists. Such meaningful phenomenal objects are the counterparts in conscious experience of the behaviorists' meaningful (molar, purposive) responses, and are more nearly synonyms of the behaviorists' term *Response* than of his term *Stimulus*. Once such a translation is essayed, the dispositional predictions of the social-perception theories are remarkably identical with those of the behaviorist. For example, Lewin's theory and Hull's became intertranslatable when Hull added the parameter K corresponding to Lewin's *valence*.

A tangible illustration in terms of spatial locomotor dispositions will help illustrate the common ground: Let us imagine an experimental room containing a number of boxes. In Box C is a supply of candy, ever replenished. In Box S are contacts providing an electrical shock to whomever touches it. In Box M there is sometimes candy, sometimes electric shock. Boxes A, B, and Z are empty and neutral. Children are allowed to acquire behavioral dispositions in this room. Let us bear in mind two comparisons in particular: first, the change in dispositions for a single child in the course of several explorations, and second, the differences in dispositions between two children, one for whom Box M has always provided candy, the other always shock.

In the cognitive, phenomenological, perceptual theories, one might describe the change with experience as a change in the perception of the situation and the objects in it. Whereas initially the life space or cognitive field was unstructured, now it is structured with regions, valences, and paths. The two children looking at Box M perceive or experience differing objects, live in different behavioral environments, have different life spaces, etc. On the behaviorist side, the same facts and the same predictions of future behavior would be stated in terms of learned approach response to the stimuli of Box C, learned avoidance responses or learned inhibition of approach responses to Box S, changes in response probabilities, etc. The differences between the two children in response to Box M would be a difference in past history of reinforcement resulting in strong habit strength for quite different S-R connections, etc. For present purposes it is not necessary to further belabor the point of equivalence or translatability, since this has been done extensively elsewhere (Campbell, 1960a.)

Modes of Acquiring Dispositions

The above example serves as a basis for illustrating another essential point: *for social beings, learning by direct experience is only one of several ways of acquiring behavorial dispositions.* The following six ways seem distinguishable:

1. *Learning, blind trial and error, or locomotor exploration.* Were the child to have been blindfolded, it could have learned its way about in the room in the course of a series of explorations, and finally to walk confidently and directly to the box of candy, and equally to deliberately avoid the shocking box. This is the mode of acquiring behavioral dispositions most fully developed by behaviorist learning theorists, and the one to which their theories most directly apply. Their relative neglect of other modes of acquisition has been justified by a first-things-first approach, but must be corrected for applicability to social psychology. While learning theorists usually use seeing rats and people in their studies, in their explanatory laws visual perception enters only as a nondescript signal, comparable to an isolated sound of no spatial or guiding significance. It is in contrast with the next mode of acquisition that this mode has been called blind. While blind trial and error is the least efficient mode of learning, it is in some way the most basic, the last resort, the epistemologically most primitive.

2. *Perception.* Were the child allowed upon a mezzanine balcony overlooking the room, and were the boxes open at the top so that the candy contents and the emptiness of the

various boxes were visible, the child could, through a period of stationary study, acquire behavorial dispositions equivalent to those acquired by blind trial and error. Were the child then to be blindfolded, its overt locomotor behavior might not be distinguishable from that of a child who had achieved the learning by blind trial and error. When animals are studied in tunnel mazes, perceptual acquisition is not available, while in elevated mazes, it may to some extent be employed. Tolman (1932) has noted this point in treating perceptual expectancies as coordinate with mnemonic expectancies. The delayed reaction studies also clearly show that it is possible for animals to acquire behavorial dispositions perceptually. In such studies the experimenter, in full sight of the animal, places a favorite bit of food under one of several covers, inducing in the animal a very specific behavioral disposition or stimulus-response consistency. The learning theorist may want to trace this animal's achievement to earlier learning of the blind trial-and-error sort, and this may eventually be possible in part. The social psychologist can, however, well afford to neglect this problem, and note that for the human social animals he studies, perceptual acquisition is already available, although perhaps not too important, in the acquisition of social dispositions.

3. *Perceptual observation of the outcomes of another person's trial-and-error exploration.* Take two children, both equally innocent of the contents of a room, equally lacking in any specific disposition to respond selectively to the stimuli in it. Let one child, the model, explore by trial and error, while the other child watches: sees the model go from box to box, sees the frightened withdrawal when the electric shock is encountered, sees the empty-handed exploration of most of the boxes, and the triumphant discovery of candy in Box S. As a result of the process of observing the outcomes of the model's explorations, the observing child has acquired a set of behavioral dispositions very similar to those acquired

simultaneously by the model through trial and error. Were one to observe their performance after this learning had taken place, one might not be able to tell which child had learned in which way.

The capacity to profit in this way from the experience of others may be in some degree learned itself. Even so, it is a capacity which we can count on, can reckon with in social psychology—all socialized human beings have it. The particular distinctness of this mechanism from other possible forms of imitation, such as the one that follows, shows up in the learning of avoidance habits. Some social and semisocial mammals seem innately equipped to be able to learn from the misfortunes of their fellows—e.g., through warning cries which have no utility to the unfortunate model, but which abet the survival of the observer. The instinctive dread shown by apes for inert, unresponsive, or dismembered ape bodies (Hebb, 1946) makes good functional evolutionary sense as a mechanism of this sort. And whether learned or innate, socialized human beings are usefully equipped so as to be able to learn from the experience of the more adventurous members of the species, even when, or especially when, that experience is disastrous to the model.

4. *Perceptual observation of another person's responses.* Let us suppose that by means of a low screen or some such arrangement, we allowed an observing child to watch the responses of a child who had already learned its way about in the room, but without seeing the results of his responses. It would be possible for an observing child to later mimic the model's response pattern, and produce an overt response sequence indistinguishable from that of the model. Miller and Dollard (1941) have called this *matched dependent behavior* and have demonstrated that both rats and children can learn to imitate responses independently of mode 3, in which information about the environment is obtained by observing the outcomes to another when that other explores.

5. *Linguistic instruction about the characteristics of objects.* Once one child had learned the room, he could easily induce a parallel set of behavioral dispositions in a second child by saying: "The green box will give you a shock. The red box has candy in it. The other boxes are all empty." Such verbal instructions contain no explicit reference to responses to be made, yet none the less generate specific response dispositions.

6. *Linguistic instruction about responses to be made.* The knowledgeable child could also say to the neophyte, "Take three steps forward and then two steps to your right. Open the red box and place your hand inside. Inhibit any response tendencies of approach to the green box." An obedient neophyte might as a result show a pattern of overt response comparable to that of the instructor.

These last two modes of dispositional acquisition, 5 and 6, make use of the learned mechanism of language, and are thus limited to those who share a common language. However, language is so universally present in human beings, and is such a preponderant mode in the acquisition of social-psychological dispositions, that its pervasive status as a means of acquiring behavioral dispositions merits coordinate recognition with the other modes in social psychology. For our present purposes then, the achievement of language will be assumed rather than derived.

Note that language can operate as a mode of acquiring behavioral dispositions even where the language itself is not learned. A honey bee can by trial and error discover a source of nectar or sugar. Such a discovery can produce a marked change in response dispositions. If the source is relatively inexhaustible it can produce a marked regularity in the direction of flight, i.e., in the response to environmental stimuli. Other bees in the colony can acquire this same behavioral disposition without going through the trial-and-error process themselves, and without following the lead of the successful explorer (although this means is used also, especially among the social ants). Von Frisch (1950) has described how the successful explorer among the bees can instruct the others as to the direction and distance of a discovery through a particular "wagging dance." The other bees then fly directly to the new source of nectar, manifesting a behavioral disposition acquired through this primitive and rigid, but withal remarkably flexible, quasilinguistic instruction.

Without designating additional modes, it should be noted that frequent reference will be made here to combinations of 3 and 4 with 5 and 6, as in linguistic instructions about others' responses or the outcomes of others' explorations.

These several modes of acquiring dispositions are regarded as coordinate or intersubstitutable insofar as equivalent behavior tendencies can be acquired through each. A further point is that dispositional tendencies acquired through one mode can summate or combine with those acquired through other modes to produce a net dispositional tendency. A child who has once through trial and error confirmed the rewardingness of Box C and who has also been told of its goodness by a friend, has a stronger disposition than would result from either source alone. Such combinations are demonstrated in the classic studies of Hilgard and Humphreys (Hilgard, 1938; Hilgard & Humphreys, 1938) of the additive and subtractive effects of combining direct eyelid conditioning (classified with mode 1, direct trial-and-error encounter with the environment) with verbal instruction about responses to be made.

Conformity research is typically research in composite dispositions. Conformity research is usually centered around instances of incompatible dispositional tendencies induced on the one hand by individual modes such as trial-and-error and vision; and on the other hand by social modes such as observation of another's response, verbal instruction about another's response, or the like. (Conformity research can also deal with conflict among socially induced dispositions, as between those induced in the past, internalized, and those induced through contemporaneous models or instructions.)

Differences in the degree of conformity are differences in the degree to which the different modes (e.g., the personal, 1 and 2; or the social 3, 4, 5, 6) *are weighted in achieving a composite.* This paper is primarily an effort to summarize conformity research in terms of laws of relative weighting.

Note that we have already made some commitments on the meta-issue of the rationality of conformity behavior: the issue has been translated into the issue of the rationality of giving some weight to the observations of, or the reports on, the experience of others. As Asch (1952) and Rokeach (1960) have correctly emphasized, social life is dependent upon, made possible only by, our willingness to make use of knowledge provided by others. We are all conformant to some extent. In other terms, the organism, the knower, recognizes the fallibility of each mode of knowing, and the gain in predictive certainty achieved through triangulation through separate modes (Campbell, 1959). We are all rationally conformant to the extent that we are more certain (our response tendencies are stronger) when our own observations are confirmed by those of others than when contradicted. The idea that conformity experiments can be completely explained on the basis of an irrational "wanting to be like other people" is contradicted by the pioneer experiments of Warner Brown (1916) on suggestibility. His subjects chose to be *dissimilar* to the reported majority when the instructions were, "Most people make the mistake of judging this line to be longer than it really is."

In many instances, certainly, so-called conformity behavior is an intelligent part of a rational search for valid knowledge about a fallibly and indirectly known world rather than merely an interest in being like other persons whether or not they are correct. While the problem of rationality is not entirely central to this paper, nor the "rational" portrait of man wholly admirable, it seems valuable to join Asch (1952) in alerting the reader to the rationality aspect of the conformity problem. As a minor theme at least, it will recur throughout.

The problem, then, is what weights are given self vs. other when these modes of dispositional acquisition are in conflict and are combined in a net decision. Three modes of combination must be distinguished: 1. Resolved Composites; 2. Dominated Composites; and 3. Compromised Composites.

RESOLVED COMPOSITES. In these instances each of the sources provides information that is equivocal but not necessarily incorrect or errorful. The resolution achieves an interpretation which is perfectly compatible with each, which falls within the equivocal equivalence set of each, the combination of the two removing the equivocality. This is the type of composite particularly emphasized by Asch (1940; 1948; 1952). It is clarifying to illustrate all three forms of composite through analogy to binocular fusion: imagine that in order to achieve a single estimate, the right eye had to be "suggestible" to, "conformant" to, the left eye. Consider a stereoscope slide, in which the left eye views two vertical lines 10 degrees apart, while the right eye views two vertical lines 5 degrees apart. The left eye's view is equivocal in that there are many combinations of vertical lines at varying distances which will subtend this same angle, provide this same image. Similarly for the right eye's view. The two disparate images can be *resolved* by an interpretation that some 7 to 10 inches away there are two vertical lines, the leftward one lying some three inches behind the rightward one. (For full removal of equivocality, the angle of convergence of the eyes must also be added.) The resolution is completely compatible with each, makes full use of each. The inherent equivocality of each eye's view has been greatly reduced by adding of another, slightly different perspective. Each eye's contribution contains much information, in that it alone would rule out the great bulk of conceivable external-object combinations in the visual field. But together the residual equivocality is still further reduced *when a resolution solution can be found,* i.e., when within the equivocally equivalent sets of each a common member exists and is discovered.

Much of human behavior in so-called suggestibility, conformity, or yielding experiments can be analogously visualized. Two social beings view a common situation from disparate vantage points, verbally communicate their individual observations to each other, and are influenced to resolve the two reports into an interpretation of the external world compatible with both of their views, in a triangulation characteristic of the most powerful knowledge processes (Campbell, 1959; Feigl, 1958). The conformity study which comes closest to illustrating such a process is that of Asch (1940) on the judgment of the intelligence characteristic of the professions of *politics.* The term *politics* has equivocal reference. When Asch's students were told that 500 college students had previously ranked *politics* first among 12 professions for intelligence, they interpreted the *politics* as synonymous with *statesman:* when told that *politics* had ranked last, they interpreted it as synonymous with *wardheeler.* Conceivably, neither interpretation need have contradicted or changed the students' own view of the division of labor and the correlated intelligence requirements. The knowledge instead could have led them to select among their sets of equivocal interpretations of the word *politics.* They could thus have solved by a discovered resolution any conflict between their own initial response tendencies and that of the 500 competent and to-be-respected college students.

DOMINATED COMPOSITES.   In other instances the reports of the two eyes in the stereoscope are so disparate that no resolution is possible. Where each eye views a different complexly contoured meaningful image, one view dominates over and suppresses the other. Which dominates becomes a function of relative strength or weighting factors, and for this reason such stereoscopic presentations have been found useful in measuring attitudes (e.g., Bagby, 1957; Engle, 1956). Similarly, in some experimental conformity situations the disparity of the sources is so great that resolution is impossible, one source must be regarded as false, incompetent, to be disregarded. Which is suppressed depends upon weighting factors, or upon relative faith in the sources.

COMPROMISED COMPOSITES. If the two stereoscope slides contain different colors, the resulting net image may be neither of these colors but instead some average or intermediate. Similarly, two disparate estimates may be averaged. For probabilistically disturbed channels, for imperfect knowing in many settings, such averaging is as rational, if not as intriguing, as is the resolved composite. Averaging processes do reduce random error.

The Resolved Composites evade the relative weighting problem by finding an interpretation which, so to speak, weights each source 100 percent. For the Dominated Composites, the details of the relative weighting leading to dominance are obscured, except as revealed in the distributions of dominance over a population of subjects. For the Compromised Composites the relative weighting of sources is most directly apparent, and this will become, therefore, our major conceptual referent as we consider the factors leading to different relative weightings. (See Campbell, 1956, for another illustration of composite dispositions.)

Consider, for example, some data collected for an unpublished study by Jacobs and Campbell using the Sherif (1936) autokinetic situation. Under conditions in which solitary judges saw autokinetic movements averaging 3.8 inches, a confederate in a two-person group made judgements averaging 15.5 inches, leading the naive member to make judgments averaging 12.2 inches. We interpret this resultant as a composite disposition as follows: individual perception produces a tendency to respond at 3.8 inches; observation of another a tendency to a response of 15.5 inches. If the naive member regarded the other's judgment as equally valuable as his own, the resulting average would have been 9.7 inches. Instead, the average of 12.2 reflected a tendency to weight the judgments of the other 2.6 times as heavily as one's own in achieving the compromise.

While Asch's (1940) study of the ranking of *politics,* with its unusual data collection on how persons interpreted the stimulus, makes an excellent example of the Resolved Composite, his actual data also fit in well to the Compromised Composite model. If we take his control group as representing what "own observations" would have been, we find under the high-intelligence suggestion this situation: Own observation, 8.1; reported other, 1.0; with the resulting net response, 4.1, falling about half way between, weighting the reported judgment of 500 other students 1.3 times as much as own observation. For the low-intelligence suggestion, own observation, 8.1; reported other, 10.0; resulting net about half way between at 9.1, which is weighting the 500 others 1.1 times own observation in fairly good agreement with the 1.3. The respect for others in this situation was obviously much less than found in the autokinetic situation, due presumably to the much greater ambiguity of the latter (see principle 2.a, below).

The frequent finding that the more deviant the person's opinion from the group norm, the more he is influenced, or the greater the disparity between own opinion and reported norm the more the conformity induced shift (e.g., Goldberg, 1954; Helson, Blake, & Mouton, 1958b; Raven, 1959; Scott, 1959; Wiener, 1958) is not included in the principle list below because, from the relative weighting perspective, it is uninterpretable in this form. That is, even if all persons were weighting the opinion of others equally, this is exactly what would be found. Thus in the Asch (1940) example just cited, had the high-intelligence (1.0) suggestion group moved from 8.0 to 4.5; and the low-intelligence (10.0) suggestion group from 8.0 to 9.0, the weighting ratio would have been equal in both cases (1.0), both groups equally conformant, even though one moved 3.5 points, the other only 1.0. Were relative weighting ratios to be computed, some such finding might be discovered, although it is doubtful. As a matter of fact, in natural groups with only truly deviants being so classified (i.e., excluding the making of persons with actually central attitudes seem deviant), the deviants would be predicted to weight group opinion less heavily. (See principle 4.i, and the special analysis of extreme deviates in Raven, 1959.) Goldberg (1954) reports uniform proportional influence, for three drastically different discrepancy pressures: in our terms; a tendency to weight the opinion of one or two others only .43 times as much as one's own; in judging intelligence of Negroes from photos. His trends are for less weighting of others under most extreme discrepancies. In an all-or-none conformity situation, Blake, Helson, and Mouton (1957) found more conformity for small deviations.

Note the similarity in perspective to that of Kelley and Thibaut (1954, pp. 744–746). While they treat of group decision reaching rather than the conformity per se, and with group weighting processes rather than individual ones, they discuss the *weighting* problem in a manner quite compatible with the present one, including "weighting produced by direct social pressure" and "self-weighting."

Our normative model is thus one in which *all* persons give *some* weight to all dispositional sources. Differences in relative weighting in achieving the composite thus become the research issue.

Principles of Relative Weighting (Conformity)

In all of the principles which follow, it will be assumed that a situation of conflict exists between an individual dispositional source (1 or 2) and a social one (3, 4, 5, or 6). Giving heavy weight to the social source will be regarded as synonymous with conformity, suggestibility, persuasibility, or yielding, as these terms have been used in the literature. It follows from the Compromised Composite model that any strengthening of an individual dispositional source will lead to decreased conformity, whereas strengthening of a social source will lead to increased conformity. (See Hollander, 1958; Mausner, 1955; & Zetterberg, 1957—for partially parallel analyses.)

1. *Learning and competence*

1.a. The stronger the specific individual disposition (attitude, habit, knowledge, belief, response-tendency, expectancy, etc.) against which social-dispositional sources conflict, the less the conformity.

1.a.1. The more frequently the individually learned disposition has been activated or exercised in the past, the more resistant to conformity pressures, the more heavily it will be weighted in achieving the composite. Sherif (1936) illustrated this principle in showing that group norms were established more slowly after individual norms had been established.

1.a.2. The more difficult the subject material, i.e., the less well learned and unfamiliar the task, the more the conformity (Blake, Helson, & Mouton, 1957; Coffin, 1941; Coleman, Blake, & Mouton, 1958; Patel & Gordon, in press).

1.a.3. The greater a person's knowledge on a subject, the less conformant he is (e.g., Coffin, 1941).

1.a.4. The older a person is, the more established his dispositions, and therefore the less conformant he is

(Marple, 1933); Patel & Gordon, in press). (See also 1.b.3 and 1.b.4 below, for other explanations of this age trend.)

1.a.5. Commitment to an individual disposition before exposure to social sources strengthens the individual-dispositional weighting and thus reduces conformity. The more recorded and the more public the commitment, the less the conformity (Deutsch & Gerard, 1955).

1.a.6. Reactivating or otherwise increasing the strength of certain attitudes reduces the conformity to counter-attitude dispositional sources. Thus increasing the salience of religious group membership decreases conformity to discrepant menages (Kelley, in Hovland, Janis & Kelley, 1953). The more group membership is valued, the more resistant to external contrary persuasion the person is (Gerard, 1952; Kelley & Volkart, 1952).

1.a.7. The more rewarded the disposition in the past, the less conformity there will be.

1.a.8. The more certain the person is about a judgment, the less conformity he will demonstrate (Wiener, 1958).

The above principles deal with the strength of the specific disposition against which conformity pressures are brought to bear. Anything strengthening a disposition—all of the laws of learning—are relevant here. The subsequent principles deal with the capacity for learning or for generalizing from past learnings, and are thus not specific to the strength of a single disposition.

1.b. The more competent the person has been in learning, problem solving, generating valid dispositions through individual modes, the more heavily he will weight individual modes over social ones.

1.b.1. The more a person's problem-solving efforts, responses, judgments, have been rewarded in past situations (and the more similar such situations) the less conformant he will be (DiVesta, 1959; Kelman, 1950; MacBride, 1958; Mausner, 1954a; Mausner & Bloch, 1957).

1.b.2. The more competent a person is led to believe he is on the task at hand, the less conformant he will be (Samelson, 1957).

1.b.3. The more intelligent and generally competent a person is, the less he will conform (Crutchfield, 1955; Nakamura, 1958; Tuddenham, 1959).[2] This is interpreted as reflecting the incompetent person's frequent past experience of finding his own judgment wrong. For the truly stupid person, it is intelligent and rational to be conformant, i.e., to weight other person's judgments more heavily than one's own in achieving a net composite.

1.b.4. The higher the person's status, the greater his influence on others, the less conformant he will be. Leaders are less conformant or persuasible than nonleaders (Crutchfield, 1955; Kelley & Volkart, 1952; Tuddenham, 1959). Persons of high social status and education are less conformant (Tuddenham, 1959).

1.c. The greater a person's self-perceived own ability, the less his conformity. The more self-esteeming, self-assured, ascendant, nonsubmissive, aggressive, impulsive, self-confident, nonself-devaluating, nondepressed, nondependent, etc. persons are less conformant (Beloff, 1958; Helson, Blake, & Mouton, 1958; Hochbaum, 1954; Hovland, Janis, & Kelley, 1953; Jakubczak & Walters, 1959; Janis et al., 1959; Mouton, Blake, & Olmstead, 1956; Schroder & Hunt, 1958; Thorndike, 1938a; Tuddenham, 1959).

[2] Negative results were reported by Janis et al. (1959).

1.d. The greater the general value placed upon individual achievement, the less conformity will occur.

    1.d.1. Instructions emphasizing individual achievement produce less conformity (Grossack, 1954); introducing a task as an intelligence test reduces conformity (DiVesta, 1959).

    1.d.2. Individuals valuing individual achievement are less conformant. Persons valuing self-approval are less conformant (Moeller & Applezweig, 1957). Introspective persons are less conformant (Tuddenham, 1959). Orientation toward creativity is associated with less conformity (Barron, 1955). High need for individual achievement goes with less conformity (Krebs, 1958; Tuddenham, 1959; but the need for achievement results are complex, e.g., Samelson, 1957).

2. *Perception*

2.a. The clearer and more distinct the perceptual situation, the stronger the perceptual disposition, the less conformity is likely to occur (Coffin, 1941). The larger the contrast in a discrimination judgment, the less conformity will occur (Asch, 1948; Asch, 1956; Crutchfield, 1955; Luchins, 1944; Thrasher, 1954). The more ambiguous the stimulus, the more conformity will result (Luchins & Luchins, 1955a; Wiener, 1958). The more difficult the observational conditions, e.g., the speeded presentation of clicks, the more conformity will occur (Blake, Helson, & Mouton, 1957).

2.b. The poorer the person's eyesight, the greater the conformity resulting in an Asch-type situation. Tuddenham (1959) found this, although for men only. Though the results are not yet clear-cut, this provides an excellent illustration of the rationality of depending upon the verbal reports of the visual perceptions of others. Similarly, tasters are less conformant than nontasters in a tasting judgment (Kelley & Lamb, 1957).

2.c. Perceptually induced dispositions, like any other dispositions, decay with time. Judgments based upon memory are more subject to conformity influence than those based upon immediate perception (Deutsch & Gerard, 1955).

3. *Observational learning*

3.a. *Simple vicarious reinforcement.* A person observing the behavior of a model will acquire the same incentives (K in the Hull-Spence theory) or valences which the model is acquiring, providing the conditions of observation and communication are adequate to inform the observer of the rewards and punishments being received by the model (Lewis & Duncan, 1958, with qualification). *The more rewarded the model* for the act or response, *the more conformant will be the observer.* The more punished the model, the more the observer will tend to inhibit the punished act. (If such inhibition were to be in conflict with the observer's own disposition, such inhibition might be regarded as conformity. But usually conformity would be a direct matching of the model's behavior.) (I must with regret report that Miller [1959] failed to find white rats social animals by this criterion.)

3.b. *Prestige generalization across behavior samples for one model.* A person observing the responses of a model in a situation in which the reinforcement for the model cannot be observed, will acquire positive valence and incentive for the response being made by the model to the extent that the responses of the model have been observed to be rewarding to the model in previous situations. *The more previously rewarded the model, the more conformant will be the observer.*

Note that it is usual in conformity experiments to use situations in which the correctness of the specific response of the model is not revealed. Conformity under 3.a above is too rational for it even to be considered a conformity situation. Conformity under 3.b seems, however, a rational extension under conditions of uncertainty. Experimental demonstration of this effect has been provided (Jones, Wells, & Torrey, 1958; Lanzetta & Kanareff, 1959; Luchins, 1944; Luchins & Luchins, 1955b; Mausner, 1954b; Mausner & Bloch, 1954; Schein, 1954). Mausner and Bloch (1957) found this effect much stronger than 1.b, one's own reinforcement. The greater conformity to the opinions of the more successful groups is also interpreted as a multiple model demonstration of this principle (Kidd & Campbell, 1955; Shelley, 1954).

3.b.1. Intelligent, strong, successful, high status persons will induce more conformity than low status ones (Harvey & Rutherford, undated; Lefkowitz, Blake, & Mouton, 1955; Lippitt, Polansky, & Rosen, 1952).[3] Adults induce more conformity in children than do peers (Jakubczak & Walters, 1959). Older students as models induce more conformity than younger ones (Patel & Gordon, in press). More competent models are imitated more, even if the observer has to evaluate competence without confirmation and while conforming (DiVesta, 1959). More talkative and dominant persons are more influential (Riecken, 1958).

3.b.2. Extending the principle to persons whose past receipt of reward has been announced, it follows that high prestige persons will be more imitated, conformed to, than low prestige persons. Experts and celebrities will induce more conformity than nonentities (Haiman, 1949; Hovland, Janis, & Kelley, 1953; Mausner, 1953).

3.b.3. The prestige generalization is greater the more similar to the present situation were the past rewarded acts of the model (Schein, 1954). Of two models, equally rewarded in past observed acts, the one whose acts were

---

[3] It should be noted that Harvey (undated) found persons with middle status more conformant than those with low status.

most similar to the present act will induce the most conformity. With equal past receipt of reward, the expert (i.e., the one whose past rewarded acts are specific to the topic at hand) will have more prestige than the celebrity whose rewarded acts were along other lines.

3.c. *Prestige generalization across models.* A person observing the behavior of a novel model under conditions in which the outcome to the model cannot be observed, will acquire incentive (valence) for that act to the extent that the behavior of other similar models has been observed to be rewarded.

Persons raised by the more competent, effective parents, and surrounded by the more effective adequate, teachers and peers will be the more gullible and conformant to a novel model. Persons raised by ineffectual parents, and surrounded by failures, will be less conformant to a novel model. Persons raised in broken homes are less conformant (Crutchfield, 1955). These statements are supported by the placid, optimistic, socialized self-portrait of Barron's (1953) and of Tuddenham's (1959) yielders.

3.c.1. The more similar a novel model to past rewarded models, the more conformity it will induce.

3.c.2. The more recently observed the model's behavior, the more conformity it will induce (Canning & Baker, 1959; Duncker, 1938).

3.c.3. Familiar models will induce more conformity than novel models (Mausner & Bloch, 1957; Thrasher, 1954).

3.c.4. The average person from a stable social background will tend to conform to novel models. Since the past models were themselves learners, they tended to eliminate punished responses and repeat rewarded ones, if the situation were stable enough so that learning were possible. Thus most of the responses of others observed by the average person were rewarding to those others.

Generalizing to novel models, the observer must expect the average response of another to be reward-producing, adequate, competent, worthy of emulation. The principle is compatible with the conformity effects almost universally found in the laboratory (e.g., Blake & Mouton, 1957; Sherif, 1936).[4] An instinctive presumption to this effect may be present in rats (Angermeier, Schaul, & James, 1959).

3.c.5. Those persons viewing the average other as competent and worthy of respect will be more conformant (Steiner & Peters, 1958). Those who address others with deferential titles will be more conformant (Barry, 1931). (This view of the world is presumed here to be a product of the past history of reinforcement described under 3.c above.) Those who disrespect the average other will be less conformant.

3.d. The more numerous the models modeling the same act, the stronger the incentive for that act. From the rational model implied, or from the standpoint of getting valid information from noisy channels, the greater the number of independent channels conveying the same message, the more likely that message is to be correct. It is noted with regret that this principle has had only partially consistent confirmation, or that the asymptote occurs at a very low number of others. With groups of four, five, and six, Thorndike (1938b) found more conformity in the larger groups. More recently, Goldberg (1954) and Kidd (1958) found no significant difference between one and three others, even with large numbers of groups, though slight trends were in the predicted direction. Asch (1951) found three others more persuasive than one or two, but more numerous models had no additional effect. Jacobs and Campbell (unpublished) found two others more persuasive than one, but three no more persuasive than two.

[4] See Campbell (1951) for review of earlier literature.

Note that persuasive efforts change recipient's estimates of majority of opinions (Parrish & Campbell, 1953) and the persuasive effect may actually be thus mediated (McKeachie, 1954; Sawyer, 1955).

3.d.1. The more dilute the majority, the more partners in minority status the subject has, the less the conformity (Asch, 1951; Hardy, 1957; Mouton, Blake, & Olmstead, 1956; Thorndike, 1938a).

Parentheses on rationality and Asch: The above set of principles, 3.a to 3.d, are rational in the sense that they follow strategies for behavior under condition of uncertainty which a purely normative information theory might recommend; rational in the sense that if followed they would lead to greater adequacy in predicting future environmental reinforcements. They involve a number of primitive assumptions about the nature of the world. These include: stability in the reinforcing characteristics of the world from time to time (an assumption in all learning); stability in the reinforcing characteristics of the world across actors, i.e., what is reinforcing for "him" will be so for "me" (a fundamentally social presumption); stable individual differences in competence and wisdom—he whose responses have been wise and rewarded in the past will be likely to have wise and rewarded responses in the future; generalizability from known persons to unknown persons; trust in the general honesty and striving for rewarded responses on the part of other persons, at least in those situations in which they have no obvious motive for deceit.

The imputed rationality carries no necessary connotations of conscious decision making. The worker bee who trusts the scout's dance and flies off in the indicated direction (von Frisch, 1950) and the rabbit who is terrorized by the desperate squeal of another are behaving rationally in this sense, as is the rat who returns to the spot in the maze where he found food before. The scientist has to know something of the ecology before he can judge such rationality, including the trustworthiness of scout bees and squealing rabbits who may occasionally cry "wolf wolf" without cause.

For this social mode of knowing, however, at least at the levels of 3.b and 3.c, a collective rationality puts a curb on "rational conformity." If we characterize social life as a coalition against nature, a social contract to pool observations for maximum adaptiveness of response, then collective knowledge is maximized when each person so behaves as to be in his turn a valid dependable model for the others. Each acts as both model and observer. Thus, in Asch's famous situation, the single true subject might rationally decide that, since everybody's eyes are imperfect, and since it would be so extremely infrequent that so many Swarthmore students would deliberately lie in a situation like this, it is more probable that his own eyes are wrong than that all of the others are wrong. He might, therefore, rationally decide that, if asked to bet, he would bet with the majority. But if he, therefore, fails to report out loud on how he himself sees the situation, he becomes an undependable model to the others, and reduces the collective validity of the social decision making. The best response, from the point of view of the *collective* rationality is for him to say: "You fellows are probably right, but I definitely see line B as longer," i.e., both rationally respecting others as a source of information about the world, and so reporting that others can rationally depend upon his report in turn. It is failure in this latter respect that instigates our moral indignation at the conformant chameleon character, who parasitically depends upon the competence of others but adds no valid information, no clarifying triangulation, to the social pool.

This all is, of course, just an oversimplified translation of Asch (1952) in his difficult and subtle treatment of the essentially social nature of man, of the rationality of conformity in the sense of trust and respect for the observations of others, and of the essentiality of trustworthiness in report if sociality is to be advantageous.

Equivocality remains. The principles of this section emphasize attention to other's experiences as a source of valid cognizance of the external world. The emphasis is upon the rewardingness of the model's acts *to the model,* or "informational social influence" (Deutsch & Gerard, 1955). The principles of the next section center around the reward *to the observer* of the act of imitating, to conformity as an end in itself rather than a means to valid knowledge about the environment, or conformity as an aspect of group coordination, "normative social influence" (Deutsch & Gerard, 1955). Both such processes have been demonstrated. But in the usual conformity research they are confounded, in that either interpretation will explain the data, both theories make the same prediction. The distinction is clear where the model is punished, but where the model is rewarded, the principles are apt to be confounded. Thus much of the research cited above could also be cited in support of principles to follow.

The focus of the following section is on observer responses imitating the responses of the model, rather than on vicarious exploration of the environment through the agency of the model. When generalized, however, the two modes become less distinct. The focus is also upon reinforcement of the observer's imitative response, and through this the reinforcement of a meta-response of imitating. (But note Solomon & Cole's [1954] failure to find such a generalization of imitation.) Even if there were to be some instinctive tendency to follow or to imitate (e.g., Angermeier, Schaul, & James, 1959), the assumption of such a tendency as the sole determiner would fail to provide the variety of differential predictions which an emphasis upon the reinforcement of imitating makes possible.

4. *Reinforced imitative responding*

4.a. Reinforcement of imitative responses. Rewarding observers for imitative responses leads to increased imitating of a given model (Church, 1957; Miller & Dollard, 1941). In the studies of animals and children by Miller and Dollard, this is clearly independent of learning the model's cues, and probably of the learning of the rewards given the model. (In the studies of Schein in 1954, and Lanzetta & Kanareff in 1959, these are confounded. Schein's interpretation is closer to the latter.)

4.a.1. The more frequently, strongly, consistently, and recently the observer has been reinforced for imitating a given model, the more conformant is the observer (Lanzetta & Kanareff, 1959).

4.a.2. The more similar the task or response of the model to responses which the observer has been reinforced for imitating previously, the greater will be the observer's conformity (Schein, 1954).

4.b. Imitation generalizes across models. Observers reinforced for imitating a given model will tend to imitate novel similar models (Miller & Dollard, 1941).

4.b.1. The more models for which the observer has been rewarded for imitating, the stronger will be the tendency to imitate a novel model.

4.b.2. The more recently the model's behavior has been observed, the greater will be the observer's conformity (Canning & Baker, 1959).

While it has been clearly demonstrated that such learning is possible, what immediately becomes of interest to the social psychologist is how general such training is. To what extent has response matching been reinforced in the average socialized person? It seems likely that in language learning and many other areas of infant training, the imitating response is rewarded. At the adult level, the action of aggregates en masse may be often most mutually reinforcing if similar. But note that the essential social invention of the division of labor requires coordinated dissimilar, though complementary, behavior, which would be sabotaged by any mass homogeneity. It seems more probable that each socially needed response, complementary or similar, is reinforced specifically in the social setting in which it is required.

Another source of imitative behavior is suggested in the circular reflex of Allport (1924) and Mowrer (1950) which points to the secondary reinforcement gained by making stimulus producing responses for which the stimulus is similar to stimuli associated with the rewarding acts of other persons.

4.c. The more rewarding a model has been, the more an observer will tend to imitate the model's acts in the model's absence. The more a model is liked, the more influential the model will be (Horowitz, Lyons, & Perlmutter, 1951; Janis *et al.*, 1959; Mussen & Distler, 1959; Steiner & Peters, 1958; see also principle 3.c.3 above).

4.d. The more an observer has been punished for imitating, the less imitating and the more nonimitating will he exhibit (Miller & Dollard, 1941). An observer imitating an incompetent model may be more punished than rewarded for such imitating, analogously to 3.c above.

4.e. The more an observer has been rewarded for nonconformity, the less conformant he will be. Persons who in their past experience have been successfully inventive or innovative will be less conformant. Those with earlier (and presumably stronger) independence training are less conformant (Krebs, 1958). Those more disposed toward originality, presumably through past reward for originality, are less conformant (Barron, 1955).

4.f. The more a person has been punished for non-conformity, the more conformant he will be (holding reward for conformity constant).

4.f.1. The more a person anticipates punishment for nonconformity the more conformant he will be (Kipnis, 1958). The more a person feels accepted by the group, the less conformant he will be (Dittes & Kelley, 1956; Menzel, 1957).

4.f.1.a. The more a person values group membership, the more conformant he will be (Back, 1951; Schachter *et al.*, 1951). Source-oriented persons are more conformant (McDavid, 1959); those more lacking in interpersonal confidence are more conformant (Berkowitz & Lundy, 1957).

These principles seem likely to be more predictive than 4.a and 4.b, reward for conformity, in that more ubiquitous forces leading to such punishment seem present. On the individual psychology side can be noted the internal cognitive dissonance created by learning that others disagree with us (Sourian, 1881, p. 30; Festinger, 1954; Festinger, 1957). This dissonance can be resolved, in part, by changing one's own opinion. But the dissonance can also be resolved by changing the others, and this produces pressure on the nonconformist from all of those for whom he is causing dissonance (Festinger, 1950; Festinger & Thibaut, 1951; Emerson, 1954).

It may also be seen that if each person is a part of the maze which each of the others has learned, a change in this maze disrupts the learned adaptations of the others, reduces temporarily at least the reward value of their behavior to themselves, and produces efforts to reconstitute the maze, or to sever interdependence by expulsion of the nonconformist from the group. From the ubiquity of these processes we get the following principle.

4.f.2. The average person has negative incentive for a nonconformant act.

4.f.3. The average person has more negative incentive for a nonconformant act the more public and visible to others that act is. In conformity and persuasion studies, private expression of opinion uniformly shows less conformity than does public expression (Argyle, 1957; Asch, 1951; Gorden, 1952; Deutsch & Gerard, 1955; Dittes & Kelley, 1956; Jones, Wells, & Torrey, 1958; Menzel, 1957; Mouton, Blake, & Olmstead, 1956; Raven, 1959).

This finding, it should be pointed out, is directly contradictory to the emphasis above which stressed the contribution to adequate group problem solving through the expression of dissident observations even when one is convinced that the others are correct. From that perspective, optimal social rationality would be to show less conformity in overt expression, in which one is contributing to the group's total perspective and informational pool, and more conformity in private expression of one's bet as to the nature of reality.

To understand how a social process might seem to be maladaptive, a selective survival view of culture history must be invoked. Such a view points to an inherent conflict between mechanisms preserving valuable customs and social knowledge already achieved, on the one hand; and mechanisms for innovation and the improvement of customs, on the other hand. An analogous conflict exists between the rigid chromosome and gene duplication preserving an organism's achieved adaptive complexity, and the mutation process which both threatens this valuable cumulation and makes possible any further improvement. In this instance, most innovations are deleterious, and conservative geneticists worry about increasing man's mutation rate, though some degree of mutation is certainly desirable; and evolution seems to locate minimax solutions, without obviating the essential incompatibility. Similarly, in individual wisdom and in science there may be some inherent incompatibility between erudition and creativity (Campbell, 1959; Campbell, 1960b; Sourian, 1881). The social and psychological forces seen working in conformity pressures indicate for the past culture of our subjects a greater pressure to preserve than to innovate. Further, one may see in the dissident private opinions latent potentiality for rapid custom change analogous to the potentiality for rapid response to environmental change made possible in organic evolution through heterozygosity under genetic dominance.

This aspect of conformity pressures is well illustrated by the recent study of Barry, Child, and Bacon (1959), in which it is shown that conformity training in childhood is much greater in those subsistence cultures engaged in tillage and dependent upon loyal adherence to detailed practices, than in those subsistence cultures of comparable size and complexity depending upon hunting and fishing. Our modern European cultures are based upon predecessor cultures involving complex, interlocking, efficacious customs, often superstitiously justified on tangential grounds. With the modern rationalization of social process (in Weber's sense), the justifications for required performances may become more validly explicit; cooperation more elicitable through enlightened self-interest; and a superstitious, ritualistic conformity less functional, and less present. In these terms, the present generation is probably less conformant than its European ancestors of 100, 1000, or 10,000 years ago. But let us not digress into the problem of values for the future. At the present time, nonconformity seems on the average to be unpleasant.

4.f.4. Where conformity serves the social role of group coordination, conformity will be greater. Aggregates interpreting themselves as interdependent groups will be more conformant than those which do not (Deutsch & Gerard, 1955). Cooperative joint product evaluation instructions induce more conformity than do competitive ones (Grossack, 1954). Group-centered classes achieve more conformity (McKeachie, 1954). More cohesive groups induce more conformity (Festinger, 1950; Thibaut & Strickland, 1956). Under group set, increased conformity pressure increases conformity, while it does not for task set (Thibaut & Strickland, 1956).

The emphasis upon the discomfort of nonconformity leads to this prediction, supporting 4.a. and 4.b.

4.g. The more the person has been reinforced for the cessation of nonconformity, the more conformant he will be.

Considering these principles of reward for conformity and punishment for nonconformity collectively, we can predict as follows.

4.h. Those persons raised in authoritarian manners—rewarded for conformity and punished for nonconformity—will be more conformant (Hoffman, 1953; Janis *et al.*, 1959). While the inference chain is much too indirect to be satisfactory, this may be confirmed by the fact that those persons scoring high on the F scale are more conformant[5] (Beloff, 1958; Canning & Baker, 1959; Crutchfield, 1955; Janis *et al.*, 1959; Nadler, 1959; Small & Campbell, 1961; Wells, Weinert, & Rubel, 1956).

4.i. Persons who have no chance of being fully accepted for conformity or of being rewarded for cessation of nonconformity will be less conformant. Thus, social isolates are less conformant (Hovland, Janis, & Kelley, 1953).

[5] This is certainly one of the best cross-validated findings available about conformity.

Minority group members will be less conformant. There is no real evidence on this except for a study of experimental marginals by Kelley and Shapiro (1954).

4.j. Those who value social approval highly will be more conformant (Moeller & Applezweig, 1957). (This principle, and the research cited, may be essentially saying that those diagnosed as conformant by self-description of values and attitudes prove to be conformant by objective test.) Conventional persons are more conformant (Barron, 1953; Beloff, 1958; Hochbaum, 1954; Hoffman, 1953). Submissive persons are more conformant (Helson, Blake, & Mouton, 1958; Mouton, Blake, & Olmstead, 1956). Other-directed persons are more conformant (Bell, 1955; Janis *et al.*, 1959). Those tolerant of nonconformity are less conformant (White, 1957).

The distinction between verbal instruction about the nature of objects and verbal instruction about responses is important for the general integrative perspective, as representing the cognitive and response-oriented theories in the verbal area. However, for the present chapter no useful purpose is achieved by maintaining the distinction, and principle 6 will here be combined with 5.

The distinction between differences in impact depending on the one hand upon the success status of the source, and on the other, the reward experience to the follower is maintained in parallel with the distinctions between sections 3 and 4 above; the argument has thus already been developed in large part. Many of the citations in sections 3 and 4 could have been with equal appropriateness cited here.

5. *Verbal instruction*

5.a. The more a communicator's own responses have been known to have been rewarding to the communicator, the more his communications about the goodness and badness of object regions and actions will lead to positive and negative incentives for those objects and actions.

5.b. The more that similar communicators have been observed to have their own actions rewarded in the past, the more influential a novel communicator will be.

5.c. The more the listener has been rewarded in the past for following the verbal instructions of the communicator, the more influential will be the communicator. Thus, Scott (1959) found those reinforced for parroting a given argument were more changed by it.

5.d. The more the listener has been rewarded in the past for following the instructions of similar communicators, the more influential will be a novel communicator.

5.e. The more similar the communicator to past effective communicators (in the senses of 5.a and 5.c), the more persuasive he will be. For these reasons, *ceteris paribus,* movie and TV presentations are more effective than radio, which is more effective than the printed page.[6]

Summary

As a part of an effort to combine dispositional theories, this chapter has borrowed freely from both cognitive and behavioristic sources. Social-observational modes of acquiring dispositional strength have been given particular emphasis. The conformity situation in usual research is typified as one in which individual dispositional sources (learning and perception) are in conflict with social sources (observation, imitation, and verbal instruction). Three modes of achieving composite dispositions in such conflict are the Resolved Composite, the Dominated Composite, and the Compromised Composite. The laws of conformity become laws of the relative weighting of dispositional sources, most conveniently manifest in the Compromised Composite. Any factor strength-

---

[6] For a review of the conflicting evidence on this, see Hovland (1954). For trends not significant in this direction, see Blake & Mouton (1957).

ening or weakening either component in the conflict becomes a factor in conformity. Some two dozen such principles have been offered, many with research citation. Throughout Asch's emphasis upon the rationality of so-called conformity behavior has been argued.

REFERENCES

Allport, F. H. *Social psychology.* Boston: Houghton Mifflin, 1924.

Angermeier, W. F., Schaul, L. T., & James, W. T. Social conditioning in rats. *J. comp. physiol. Psychol.,* 1959, **52**, 370–372.

Argyle, M. Social pressure in public and private situations. *J. abnorm. soc. Psychol.,* 1957, **54**, 172–175.

Asch, S. E. Studies in the principles of judgments and attitudes: II. Determination of judgments by group and ego standards. *J. soc. Psychol.,* 1940, **12**, 433–465.

Asch, S. E. The doctrine of suggestion, prestige, and imitation in social psychology. *Psychol. Rev.,* 1948, **55**, 250–277.

Asch, S. E. Effects of group pressure upon the modification and distortion of judgments. In H. Guetzkow (Ed.), *Groups, leadership, and men.* Pittsburgh: Carnegie Press, 1951.

Asch, S. E. *Social psychology.* New York: Prentice Hall, 1952.

Asch, S. E. Studies of independence and conformity: I. A minority of one against an unanimous majority. *Psychol. Monogr.,* 1956, **70**, No. 9 (Whole No. 416).

Back, K. The exertion of influence through social communication. *J. abnorm. soc. Psychol.,* 1951, **46**, 9–23.

Bagby, J. W. A cross-cultural study of perceptual predominance in binocular rivalry. *J. abnorm. soc. Psychol.,* 1957, **54**, 331–334.

Barron, F. Some personality correlates of independence of judgment. *J. Pers.,* 1953, **21**, 287–297.

Barron, F. The disposition toward originality. *J. abnorm. soc. Psychol.,* 1955, **51**, 478–485.

Barry, H. A test for negativism and compliance. *J. abnorm. soc. Psychol.,* 1931, **25**, 373–389.

Barry, H., Child, I. L., & Bacon, M. K.   Relation of child training to subsistence economy. *Amer. Anthrop.*, 1959, **61**, 51–63.

Bell, E. G.   Inner-directed and other-directed attitudes. Unpublished doctoral dissertation, Yale Univer., 1955.

Beloff, H.   Two forms of social conformity: Acquiescence and
conventionality. *J. abnorm. soc. Psychol.*, 1958, **56**, 99–104.

Berkowitz, L., & Lundy, R. M.   Personality characteristics related
to susceptibility to influence by peers or authority figures. *J.
Pers.*, 1957, **25**, 306–316.

Blake, R. R., Helson, H., & Mouton, J. S.   The generality of
conformity behavior as a function of factual anchorage, difficulty of task, and amount of social pressure. *J. Pers.*, 1957, **25**,
294–305.

Blake, R. R., & Mouton, J. S.   The study of social conduct within
the framework of adaptation-level theory. In M. Sherif and
M. O. Wilson (Eds.), *Emerging problems in social psychology.*
Norman, Oklahoma: Institute of Group Relations, Univer. of
Oklahoma, 1957.

Brown, W.   Individual and sex differences in suggestibility.
Univer. Calif. Publ. Psychol., 1916, **2**, 291–430.

Bryant, H. A., Dobbins, D. A., & Bass, B. M.   Group effectiveness,
coercion, change and coalescence among delinquents compared
to non-delinquents. *Tech. Rept. 15*, Contract N7 ONR 35609,
Louisiana State Univer., 1958.

Campbell, D. T.   On the possibility of experimenting with the
bandwagon effect. *Int. J. Opin. Attitude Res.*, 1951, **5**, 251–260.

Campbell, D. T.   Enhancement of contrast as composite habit.
J. abnorm. soc. Psychol., 1956, **53**, 350–355.

Campbell, D. T.   Methodological suggestions from a comparative psychology of knowledge processes. *Inquiry* (Univer. Oslo
Press), 1959, **2**, 152–182.

Campbell, D. T.   Social attitudes and other acquired behavioral
dispositions. In S. Koch (Ed.), *Psychology: a study of a science.*
Vol. 6. *Investigations of man as socius: Their place in psychology and the social sciences.* New York: McGraw-Hill, 1960a.

Campbell, D. T.   Blind variation and selective retention in
creative thought as in other knowledge processes. *Psychol.
Rev.*, 1960b.

Canning, R., & Baker, J.   Effect of the group on authoritarian and non-authoritarian persons. *Amer. J. Sociol.,* 1959, **64,** 579–581.

Church, R. M.   Transmission of learned behavior between rats. *J. abnorm. soc. Psychol.,* 1957, **54,** 163–165.

Coffin, T. E.   Some conditions of suggestion and suggestibility. *Psychol. Monogr.,* 1941, **53,** No. 4 (Whole No. 241). Pp ix–125.

Coleman, J. F., Blake, R. R., & Mouton, J. S.   Task difficulty and conformity pressures. *J. abnorm. soc. Psychol.,* 1958, **57,** 120–122.

Crutchfield, R. S.   Conformity and character. *Amer. Psychologist,* 1955, **10,** 191–198.

Deutsch, M., & Gerard, H. B.   A study of normative and informational social influences upon individual judgment. *J. abnorm. soc. Psychol.,* 1955, **51,** 629–636.

Dittes, J. E., & Kelley, H. H.   Effects of different conditions of acceptance upon conformity to group norms. *J. abnorm. soc. Psychol.,* 1956, **53,** 100–107.

DiVesta, F. J.   Effects of confidence and motivation on susceptibility to informational social influence. *J. abnorm. soc. Psychol.,* 1959, **59,** 204–209.

Duncker, K.   Experimental modification of children's food preferences through social suggestion. *J. abnorm. soc. Psychol.,* 1938, **33,** 489–507.

Emerson, R.   Deviation and rejection: an experimental replication, *Amer. sociol. Rev.,* 1954, **19,** 688–692.

Engle, E.   The role of content in binocular resolution. *Amer. J. Psychol.,* 1956, **69,** 87–91.

Feigl, H.   The "mental" and the "physical." In H. Feigl, M. Scriven, and G. Maxwell (Eds.), *Concepts, theories, and the mind body problem.* Vol. II. *Minnesota studies in the philosophy of science.* Minneapolis: Univer. Minnesota Press, 1958.

Festinger, L.   Informal social communication. *Psychol. Rev.,* 1950, **57,** 271–282.

Festinger, L.   A theory of social comparison processes. *Hum. Relat.,* 1954, **7,** 117–140.

Festinger, L.   *A theory of cognitive dissonance.* Evanston: Row Peterson, 1957.

Festinger, L., & Thibaut, J.   Interpersonal communication in small groups. *J. abnorm. soc. Psychol.*, 1951, **46**, 92–99.

Frisch, K. von.   *Bees, their vision, chemical sense, and language.* Ithaca: Cornell Univer. Press, 1950.

Gerard, H. B.   The anchorage of opinions in reference group. *Amer. Psychologist*, 1952, **7**, 328. (Abstract)

Goldberg, S. C.   Three situational determinants of conformity to social norms. *J. abnorm. soc. Psychol.*, 1954, **49**, 325–329.

Gorden, R.   Interaction between attitude and the definition of the situation in the expression of opinion. *Amer. sociol. Rev.*, 1952, **17**, 50–58.

Grossack, M. M.   Some effects of cooperation and competition upon small group behavior. *J. abnorm. soc. Psychol.*, 1954, **49**, 341–348.

Haiman, F. S.   An experimental study of the effects of ethos in public speaking. *Speech Monogr.*, 1949, **16**, 190–202.

Hardy, K. R.   Determinants of conformity and attitude change. *J. abnorm. soc. Psychol.*, 1957, **54**, 289–294.

Harvey, O. J.   Status and conformity to pressures of informal groups. *Tech. Rept. 6*, Contract NONR 2149 (02), Group Psychology Branch, Office of Naval Research (undated).

Harvey, O. J., & Rutherford, J.   Relationship of status in the informal group to influence and influencibility at differing age levels. *Tech. Rept. 3*, Contract NONR 2149 (02), Group Psychology Branch, Office of Naval Research (undated).

Hebb, D. O.   On the nature of fear. *Psychol. Rev.*, 1946, **53**, 259–276.

Helson, H., Blake, R. R., & Mouton, Jane S.   Petition-signing as adjustment to situational and personal factors. *J. soc. Psychol.*, 1958a, **48**, 3–10.

Helson, H., Blake, R. R., & Mouton, Jane S.   An experimental investigation of the effectiveness of the "big lie" in shifting attitudes. *J. soc. Psychol.*, 1958b, **48**, 51–60.

Hilgard, E. R.   An algebraic analysis of conditioned discrimination in man. *Psychol. Rev.*, 1938, **45**, 472–496.

Hilgard, E. R., & Humphreys, L. G.   The effect of supporting and antagonistic voluntary instructions on conditioned discrimination. *J. exp. Psychol.*, 1938, **22**, 291–304.

Hochbaum, G. The relation between group members' self-confidence and their reactions to group pressures to uniformity. *Amer. sociol. Rev.*, 1954, **19**, 678–687.

Hoffman, M. L. Some psychodynamic factors in compulsive conformity. *J. abnorm. soc. Psychol.*, 1953, **48**, 383–393.

Hollander, E. P. Conformity, status, and idiosyncrasy credit. *Psychol. Rev.*, 1958, **65**, 117–127.

Horowitz, M. W., Lyons, J., & Perlmutter, H. V. Induction of forces in discussion groups. *Hum. Relat.*, 1951, 4, 57–76.

Hovland, C. I. Effects of the mass media of communication. In G. Lindzey (Ed.), *Handbook of social psychology*. Cambridge, Mass.: Addison-Wesley, 1954.

Hovland, C. I., Janis, I. L., & Kelley, H. H. *Communication and persuasion*. New Haven: Yale Univer. Press, 1953.

Jacobs, R. C., & Campbell, D. T. The perpetuation of an arbitrary tradition through several generations of a laboratory microculture. Unpublished manuscript.

Jakubczak, L. F., & Walters, R. H. Suggestibility as dependency behavior. *J. abnorm. soc. Psychol.*, 1959, **59**, 102–107.

Janis, I. L., Hovland, C. I., Field, P. B., Linton, H., Graham, E., Cohen, A. R., Rife, D., Abelson, R. P., Lesser, G. S., & King, B. T. *Personality and persuasibility*. New Haven: Yale Univer. Press, 1959.

Jones, E. E., Wells, H. H., & Torrey, R. Some effects of feedback from the experimenter on conformity behavior. *J. abnorm. soc. Psychol.*, 1958, **57**, 207–213.

Kanareff, V. T., & Lanzetta, J. T. The acquisition of imitative and opposition responses under two conditions of instruction-induced set. *J. exp. Psychol.*, 1958, **56**, 516–528.

Kelley, H. H., & Lamb, T. W. Certainty of judgment and resistance to social influence. *J. abnorm. soc. Psychol.*, 1957, **55**, 137–140.

Kelley, H. H., & Shapiro, M. An experiment on conformity to group norms where conformity is detrimental to group achievement. *Amer. sociol. Rev.*, 1954, **19**, 667–677.

Kelley, H. H., & Thibaut, J. W. Experimental studies of group problem solving and process. In G. Lindzey (Ed.), *Handbook of social psychology*. Cambridge, Mass.: Addison-Wesley, 1954.

Kelley, H., & Volkart, E.   The resistance to change of group-anchored attitudes. *Amer. sociol. Rev.*, 1952, **17**, 453–465.

Kelman, H. C.   Effects of success and failure on "suggestibility" in the autokinetic situation. *J. abnorm. soc. Psychol.*, 1950, **45**, 267–285.

Kidd, J. S.   Social influence phenomena in a task-oriented group situation. *J. abnorm. soc. Psychol.*, 1958, **56**, 13–17.

Kidd, J. S., & Campbell, D. T.   Conformity to groups as a function of group success. *J. abnorm. soc. Psychol.*, 1955, **51**, 390–393.

Kipnis, D.   The effects of leadership style and leadership power upon the inducement of attitude change. *J. abnorm. soc. Psychol.*, 1958, **57**, 173–180.

Krebs, A. M.   Two determinants of conformity: Age of independence training and achievement. *J. abnorm. soc. Psychol.*, 1958, **56**, 130–131.

Lanzetta, J. T., & Kanareff, V. T.   The effects of a monetary reward on the acquisition of an imitative response. *J. abnorm. soc. Psychol.*, 1959, **59**, 120–127.

Lefkowitz, M., Blake, R. R., & Mouton, Jane S.   Status factors in pedestrian violation of traffic signals. *J. abnorm. soc. Psychol.*, 1955, **51**, 704–706.

Lewis, D. J., & Duncan, C. P.   Vicarious experience and partial reinforcement. *J. abnorm. soc. Psychol.*, 1958, **57**, 321–326.

Linton, H. B.   Rorschach correlates of response to suggestion. *J. abnorm. soc. Psychol.*, 1954, **49**, 75–83.

Lippitt, R., Polansky, N., & Rosen, S.   The dynamics of power. *Hum. Relat.*, 1952, **5**, 37-64.

Luchins, A. S.   On agreement with another's judgments. *J. abnorm. soc. Psychol.*, 1944, **39**, 97-111.

Luchins, A. S., & Luchins, E. H.   Previous experience with ambiguous and non-ambiguous perceptual stimuli under various social influences. *J. soc. Psychol.*, 1955a, **42**, 249–270.

Luchins, A. S., & Luchins, E. H.   On conformity with true and false communications. *J. soc. Psychol.*, 1955b, **42**, 283–303.

MacBride, P. D.   Studies in conformity and yielding. IX. The influence of confidence upon resistance of perceptual judgments to group pressure. *Tech. Rept. 10*, Contract NR 170–159,

Univer. of California (R. D. Tuddenham, Principal Investigator), 1958.

McDavid, J. Jr.   Personality and situational determinants of conformity. *J. abnorm. soc. Psychol.*, 1959, **58**, 241–246.

McKeachie, W. J.   Individual conformity to attitudes of classroom groups. *J. abnorm. soc. Psychol.*, 1954, **49**, 282–289.

Marpel, C. H.   The comparative susceptibility of three age levels to the suggestion of group versus expert opinion. *J. soc. Psychol.*, 1933, **4**, 176–186.

Mausner, B.   Studies in social interaction: III. Effect of variation in one partner's prestige on the interaction of observer pairs. *J. appl. Psychol.*, 1953, **37**, 391–393.

Mausner, B.   The effect of prior reinforcement on the interaction of observer pairs. *J. abnorm. soc. Psychol.*, 1954a, **49**, 65–68.

Mausner, B.   The effect of one partner's success in a relevant task on the interaction of observer pairs. *J. abnorm. soc. Psychol.*, 1954b, **49**, 557–560.

Mausner, B.   Studies in social interaction: I. A conceptual scheme. *J. soc. Psychol.*, 1955, **41**, 259–270.

Mausner, B., & Bloch, B. L.   A study of the additivity of variables affecting social interaction. *J. abnorm. soc. Psychol.*, 1957, **54**, 250–256.

Menzel, H.   Public and private conformity under different conditions of acceptance in the group. *J. abnorm. soc. Psychol.*, 1957, **55**, 398–402.

Miller, N. E., & Dollard, J.   *Social learning and imitation.* New Haven: Yale Univer. Press, 1941.

Miller, Norman.   Acquisition of avoidance dispositions by social learning. Unpublished doctoral dissertation, Northwestern Univer., 1959.

Moeller, G., & Applezweig, M. H.   A motivational factor in conformity. *J. abnorm. soc. Psychol.*, 1957, **55**, 114–120.

Mouton, Jane L., Blake, R. R., & Olmstead, J. A.   The relationship between frequency of yielding and the disclosure of personal identity. *J. Pers.*, 1956, **24**, 339–347.

Mowrer, O. H.   *Learning theory and personality dynamics.* New York: Ronald, 1950.

Murphy, G. *Personality.* New York: Harper, 1947.

Murphy, G., Murphy, L. B., & Newcomb, T. M. *Experimental social psychology.* (rev. ed.) New York: Harper, 1937.

Mussen, P., & Distler, L. Masculinity, identification, and father-son relationship. *J. abnorm. soc. Psychol.,* 1959, **59,** 350–356.

Nadler, E. B. Yielding, authoritarianism, and authoritarian ideology regarding groups. *J. abnorm. soc. Psychol.,* 1959, **58,** 408–410.

Nakamura, C. Y. Conformity and problem-solving. *J. abnorm. soc. Psychol.,* 1958, **56,** 315–320.

Parrish, J. A., & Campbell, D. T. Measuring propaganda effects with direct and indirect attitude tests. *J. abnorm. soc. Psychol.,* 1953, **48,** 3–9.

Patel, A. S., & Gordon, J. E. Some personal and situational determinants of yielding to influence. *J. abnorm. soc. Psychol.,* 1961, in press.

Raven, B. H. Social influence on opinions and the communication of related content. *J. abnorm. soc. Psychol.,* 1959, **58,** 119–128.

Riecken, H. W. The effect of status on ability to influence group solutions of problems. *Tech. Rept. 1,* Contract N8 ONR 66216, Univer. of Minnesota, 1958.

Rokeach, M. *The open and the closed mind.* New York: Basic Books, 1960.

Samelson, F. Conforming behavior under two conditions of conflict in the cognitive field. *J. abnorm. soc. Psychol.,* 1957, **55,** 181–187.

Sawyer, T. M. Shift of attitude following persuasion as related to estimate of majority attitude. *Speech Monogr.,* 1955, **22,** 68–78.

Schachter, S., Ellerton, N., McBride, D., & Gregory, D. An experimental study of cohesiveness and productivity. *Hum. Relat.,* 1951, 4, 229–238.

Schein, E. H. The effect of reward on adult imitative behavior. *J. abnorm. soc. Psychol.,* 1954, **49,** 389–395.

Schroder, H. M. Dispositional effects on reactions to the source of disapproval. *Tech. Rept.* No. 2, Contract NONR 171–055, Princeton Univer. (undated).

Schroder, H. M., & Hunt, D. E.   Dispositional effects upon conformity at different levels of discrepancy. *J. Pers.*, 1958, **26**, 243–258.

Scott, W.   Attitude change by response reinforcement: replication and extension. *Sociometry*, 1959, **22**, 328–335.

Shelley, H. P.   Level of aspiration phenomena in small groups. *J. soc. Psychol.*, 1954, **40**, 149–164.

Sherif, M.   *The psychology of social norms.* New York: Harper, 1936.

Sherif, M., & Sherif, C. W.   *An outline of social psychology.* (rev. ed.) New York: Harper, 1956.

Small, D. O., & Campbell, D. T.   The effect of acquiescence response-set upon the relationship of the F scale and conformity. *Sociometry*, 1960, **23**, 69–71.

Solomon, R. L., & Coles, M. R.   A failure of generalization of imitation across drives and across situations. *J. abnorm. soc. Psychol.*, 1954, **49**, 7–13.

Sourian, P.   *Theorie de L'invention.* Paris: Hachette, 1881.

Steiner, I. D., & Peters, S. C.   Conformity and the A-B-X model. *J. Pers.*, 1958, **26**, 229–242.

Thibaut, J. W., & Strickland, L. H.   Psychological set and social conformity. *J. Pers.*, 1956, **25**, 115–129.

Thorndike, R. L.   The effect of discussion upon the correctness of group decisions, when the factor of majority influence is allowed for. *J. soc. Psychol.*, 1938a, **9**, 343–362.

Thorndike, R. L.   On what type of task will a group do well? *J. abnorm. soc. Psychol.*, 1938b, **33**, 409–413.

Thrasher, J.   Interpersonal relations and gradations of stimulus structure as factors in judgmental variation: an experimental approach, *Sociometry*, 1954, **17**, 228–241.

Tolman, E. C.   *Purposive behavior in animals and men.* New York: Century, 1932.

Torrance, E. P.   The influence of experienced members of small groups on the behavior of the inexperienced. *J. soc. Psychol.*, 1959, **49**, 249–257.

Tuddenham, R. D.   Correlates of yielding to a distorted group norm. *J. Pers.*, 1959, **27**, 272–284.

Wells, W. D., Weinert, G., & Rubel, M.   Conformity pressure and authoritarian personality. *J. Psychol.*, 1956, **42**, 133–136.

White, M. S.　Attitude change as related to perceived majority opinion. *Research Report AFPTRC-TN-57-59;* ASTIA Document No. 131431, Texas: Crew Research Laboratory Randolph Air Force Base, 1957.

Wiener, M.　Certainty of judgment as a variable in conformity behavior. *J. soc. Psychol.*, 1958, **48**, 257–263.

Zetterberg, H. L.　Compliant actions. *Acta Sociologica*, 1957, **2**, 179–201.

CHAPTER 4

Issues in the Study of
Social Influences on Judgment

SOLOMON E. ASCH

Swarthmore College[1]

It was my original intention to give a sober historical account of the experimental investigation of conformity, to consider the principal problems that occupied investigators during the empirical period which opened roughly at the turn of the century, to detail the steps that were taken and the knowledge that was amassed. Unwittingly my pen led me elsewhere. Another theme, to which I finally succumbed, kept intruding. This has become an examination of one dominant motif of theorizing and experimentation in this region, one that has, in my opinion, hampered a deeper understanding of the processes of social influence. What follows is a critical, perhaps even a censorious, essay. My only excuse is that it may throw some light on the situation we face currently, and that it may provoke an equally critical discussion.

The investigation of conformity has always been guided by a schematic and inclusive conception of social influence. The empirical data have, as a rule, appeared to confirm the initial theoretical assumptions. It will be my contention that investigation has not subjected these assumptions to searching test; that the empirical findings have failed to refine or to modify them; and that one consequence of this theoretical

[1] Now at the Institute for Advanced Study, Princeton, New Jersey.

starting point has been to restrict unduly the range of observation. I propose to examine the reasons and consequences of this situation. It is not easy to appreciate what happened in this area if one ignores the background of ideas out of which investigation grew.

Historical Perspective

One source of thinking about social influence traces not directly to psychology but to the social disciplines. One can best illustrate it by noting the radical difference of perspective between the students of social influence and the "objects" of their investigation—the subjects. The person who is immersed in action and faces decisions considers his opinions and beliefs to rest on evidence, on the assessment of probabilities. He will insist that these operations require intelligence, perhaps even imagination. He will not question that he can go wrong, that preconceptions, personal interest, and the opinions of others play their part, but he will not lose sight of the problem-solving character of these activities. The social psychologist has traditionally come to these phenomena with a different orientation. He starts with the postulate of the relativity of belief and opinion, when these concern issues of social import. Historical evidence, and the data of anthropology, have taught the social psychologist that there are serious differences between the practices, beliefs, and values of societies. Nor does it escape him that the adherents of each of these traditions agree in one respect: each regards its assumptions and conclusions to be sensible and valid. These partialities confirm his belief that people tend to adhere dogmatically to their respective ways. The investigator notes further that few persons are aware of the historical circumstances responsible for their opinions. He therefore considers that his relativistic frame is superior, since it is capable of handling divergent beliefs in a consistent manner.

TRENDS AND CIRCUMSTANCES. In the course of this century a number of additional circumstances have strengthened this initial approach. The study of public opinion has concentrated on the regional determination of economic and political opinion. Race relations have made questions of prejudice prominent in studies of the psychology of attitudes. The workings of propaganda have attracted increasing attention. Finally, the growth of a mass society, with its increasing emphasis on the deliberate and impersonal manipulation of preference and beliefs, has converged with the other trends to create the climate that we meet today in social psychology. These conditions and conceptions have formed a potent direction for thinking about the social determination of opinion. They also contained the rudiments of a psychological interpretation, which was shortly to become more explicit and systematic. We will see that there were ready at hand certain psychological ideas that appeared to provide the necessary foundation.

THE ROLE OF SUGGESTIBILITY. It is perhaps more than a historical anomaly that the first impetus to concrete investigation of social influence came from abnormal psychology, in the form of observations of hypnotic phenomena. The medical men who worked with hypnosis as a therapeutic procedure were not concerned with the issues of social psychology, but the relation became apparent to those who followed them. This impact is symptomatic of a climate in which the special and abnormal are seen as not far removed from the everyday, and the psychological as belonging to the circle of biological events. Even so, the study of hypnosis did not directly lead into social psychology; several intervening steps were necessary to secure the connection. The first came from Liébault and Bernheim (1888), who argued that hypnotic phenomena were normal, continuous with waking suggestibility; and that they illustrated a most general principle of psychological functioning—the association of ideas. This formulation prepared the way for the study of waking suggestibility, of which the work of Binet (1900) is an early example.

The phenomena of suggestion figured at first as part of individual psychology in the traditional sense; their social relevance was still to be demonstrated. This was the work of a number of sociological writers (among them Tarde, Le Bon, Ross), who undertook to show that a great range of group phenomena—of leadership, fashion, crowd action—were manifestations of suggestion. Their contribution introduced a considerable change. While hypnosis and suggestion initially referred mainly to a dyadic relation, these writers extended the relevance of the phenomena to group settings. Further, they proposed that the area of relevance included the most typical group interactions. Thus they naturalized the unusual observations of hypnosis for the social disciplines. This conjunction and elaboration of ideas from medical psychology and sociology prepared the way for the subsequent developments in social psychology.

The entrance of the suggestion theme into social psychology was gradual and somewhat delayed. It was not until the 1920's that we find the consistent reappearance of the suggestion experiment, but now oriented directly to the issues of social psychology. We are referring to investigations demonstrating the power of groups to alter judgment on the most diverse issues. Despite its familiarity, let us review the main features of the suggestion experiment, which has served as a paradigm.

ALTERING GROUP JUDGMENTS. The investigator establishes the subject's preference, belief, or judgment concerning some particular matter. He then introduces the subject to the purported judgment of an identified group or authoritative figure, which deviates substantially from that of the subject. The discrepant view is usually spurious, but the subject is not aware of the simulation. The final step is to establish whether and how the subject has shifted from his initial position. This procedure aims to trace how an individual copes with social difference or opposition; since observation of actual opposition is hard to obtain, the procedure aims to contrive a convincing duplication.

This procedure uniformly produced positive results; there is hardly an instance on record of a failure to find a measurable shift to the position of majority or expert. This trend is noteworthy when one considers that the subjects, unlike those in the hypnosis (or suggestion) experiment proper, are not told what they will perceive or feel. Even more notable is the observation that these shifts take place in the absence of new information or reasons. Apparently there is much sensitivity to the opinions of equals and authorities.

There is much of interest and worthy of careful study in investigation of this kind. But for a considerable period students were content to demonstrate the effect repeatedly, without carrying the inquiry much further. They believed that they were observing under controlled conditions the essentials of a fundamental social process for which they had an adequate interpretation, and which hardly required further analysis. They first referred the effects to suggestibility, which was, to be sure, hardly enlightening. But soon there was to be a marked change, when a prevailing theory of learning was pressed into service to provide an apparently exact interpretation. It was easy to assimilate the action of groups, their power to control individuals, to the operation of rewards and punishments. Conformity was taken as an instance of the learned tendency to follow group dictates because to do so was rewarding; avoidance of deviation was related to the threat of punishment. Thorndike (1935) showed that the structure of the law of effect experiment was formally identical with the paradigm described above. The subsequent studies of imitation by Miller and Dollard (1941) went in the same direction. The stimulus-response psychology of learning was remarkably suited to provide the theoretical basis for the doctrine of the relativity of social judgment.

A Turning Point

The work of Sherif (1935, 1936) struck a different and important note. More than other investigators, he started with an independent assessment of the nature of social fact. In particular, he saw the formation and change of standards or norms as a central fact of social existence, and he undertook to explore this fact from the psychological side. His experimental contributions owe much to this starting point, both in enlarged perspective and in detail. In the first place, his experimental efforts derived vitality from a preceding analysis of social data. The more usual procedure reverses this order; the psychologist is inclined to start from within the psychological perspective, which is likely to be individualistically oriented, and to conclude with a hint, often conveniently general, that his findings are socially relevant. Connected with this approach is an important property of the first contributions of Sherif, one that has not been, to my knowledge, sufficiently noted. He sought to study the mutual interaction between persons as they formed a group product. This procedure departs from the one we have been describing, which observes a division of labor between those who influence and those who are being influenced. It seems right to say that Sherif was concerned to trace a group process that had the character of an achievement, and which under certain circumstances might be a productive achievement, at a time when most investigators were concentrating on the misleading effects of group interaction. To be sure, other investigators have followed the design of the Sherif experiment, but they have done so mainly for reasons of method; they have profited less from his fundamental orientation.

OTHER CONCERNS OF SOCIAL PSYCHOLOGY. At this point it may be in order to note that conformity has not always been the principal concern of social psychology. During the first quarter of this century one finds considerable stress on the quality and quantity of performance under group conditions. The question to which Triplett (1897), Moede (1920), Allport (1924), and others addressed themselves is quite indigenous to our field. They aimed to trace the differences between solitary performance and performance in the presence of other persons. One leading assumption was that the sheer presence of other persons, especially when they are engaged in similar activities, would have perceptible effects on energy output, efficiency, and also on thinking and imaginal activities. A related question was whether group performance was superior to the contributions of its individual members. There were findings of distinct interest, among them that of Allport concerning the inciting effects of emulation when no direct interaction occurred, and also his report that the sheer presence of others had the effect of moderating affective judgments. In retrospect, this work is notable for its concern with the constructive sides of psychological functioning. This line of activity has not been pursued strongly into the present; we should look forward to a resumption of this interest.

Recent Trends

Returning to our main theme, the study of conformity during the last decade has much extended the range and detail of observation, but the initial theoretical assumptions have not altered appreciably. Interest has increasingly centered on the specific conditions of conformity, and it may appear that theoretical concerns have receded into the back-

ground. But they continue their dominance from this pro-
tected position. We need to scrutinize them more closely.

COMPLEMENTARITY, CONFORMITY, AND SOCIAL INTERACTION.
One notes first the tendency to equate conformity with the
entire range of social influence. The center of interest is with
the kind of social control that results in uniformity of belief
and action. The obvious importance of conformity accounts
for this emphasis, but the assumption of representativeness is
unfortunate. The far more fundamental pattern of social
interaction is that of complementarity. As a rule, A acts and
B helps, or hinders, advises, criticizes, praises. The relationship is typically more that of question to answer than of
reduplication; the point of significance is generally how the
action of A fits to that of B. Indeed, conformity itself should
be considered as a particular way of establishing an appropriate or fitting relation.

The concentration on the conforming aspects of judgment
has had a restrictive effect. One need only consider the phenomena just mentioned—of helping and hindering, of criti-
cizing and praising—to realize how limiting this stress is if
the aim is to formulate a theory of social influence. It is also
in order to ask whether the phenomena of conformity constitute a natural division for the purpose of investigation, a
matter to which we shall return.

THE IMPORTANCE OF STIMULUS CONDITIONS.   The concentration on conformity has appeared to confirm and to give
special prominence to the thesis of the subjectivity of socially
induced effects, and to obscure a range of other operations.
The effects selected for examination have generally involved
decreased sensitivity to perceived conditions. They appeared
to show that one can manipulate judgment arbitrarily, in
disregard of the given circumstances. The principal conclu-

sion that psychologists have drawn in this region is that one can induce persons to believe as others do for no other reason than that they do so, and that the most basic operation of profiting from experience compels this outcome.

We will ask subsequently whether this is an adequate formulation; for the present we note that it is so readily taken for granted as to obscure the radical thought it contains. The critical property of the social induction of opinion is the apparent—often flagrant—disregard by the individual of the actual conditions to be evaluated. But in every field of human inquiry, whether in the social disciplines generally or in psychology, the properties of the situation have a decisive place in the interpretation of action. The historian relates the alignments and decisions of groups to the problems urgent at the time. To move to a distant extreme, the student of psychophysics anchors his data to the objective properties of the stimulus. The student of learning knows that he can teach his subject to go either to the right or left, but he does not lose sight of the fact that what the subject eventually comes to do is related to the position and nature of the goal. In each department of investigation, whether the concern is with intellectual or emotional activities, and regardless of whether they are vertical, the starting point for thinking is that the psychological operations must be related to the circumstances to which they refer. This is the case whether one treats of the birth of a scientific idea or of a delusion. It is therefore remarkable how little is said in this area about the stimulus conditions or objects of judgment. To be sure, they are described, but they serve mainly as a point of departure for the induction of distortion. And indeed, the intent of investigation has been precisely to demonstrate that actual conditions play at best a secondary role, that between them and the person stands the group, which can freely impose its direction. (Further supporting this interpretation is the belief that social issues are by their nature subjective, that therefore their resolution must be equally so.)

It was not the intent of the preceding comments to question the reality of subjective forces, or the power of social conditions to distort thinking and feeling, or the importance of conformity. What we noted was a one-sidedness in the selection of phenomena for observation. Further, we questioned whether the phenomena of conformity can be studied in isolation from other social effects.

Other Problems

We now turn to a different, though related, question. The partiality of a theory or a method need not be a shortcoming in a final sense, since empirical procedures aim to be self-corrective. Seen in this light, the experimental effort in this region must be judged defective. It has not strictly tested its basic assumptions; it has not substantially revised or improved them. It has established at best a gross correspondence between a hastily formulated conceptualization and inadequately analyzed data.

The phenomena of conformity rest on cognitive and motivational processes of some complexity. The subject faces the problem of reconciling disparate sets of evidence, and often he also has to decide between conflicting emotional demands. These operations, which intervene between the conditions the experimenter has created and the final outcome, constitute the subject's definition of the situation and the basis for his decisions. It cannot be said that these intellectual affective operations have received serious study. Investigation has generally concentrated on the quantitative relations between conditions as objectively defined, and an objective index of the effect. The psychological content of the conditions and their effects has suffered neglect. These circumstances have been largely responsible for the failure of theory to advance appreciably beyond the initial starting point.

SOME PRECAUTIONS. The following are instances of the slighting of pertinent observations. Even cursory observation shows that, in the usual experimental situation, subjects attempt to reconcile the discrepant data. Since this is the basis of all further effects, it is by no means unimportant to clarify the grounds of this striving. It has seemed to me that, as a rule, the experimental conditions are such as to demand consensus for objective reasons. The desire for agreement has also other sources, but the objective requirement is often central. One observes, further, that subjects generally try to evaluate the sources of discrepant information, to weigh their merits, and that these considerations play a part in the outcome. One is not likely to reach clarity by ignoring these obvious but not insignificant operations. At least they serve to caution the investigator against the assumption of automatic, unthinking conformity.

Such observation would also have sufficed to convince investigators that it is not sufficient to concentrate on conformity, that they must be equally concerned with the conditions of independence. It may appear that to study the one is automatically to study the other, but the distinction is quite real. Independence is not simply the weakening of conformity, nor is conformity the dilution of independence. The respective trends are in opposition to each other, and they have their sources in distinct considerations and motives; the final action of the subject represents, as a rule, the balance he has struck between them. A careful attention to the happenings within the usual experimental situations would reveal that the trend to independence is usually present, often quite strong, and at times stronger than other trends. It is misleading to speak of studies of conformity when one is regularly dealing with the relation of the forces of independence and conformity.

To these circumstances we owe also the emphasis on the measurement of effects and the failure to assess their significance. Treating the subject as a "black box" threatens adequate understanding, and indeed, the proper description of data. It should be plain that the responsiveness to social influence that we call conformity is not a psychological category, but an external classification, which may include quite heterogeneous phenomena. One can reach agreement with others on the basis of independent judgment. One may delegate responsibility to those whose expertness and intentions one trusts. When uncertain, one may quite deliberately decide to give the benefit of the doubt to the urgings or advice of others. There is also a more immediate persuasiveness that persons and groups exert; this has been the main concern of students, although its conditions have hardly been formulated. This enumeration is far from complete; there are other circumstances that produce what we call conformity. It is an extreme simplification to consider conformity a psychologically homogeneous phenomenon.

Why are these obvious distinctions missing from discussion? General experience has made them sufficiently familiar; it has also taught us that firmness and a desire for independence are not strangers on the human scene. There must be strong theoretical grounds for the selectiveness we have noted in the choice of phenomena and the mode of their observation. The principal reason is, it seems, the commitment to apply the schema of a stimulus-response psychology, derived from another region, that of animal investigations of learning, to the present problems. The following may serve as an illustration of this commitment.

PROBLEMS OF INTERPRETING IMITATIVE BEHAVIOR.   We will consider the well-known interpretation by Miller and Dollard (1941) of a form of imitation in children. One child observed another, who regularly preceded him, when the problem was to find a piece of candy in one of two boxes, which differed in position. The first child, acting on instructions, varied his choices randomly on successive trials. The experimenter made the success of the second child conditional on whether he duplicated the choice of the first child. One group of children was successful only when they repeated the choice of their companion; a second group was successful only when they chose the other alternative. Both sets of children, of course, solved these problems quite readily.

Miller and Dollard proposed that these solutions were instances of learning essentially identical with those they observed when they taught rats in a maze to make the same (or opposed) choice as a rat that preceded them. They formulated that the choice of the first child was a cue for the second; that the tendency to choose the first child's choice (or the other alternative) was the "response" which was strengthened by "reinforcement," or the finding of the goal object. In brief, they proposed that the imitation they studied was an instance of learning, and that the concepts of drive, cue, and reinforcement provided a satisfactory account. Field (1947) repeated this investigation and also varied the conditions. The principal innovation was to question the children about the reasons for their choices. It became convincingly clear that the children proceeded in a way that does not conform to the preceding account. In the first place, they constantly formulated hypotheses about the situation, which also included reference to the hidden plans of the experimenter. Quite soon they formulated to themselves that, for some unaccountable reason, their candy was always in the same place where the first child found his, or that it was always in the other box. Many eventually stated that the experimenter regularly placed two pieces of candy in one box on each trial, or that the experimenter always distributed the candy between the two boxes. They were puzzled no end that the first child was unfailingly successful. In a further variation, this procedure was repeated, but the first child always returned empty-handed. No learning was required to get the experimental children to go to the other position, but it was very hard to teach them to go to the place where their predecessor had just failed. Evidently the children took into account not only the response of their companion, but also the outcome of his action. Finally, the children did at least as well when the game involved the finding of a marble as when they ran for candy; and they preferred the former incentive. This is, of course, not a critique of a stimulus response theory of learning. It does illustrate the dangers of ignoring operations of thinking, and of applying an interpretation that may be plausible in one region to inadequately examined data in another. This procedure has, I believe, been implicit in much of the work in this region.

This account of a particular theme has omitted much that is relevant to the general topic. There has, to cite but one example, been no mention of the growing interest in the personal determinants of independence and conformity. The aspect on which I concentrated is, it seems, pertinent to the most varied lines of investigation, whether they follow the usual procedures of experimentation, observe the activities of groups, or concentrate on clinical analysis.

Summary

The phenomena of group pressure are part of the more inclusive operations of social influence, which include teaching and learning, or the imparting of ideas and skills, the generating of enthusiasm and purpose, and the exercise of outright coercion. It is an error to equate conformity with the effects of social influence. The operations of conformity need to be placed in their context. The danger of a narrow starting point is not simply that one may assert what is wrong, but that one may neglect other data that should limit and modify what is observed in a local region. Conformity is not a psychological category; it includes a number of heterogeneous conditions, each of which must be characterized in psychological terms.

If one restricts oneself to socially induced modifications of opinion in the absence of adequate information or reason, or in violation of these, it is necessary to include reference to the tendencies of conformity *and* independence, both of which are as a rule simultaneously active. The sources of independence and conformity are not the same, although they are always in relation. Failure to observe this requirement produces a misleading emphasis on subjective determinants of judgment, and a neglect of the striving toward validity, which is active even when it does not prevail. More generally, the study of conformity needs to consider the productive tendencies of persons, as well as productive effects of groups.

The investigation of the effects of social pressure requires the analysis of cognitive and emotional activities. It is not sufficient to establish quantitative relations between conditions and effects whose psychological content is only sketchily known. Such a procedure promotes reliance on questionable interpretations and hampers searching experimentation.

REFERENCES

Allport, F. H. *Social psychology*. Boston: Houghton Mifflin, 1924.

Asch, S. E. *Social psychology*. New York: Prentice-Hall 1952.

Bernheim, H. *Die Suggestion und Ihre Heilwirkung*. Leipzig und Wien: Franz Deuticke, 1888.

Binet, A. *La suggestibilité*. Paris: Schleicher, 1900.

Field, A. Hypothesis formation of children in problem solving. Master's thesis, New School for Social Research, 1947.

Miller, N. E., & Dollard, J. *Social learning and imitation*. New Haven: Yale Univer. Press, 1941.

Moede, W. *Experimentelle massenpsychologie*. Leipzig: S. Hirtzel, 1920.

Sherif, M.   A study of some social factors in perception, *Arch. Psychol.*, 1935, **27**, No. 187.

Sherif, M.   *The psychology of social norms*. New York: Harper, 1936.

Thorndike, E. L.   *The psychology of wants, interests and attitudes.* New York: D. Appleton-Century, 1935.

Triplett, N.   The dynamogenic factors in pacemaking and competition. *Amer. J. Psychol.*, 1897, **9**, 507–533.

CHAPTER 5

Conformity-Deviation, Norms, and Group Relations

MUZAFER SHERIF

The University of Oklahoma

There are certain questions that should be raised at the outset in dealing with the problem of conformity and deviation. I shall start by raising them. Then some laboratory studies of the normative process which underlies conforming or deviating behavior will be summarized, and limitations of the confines of the traditional laboratory in handling basic problems of conformity and independence will be discussed. This will lead us to the necessity of research on normative process within the framework of the properties of groups. It will be concluded that research and experimentation thus formulated will yield a basis for realistic evaluation of the norm system of a group from the point of view of social stability and social change.

Problem of Conformity and Deviation

An item of behavior, taken in and by itself, cannot be labeled either conformity or deviation. There is no such thing as conforming or deviating behavior in the abstract. The terms "conformity" and "deviation" make sense when at least the following questions are raised:

1. Conformity to *what?* Deviation or departure from *what?* Always, conformity is conformity to *something*. Deviation is

departure from something, whether the referent of that "something" is made explicit or not.

What is that "something"? The referents may be the prevailing, the usual, or expected ways of doing things in the individual's surroundings. This is the *normative* basis of the problem. The referents may be the individual's particular place or position in the scheme of interpersonal or group relationships. This is the *organizational* basis of the problem. Does the individual accept and behave in terms of the place and position expected of him and his kind in the scheme of things?

2. What is the relative importance of the behavior area in which conformity or deviation occurs? For example, is it a matter of whether a father takes care of his family as he should, or is it a question of whether he keeps up with the baseball scores in the World Series as his friends do?

3. Is the normative basis of the behavior in question shared and upheld by other groups to which the individual is related in some capacity? Or do his multiple groups put contradictory or even conflicting demands and expectations on the individual for his behavior in given dimensions? This of course relates to the problem of integration or conflict of social values in the psychological world of the individual.

4. The fourth question concerns whether conformity and deviation occur primarily through coercion or threat of subsequent coercion and force, or whether the behavior in question is prompted by the individual's inner convictions and personally cherished values.

5. What are the *alternatives* available for the individual in the stimulus situation with respect to the area of behavior in question? Are there many, few, or none? Are they clearly defined or difficult to distinguish? In other words, what situational factors enter into the picture, both as to the physical setting and the other people involved?

When studied in the context of these questions, conforming or nonconforming behavior can be taken as an index of the degree of stability or the extent of change in the human relationships of a given setting and specifies whether stability or change occurs primarily as a consequence of coercion or primarily through the voluntary interaction of individuals. Thus viewed, conforming behavior and nonconforming behavior can serve as a basis of evaluating the trends in human relationships: how a group is doing and in what directions it is headed.

These are among the basic problems for any human group. They are all the more vital in this modern shrinking world. Whether we like it or not, peoples and groupings are being brought into closer functional relationships. Scarcely a group is left which is contained within itself as a closed system. What a particular group is doing and where it is headed have wide impacts on other peoples. The implication of this enlarging interdependence of peoples is rather obvious, namely a normative system which transcends restrictive, monopolistic loyalties and conformities still surviving from relatively more closed group patterns of previous periods.

RESULTS OF NEGLECT OF ISSUES.   Apart from the questions just raised, that is, questions of the referents of conforming behavior, of the relative importance of the area of behavior, of the integrated or conflicting character of the normative bases of the behavior in question, of how conformity is brought about, conforming and nonconforming behavior cannot be studied as a scientific problem. Neglect of one or the other issues raised here has resulted in a spate of literature in recent years by social psychologists, social scientists, and essayists, which at its best is healthy social critique and at its worst boils down to a romantic protest and a cry for heroes.

We even read discussions of whether man is by nature a conformist, a submissive prey of social winds and tides, or whether by nature he is a seeker of truth, hence required by his own nature to be independent. Such formulations are reminiscent of the old controversies over human nature by instinct theorists of whether man is altruistic or selfish, co-operative or competitive, acquisitive or sharing. Now the argument seems to be transferred to the cognitive sphere.

By implication, those who would define "human nature" as basically conformist or as basically independent praise one kind of behavior and damn the other. Yet by formulating the problem in this dichotomous form in the abstract, conforming behavior or deviating behavior cannot be evaluated in a consistent fashion.

Taking a stand as an apologist of conformity can amount to the praise of blind subservience. On the other hand, singing the praise of nonconformity apart from evaluation of the norm or value to which it is related may lead to an absurd dilemma. Let's just cite a few cases of nonconforming behavior, such as driving down the middle of the road, monopolizing a conversation, deliberate plagiarism, or stealing. Of course, those who see virtue in nonconformity in its own right would protest these crass examples. For praise of nonconformity is made of righteous nonconformity. This is exactly the point. Nonconformity or conformity cannot be evaluated in its own right apart from its referent, namely the normative basis of the behavior in question.

Normative Process in the Laboratory

I shall first consider the formation of the normative process as studied in the psychological laboratory, with special reference to variations in results owing to the kind of controlled stimulus setup presented to the subjects.

The study of norm formation in the laboratory has been undertaken through producing a characteristic mode of behavior relative to the aspect of the stimulus situation experimentally introduced. This production embodies the bare essential of norm-regulated behavior.

MODES OF BEHAVIOR AND STIMULUS PROPERTIES. If the stimulus arrangement provided by the experimenter is objectively well graded or has compelling anchorages, the ensuing uniformity of behavior relative to it is determined by these salient features of the stimulus conditions. As a result of repeated encounters with them, characteristic modes of behavior come into close fit with the stimulus properties.

Tresselt and Volkmann (1942) clearly demonstrated the principle in their study dealing with the production of uniform opinion by nonsocial stimulation. These authors formulated the principle in question as follows: "Each person in a group says what he does not only because he has been persuaded by argument, induced by reward, compelled by pressure, guided by past experience, or influenced by the voiced opinions of other people; he says it also because he faces a restricted range of social or nonsocial stimulation, and this range has determined his scale of judgment" (p. 243).

When stimuli are presented serially over a period of time, the range representing categories of behavioral uniformity to particular items is appropriate evidence for inferring the formation of a *psychophysical scale*.

The study of stimulus relationships affecting the formation and functioning of psychophysical scales cannot occupy our attention further at this time. It has been carried to a rather sophisticated level in recent years through the efforts of such contributors as Graham (1952), Helson (1959), Johnson (1955), Stevens (1957), Volkmann (1951), and others.

For the present discussion it is sufficient to emphasize that the normative process can be determined primarily by the range and salient anchorages of the stimuli to which individuals are exposed repeatedly. I strongly suspect that the principles to which we have alluded underlie the similarity in characteristic modes of outlook in technological matters by various human groupings scattered over wide geographic regions, but exposed to similar technology (Sherif, 1948;

Sherif & Sherif, 1956). If so, the rapid shift in psychophysical scales following the introduction of new stimulus values may be pertinent to understanding the relatively faster assimilation of new technological items as compared with new social concepts. This refers, of course, to the well-known empirical facts formulated by sociologists and anthropologists as the "cultural lag."

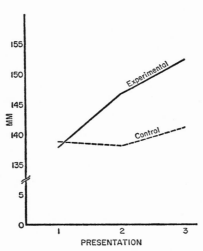

FIGURE 5.1. Mean ratings of moderately undesirable behavior items. (Drawing based on data from Cohen [1957].)

Of course, weights, lines, and sounds do not have an exclusive copyright on compelling stimulus characteristics. Stimuli with social relevance, including verbal statements, may have such compelling properties as well. In his study on stimulus conditions as factors in social change, Cohen (1957) at the University of Oklahoma studied changes in norms as a function of alteration in the range of social stimulation faced by the subjects. By scaling statements of undesirable behavior of the kind used earlier by McGarvey (1943), Cohen selected moderately undesirable acts, such as "fishing without a license." Subject pairs were to come to an agreement in rating how desirable or undesirable these acts were. Exposed to the restricted range of items, control and experimental pairs rated them similarly (see Figure 5.1). In the second experimental presentation, very undesirable behaviors, such as "kidnapping a baby for ransom," were included. As Figure 5.1 shows, the somewhat undesirable behaviors were agreed to be more desirable, thus showing the well-known contrast effect owing to the dastardly acts introduced in the second presentation. The differences between the experimental and control subjects were maintained in the third session when individuals rated the behaviors alone, indicating a normative process primarily determined by the exposure of interacting individuals to specified ranges of stimulus items. It is in this sense that conformity is related to the formation of psychophysical scales.

Laboratory Studies

Now let's turn to laboratory studies on the formation of *psychosocial scales:* scales of characteristic modes of behavior whose formation may be influenced by the relationships among interacting individuals. Features of man's relationships with man become most salient as determinants of his conformities precisely when the stimulus situation they face together is highly fluid and provides various alternatives.

This observation has been made time and again by social scientists. I was first impressed with it upon reading Durkheim's accounts of the formation of *representations collectives* in out-of-ordinary interaction situations and the accounts of Chicago sociologists—notably Clifford Shaw, Thrasher, and Zorbaugh—of small group functioning in interstitial areas of large cities. Even in the midst of "social disorganization," in the sociological sense of that term, an orderliness prevails in the social life of these small groups. How does the normative process take shape under such conditions? How do new standards of conduct arise in out-of-ordinary situations, times of crisis and the breakdown of established conformities?

RESEARCH ON NORM FORMATION. These were among the questions that led to the laboratory norm-formation experiments which utilize the autokinetic setup as a fluid stimulus in the dimension in question amenable to various alternative modes of behavior (Sherif, 1935; 1936). The problem was conceived in terms of stabilization of behavior over a period of time, and not as a question of whether an individual is susceptible to suggestion in this or that particular round of judgment. Contrary to Durkheim's view, even when the individual is alone and not interacting with others, his psychological functioning becomes organized and exhibits emergent properties. This was the finding of the individual sessions. As some of you know, after the individual faces such a situation repeatedly, his behavior stabilizes within a characteristic range and around a modal point with reduced variability.

When individuals face the autokinetic setup together, over a period of time a convergence of the individual behaviors occurs, resulting in similarities not initially present. But the norm that emerges during interaction is not an average of the individual norms. Nor is it necessarily identical with the initial behavior of one or the other individual, although a large prestige or status differential may almost produce this result. To specify the normative outcome further, the relationships of individuals in a particular interaction process have to be delineated. However, once formed, the convergent behavior is not dependent upon the *immediate presence* of other individuals. In subsequent sessions when the individual was alone, behavior was still regulated by the normative process.

It was suggested that when the individual changes his verbal reports in the presence of another person making somewhat different judgments, he is not really *seeing* the stimulus any differently, but is simply changing his behavior in order to avoid disapproval and appear agreeable. Certainly this does happen in some situations. A recent experiment by W. R. Hood and the writer (1957) was designed to investigate whether or not behavior in the highly unstructured autokinetic situation represented such public compliance. Procedures were planned to eliminate suspicion that the experiment had anything to do with social influence and to remove the immediate presence of another person or the sound of his voice at the time judgment was rendered. The subject simply overheard another person making 20 judgments while waiting his turn to make estimates by himself.

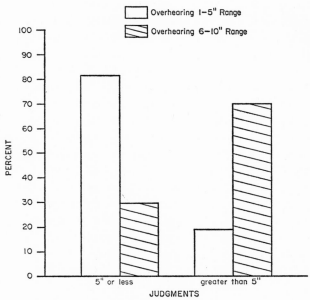

FIGURE 5.2. Proportions of judgments 5″ or less and greater than 5″ for two conditions. (From Hood & Sherif [1957].)

One sample overheard judgments ranging from 1 to 5 inches and another sample overheard reports ranging from 6 to 10 inches. Figure 5.2 summarizes judgments made when the subjects were alone, by showing the proportions of judgments 5 inches or less and 6 inches or more under these two conditions. Later, when asked what extent of movement they had usually seen, the subjects' estimates did not differ significantly from their own median judgments in the situation. We may conclude, I believe, that in this situation, individuals "call them as they see them" and they see them as influenced by judgments previously overheard. There is no evidence of a discrepancy between judgment and verbal report.

JUDGMENTS AND LIMITS.   Can we say, then, that in highly fluid situations, the relationships among individuals determine behavior altogether, and that the "sky is the limit" as far as the extent of social influence that can be achieved? We cannot. For even in this highly unstructured situation, the size of the room, as the individual can determine it—from finding his way about, from echo and the like (Sherif & Harvey, 1952)—the subject-to-light distance, exposure time, intensity of the light, and other stimulus arrangements set rather definite limits upon the extent of movement perceived. If another person's judgments exceed these limits too far, they are unlikely to exert any determining role at all.

Whittaker (1958) showed this at the University of Oklahoma by having planted subjects make judgments which exceeded the individual's largest estimate made previously when he was alone. For different samples, the "plant" made judgments ranging upward from magnitudes 1 inch larger, twice, eight, or twelve times larger than the maximum estimate the individual had given when alone. Figure 5.3 summarizes the results in terms of the average difference between means of the individual and together sessions. It may be seen that the partner's judgments had a significant effect when they exceeded the previous maximum estimate by 1 inch and upward, that the effect decreased when his judgments were twice as great, and that no significant effect was found when the partner's judgments were eight or twelve times as large. These latter changes do not differ significantly from those for the control group, which simply judged alone a second time. Analysis in terms of frequency of judgments exceeding the individual's initial range when alone leads to the same conclusion. We conclude "the sky is *not* the limit" in the effectiveness of attempted influence even in a highly unstructured situation.

Furthermore, once a psychosocial scale has been established, the experimenter cannot play around indefinitely,

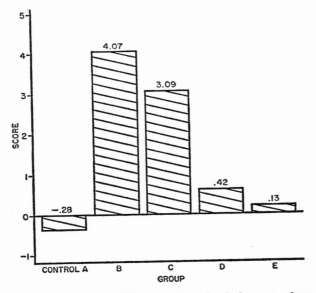

FIGURE 5.3.   Mean difference scores for judgments alone and with "plant." (From Whittaker [1958].)

introducing new social anchorages in order to change it. This is in some contrast to laboratory findings on psychophysical scales, which reveal strikingly quick adaptations to changes in the stimulus values presented. The successive introduction of conflicting social anchorages produces breakdowns of a psychosocial scale, as Norman Walter's experiment at the University of Oklahoma (1955) shows. Walter was interested in what would happen to an established psychosocial scale for judging autokinetic movement when conflicting reports from equally good sources were presented successively. A few days after the individual established a characteristic range and mode of behavior alone, he was informed casually of the performance of students at a university with high prestige in his eyes. The figure given was actually either the 90th or 10th percentile of his own previous estimates. The result was a significant shift toward the figure introduced, with greatly reduced variability, even a greater reduction than for control subjects whose variability decreased regularly during four sessions on different days without procedural changes. At a third session 3 or 4 days later, a second "data report" opposite in direction to the first was given experimental subjects, this one from another institution of about equal prestige in his eyes. The typical result was a shift in behavior back to the region of the initial norm established when alone, but with increased variability. Finally at a fourth session, the experimenter discredited both reports by saying the results were suspected of error. The result was further marked increase in variability such that a breakdown in the normative process ensued.

ANCHORAGE POINTS AND BEHAVIOR. The effect of systematically reducing the number of anchorages available in the stimulus arrangement is to increase the probability that characteristic behaviors developing as individuals face the situation repeatedly will be significantly influenced by relationships among the individuals. This generalization is supported by the findings of various studies, and James Thrasher (1954) tested it in a single design. His stimulus setups represented three gradations of stimulus structure. Judgments were obtained from individuals alone, then in pairs composed either of good friends or initially neutral persons. In the situation with the most stable anchorages available in the stimulus setup, neither friends nor neutral individuals affected each other's behavior significantly. But in the least structured situation, the relationship among the individuals as friends or as initially neutral decidedly affected the normative process. The intermediate situation produced results intermediate between these two.

Limitations of Laboratory Confines for Valid Research Strategy

The general conclusion to be drawn is that the choice of the stimulus setup in the laboratory determines to a great extent how effective social factors introduced by the experimenter will be. If the structural properties of the stimulus arrangements allow no alternatives, social factors introduced will play relatively little part in patterning characteristic behavior. If the stimulus conditions provide alternatives in his sizing up of them, the likelihood of compliance to social influences introduced by the experimenter will increase. There are a good many combinations and gradations in between the stimulus situations representing these two extremes. If space permitted, we could draw upon experiments by Asch (1952), Coffin (1941), Luchins (1944), Mausner (1953; 1954), and others to accentuate this conclusion.

Frequently, the manipulator in public relations, the demagogue in public affairs enjoys a cynical glee at the compliance and malleability of people owing to the muddied atmosphere which the manipulator and demagogue themselves have helped manufacture. It is a laudable antidote against such cynical views of human affairs to set up experiments in the laboratory with clear-cut stimulus arrangements and to present results showing that people are independent in their appraisals of the situation, that they do not blindly succumb to false social influences. However, the demagogue himself seldom works with a situation as clear-cut as, say, matching a pencil to a yardstick, when he attempts manipulations. He fishes in muddied waters, unless he feels that brute force is on his side.

COUNTERACTING MANIPULATION. Perhaps the more effective way of counteracting such situations may be a concentration on analysis of conditions which render people susceptible to manipulative influences. Here one problem is *what* is presented at all, in the first place. All the information, all the news fit to be presented in speech and mass communication media on vital matters which lie far beyond the individual's perceptual range come to him through the *selectivity* of people in control of the mass media. Especially in the contemporary scene, when man is faced with the problem of taking sides, making decisions, and expressing opinions on issues that relate to the use of atomic energy, foreign aid in distant lands, or the merits or demerits of a balanced budget, he gets most of his information through the mass media or from other persons who got it from the mass media. The problem of *selectivity* in *what* is presented is at least as important as that of the presence or absence of alternatives once a situation requiring a decision is encountered. Furthermore, we suspect that in problems such as those just mentioned, man's ethnic, religious, and political ties may be weighty factors in determining which side is taken and which decision is made. If so, it is a bit unrealistic to study conformity and noncomformity in an arbitrary situation within the confines of the traditional laboratory and to declare the generalizations reached on this basis as the verdict of psychological science.

The study of the relative contribution of selected stimulus factors, in which almost infinitely fine gradations of structure are possible, and of selected social factors, which are also numerous, is an interesting psychological problem. A good many psychologists could devote their whole lifetimes to it. But no amount of concentration on all the variations between a sharply defined stimulus setup at one extreme and a highly fluid setup at the other, and no amount of technical refinement within the traditional laboratory setting will settle for us the important question of what are *typical* conditions conducive to the production of various modes of compliance and independence to social influences.

It is not yielding or being independent to discrete and transitory social influence that brought about concern over problems of conformity and independence in human affairs on the contemporary scene. That is why my brief report of experiments dwelt mainly upon studies of the normative process producing a characteristic attitude and mode of behavior to its referents over a span of time. Studies of yielding and independence in relation to one-episode social influence are reminiscent of Allport's early studies of "social decrements," "social increments," and "social subvaluents" through what is referred to as the study of "pure social effect." Such studies have only limited bearing on problems of conformity and deviation in which the individual's self-esteem, status, and work in relation to other persons significant in his scheme of things are at stake.

INTERACTION CONDITIONS.   The settings in which compliance and noncompliance become important problems cannot be determined within the confines of the traditional laboratory setting. Here we have to extend our research perspectives and put validity checks upon ourselves to catch the essential properties of actual situations conducive to various modes of compliance or independence. In order to achieve this perspective, intimate familiarity must be achieved first with interaction settings in which an integral aspect is that of compliance or independence in behavior. And the proper focus for developing valid research strategies is upon the formation and functioning of actual groups in both their ingroup and intergroup interactions.

Conformity and Nonconformity in Group Relations

This brings us to the central part of my presentation. The representative, the typical, problems of conformity and non-conformity can be more effectively singled out through due recognition of man's behavior relative to significant other persons. Significant other persons stand in specifiable relationships to the individual—friendly or unfriendly, pulling together or pulling apart. Conforming or noncomforming behavior makes very little sense when it is not analyzed within a framework of these relationships. An observation will illustrate the point. In 1958, a group of liberal students at a southwestern university were interested in persuading restaurants and soda fountains in the area to cater to Negro students. The representative response of the shopkeepers was that they were willing to do so but each individual was concerned about what the other shopkeepers in the area would do. Our image of ourselves, our appraisals of our own practices, are not self-generating. They are not independent of our relatedness to people significant in our eyes, whether these significant people are seen as friend or foe. This point will be specified further in connection with the properties of groups and ingroup and outgroup demarcations.

It may not be too far off the mark to maintain that man's relation to significant others is, on the whole, in terms of his membership in various groups, such as family, club, fraternity, occupational outfit, religious or political outfit of some sort. If the problem of conformity and independence is formulated within a framework of the individual's group setting, we are confronted head on with relationships in which the problem is an ever-present, integral aspect of interaction situations day in and day out, and not an incidental side issue. If the problem is formulated within the concreteness of group relations, as these relations unfold in the actualities of social life, then conformity or noncomformity acquires a functional significance which is mutilated when either is considered apart from these relations, as by those who advocate a doctrine of an irreconcilable individual—group dichotomy. The social philosophy which puts issues in dichotomous either-or form, that is either *for* the individual or *for* the group, starts with the categorical assumption of individual and group as irreconcilable entities or antithetical polarities, as though demands and interests of one are necessarily in conflict with the interests of the other for all occasions. Within the framework of man's ties with other men in lasting relationships, the conflicting or harmonious character of interests is itself a problem of study. With the vantage point thus gained, the external stimulus, whether it be sharply defined or fluid and uncertain, can be studied as it becomes relevant to relationships among individuals facing definable problem situations.

Member's Experience of Conformity and Independence, and Properties of Groups

A rounded analysis of the important problem of the individual's experience when he complies and when he is independent in specific instances of his group relations should start with specification of the essential properties of the group itself and the individual member's psychological relationship to these properties.

The concept "group" means all things to all people. Various concepts are offered in the academic market place today in the name of operational definitions. Not infrequently, the model and technique are derived from more established sciences without due concern for their appropriateness as tools for valid study of human group problems. Unless the appropriateness of the proposed techniques and models is examined relative to the essential properties of actual groups, they are doomed to inefficacy in yielding valid results which can be generalized to handle the individual's behavior in his actual group setting.

EARLY STUDIES.   Prompted by this serious methodological concern with formulation of valid problems, we undertook an extensive survey of sociological field studies dealing with properties of small groups. We turned to this literature for the simple reason that sociologists have priority in their concern with the properties of actual small groups and have collected considerable empirical data on the topic (Faris, 1953). These surveys were a first step in our ongoing research program on formation and functioning of groups in both their ingroup and intergroup relations, in which the problem of conformity and deviation is an integral part. They are presented in various publications (Sherif, 1948, Chs. 5 and 6; Sherif & Cantril, 1947, Ch. 10; Sherif & Sherif, 1953, Ch. 8; Sherif & Sherif, 1956, Chs. 5, 6, 7).

These early surveys deliberately centered on informally or spontaneously formed small groups in order to start with group formations which are the creation of voluntary and free interaction among the individual members, and not the product of an organizational blueprint with rules and by-laws handed down by a governing body with outside authority. From this survey, several generalizations about the properties of small groups were extracted. Here we touch only on the minimum essentials.

It is extracted that any small group functions as a delineated social unit. The members have a rather clear notion who is in, who is out, and also the marginal ones who did not quite make it at the time.

It is extracted that the individuals who achieve accepted membership in groups can be ordered at a given time along a status hierarchy from the leader down to the position at the bottom. This property of status differentiation need not be brought about through a formal vote or through formal codification on paper. The relative status position that a given individual member occupies is operationally inferred from the relative frequency of *effective initiative* that he achieves in starting and carrying out activities and projects in which the membership as a whole participates. This result is confirmed by sociometric choices of the group members along dimensions of effective initiative as well as popularity. The status differentiation of the members constitutes the *organization* of the group and embodies the *power* aspects of relations within the group.

The psychological counterpart of the emergence of group structure or organization is revealed through reciprocal performance expectations of members, not through dictates of an outside authority, but on the basis of their experiences of the relative contributions of each member in previous efforts towards solution of common problems.

PROPERTIES OF "GROUPNESS."   Another essential property of groups, extracted from a survey of empirical field studies, is a set of values or *norms* shared by group members. It can be said that the "groupness" of the group as a more or less lasting social unit may be best defined in terms of these essential properties, viz., organization or structure and a set of values or norms (Homans, 1950). More transitory social situations which lack these properties may be referred to as mere aggregates or togetherness situations.

The set of values or norms of a group (variously referred to as its code, standards, or rules) has probably a more direct bearing on the problem of conformity and deviation. There would be no persistent problem of conformity or deviation if there were no norms to conform to or deviate from: a question raised at the start of this discussion. As long as there are values or norms shared, upheld, and cherished by group members, compliance to and deviation from them are ever-present concerns.

In the literature, there is confusion in regard to the concept "group norm." As long as a norm is property of the group, upheld by members as "theirs," a norm is an expected and even ideal mode of behavior for them and does not refer necessarily to the statistical average of the behavior of members (Freeman *et al.*, 1952).

The *social attitude* of the individual, determining characteristic and persistent modes of behavior to relevant stimuli, be they other persons, groups, activities, institutions, or symbols, is derived from those expected, or even ideal modes of behavior referred to as a group norm. A norm is a group property and, as such, is a sociological designation. The individual's social attitude is the consequence of internalization of the norm by the individual. Social attitudes define the individual's relatedness to stimuli in question—to other persons, groups, symbols, etc.—and his stance for or against them. As such, social attitudes may be referred to as his ego-attitudes or, if you like, self-attitudes. The individual's experience of self-identity, his feelings of stability (security), his strivings toward expected and ideal goals consist in large part of ego-attitudes derived from his membership character in given groups during his life history.

This being the case, norms are not rules or standards of behavior devoid of motivational and emotional warmth. Social attitudes formed relative to group norms define a substantial part of the individual's goal-directed behavior, which is the earmark of any motivational state.

The motivational-emotional character of norm-regulated behavior is not a mystery if we consider the rise and stabilization of norms in spontaneously formed groups. Small groups arising on an informal basis in actual life are outcomes of interaction among individuals with motives perceived as common, be they common deprivations and frustations—

such as those experienced by youngsters in slum areas—or desires for social distinction and exclusiveness with appropriate facilities and prestige symbols—such as those characteristic of clubs mushrooming in residential extensions of large cities like Los Angeles, Houston, and Chicago. As anyone familiar with the history of labor organizations in this country knows, it was the common urge for mutual protection and improvement of working and wage conditions which prompted the banding together of laborers in the latter half of the 19th century, at first secretly and then in public forms which foreshadowed the modern labor unions. The norms cherished as almost sacred and upheld most tenaciously in word and deed by labor organizations to this very day are those related to the motivational issues that brought the early workers together—collective bargaining, the right to strike, seniority rights, the closed shop, minimum wage, and so on. The motivational bases of such norms are readily seen when one of the members deviates from the hard-won standards. Not just a few administrators, but the rank and file have coined labels and developed corrective measures for deviations they consider as selling out their interests. A similar analysis of motivational bases in the rise and functioning of norms can be applied to management and business organizations.

In short, norms arise and are stabilized relative to motivationally important relationships and activities. Serious issues of conformity and noncomformity arise relative to norms pertaining to matters of consequence to the group, its existence, its perpetuation, its solidarity and its effective functioning toward central interests and goals. Therefore, it is somewhat unrealistic to dwell upon cases of conformity or nonconformity in matters considered peripheral to the scheme of things by the group in question, such as the hobbies engaged in by members privately. This question of the relative importance of the behavior area was one of those which opened this presentation. In this connection, it is essential that the investigator recognize that the importance of a norm in the scheme of a particular group may or may not correspond to the importance and seriousness of the issue in question in determining the course of human relations in a larger sense. For example, in this country until recently, many organizations, including labor, considered political matters as the politician's realm.

Latitude of Acceptable Behavior Defined by Norm

Now we turn to discussion of a concept which will provide us with a baseline for classifying given behavior as conforming or deviating and for evaluating unique personal variations of individuals in this respect. Norm-regulated behavior cannot be represented as a single point. The expected or ideal behavior within the bounds of a given norm is represented by a range of behaviors, which we have referred to as a "range of tolerable behavior" and "latitude of acceptance," and shall here term "latitude of acceptable behavior" (Hovland, Harvey, & Sherif, 1957; Sherif & Sherif, 1953, pp. 198, 207f.; Sherif & Sherif, 1956, pp. 171, 533).

As long as behavior falls within bounds defined by this range, it will not call for correctives applied to cases of deviation (Jackson, 1960). Behavior outside the limits is viewed as objectionable by other members and will arouse spontaneous correctives from the membership, even without deliberate formal action. In our present ongoing research on naturally formed groups in settings differentiated as to social rank in several southwestern cities, we find that an important difference between groups distinguished as to their solidarity is the extent to which the membership actively participates in correctives for deviating behavior (Sherif, 1959; Sherif & Sherif, 1960). Solidarity is measured by members' behaviors when the leader is present and absent, by their secrecy and exclusiveness relative to outsiders, by relative coordination of role performance in the face of mildly threatening situations. The group with greater solidarity by these measures is also the group whose members react to a man when a member deviates from an important norm.

Of course, the usual routines of social life run within the bounds of acceptable behavior. Like the oxygen in the air which is noticed only when the concentration falls, the reality of norms and their limits are seen most strikingly when correctives and constraints are aroused by deviation, as Durkheim so aptly noted.

NORMS, LATITUDE, AND BEHAVIOR.   The latitude of acceptable behavior varies in magnitude according to the importance of the norm for the group. The more consequential the issue at hand, the more constricted the latitude of acceptable behavior. Conversely, the more peripheral the issue, the greater the variability encompassed by the latitude of acceptable behavior. In matters bearing closely on the existence and perpetuation of the group, the latitude of acceptable behavior is constricted, unless the group is in a state of disorganization. And, at times when the well-being of the group becomes an acute problem, it is constricted still further. In our experiments on group formation and intergroup relations in 1949 and 1954, groups met in intense competition for a single goal over a period of several days. At the height of the group conflict growing out of this competition even a slightly kind word about the out-group was seen as almost treasonable; whereas, a little earlier, similar acts were acceptable in the spirit of good sportsmanship (Sherif & Sherif, 1953; Sherif *et al.,* 1954). It is not hard to find parallels of this constriction of the latitude of acceptable behavior in the political scene of recent years.

Along the lines of previous studies in relation to the closed-shop issue in 1948 by Hovland, Volkart, and Sherif and the prohibition issue in Oklahoma by Hovland, Harvey, and

Sherif (1957), our study during the 1956 election campaign (Sherif & Hovland, manuscript) verified the constricted latitude of acceptance in matters vital to the existence of a group. In this experiment, the task was to indicate acceptance and rejection of nine statements ranging from extremely pro-Republican (labeled A) to extremely pro-Democratic (labeled I) on the issue of the election of presidential and vice-presidential candidates of the two parties. The finding pertinent to our present discussion was that identified members who were actively campaigning at the time for their respective parties, viz., members of Young Republican and Young Democratic organizations in several universities in the Southwest, included fewer stands in their latitudes of acceptance and rejected an extended range of stands as compared with individuals not identified organizationally with either party, who had more extended latitudes of acceptance around the stand they endorsed (see Figure 5.4).

BEHAVIORAL LATITUDE AND POSITION IN THE GROUP. The latitude of acceptable behavior on a given issue varies also with the position the individual occupies in the group. I strongly suspect that position in the group and importance of the norm interact in rather complex fashion to define the limits of the latitude of acceptable behavior for a particular individual relative to a particular norm. But it should be mentioned that the leader, as a member of a group, is not immune to correctives. If his nonconformity pertains to a matter of sufficient importance, the end result may be his decline in the power hierarchy.

The concept of latitude of acceptable behavior is explicit recognition of the fact that no two individuals in the same group uphold the norms to the same degree, nor are cases of nonconformity involving different individuals ever identical. There are individual variations in both conformity and nonconformity owing to unique personal characteristics of the individuals in question. These individual variations are psychological facts which should be included in an adequate conceptualization. Perhaps some of the difficulty encountered in doing so stems from the tendency in psychology to categorize individual variations as though they referred to events in an altogether different universe of discourse than social behavior. If unique individual variations are ordered relative to a baseline defined by the latitude of acceptable behavior and the range of rejected behavior on the issue in question, we may achieve a reference scale more meaningful than hypothetically constructed scales dictated by worn-out typologies and computational convenience (Hood & Sherif, 1955).

Conformity-Deviation and Change in Intergroup Relations

As concluded in the last section, a norm emerges in relation to significant aspects of the existence and activities of the group. The prevailing pattern of relations of a given group with others is certainly a significant concern for its members. In the course of friendly or hostile, cooperative or competitive traffic between groups, norms emerge which regulate the intergroup attitudes and behavior of the members of the ingroup toward the outgroup and its members. If the character of this traffic is positive, if the goals of the respective groups do not conflict, if interests of groups do not clash, the norms regulating attitude and behavior are friendly and favorable. If the groups are striving towards goals whose attainment implies gain for one group while signifying loss and defeat for the other, the intergroup norms are unfavorable and hostile. In line with the specific character of the norms, qualities or stereotypes are attributed to the outgroup, being positive or negative depending on the character of the intergroup relations. This process underlies the close or remote "social distance" at which another group and its members are kept.

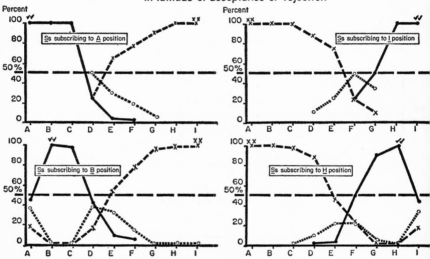

Legend:

●———● Acceptance
x———x Rejection
o·······o Noncommittal
✔ ✔ Most Acceptable position
x x Most Objectionable position
50% Horizontal line: Criterion for inclusion
in latitude of acceptance or rejection

FIGURE 5.4. Latitudes of acceptance and rejection for stands on a political issue by individuals upholding different positions: A (extreme pro-Republican) to I (extreme pro-Democrat).

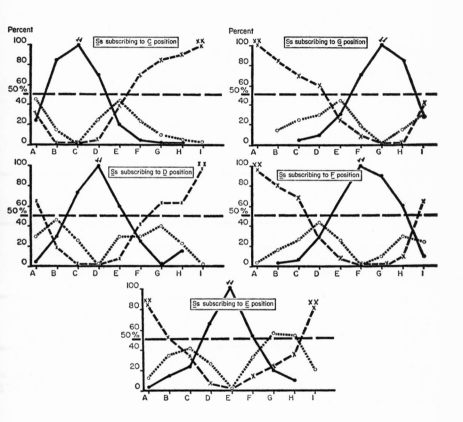

GROUPS AND NEGATIVE STEREOTYPES. In our 1949 and 1954 experiments on group relations mentioned earlier, groups in conflict developed unmistakable negative stereotypes and each group viewed the other through the widening gap of social distance which appeared irreconcilable to the members of both groups. In the 1954 experiment, these negative stereotypes were changed and the social distance between the groups reduced to the point of mutual acceptance. A brief background is necessary to explicate the conditions bringing about this positive change.

In these experiments, groups formed as social units when individuals who were initially unacquainted were brought together in activities with compelling goals whose attainment required joint and coordinated action on the part of all individuals. As a consequence of interaction in such conditions over a period of time, groups emerged with organizations and with norms, as is characteristic of groups in actual life. When two groups had thus developed independently as social units, they were brought together for the first time in the second stage of the experiment, in a series of reciprocally competitive activities, in which the victory of one meant the defeat of the other, with attendant reward and glory for the victor and disappointment and frustration for the vanquished group. In the course of these encounters, the initial sportsmanship toward the adversary went into a sharp decline and was supplanted by derogatory invectives and open expressions of hostility. In time, unfavorable adjectives, such as "stinkers," "cheats," "sneaks," became stabilized in word and deed as the picture of the adversary. As intergroup conflict increased, cooperation and solidarity *within* each group reigned supreme.

At this point, members of each group were disinterested in any *information* about their adversary which might have changed their views of them; they were adamant in their insistence that they did not even want to be in the same situation as the other group. Therefore, the ground was not favorable for *negotiations between the leaders.* When brought into physical proximity in activities enjoyable to each group separately, the *social interaction situations* were utilized for furthering the mutual derogation.

None of the measures just mentioned could have been effective in changing the reciprocal hostility to intergroup cooperation or in changing the highly unfavorable stereotypes to a congenial picture of the outgroup. Of course, the threat of a common enemy is usually conducive to burying the hatchet for the time being, but this measure, which had been effective in 1949, was discarded because of its temporary nature and because it simply widened the sphere of group conflict.

THE OUTGROUP AND ATTITUDE CHANGE. The experimental procedure that proved to be effective in changing attitudes and behavior toward the outgroup was the same in conception as that which had resulted in the individuals banding together in group organizations in the first place: viz., the introduction of problem situations and goals which individuals could not ignore but whose solution and attainment required that all of them pull together. When the problem situation involves two or more groups, the goals conducive to opening interchange between their respective members and laying the ground for mutual efforts could only be those with *urgency* for members of all the groups involved, but which cannot be attained by the resources and efforts of the groups separately. The coordination of all efforts in the same direction must be required to reach the goal, which may be avoiding a common disaster or may be ends mutually beneficial and satisfying to all. Such goals are *superordinate* to each of the groups in question. Through the introduction of, not one, but a *series* of superordinate goals, social distance between the groups in the experiment was reduced and stereotypes changed from largely unfavorable to generally favorable pictures of the outgroup. Figure 5.5 shows the combined ratings of the outgroup on several traits made by members of the respective groups first at the height of intergroup conflict, and later, following the series of superordinate goals.

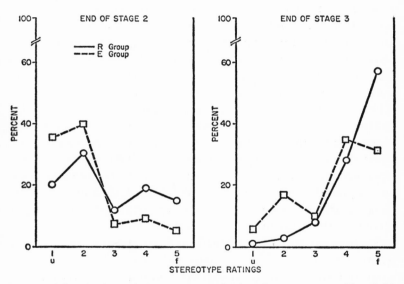

FIGURE 5.5.   Rating of the outgroup during intergroup conflict (left) and reduction of conflict (right). (From Sherif *et. al.* [1954.])

The process of change involved shifts in conforming behavior and changes in what constituted nonconformity. The friendly interchange and mutual cooperation between members of the different groups which characterized their relationships following the series of superordinate goals were viewed by members of each group as conforming to the developing group trend. They were not considered deviation, as they certainly would have been during the earlier period of intergroup hostility when a friendly gesture would have been regarded as "indecent."

Conformity-Deviation and Social Change in the Larger Setting

Conformity and deviation have been discussed in this paper in terms of normative process in small groups spontaneously organized by individuals with motives and problems seen as common, whether these motives relate to common conditions of the natural settings or to experimentally created problem situations. In such groups, whatever the organizational form and the character of the norms may be, they are not handed down by an outside authority. They are outcomes of the interaction process among the individual members, of course, as influenced by their previous group memberships and the setting in which they function. Each individual attains a position in the group through his relative contribution and efforts, and his position is not fixed once and for all. Each had some hand in shaping the norms of the group and can have a hand in changing them through further interaction.

Such is not the case in traditional groups and formally organized groups in the larger cultural setting. We cannot adequately touch upon the questions raised at the beginning of this paper without at least mentioning conformity and deviation as they occur in such organizational frameworks

LARGER SETTINGS. Many organizations in the larger setting are handed down through the generations and some are deliberately organized with blueprints, rules, and regulations put down on paper by personages or governing bodies in power. As a result many individual members have had nothing to do with shaping the organizational patterns and normative system. Not infrequently, the norms and organizational forms, which might have been appropriate under conditions at the time of their appearance, prevail now more through the heavy hand of tradition or through active efforts of those interested in their perpetuation.

The larger setting is further confounded by multiple groups in which individuals may have overlapping memberships, and by sizable power differentials between various groups in the scheme of things. In the highly differentiated modern scene, the individual may be faced with contradictory, even conflicting modes of compliance from his multiple groups. He may also experience in a personal way the power differential between his own groups and others in the setting.

Problems suggested by formal organizations and multiple groups have been investigated especially by sociologists— Durkheim, the Lynds, Merton, and Williams, to mention only a few. Here I can only cite a few of the psychological questions these topics impose upon us without marshalling factual evidence.

We may note, first of all, that when normative systems are upheld by the heavy hand of tradition and coercion, with little voluntary acceptance by the bulk of the individuals involved, informal groups usually arise within the formal outfit, as has been observed in industrial and military organizations. In such cases, the individual's compliance with inner acceptance is to norms of the informal groups to which he actively contributes. It may be suggested as a hunch to be tested that the greater the appeal of informal groups within formal organizations, the greater the secrecy observed in maintaining the existence of informal groups, the greater is the likelihood that the norms and rules of the formal organization have lost their effectiveness in regulating the behavior of the individuals involved.

The formal organization is one of the settings, so prevalent in modern differentiated societies, in which an individual's membership group (in this case, the formal organization) may not be his reference group, that is the group to which he relates himself psychologically or aspires to belong. Other common instances of discrepancies between the individual's membership groups and his reference groups owe their existence to the anchoring effects of the more powerful groups for individuals situated at lower levels in a setting which sanctions upward mobility.

CONFLICT AND THE INDIVIDUAL IN THE GROUP. The individual living his existence in membership groups with set modes of conformity while simultaneously relating himself psychologically to other groups or aspiring to belong to other groups is bound to experience frustration and personal conflict, at least at times. Many a man, dissatisfied and frustrated in his association with a given group, in which whatever compliance he observes is through coercion or fear of coercion, strives to break away from it and its norms. However, the efforts toward the break are not the end point in this picture. Usually the break, when it is made, is from one constellation of human relationships toward another. Thus, resistance and tendencies to deviation from the norms of one group are supplanted by active searching for new anchorages which the individual can accept as his own.

Perhaps this picture may have some relevance for issues of change. It suggests that active nonconformity to the norms of a membership group which require coercion for their observance, which arouse frustration in man and conflict between men rather than understanding and cooperation, is but one part of the picture. The completed picture is not a state of normlessness, but a search for normative bases which are not conflicting, not frustrating, not self-degrading to the individual.

The elevation of nonconformity alone to the level of a slogan has its roots in an untenable dichotomy between individual and group, in a preconceived inevitability of clash between the two. Such a stand cannot account for changes in human relationships or their normative bases.

If normlessness is not the end result of social change, then the human sciences face a more vital and difficult task than merely demonstrating the blinding and degrading effects of certain norms. The task requires some valid criteria for singling out prevailing norms which produce these effects and for deliberate choice of values and organizational forms conducive to behavior which is enriching and "self-actualizing" for individuals in their social relationships.

Summary and Conclusions

In all phases of his daily living—social, political, economic, religious—man is confronted today with pressures and exhortations to regulate his behavior within advocated molds and directions.

Concerned with the plight of those of their fellow men who have fallen prey in blind conformity to such pressures and exhortations, psychologists and social scientists have advanced various antidotes. One attempt in this direction is the cult which almost elevates nonconformity in its own right to a pedestal of virtue. Such attempts are laudable from the point of view of intent. But their realistic adequacy as effective measures is a different matter.

Even the most ardent proponent of nonconformity would not praise stealing simply because it is a nonconforming deed. Indeed, conformity is condemned because of concern over widespread degradation of moral and artistic values, of repressive restrictions on human expression and the rights of man, of arbitrary limitations to human dignity and potentialities. In short, the plea for nonconformity is made in the name of values or norms which were themselves formulated through a long and arduous stretch of human history. But as long as the analysis and the plea center on conformity or nonconformity in the abstract, there is no adequate basis for evaluating conforming or nonconforming behavior. And the exhortation to individual man to assert his independence of a mountain of social pressures may not be an adequate way to move the mountain.

An item of behavior, whether in social, political, religious, or economic spheres, cannot be characterized by itself as either conforming or deviating. It is always conformity or deviation relative to some premise, canon, standard, or value —in short, to some norm. Therefore, the primary question to be raised becomes: "Conformity or nonconformity in relation to what practice, what value, what moral standard, or what norm?"

Social values, moral standards, or norms are products of interaction among human beings over a period of time in matters of consequence to their mutual and individual concerns. Thus, issues of conformity and nonconformity which make the problem so urgent for study are not one-episode affairs involving momentary, transitory social influence on inconsequential matters. For these reasons, the traditional laboratory setting is far from adequate for studying significant problems of conformity and deviation.

On the whole, the traditional laboratory experiment takes the individual from a context of relationships with other people involving matters of mutual importance to expose him briefly to a momentary situation arranged by the experimenter. There is sufficient evidence to conclude that the experimenter's success in demonstrating susceptibility to conform in the laboratory is inversely related to the degree of structure, the number and clarity of alternatives available in the stimulus situation the experimenter has arranged for the subjects. Thus in a highly unstructured situation with various alternatives, the subject may conform almost invariably to definitions introduced by the experimenter. To conclude, therefore, that he is basically a conformist would be quite in error. Likewise, demonstration of righteous protests by individuals exposed to easily discriminable stimuli and a fantastically false consensus by others is scarcely evidence for man's basic independence.

The attribution of either blind subservience to the group or independence to the basic nature of man rests on an untenable dichotomy between individual and group. An adequate approach must begin with a clear statement of the place of norm-regulated behavior in psychological functioning. Even a single individual faced with a perceptual situation for which he has little in the way of established guideposts for evaluation, comes *in time* to a stabilized mode of behavior, as experiments have shown. At the basis of this tendency toward stabilization lies man's capacity to regulate his behavior through conceptual categories.

Normative regulation of behavior is also conceptual regulation, and without it, human morality of any kind would be inconceivable. It is precisely the normative regulation of behavior that permits human action to transcend demands of the immediate social surroundings, as well as to conform to them, to delay momentary impulses, and to resist the promptings of transitory emotional states. Normative regulation, properly conceived, is not alien to man's nature, but one of its distinctive features. In specific situations, the process may lead either to conformity or nonconformity.

Those canons, values, or norms relative to which conformity or nonconformity become important problems are integral aspects of man's relations with other men. These relations involve lasting expectations, reciprocities, and responsibilities, and their patterns constitute the individual's group relations. Thus the realistic, the significant setting for study and analysis of conforming behavior is the setting of human groups, large and small.

Some kind of norm system is one of the essential features of any human group, be it a club or church, a sect or professional group, or even a group whose major tenets involve nonconformity to prevailing societal norms.

When man enters into repeated interaction with others, directed toward similar concerns and goals, he takes part in a process of norm formation and stabilization. Once a normative system is stabilized, the individual member who took part in its creation regulates his behavior within the bounds it defines as acceptable, even without external pressures and sanctions. Both our research and considerable empirical findings demonstrate that the bounds defined by group norms are perceived by the single member as his own *latitude of acceptable behavior*. Behavior outside of this range is evaluated as objectionable. Henceforth, social control is achieved in part through the autonomous regulation of behavior by individual members. And when it relies exclusively on external pressure and coercion, changes in the normative structure may be anticipated.

Therefore, the question of concern to those who are disturbed with the plight of men caught in pressures toward certain molds of conformity should not be evaluation of conformity or nonconformity in the abstract. The first question must be conformity to what norm? Answers to this question entail not only the external referent of the behavior, but the context of group relationships in which it occurs and the voluntary or coercive nature of its regulation. Then analysis of the appropriateness or inappropriateness of the norm in question for the situation and in terms of other criteria may begin with an adequate basis. If on this basis, norms are found inappropriate, a related task becomes discovering the processes leading to perpetuation of dysfunctional norms, including notably, interested parties engaged in active efforts to that end.

A closely related task is assessing the demands placed upon the individual by conflicting norms—for example, norms of altruism preached on Sunday and norms for the hard facts of business and professional practice. The existence of mutually conflicting values or norms characteristic of highly differentiated Western societies today, as various social scientists have pointed out, is responsible in no small part for psychological conflict with attendant wear and tear and restlessness so widely reflected in contemporary novels and social science literature.

If, as it would seem, the interdependencies of human development and human groups are becoming increasingly closer and wider in scope, then the analysis demands a flood of light upon the consequences of maintaining obsolete, constrictive norms perpetuated through ethnocentrisms and activities of particularly interested groups. The appropriate changes in norms are, of course, part of the problem of social change. If the social scientist or psychologist backs away from this problem, he is backing away from the course of intellectual history. For good or evil, human relationships and their norms have changed and they will change. The challenge of understanding the process and the directions it takes must be met if we are seriously concerned with man's creative development and larger self-fulfillment. The two are not independent.

REFERENCES

Asch, S. E.   Effects of group pressures upon the modification and distortion of judgments. In G. E. Swanson, T. M. Newcomb, and E. L. Hartley (Eds.), *Readings in social psychology.* (2nd ed.) New York: Holt, 1952.

Coffin, T. E.   Some conditions of suggestion and suggestibility: A study of certain attitudinal and situational factors influencing the process of suggestion. *Psychol. Monogr.,* 1941, No. 241.

Cohen, Edwin   Stimulus conditions as factors in social change. *Sociometry,* 1957, **20**, 135–144.

Faris, R. E. L.   Development of the small group research movement. In M. Sherif and M. O. Wilson (Eds.), *Group relations at the crossroads.* New York: Harper, 1953.

Freedman, R., Hawley, A. H., Landecker, W. S., & Miner, H. M. *Principles of sociology.* New York: Holt, 1952.

Graham, C. H. Behavior and the psychophysical methods: An analysis of some recent experiments. *Psychol. Rev.,* 1952, **59,** 62–70.

Helson, H. Adaptation level theory. In S. Koch (Ed.), *Status and development of psychology.* Vol. 2. New York: McGraw-Hill, 1959.

Homans, G. C. *The human group.* New York: Harcourt, Brace, 1950.

Hood, W. R., & Sherif, M. Appraisal of personality-oriented approaches to prejudice. *Sociol. soc. Res.,* 1955, **40,** 79–85.

Hood, W. R., & Sherif, M. Verbal report and judgment of an unstructured stimulus situation. Paper read at Southwestern Psychological Assn., Little Rock, April, 1957.

Hovland, C. I., Harvey, O. J., & Sherif, M. Assimilation and contrast effects in reactions to communication and attitude change. *J. abnorm. soc. Psychol.,* 1957, **55,** 244–252.

Jackson, Jay M. Structural characteristics of norms. In G. E. Jensen (Ed.), *Dynamics of instructional groups.* Chicago: Univer. of Chicago Press, 1960. (Mimeographed)

Johnson, D. M. *The psychology of thought and judgment.* New York: Harper, 1955.

Luchins, A. S. On agreement with another's judgment. *J. abnorm. soc. Psychol.,* 1944, **39,** 97–111.

McGarvey, H. R. Anchoring effects in the absolute judgment of verbal materials. *Arch. Psychol.,* 1943, No. 281.

Mausner, B. Studies in social interaction. III. Effect of variation of a partner's prestige on the interaction of observer pairs. *J. appl. Psychol.,* 1953, **37,** 391–394.

Mausner, B. The effect of prior reinforcement on the interaction of observer pairs. *J. abnorm. soc. Psychol.,* 1954, **49,** 65–68.

Sherif, M. A study of some social factors in perception. *Arch. Psychol.,* 1935, No. 187.

Sherif, M. *The psychology of social norms.* New York: Harper, 1936.

Sherif, M. *An outline of social psychology.* New York: Harper, 1948.

Sherif, M. Operational report to the Hogg Foundation for Mental Health, The University of Texas. Description of research work on natural groups (1958–1959). (Mimeographed)

Sherif, M., & Cantril, H. *The psychology of ego-involvements.* New York: Wiley, 1947.

Sherif, M., & Harvey, O. J. A study of ego functioning: Elimination of stable anchorages in individual and group situations. *Sociometry,* 1952, 15, 272–305.

Sherif, M., Harvey, O. J., White, B. J., Hood, W. R., & Sherif, C. W. *Study of positive and negative intergroup attitudes between experimentally produced groups: Robbers Cave study.* Univer. of Oklahoma, 1954. (Multilithed)

Sherif, M., & Sherif, C. W. *Groups in harmony and tension.* New York: Harper, 1953.

Sherif, M., & Sherif, C. W. *An outline of social psychology.* (rev. ed.) New York: Harper, 1956.

Sherif, M., & Sherif, C. W. Self-radius and goals of group members and their age-mates in differentiated sociocultural settings. Report to Institute of Group Relations, Univer. of Oklahoma, 1960. (Mimeographed)

Stevens, S. S. On the psychophysical law. *Psychol. Rev.,* 1957, 64, 153–181.

Thrasher, J. D. Interpersonal relations and gradations of stimulus structure as factors in judgmental variation: an experimental approach. *Sociometry,* 1954, 17, 228–241.

Tresselt, M. E., & Volkmann, J. The production of uniform opinion by non-social stimulation. *J. abnorm. soc. Psychol.,* 1942, 37, 234–243.

Volkmann, J. Scales of judgment and their implications for social psychology. In J. H. Rohrer and M. Sherif (Eds.), *Social psychology at the crossroads.* New York: Harper, 1951.

Walter, N. A study of the effects of conflicting suggestions upon judgments in the autokinetic situation. *Sociometry,* 1955, 18, 138–146.

Whittaker, J. O. Effects of experimentally introduced anchorages upon judgments in the autokinetic situation. Paper read at the International Congress of Psychology, Brussels, June, 1957; Ph.D. Thesis, Univer. of Oklahoma, 1958.

CHAPTER 6

Competition, Communication, and Conformity[1]

ROBERT R. BLAKE and JANE SRYGLEY MOUTON

The University of Texas

When an individual cherishes membership in a group, the directions characteristic of his personal behavior, whether constituting crass conformity or depicting devilish deviation, cannot possibly be accounted for either from his knowledge of the immediate task, the reactions to him by others, or appeal to psychodynamic aspects of personal adjustment. Under these circumstances the characteristics of individual action can be understood *only* against the background of *primary* group interests, in terms of the attainment of the goals of the group, and most important, in terms of outgroup pressures, either real or imagined. It is the arousal of conformity under intergroup conflict we want to tackle in the present report. Our thesis is that even *without* communication between members, personal behavior is meaningful only when considered in the light of valued membership interests. Then a person will conform to protect or to enhance his group; he will resist outsiders to reduce threat to his group, or he will launch an attack to weaken the position of an adversary relative to the strength of his own. Conformity takes

[1] Research reported in this study was supported in part by Grant M-2447 (c1), "Behavior of group representatives under pressure." National Institute of Mental Health. Department of Health, Education and Welfare: Bethesda, Maryland.

on entirely new implications when viewed in these terms, as the following studies show.

The investigations reported below are ones in which persons *value* their membership. Their group is under threat of defeat in a competitive situation, but it also has the prospect of achieving victory. When the dominant theme of action is to win, individual member reactions are remarkably uniform, constituting a high degree of conformity in the direction of protecting group interests through actions which move the group toward victory. The experimental situations are such that conformity is demonstrated even without communication between group members to develop a "party line." We show that it is not necessary to generate a discrepancy or an imbalance in perception in order to press a person toward conformity or to arouse him to maintain independence of judgment. Rather the "party line" already is present in the thoughts and feelings of each individual, without his being told what constitutes appropriate action or which way to go. The significant factors are the ingroup and the intergroup relationship aspects of the situation. The studies, each designed to investigate some aspect of conformity dynamics under conditions of intergroup competition, are only typical. Many more experiments of similar character, not reported in detail here, bring forth in bold relief the highly regular nature of the phenomena reported.

Creating Conflict among Competitors

THE GENERAL SETTING. All studies were undertaken in connection with human relations training laboratory programs (i.e., *Proceedings*, HRTL, 1959) with laboratory populations ranging between 24 and 50 people each.[2] Participants

[2] Appreciation is expressed to Muzafer Sherif of the University of Oklahoma who collaborated with us in designing some of our original investigations. The general design followed in conducting these experiments and results obtained parallel Sherif's earlier work with children's groups (Sherif & Sherif, 1953).

represent all ages from 25 to 65 and all ranks in the management hierarchy of organizations from shift foreman to department or division head to president.

To create optimal laboratory conditions participants move off the job for a two-week stay on a "cultural island." The program starts off, say, on a Sunday afternoon. An introduction points to the significance of experimenting with behavior in order to experience new and more effective ways of acting that may not have been tried before. The "kickoff" calls attention to the importance of understanding ideas and principles of behavior which can themselves serve as blueprints for more effective action in achieving productive collaboration among individuals within an organization. The two weeks are probably as busy and involving as any a person is likely to spend. But central to our present interest is the fact that each person becomes a member of an 8-to-12-man Development Group which meets in two-hour stretches once or twice a day for a total of 40 to 50 hours over the two-week period.

From the person's point of view, he is not an S in some massive experimental design. He is a participant in a vital, real life learning situation of high significance to his own personal growth and development. He is ready to investigate principles of behavior in the most rigorous scientific sense once he comes to see the richness of insight possible from critiquing the results of a range of experimental treatments. But to conform with stylistic specifications we will call him an S!

PARTICIPANTS IN THE STUDIES.   The experiments were conducted in 21 different laboratory training programs, representing 66 groups and totaling about 575 Ss. Any given laboratory was composed of from two to four groups. All of these training programs were conducted in basically the same manner, but after sufficient data collection on one problem, a twist was introduced for the next few programs in order to investigate another feature of intergroup competition. Thereafter, still other angles would be investigated. You might say that it is a "rolling" design with one problem investigated through four or five laboratory sessions, another through four or five more laboratory sessions, and still another through four or five more, and so on; but all were conducted within the broad specifications described below.

EVOLUTION, OPPOSITION, AND RESOLUTION OF DIFFERENCES BETWEEN GROUPS.   The general arrangements for creating "live" groups, for generating opposition among groups, and for resolution of these differences are described below. More specific details and a description of particular measurements taken are provided in connection with each investigation.

Composition and evolution of groups. Groups were matched according to education, occupation, and levels within their home organizations. The groups were assembled to study group decision making under autonomous conditions (Blake & Mouton, 1961). Groups devoted from 6 to 18 hours to ingroup activity over a period of two to four days up to the time when intergroup relations were inaugurated. Three to four groups were assembled and treated in this way in each session of a laboratory.

Creation of intergroup differences. After completion of the phase above, each group had three hours to develop its own approach to the solution of an assigned problem. The problems used in various laboratories involved such considerations as "ways to improve labor-management relations," "power use in the organization," "criteria for evaluating the effectiveness of an organization," or "useful procedures for resolution of intergroup disputes." Only one of the problems was used in any particular laboratory. Members recognized that their solutions would provide a measure of their effectiveness as a problem-solving group. It was understood that the solutions would be evaluated and winning and losing groups determined. Evaluations were done either through voting, through the interaction of members, by representatives elected to speak for their groups' points of view, or through neutral judges. As is true in most intergroup competitive situations, here too, members looked forward to their solution being selected over the others as best in a win-lose sense.

Election of representatives. In all situations representatives interacted to determine the outcome. They were elected by members rank ordering each other without the opportunity of discussion or of electioneering, according to the criterion, "Rank order the members of your group, including yourself for serving your group as its representative." The representative in some instances served only to clarify the position taken by their groups, while in others, actual determination of the winning, intermediate, and losing solutions was their responsibility. Only the *ranking* for representative took place at this stage; interactions between representatives occurred at a later stage.

Clarification of group positions. Solutions were then dittoed and exchanged between groups. Before intergroup interaction members judged the solutions in private, with approximately two hours devoted to discussing the merits of each. Members were urged to increase their understanding of the positions of the other groups by noting similarities and differences and points needing clarification or elaboration. Private evaluations were again made, followed by a public vote. No contacts among groups occurred during this phase or at any earlier time.

Interaction of representatives. The person from each group who had been elected as its representative explained and clarified his group's solution in response to questions raised by the representatives of other groups. The explanation and clarification phase lasted an additional one and a half to two hours. When group members reported that further interaction among representatives would not increase their understanding of the other group's statements the representatives ranked the solutions from "best to worst." When a clearcut decision could not be reached by representatives, *member* pairs from contending groups discussed and evaluated the solutions in some of the experiments, and in other experiments member pairs interacted *before* the public negotiations occurred between representatives. When these approaches also failed, as they routinely did, impartial judges rendered a verdict.

Post competition. Groups again met for further ingroup discussion and study of problem solving following the verdict. In some of the experiments after the intergroup competition was completed, a phase of intergroup collaboration followed an interim period of 15-25 hours of renewed ingroup activity.

Dynamics of Intergroup Conformity and Resistance

CHANGES IN COHESION. Cohesion generates quickly during the phase concerned with the evolution of groups. There is a lot of pride in membership. Then groups enter competition to determine which is the most effective in problem solving. Members sense their ability to perform and their status as an effective group is challenged when confronted with competition. The result? A strong motive to win, as is true for any group which is challenged.

Cohesion is a variable through which changes in personal adjustments to group organization may be seen under condition of competitive relations. Subjective evaluations of the "goodness" of one's own group can be taken as an approximate measure of the attractiveness of the group to each of its individual members and, therefore, they provide an index of group cohesion. Members indicate how good they think their groups to be at the end of each Development Group period. The question "How do you feel about your group?" is answered on a nine-point scale from "worst possible" to "best possible" group. The same scale also is answered at points along the way during the intergroup competition and afterwards as well.

Figure 6.1 shows the feelings of cohesion reported by 12 different Development Groups with each block showing the

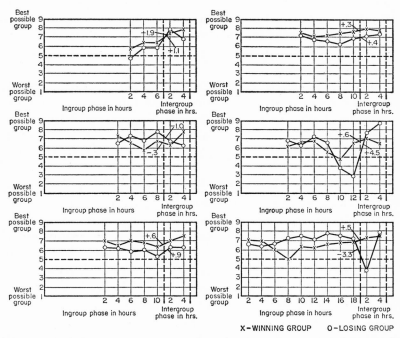

FIGURE 6.1. Development group trends in cohesion during ingroup and intergroup phases.

results for experiments where groups were competing with one another two at a time. From Figure 6.1 it is apparent that Development Group members rarely think themselves to be as low as "average" even before competition is introduced. All groups rate themselves to be something better than average. Here in itself is an interesting phenomenon of norm formation and conformity to it. What does it mean? It points to the natural "superiority complex" of groups. It looks as though a commonly shared norm, regardless of the group in which one holds membership is that, "poor though it may be my Development Group is at least a little above average!" In almost all of the group ratings in Figure 6.1, or 60 out of 64 times, cohesion is scored as above average even before intergroup competition begins.

What happens when intergroup competition begins? Interestingly enough, 9 of the 12 groups show an even further increase in the degree they think their groups to be "good." This increase also is accompanied by a decrease in the range on the cohesion scale. This conclusion is based on the results shown in Table 6.1 where it can be seen that prior to com-

TABLE 6.1. Range on the Cohesion Scale for Meetings Occurring Prior to and Immediately Following Introduction of Competition for Sixteen Different Groups

Time of Meeting	Range between Lowest and Highest Ratings on a Group-by-Group Basis		
	1 to 2	3 to 6	7 to 8
Before competition	2	10	4
During competition	6	10	0

petition in four of the 16 groups the range in the ratings by different members on the cohesion scale was between 7 and 8, in ten groups between 3 and 6, and in two groups between only 1 and 2. After the introduction of competition, group members became much more single-minded in appraising goodness of their groups; and none of them show as much variation as would be indicated by a range of 7 or 8 points. Ten used from 3 to 6 intervals and six reduced the range of differences to 1 or 2. The chi square of 6.0 is significant beyond the 5 percent level. Here is evidence that pressures from outside result in a significant increase in uniformity of judgments regarding attitudes towards one's own group.

Why is it that competition heightens positive attitudes toward one's own group through making members of a group uniformly feel it is even a better group than it was before it entered into competitive relations? Here is an item of the first significance. Under competition, members close ranks. They become more single-minded. Then they have a clearer goal—to win—which produces increased conformity effects. The unity of direction achieved is not deliberate. Members do not focus the issue for discussion on whether "our" group is better. They know! One's own group is compared with the competitor and uniformly members feel that their group is a good one, even better than it was prior to the introduction of competition. Here is evidence of concordance in feelings linked to membership affiliations under competitive conditions.

JUDGMENTAL TRENDS FOR OWN AND COMPETITORS' SOLUTIONS. The usual procedure in a 32-man laboratory with four groups of 8 members each to place pairs of groups in competition. Solutions are reproduced without identification and exchanged among all groups for comparison.

First it is possible to assess how groups consider each of the four solutions when they only know the identity of their own, since none of the groups are informed as to which set of two groups each will later be competing in pairs. Private ratings, without the possibility of communication influencing the specific judgments that are given, are made *prior* to discussion among members. Each person, however, holds membership in one group and the group goal always is to win. In this context each individual's adjustment is easy to forecast without being clairvoyant: the dominant direction is to further group interests and to avoid defeat. The prediction is that members will single out their own solution and give it a more favorable judgment than the other solutions contending for victory.

Typical results are in Figure 6.2. The bars with heavy stippling represent the average judgment by a group of its own solutions as evaluated on a 9-point scale with intervals ranging from 1, "totally inadequate," to 9, "totally adequate."

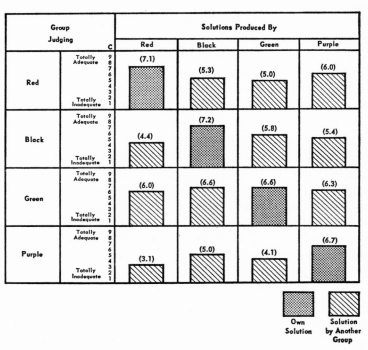

FIGURE 6.2. Judgmental tendencies for own and other's solutions when adversaries are not identified. The significant trend is for group members to place a higher assessment on their own group's product than on products by other groups developed under the same circumstances.

The bars with diagonal hash marks represent each group's evaluation of the reports submitted by the other three. To cancel order effects, the situation is arranged so that each solution is evaluated by another as often before judging one's own group's solution as afterward.

Results are clear, showing that group members prize their own solutions as higher in quality than solutions by the three unidentified, yet competing groups. This is seen in the heavy stippling bars running in diagonal from the upper left to the lower right side of the figure and having the values of 7.1, 7.2, 6.6, and 6.7. In only one of the 12 comparisons is another group's solution, in this case *Green,* accorded the same quality group members ascribe to their own solution. The same kind of results, with consistent elevation in judgment of one's own solution relative to that by another group, have been obtained in 20 replications employing the same basic design.

What do findings such as these indicate? They give clarity to the general idea that group members have a solid identification with their own group's position. The result is strong pressures toward conformity behavior which lead to a more favorable evaluation of own solution with rejection, or at least downgrading, of solutions by other groups. The striking aspect is that these similarities in group members' behavior appear without opportunity of communication among members to influence understanding or to pressure toward agreement.

ATTACK: "PING" THE ADVERSARY: DISREGARD THE NEUTRALS. After the judging phase described above, solutions are identified as to which two-group pairs will be in competition with one another for victory or defeat. An additional ingroup discussion period then occurs during which groups are encouraged to formulate questions for purposes of clarification, with the questions to be answered later on. The point-blank prediction is that group members will ask the greatest number of questions of the group which has the most ambiguous or complex solution. The reason is, "we need questions answered to improve our understanding." However, against the background of group interests, one's intuition is that this logical prediction will fall as many others do. Behavior among group members is highly predictable in another direction: to protect group interests. Competitive relationships among the groups define the strong and weak lines of communication between them. The significant consideration is not the quality of the solution itself, but whether it belongs to a group which is neutral with respect to the competition or to an adversary. The better prediction, then, is that questions will be asked of the adversary more than neutrals, without regard for quality.

To which groups, the adversary or the two neutrals, are the largest number of questions addressed? Figure 6.3 gives the answer: neutrals are *disregarded*—adversaries are challenged. Group 1, for example, asks 12 questions of its adversary, but only 6 of one neutral and 4 of the other. The comparable values for Group 2 are 12, 1, and 3; for Group 3, they are 9, 4, and 6. Group 4 shows the trend most dramatically. Values here are 13, 1, and 0!

Results such as these, which have been replicated in several other laboratories, have implications which are all too obvious. Groups challenge, ping, pick at, and push at other groups who are threatening to them, but they tend to ignore and disregard groups toward whom they feel neutral. Furthermore, trends are independent of the quality of solutions! Independence of personal judgments of quality is overruled by one's membership, and behavior is oriented toward protecting one's position and attacking the contenders.

An analogy of this trend is evident in the United Nations. Countries that feel competitive with one another tend to belittle each other's positions while ignoring proposals submitted by countries who stand as neutrals. A similar analogy can be drawn between the findings reported here and the typical reactions in a company representation election. The two strongest groups, from the standpoint of representing wage earners, are likely to launch attacks on one another, and at the same time to disregard the positions by other groups which don't have sufficient strength to be threatening. Individual adjustment, then, again is conditioned by membership considerations. The target of a group's attack, in other words, is the group which is considered its strongest

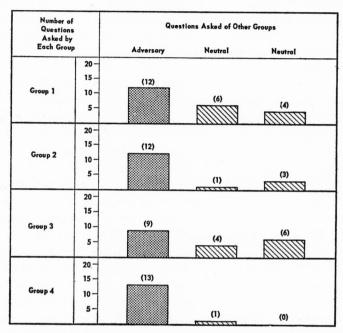

FIGURE 6.3.   Number of questions sent to adversaries and to neutrals during intergroup competition. When provided the opportunity to challenge the quality of another group's product, neutrals are more or less disregarded, but adversaries are targets of attack.

adversary, not the group which seems to have the most unclear solution or the most complex one.

JUDGMENTS OF SOLUTIONS ASSOCIATED WITH VESTED INTERESTS. A common observation is that problem solving between individuals is influenced by the vested interest of members. The idea is that when an individual has a vested interest, he is less able to think analytically and objectively than when his attitude toward the product being judged is neutral. Vested interest, in other words, is a significant factor in producing conformity behavior on the part of group members. Some of the conditions under which vested interests operate and the influence of vested interests on judgmental behavior are reported in the following study.

The definition of vested interests in the context of its use here is related to a member's identification with a group that has produced a product which is in competition, on a win-lose basis, with the product produced by other groups. Five different degrees of vested interest are involved. The control condition is where neither of the individuals engaged in judging group products has membership in the groups which produced those products, and when the outcome of their decision can in no way affect the standing of their own group. This is the base-line condition against which to evaluate the influence of conformity pressures acting in the interests of victory. *Partially vested interests* arise when one of the judges has membership in *one* of the groups that produced the two products, but the other judge does not have membership in either of the groups which produced the two products. *Competitively vested interests* occur in the situation where one of the judges belongs to the group which produced one product and the other belongs to the group which produced the other. *Supportive vested interests* originate when both judges have membership in the same group; that is, when two persons from the same group evaluate their own solution in comparison with that of a competitor.

The operation of vested interests can be evaluated against the first condition as an objective assessment of the relative merits of any two group products. The prediction is that heightened evaluation of one's own product occurs in subtle relationship with the composition of the vested interests represented in the paired situation.

The general design is as follows. Four groups designated A, B, C, and D, engage in intergroup competition. A is pitted against B, but not against C and D, and C is competing with D, but not A and B. Under these conditions, evaluations are made by every member of each group interacting in a paired relationship with a member from another. Pairs are instructed to evaluate the solutions of all four groups, judging solutions which have been pitted against one another. Judging by members from A and B of the solutions produced by C and D constitutes base-line or objective measurements. Judging by members from C and D of the solutions formulated by groups A and B also constitutes objective or base-line evaluations. For both of these conditions, there are no vested interests involved.

Judgments by pairs from A and B of solutions by A and B, and of pairs from C and D of solutions by C and D, constitute competitively vested situations; both pairs of members have a personal stake in the outcome.

If, by the objective judgments of pair members C and D, the solution by A is regarded as superior to that by B, then pairs composed of members A and C, or A and D, who are judging solutions A and B are *partially* vested with one member from the winning group, or the group with the best solution by an objective criterion, and one neutral. In addition, pairs composed of B and C, and B and D, judging solutions A and B are partially vested pairs with one member from the losing group. Parallel conditions of vestment also apply when judgments are made for solutions C and D.

Typical results for conditions differing in type of vested interest combinations are shown in Figures 6.4 and 6.5. Data in Figure 6.4 show that, in terms of the average ratings by the neutral pairs, the winning solution was judged to be significently better than the losing solution. When pair members *both* have a vested interest in the outcome, commitment to own-group solution results in predictable defense to one's own position. Solutions judged under competitively vested

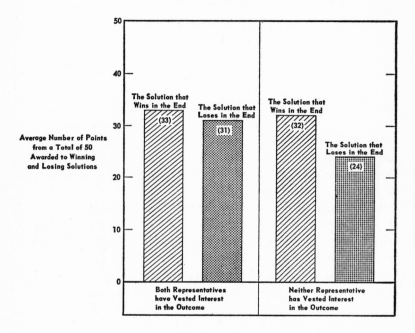

FIGURE 6.4. Evaluation of the same two group solutions by pairs when members are from different groups and each has a vested interest and when neither has a vested interest in the outcome of the judging. Representatives with vested interests are unable to agree on differences in the quality of two solutions; those without vested interests can agree on differences in the quality of the two solutions.

conditions are not evaluated as being significantly different from one another in adequacy. Individual group members have difficulty in disentangling objective attitudes toward the solution from attitudes which are saturated with membership emotions.

Data in Figure 6.5 tell what happens under partially vested

conditions. When one member has a vested interest in the solution that wins in the end, and the other doesn't have a vested interest because his group's solution is not being evaluated, as shown on the left side of Figure 6.5, judging presents no problem. They can get together and come to

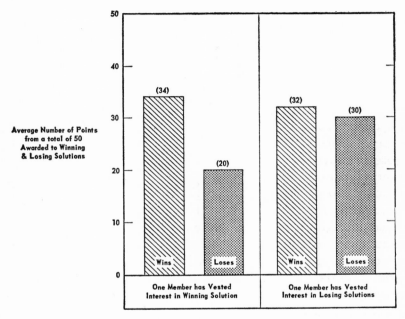

FIGURE 6.5. Reactions to group solutions by pairs of group members where one member has a vested interest in a winning solution and the other member is from a noncompetitive group.

quick agreement, correctly awarding the highest point total, 34, to the solution "owned" by the vested member and giving only 20 points to the other solution. The other section of Figure 6.5 shows the opposite side of the story. Here the vested member from the group with the objectively poorer solution refuses to give up. He is able to persuade the non-vested person to give many more points to his solution than it gets under the control or objective condition.

Cast in the context of conformity pressures, the vested individual, acting on group loyalty, distorts his judgment in the direction of elevating his own solution. The nonvested member, on the other hand, is subjected to and *yields to* conformity pressures in the immediate situation—he is free, so to speak, from his group—and, therefore, he is more likely to be pressured to agree when in contact with a commited person. Conformity and yielding are a function of where you stand, whether or not group-related personal interests are at stake!

OBJECTIVE KNOWLEDGE OF THE SOLUTION AT THE END OF COMPETITION. When competition is between groups, each of whom has its own fixed position, the identification of an individual with his group makes it difficult, if not impossible, for him to penetrate with insight and to clearly understand the position represented by the opposition. A result can be that intergroup problem solving is made more difficult because groups don't even *know* the differences in factual aspects that exist between them. Yet, when the victory in an intergroup competition is with respect to the relative quality of proposals submitted, it is important that each side have accurate and objective knowledge of the position taken by the other. Without accurate knowledge of the contents of each group's product, a verdict of victory or defeat is likely to produce invidious reactions and unrealistic attitudes. Given an adequate opportunity to study and to evaluate both the proposal of one's own group and that by a competing group, there is no *logical* reason why differences in accuracy of knowledge of one proposal over another should develop.

Yet distortion tendencies in judgments of both ingroup and outgroup products do occur as a function of ingroup membership. Without communication among members, the individual adjustment is in the direction of protecting group interests. The direction of uniformity, toward favoring one's own solution over others, already has been discussed. Intergroup competition provides an excellent opportunity to investigate distortions in intellectual understanding as they are related to membership.

At the point in the intergroup competition where members of both groups indicate full understanding of the other group's solution, as well as of their own, an intergroup knowledge test is introduced. No indication, prior to this time, has been given that participants are to be tested. The test is administered before a winner and a loser are determined.

An intergroup knowledge test, tailored to each of the competitions, is constructed. Items from written solutions are pretested by persons unfamiliar with the sequence of interaction to insure that they are fair and unambiguous. The general format described is used when two groups are in competition. Ten items are constructed, which are true for the solution of one group, but which are not contained in the other group's solution, and, which therefore, are false for the second group. Another ten items are found in both solutions. The remaining ten items are true for neither of the two solutions. Four answers are possible. Group members can indicate whether an item is true for *Own group, Other group, Both groups,* or *Neither group.*

Results from 20 groups studied under competitive conditions show that members routinely know more about their own solution than about the one submitted by a competing group. Even though the subjective experience is one of *certainty of insight* into the proposal of the competing group, in fact, objective knowledge is far less than perfect in comparison with knowledge of one's own solution. Figure 6.6 shows that in every case groups knew more about their own solution than about that produced by the competition. The sign test for the significance of differences is significant far beyond the .01 level of confidence. These findings can only mean one thing: intergroup problem solving is more difficult than it should be, if for no reason other than the fact that people have trouble understanding the position of a competitive group.

Common items are missed significantly more frequently than are those of any other type. The direction of the error,

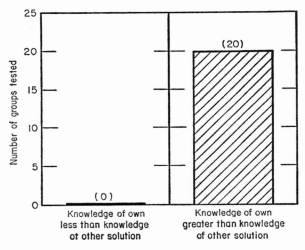

FIGURE 6.6. Knowledge of own group's solution versus knowledge of other group's solution. Even after intensive study of other group's solution, group members of the opposing group do not understand it as well as they understand their own.

as shown in Figure 6.7, is to attribute common items to one's own group's solution *only* and not to recognize that they are contained in the proposal of the competing group as well. It's as though group members fail to grasp what they share in common. To say that groups tend to act toward one another's solutions as though they had blinders on, is to make a generalization of great importance.

To state it differently: Here are two findings stemming

from trends toward uniformities in membership behavior associated with protection of group interests; both of which have unusual significance in determining barriers to the resolution of conflict between groups. They suggest that under competitive conditions members of one group perceive that they understand the other's proposal when in fact they do

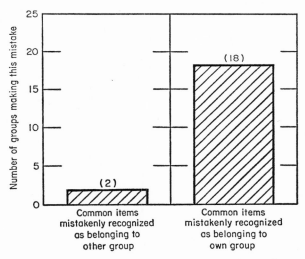

FIGURE 6.7.   Kinds of errors on common items from intergroup knowledge test. What two groups actually share in common is difficult for group members to recognize.

not. Inadequate understanding makes it all the more difficult for competing groups to view each other's proposals realistically. Areas they share in common are likely to go unrecognized and in fact be seen as being characteristic of one's own group only. Under conditions of competition, areas of true agreement go undiscovered. In combination with other results pointing to evaluative distortions that occur in the direction of protecting group interests when one group is in a competitive position to another, these data also underline the importance of viewing conformity within a group against the background of relationships between groups.

ELECTION OF SPOKESMEN: POSITIVE INGROUP ATTITUDES TOWARDS NONCONFORMITY. During the evaluation of intergroup competition, each group elects a spokesman to negotiate with the spokesman from the adversary group to determine which group is the winner and which the loser. The election is by a ranking system so that each person evaluates himself as well as all other group members from the standpoint of adequacy to serve the group as its spokesman. What is the person like into whose hands is placed his group's fate? Do members blindly elect one to speak for them, or is there perceptual selectivity in the direction of enhancing group interests?

In connection with another aspect of laboratory training, members of each group make judgments about the personal behavior of every other member. In this activity all group members give quantitative personal feedback to one another regarding how each person's behavior has been experienced by all the others according to the 24 items shown in Table 6.2. The ratings are in private, and anonymity of the raters is insured. No relationship is seen among participants between these ratings of personal behavior and the election of representatives.

Evaluations are on a 9-point scale from never, 1; hardly at all, 2; seldom, 3; a few times, 4; sometimes, 5; fairly often, 6; often, 7; almost always, 8; to always, 9. Individual scores are averaged to assign each person a rating for every item.

For five of the 11 groups, personal behavior ratings were given prior to the training sequence concerned with intergroup relations and for the others following it. Combined data are reported here since the timing of the personal evaluations reveals no significant differences in connection with assessing the perceived characteristics of represenattives.

Now it is possible to contrast the personal characteristics of those who receive a higher number of spokesman choices with those who receive a low number of nominations. The rank orderings for representatives within each group have been divided into quartiles with data from all groups combined so that each quartile consists of 22 Ss.

The averages in each quartile by personal characteristic items are presented in Table 6.2. The threefold categorization of items is on *a priori* grounds. Results can be evaluated from two points of view. One is the regularity of changes from the highest to the lowest quartiles. Progressive increases or decreases from the first to the fourth quartiles provide an indication of the stability of the relationships obtained. In addition, t's have been computed between the first and fourth quartiles to indicate the significance of differences between extremes. It is important to note that all items for which t is significant are also characterized by progressive increments or decrements from the first to the fourth quartiles.

The results are clear in showing that members who are most preferred by their peers to serve as representatives are distinguished from those who are not chosen, in terms of greater intellectual competence and higher procedural skills. They do not support the notion that highly preferred representatives possess greater social tactfulness than group members who are not chosen to serve as representatives.

Seven of the nine items evaluating an individual's procedural skills show significant differences between those most and those least preferred as representative. Examination of items shows that five are concerned with skill in aiding a group to function effectively at the task level, such as taking the lead in selecting topics, helping to get to the meat of issues, helping the group to stay on target, summarizing when needed, and encouraging a high level of productivity. The remaining two significant items are concerned with giving constructive evaluations and providing objective feedback.

TABLE 6.2. Perceived Characteristics of Individuals in Four Quartiles from Most (1st) to Least (4th) Preferred as Representatives

Type		1st	2nd	3rd	4th	t
			Mean Ratings by Quartiles			
Procedural Skill	Takes the lead in selecting topics	6.8	6.2	5.6	3.8	6.66
	Offers constructive evaluation as needed	7.1	6.8	5.7	4.8	5.34
	Helps get to the meat of issues	7.1	6.8	6.2	5.1	5.26
	Encourages group to high-level productivity	6.8	6.4	5.6	4.5	4.69
	Provides helpful objective feedback to members	6.7	6.6	6.0	5.0	4.05
	Provides good summaries when needed	6.7	6.2	5.2	4.0	3.86
	Helps group stay on target	6.8	6.5	5.9	5.2	3.41
	He likes to wander	2.9	3.2	3.5	3.3	1.42
	Blocks the group	2.2	2.4	2.5	2.4	.80
Intellectual Competence	Offers original ideas	7.1	6.7	5.9	4.7	6.85
	Helps members express their ideas	6.6	6.2	5.4	4.4	5.41
	Expresses himself clearly and concisely	7.2	7.0	6.4	5.9	3.82
	Sticks to his point arbitrarily	3.3	3.5	3.5	3.1	.46
Social Tact	Dominates and imposes his will on the group	3.5	2.9	2.6	1.9	4.10
	Runs away when faced with problems	2.2	2.3	2.8	3.2	3.44
	Yields to group pressure—conforms	4.0	4.4	4.7	5.4	3.41
	Annoys others	4.5	4.3	4.0	3.0	2.03
	Levels with other members	7.4	7.4	7.1	6.7	1.32
	Effectively senses when to talk and listen	6.8	6.7	6.3	6.3	1.25
	Makes other feel at ease	7.0	7.1	6.8	6.7	.81
	Makes others feel at ease	2.6	2.5	2.6	2.3	.53
	Listens with understanding to what others say	7.4	7.4	7.2	7.3	.39
	He shows that he likes us	6.7	6.7	7.0	6.8	.26
	Contributes without cutting others off	6.6	6.4	6.4	6.6	0

Both deal with *process* aspects of interaction which help group members steer themselves effectively; that is, they involve skill in giving reactions regarding how a person feels or how others are affecting him.

Two items fail to distinguish between chosen and unchosen representatives. They are concerned with blocking the group and with wandering off the topic. Both are actions which interfere with the group effectiveness.

Three of the four items measuring intellectual elements show progressive reductions from the first to fourth quartiles with differences in each case being significant far beyond the 1 percent level. One item is concerned with offering original ideas, with the difference between the extremes being the most significant of any in the study. The other two deal with clarity in communication: one with aiding others in expressing their ideas and the second with effectively presenting one's own ideas. The item which is not significant is related to sticking to one's own point in an arbitrary manner. As is true for the nonsignificant items under procedural skill, this is also one which interferes with group action.

Only three of 11 items concerned with tactfulness significantly distinguish degrees of preference for representative beyond the 1 per cent level. The findings for even these three are counter to what would be expected if election as a group representative were thought of as a popularity contest. Though the absolute level is low for all quartiles, individuals highly chosen as representatives dominate and impose personal will on the group more than people who are less frequently chosen. The other two significant items can be understood in the same manner. *Persons highly chosen as representatives are seen to resist group pressures toward conformity and to avoid running away when faced with problems.* This means that group members uniformly select as representatives those whom they perceive *not to be conforming* on an ingroup basis, but rather who are *independent and resistant.*

Items failing to discriminate also are counter to expectation, for they are kinds of behavior which frequently are thought of as increasing an individual's personal attractiveness and, therefore, improving his prospects of being chosen. Persons who are highly chosen are no different from those who are least preferred in terms of contributing without cutting others off, listening with understanding, making people feel at ease, sensing when to talk and when to listen, expressing liking for other members, leveling with them, and fighting rather than working. Interestingly enough, the remaining item, the only one which approaches significance, is concerned with annoying others. The results show that highly chosen members are seen as *more* annoying than are those who are not preferred to serve as representatives.

The present study demonstrates that group members agree on the perceptual level concerning the characteristics of members whom they prefer to represent their group's interests. A logical second step now needs to be taken. The question to be answered is, "Do individuals who are preferred as representatives feel free to act in a nonconforming, independent manner relative to their ingroup, when they are under intergroup problem-solving conditions?"

NEGOTIATIONS BY REPRESENTATIVES: RESISTANCE OR CONVERSION? A high degree of conformity even without communication between group members can also be seen in the behavior of group representatives who meet to evaluate their respective groups' products. Here again highly predictable relationships exist between embracing membership and acting in the interests of the group. The members, selected to represent their group, who possess in the eyes of their peers the ability to maintain independence on an ingroup basis are caught by the forces in the situation and exhibit all the signs of conformity behavior.

Negotiations between representatives occur after ingroup comparison and judgment. The person most preferred by his group as its representative explains and clarifies his own solution in response to questions raised by the competing group. The role of the spokesman is critical at this point, for his group expects him to defend them from attack and to lead the offense against the other group. The experimental situation is such that these expectations are not communicated directly to the representative.

Then representatives meet to evaluate and judge the relative merits of contending solutions. Most frequently their interaction develops into a win-lose contest, with each representative maintaining his group's position while attempting to provoke the opposing representative to capitulate. The person who exerts influence on the opposing representative and in doing so obtains acceptance of his group's position may be accorded a "hero" reaction within his group for bringing it victory. On the other hand, the representative who relinquishes his group's position, thus giving victory to the opposition, is subject to being treated as disloyal or as traitorous by members of his own group (Blake & Mouton, 1960b).

Since representatives do not want to lose status, it is rare that a spokesman capitulates. Figure 6.8 shows that the adjustment by the representative to his opposite number is highly consistent (p .01). Only 2 of 33 representatives have capitulated, and they were booed, ostracized, and treated as traitors. The repetitiveness of the phenomenon across laboratories, therefore, tells how strong the motivation to win is for the person into whose hands is placed his group's fate. Spokesmen are committed people. They elect to conform to group expectations rather than to solve the assigned problem!

If relations between groups are on a win-lose basis, as often happens when preferred positions constitute public standards announced in advance, then quest for resolution by representatives is replete with obstacles. The core of the difficulty is in the fact that representatives are committed people. From the standpoint of their own group membership they are not

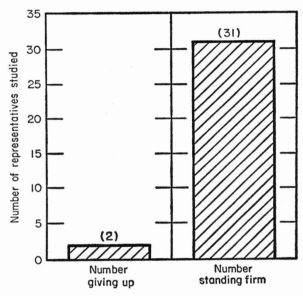

FIGURE 6.8   Loyalty of representatives to their groups during intergroup competition.

free to act in accord with fact or even to engage in compromise, if to do so would be interpreted as defeat. An interesting paradox occurs when these results are taken in conjuction with results from the preceding section describing the perceived personal characteristics of representatives. Group members do not intuitively select as representatives from among their membership persons whom they see as conforming, dependent, or lacking in initiative on an ingroup basis. Rather they elect persons who are individualistic, pro-cedurally skillful, and intellectually competent. Yet when called on to act in a problem-solving manner in the repre-sentative body, these individuals exhibit a high degree of conformity to an ingroup position. They also show great resistance to the outgroup. If the behavior of the representa-tive is viewed only in the narrow perspective of the nego-tiating situation, his actions most likely will be viewed as indicating staunch resistance against influence. Yet the simi-larity among representatives in clinging to their own group's viewpoint smacks strongly of the dynamics of conformity as the underlying theme if viewed from an ingroup perspective. Where there is conflict of interest, the situation is such that the ingroup conformity can overwhelm logic.

Conclusions

The studies described put conformity and deviation on a much stronger theoretical and practical footing than hitherto. *Conformity* is conditioned by events external to the small group as a self-contained unit. Conformity is demonstrated, even without apparent discrepancy among group members and without communication between them, where influence attempts towards unanimity might be made. The significant conditions are (1) persons value their memberships in the group, and (2) a threat is posed to the solidarity or competence of the entire group. Then members act in a highly regular way designed to defend and protect the group with clear in-dications of similarities in actions among members. Conform-ity has been demonstrated in several different forms: (1) in the elevated evaluations of one's own group and its group products, (2) in intellectual distortions regarding knowledge of own and competing groups' position, (3) in resistance in the negotiating situation by group members with vested in-terests, and (4) in adherence to ingroup position by elected representatives in the negotiating situation. Both of the latter conditions are ones of a high degree of independence or resistance to influence when viewed from the negotiation situation, but high conformity when placed in the perspective of own group membership. Yet the situation is more complicated. Representatives are perceived from an ingroup angle as independent!

These investigations compel the conclusion that the adjustment of different individuals constitutes a highly uniform trend, even when communication between members is absent. Under such circumstances there is no basis for an individual to experience a contradiction between his behavior and that of others who share his lot. Whenever the situation is one in which a person prizes his membership and his group is under the threat of defeat, individual adjustments are uniform and in the direction of protecting the group through actions which can contribute to the attainment of group's goals.

The directions taken in personal behavior must be regarded in terms of the major lines of group interest that an individual embraces by virtue of memberships. When the dominant theme of group action is to win, the impact on an individual's adjustment constitutes an example of conformity which can only be understood in terms of the competition aspects of the intergroup relationships involved.

We regard these data as providing a substantial empirical foundation undergirding Sherif's formulation of personality theory (Sherif & Cantril, 1947); for a wide range of conditions, individual expression and adjustment are *not* idiosyncratic or personally stylistic. Rather, it flows from an individual's position in the total economy of his social adjustment. Ego psychology must confront the Herculean task of reconstructing its basic premises, for studies such as these present unequivocal evidence that when an individual's behavior is seen as socially embedded, as anchored to membership interests, and as subject to external threat, the personal adjustment which occurs is predictable only in these terms.

References

Blake, Robert R., & Mouton, Jane S.   Heroes and traitors: Two patterns of representing groups in a competitive relation. *Int. J. Sociometry* (in press) 1961.

Blake, Robert R., & Mouton, Jane S.   *Training for decision-making in groups.* New York: Putnam & Sons, 1960.

Proceedings.   Bella Vista, Arkansas: The Univer. of Texas Human Relations Training Laboratory, 1959.

Sherif, M., & Cantril, M.   *The psychology of ego involvements.* New York: Wiley, 1947.

Sherif, M., & Sherif, Carolyn W.   *Groups in harmony and tension.* New York: Harper, 1953.

CHAPTER 7

Authority, Authoritarianism, and Conformity[1]

MILTON ROKEACH

Michigan State University

The task which I will set for myself in this chapter is two-fold. In the first part, I propose to analyze half a dozen or so assumptions underlying present-day formulations about the nature of authoritarianism and the closely related concept of the authoritarian personality. An attempt will be made to show that certain embarrassments, which deserve to be over-come, are posed by conventional conceptions. Some research findings relevant thereto will be discussed, and in the course of this discussion I will have occasion to propose some re-formulations. Such findings and reformulations are within the framework of a research program on the organization and modification of belief systems. In the second part of this paper, an attempt will be made to relate these reformulations regarding the nature of authoritarianism to several other conceptualizations and findings concerning the problem of conformity in every day life.

Authority and Authoritarianism

While the concepts of authoritarianism and the authoritarian personality have been, and continue to be, widely

[1] This is a modification and elaboration of a briefer paper originally presented in August, 1958, on a symposium entitled "Current Concepts of the Authoritarian Personality," sponsored jointly by the American Psychological Association and the American Catholic Psychological Association.

employed in contemporary thought and research,[2] thus far they have not been explicitly defined in a satisfactory conceptual way. In the most widely known work by Adorno, Frankel-Brunswik, Levinson, and Sanford (1950) on the authoritarian personality, the closest thing to a conceptual definition is a listing of various traits or personality characteristics, like authoritarian aggression and submission, conventionality, anti-intraception, rigidity, and projectivity which, on psychoanalytic grounds, are thought to characterize persons judged to be high on authoritarianism. But the concept itself, as far as I can tell, has not been explicitly defined in a formal way.

To my mind, there is sufficient empirical evidence now available from a variety of sources to support the hypotheses put forward by the authors of *The Authoritarian Personality* regarding at least the major personality characteristics differentiating those scoring high and low on the F scale. But I would like to raise for discussion and scrutiny a number of implicit assumptions widely held about the nature of authoritarianism which to one degree or another underlie or inhere in current conceptualizations, and which for the most part antidate the work by Adorno *et al.* These assumptions, I will argue, have profoundly influenced the direction taken by current theory and research, and are therefore worth examining in a critical way in the hope that they might lead to fresh insights and fresh directions in future research.

1. IN DEFENSE OF AUTHORITY. One assumption which is widespread is that authoritarianism is rooted in a reliance on authority while its opposite, antiauthoritarianism, is characterized by a rejection of authority and, in its place, a reliance on reason. Reasonable as this assumption may appear to be at first glance, there are grounds for assuming other-

[2] Christie and Cook (1958) cite over 200 publications through 1956 stemming from the work by Adorno *et al.* (1950).

wise. It is inconceivable that we could get to know as much as we do about the world we live in if we were not able to rely on authority and if we had only ourselves and our own powers of reason to rely on.

This idea, namely, the idea that all men *need* authority, may sound strange coming from a psychologist who, along with many others, has viewed with alarm the phenomenon of authoritarianism and the social psychological processes underlying it. But it is an idea which has been long accepted by philosophers of religion, philosophers of politics, and political scientists. Thus, Trueblood reminds us that it is a popular error to believe that "authority and reason are some-how rival ways of coming to the truth" (1942, p. 72). Charles Hendel writes: "This question of the apparent opposition of authority and freedom has long been the chief concern of political and social philosophy" (1958, p. 18). He elaborates this view at somewhat greater length as follows:

> We are further confused by an uncritical general philosophy unfavorable to authority in any form. . . . The free, responsible, self-governing individual is thought of as self-sufficient. . . . We fail to realize that man can enjoy the desired freedom and self-sufficiency only in a social order where there is an effective authority. But in popular philosophy there is no room for this truth.
>
> The mind is also closed to the need and value of authority in society by a long-prevalent optimistic notion of history. . . . The harshness as well as the crudity of primitive human existence is seen happily left behind, and authority is one of the antiquated relics of the past. . . . History is "the story of freedom" and the goal of it is a state of freedom without authority [Hendel, 1958 pp. 5-6].

Another contemporary political scientist, Carl J. Friedrich, expresses a similar view when he asks: "But are reasoning and authority so antithetical? Does authority have no basis in reason? The following analysis seeks to elucidate the proposition that authority and reason are closely linked, indeed that authority rests upon the ability to issue communications which are capable of reasoned elaboration" (1958, p. 29).

Similar views have recently been expressed by Hannah Arendt (1958) and also by Catlin who writes: "For the purposes of political science, authority is neither in itself good or bad. It carries no poison necessarily, whatever may be the warnings of psychologists and others . . ." (1958, p. 128).

Erich Fromm (1941) clearly sees the difference between authority and authoritarianism when he makes a distinction between rational authority and inhibiting authority. To compare the two he gives as examples the relation between teacher and student on the one hand, and slave and owner on the other. In the former, the aim of the relationship is to decrease the psychological distance between one and the other in order to make them more like each other. In the latter case, the aim is to increase psychological distance, one at the expense of the other.

If we had only our own reason to rely on and not authority, all of history would be forever beyond our ken; we would have no knowledge of current affairs in places we ourselves have not been; we would know nothing of advances in science and technology beyond those we have made or discovered for ourselves; and there would be no point in consulting the *Encyclopedia Britannica*.

Authority and authoritarianism. The widespread failure to make a distinction between authority and authoritarianism, which rests on the equally widespread insistence on the distinction between authority and reason, have led to a variety of ramifications, a few of which are worth mentioning briefly in passing. For example, it has led to the view that the therapist should not speak his mind to his patient, that teachers should not teach their students, and that leaders should not lead, because these all involve authoritarian relationships. Instead, it is suggested students will learn for themselves and from each other when they are ready for it, and so also with patients. And a really democratic group is a leaderless group.

There is really nothing so ugly about authority, only certain kinds of authority. And there need be no inherent contradiction between reliance on authority and reliance on reason, so long as we use independent reason to guide us in selecting the authorities we choose to influence us and so long as we use reason to tell us when to throw overboard one authority in favor of another. A person is said to be high in authoritarianism because he relies on authority while another does not. Rather, the difference lies in different notions about the *nature* of authority, different theories, if you will, about the way to employ authority as a cognitive liaison system to mediate between the person and the world he is trying to understand and adapt to.

Definition of authority. I will now define authority as any source whatsoever to which we look for information, or to which we turn to verify information already possessed about any aspect of the universe. We all look to authority in order to serve our cognitive needs to know, and to guide action designed to serve other needs. The student looks to his teacher and the concentration camp prisoner looks to his Nazi guard for information. In the former case, in order to satisfy curiosity and in the latter case in order to find out precisely what must be done and what must not be done in order to avoid being beaten or shot. Even a mathematician who has just proven a theorem by deductive logic must somewhere along the line submit the product of his thought to the scrutiny of another mathematician, if for no other reason than to make sure that he didn't make a mistake.

It is with considerations such as these in mind that the proposal has been advanced elsewhere in some detail (Rokeach, 1960) that authoritarianism and antiauthoritarianism be conceived in terms of opposing orientations in modes of reliance on authority, ranging from open orientations to authority at one extreme to closed orientations at the other.

Crucial to this analysis is what is meant by open and closed. By *open* I mean that the power of authority rests solely upon the perception of the source's cognitive correctness, accuracy, and consistency with other information, as obtained by other means—that is, from one's own cognitions, and from other information obtained from other sources. Authority which gives information in conflict with one's own cognitions will be judged unreliable and will be rejected, in order to be replaced by other authority judged to be more correct, accurate, or consistent. In *closed* authoritarian orientations to authority, however, the power of authority does not at all hinge upon cognitive correctness but solely on the ability of authority to mete out arbitrary rewards and punishments.

Content and prestige of communication sources. It is assumed that every communication received from an external authority source contains two kinds of information. It contains information of a substantive nature and it contains information about the authority source itself. Substantive information is typically obtained from the sheer content of the message. The prestige aspects of the source are obtained from the expressive and evaluative aspects of the message. And the *way* in which the communication is delivered, such as tone of voice, facial expression, the social conditions under which the message is delivered, and so on. The more open one's orientation toward authority, the more will the two kinds of information be clearly distinguished from each other and the more will each be evaluated and responded to on their respective merits. That is, the person has freedom to choose or not to choose to be influenced in a direction desired by the source, depending on his own assessment of both sets of information. However, the more closed one's orientation toward authority the more difficult it will be, by virtue of the authority's effective capability to mete out reward and punishment, to discriminate the two qualitatively different kinds of information, and consequently, to assess and act on them on their respective merits. What the external authority says is true about the world will become cognitively indiscriminable from what the external authority wants us to believe is true, and wants us to do about it. The person in such a closed state of mind will thus be forced to evaluate and to act in ways desired by the source rather than in terms of what Kohler (1938) has called "inner requiredness" and what Katz and Stotland (1959) have called "appropriateness."

From this basic distinction between the two extreme kinds of orientations to authority, it is possible to derive quite a number of other cognitive characteristics which are hypothesized to distinguish open from closed belief systems. For example, given a person incapable of distinguishing substantive information from information about the source, the parts within his belief system will be more segregated or isolated from each other, there will be less differentiation within and between various parts of the belief and disbelief system, and he will be characterized by a narrower time perspective. This is not the place to enter into a detailed discussion of why this is so. The interested reader is referred elsewhere (Rokeach, 1960) for fuller treatment of the topic and for a systematic discussion of the many cognitive variables which are conceived to differentiate open from closed belief systems or open and closed orientations toward authority.

2. IDEOLOGICAL CONTENT VS. IDEOLOGICAL STRUCTURE. All of the preceding leads me now to a second, closely related issue which has strongly influenced thinking and research on the nature of authoritarianism. Should we, in assessing the degree to which a person is authoritarian, that is, has a closed orientation toward authority, pay attention to the *content* or to the *structure* of his belief system? In the formulations of the California group, and in the construction of the F

Scale, it was ideological content rather than ideological structure which was emphasized. Consider, for example, the F Scale item: "People can be divided into two distinct classes: the weak and the strong." This item is compatible in its content with fascist ideology but not with communist ideology. I have already had occasion elsewhere (1956; 1960) to point out that the California research, by virtue of the fact that it was content-oriented, dealt only, or at least primarily, with rightist or fascistic forms of authoritarianism and not with all forms of authoritarianism. A general theory of authoritarianism has to be structure- rather than content-oriented.

How does one get at the structure of an ideology rather than at its content? Here I have found the concepts of such psychologists as Lewin (1951), Krech (1949) and, to a somewhat lesser extent, Tolman (1948) most helpful. The variables which they employ to describe the life space, the psychological field, and the cognitive map are precisely the kinds of variables which seem to get at structure rather than content. Where the content-oriented F Scale deals with such variables as conventionalism, authoritarian aggression and submission, superstition and a belief in the supernatural, the structure-oriented Dogmatism Scale deals with such variables as isolation, differentiation, time perspective, various formal aspects of the central-peripheral dimension of beliefs, and so on. In short, the items on the Dogmatism Scale are deliberately worded to avoid specific ideological content so that the structural attributes of authoritarianism being measured may apply equally well to all ideologies.

Already discussed elsewhere (Rokeach, 1956; Rokeach, 1960) so that the specifics need not be repeated here, are the individual items of the Dogmatism Scale, the structural attributes these items try to measure, and the extent to which the total scale has turned out to be successful as a measure of general authoritarianism. It will perhaps suffice here to say that even though the Dogmatism and F Scales are highly correlated, communists in England score lower than other political groups on the F Scale but higher than the same political groups on the Dogmatism Scale. Also, in contrast to the F Scale, which is significantly associated with political conservatism, the Dogmatism Scale is found to be relatively independent of liberalism-conservatism, that is, it is found with relatively equal frequency along all positions of the political spectrum.[3]

3. THE INGROUP-OUTGROUP DICHOTOMY. Psychologists and sociologists have long been accustomed to think in terms of ingroups and outgroups when addressing themselves to certain aspects of intergroup relations, social attitudes, and prejudice. A person is said to be a member of one or more ingroups, and whatever is left over are conceived to be the person's outgroups, without any further articulation of the latter concept. Similar distinctions are made between positive and negative authority, positive and negative reference groups, and between belief and disbelief. In line with such dichotomic conceptions authoritarianism has been assumed to imply an absolute acceptance, or overglorification, of the ingroup and at the same time an absolute rejection, or vilification, of the outgroup.

Continuum of outgroups. Our own conceptualizations and findings with regard to the organization of belief systems suggest that this way of thinking is inadequate to deal with certain observable facts and is therefore in need of reformulation. We find that arrayed against the ingroup is not a global, undifferentiated cluster of outgroups but rather a series of outgroups organized along a continuum of similarity to the ingroup. Furthermore, the extent to which one accepts or rejects various outgroups is, at least in part, a function of the

[3] In addition to the main references already cited, see also the factorial studies by Rokeach and Fruchter (1956) and Fruchter, Rokeach, and Novak (1958).

degree of belief congruence of outgroup to ingroup. In other words, represented within the cognitive structure of all persons is a belief system and series of disbelief subsystems arranged along a gradient of congruence to the belief system. Consider, for example, the cognitive organization we typically find for a group of Catholic college students and also, of Catholic priests. When they are asked to rank various Christian denominations in terms of similarity (belief congruence), we get the following order: Catholic, then Episcopalian, then Lutheran, then Presbyterian, then Methodist, and last, Baptist. If a group of Baptists are asked to rank these same religions for similarity, we get exactly the reverse order: Baptist, Methodist, Presbyterian, Lutheran, Episcopalian, and Catholic. The similarity continuum for Episcopalians is the same as that for Catholics, with the exception, of course, that Episcopalians judge Catholics as most similar to themselves. The similarity continua for the major religious groupings within Christianity are basically the same, with each group merely judging the other groups from the standpoint of its own position along the similarity continuum. The similarity data obtained from college students of various denominations are generally in good agreement with those obtained for clergymen of the same denomination.

The fact that we have been able to obtain stable similarity continua of this sort suggests not only that the usual dichotomous distinctions between positive and negative authority, ingroup and outgroup, positive and negative reference groups are too crude. It also suggests that the magnitude of acceptance and rejection of various outgroups will vary as some function of belief-disbelief congruence. This, indeed, turns out to be the case. We find, in general, that the more dissimilar an outgroup or a disbelief system the more it is rejected. Adherents of the six major Christian faiths all judge Jews, Mohammedans, and atheists as least similar, in that order; and they are rejected most, in the same order. And, on the average, the adherents of the six major Christian faiths reject increasingly more the Christian denominations judged to be less and less similar to themselves.

It might be mentioned here that we have found some other interesting evidence suggesting that congruence of belief systems is an important determinant of every-day behavior. For example, on the basis of these similarity continua, knowing a person's religious faith, we can predict the probability with which he will convert to or defect from one church to another. Our data show, for example, that if a Catholic leaves the Catholic Church to join another, the chances are greatest, other things being equal, that he will join the Episcopalian Church and that the chances become less and less that he will join the Lutheran Church, the Presbyterian Church, the Methodist, and Baptist Churches. Conversely, if a Baptist leaves his church to join another, the chances are greatest that he will join the Methodist Church and least (staying within the Christian fold) the Catholic Church. Similar findings are obtained for movements in and out of the Episcopalian, Lutheran, Presbyterian, and Methodist Churches. Furthermore, we get similar results which are in line with our notions about the continuous organization of outgroups or disbelief systems with respect to differential rates of enrollment in a particular denominational college by persons of various denominations. Each denominational college, it turns out, generally recruits students who are most frequently of its own denomination, next most frequently of the denomination most similar to it, and so on. Likewise with interfaith marriages. What is the probability of an interfaith marriage between a Methodist and an Episcopalian? between an Episcopalian and a Presbyterian? Again, the similarity continua I have referred to help to provide us with at least part of the answer. The probability of interfaith marriage between a Catholic and a Baptist is relatively slim as compared to that between a Catholic and an Episcopalian. And so with the probability of premarital and marital conflict in interfaith marriages. In general, we find that such conflict increases as the degree of belief system congruence decreases.

Differential reaction to belief systems. All these results would seem to suggest that in the course of socialization we somehow learn that there exist different outgroups having differing degrees of belief similarity to our ingroups and we somehow learn to react differentially to ideas, persons, and authorities associated with differing belief systems. This generalization seems to hold for all persons, regardless of individual differences in authoritarianism. But there is, nevertheless, an important difference between high and low authoritarians, as measured by the structure-oriented Dogmatism Scale. High authoritarians generally reject each and every outgroup situated along the similarity continuum at a higher level than do low authoritarians. Thus, we do indeed find that authoritarians reject outgroups *relatively* more than do antiauthoritarians; but all subjects, authoritarian and antiauthoritarian alike, reject outgroups increasingly more as they become increasingly dissimilar. All these findings strongly suggest that in thinking about authoritarianism we should keep in mind the fact that identification with authority is far from the dichotomous, black-white thing we have typically made it out to be. Rather, authoritarian and nonauthoritarian alike, seem to identify with a pantheon of authorities, positive at one extreme and with various gradations of negative as we move along the continuum. And we have differential attitudes and feelings toward positive and negative authorities occupying different positions in the pantheon.

With these points in mind, let me now refer to a study published in 1957 by Burwen and Campbell. They found that there is no evidence for a single attitude of favorableness or unfavorableness toward different kinds of authority. This finding is surprising only if we conceive of identification with authority as a dichotomous, all-or-none affair. But it is not surprising if we conceive of identification with authority in terms of positive authority and a gradation of negatve authorities.

4. AUTHORITARIANISM AS A DETERMINANT OF SOCIAL DISCRIMINATION. I come now to a fourth assumption about the nature of authoritarianism which needs to be re-examined. It is widely assumed that individual differences in prejudice or social discrimination are in large part a function of individual differences in authoritarianism. There are various kinds of evidence available from a variety of sources which do indeed seem to support this view. Recall, for example, the rather sizable correlations found in the California research between authoritarianism and ethnocentrism. However, the research I have just referred to on the relation between similarity and rejection clearly suggests that this is not the whole story. We actually find two variables which are significantly associated with the degree of rejection of a particular outgroup. One is authoritarianism. Groups scoring above the mean on the Dogmatism Scale almost always show higher mean rejection scores of various religious outgroups. The second variable, however, is sheer cognitive similarity or congruence between belief and disbelief systems. Our data clearly show that even if the individual differences in authoritarianism were altogether eliminated from the picture there would still be considerable discrimination against various outgroups on the basis of cognitive similarity alone. In fact, we find that far more of the variance is attributable to cognitive similarity than to authoritarianism as a source of attitudinal rejection and as a basis for differential preference and conflict in every day life.

5. BELIEF CONGRUENCE VS. ETHNIC OR RACE CONGRUENCE AS THE BASIS OF INTOLERANCE. Another assumption widely held is that authoritarianism involves a greater tendency to cog-

nitively categorize the world of people in terms of ethnic and racial groupings and to discriminate on this basis. A major weakness in this conception is that it is difficult to deal with certain manifestations of authoritarianism which are not at all associated with ethnic or racial discrimination, or which are indeed associated with its opposite—extreme tolerance toward ethnic or racial groups. For example, how are we to account for our finding that communists in England score higher than other political groups on authoritarianism, as measured by the Dogmatism Scale, but score lowest of all groups on a measure of ethnic and racial intolerance? And again, the phenomenon of authoritarianism may be observed in the academic world and in other areas of human activity where there is not necessarily a concomitant manifestation of ethnic or racial intolerance.

In my own view, the difficulties posed seem to arise once again from the fact that we have long been accustomed to define prejudice in terms of ideological content rather than structure. Prejudice against the Jew and Negro seem compatible with certain kinds of ideologies—for example, Fascism or the dominant ideology of the South—but not with others—for example, Marxism, socialism, or democracy. Does this mean that no instances of prejudice are to be found associated with the last-mentioned ideologies? Obviously not. The problem then becomes: how can the problem of man's intolerance to man be reformulated so that all forms of intolerance, regardless of specific ideological content, will gracefully fall under scrutiny?

In an attempt to answer this question I have previously proposed that we redefine prejudice (or intolerance or bigotry) in terms of structure rather than content, a proposal parallel to the one made in redefining authoritarianism. Prejudice is redefined in terms of the way we feel and act toward those who agree and disagree with us on specific issues we care about. In other words, the criterion is a belief criterion rather than a racial or ethnic one. The Opinionation Scale tries to get at this belief criterion. The basic idea underlying this scale is very simple. How often and to what degree will persons agree with belief statements preceded by such opinionated phrases as: "Anyone who is intelligent knows that . . . ," "Only a simple-minded fool would believe that . . . ," "Anyone with an ounce of common sense knows perfectly well that . . . ," and so on. The more such statements are endorsed by a person the more the assumed rejection of others *because* they disagree, and the more the assumed acceptance of others *because* they agree.

The results obtained with the Opinionation Scale differ from those obtained with traditional tests of prejudice, which as has already been mentioned, contain references to ethnic and racial groups. English Communists who score relatively low on the California Ethnocentrism Scale score high on the Opinionation Scale. Other groups which score high on the Ethnocentrism Scale also score high on the Opinionation Scale. These results, as well as a variety of other results presented elsewhere (Rokeach, 1956, 1960) suggest that at most, only the rightist form of authoritarian categorizes and discriminates in terms of ethnic and racial groups. But such categorizations cannot be considered a general attribute of authoritarianism.

In fact, we have gone one step further to suggest that even those social discriminations which at first glance appear to be based on racial and ethnic considerations may, from a psychological standpoint turn out to be more due to belief than to racial or ethnic discrimination. Our subjects—white college students at Michigan State University—seem to prefer more as friends Negroes who agree with them on various issues than whites who disagree with them on the same issues. For example, 42 out of 65 white subjects—two out of three— rated more favorably on a friendship scale a Negro who agrees with them on the desegregation issue than a white who disagrees with them on desegregation. Fifty-five out of the 65 subjects—11 out of 13—preferred friendship with a Negro who believes in God to a white atheist. Our findings for Southern college students are very similar. On the issue of desegregation in education, 92 out of 136—again 2 out of 3— preferred friendship with a Negro who agrees than with a white who disagrees; 110 out of 136—again 11 out of 13— preferred friendship with a Negro who believes in God to a white atheist. Similar results are obtained with Jewish children between the ages of 7 and 16. We find that they overwhelmingly prefer friendship with Gentiles who agree with them on various issues than with Jews who disagree with them.

Belief congruence is basic. All these findings indicate that a basic principle of organization and categorization, for authoritarian and nonauthoritarian alike, is belief congruence rather than racial or ethnic congruence. We find that when belief is held constant, there are relatively small differences in preferences of white over Negro, and, in the Jewish children, in preferences of Jew over Gentile. But when race or ethnic group is held constant, we find enormous differences in preference for those who agree over those who disagree with the subject's views. These differences are greater for those who are authoritarian than for those who are less so, suggesting that authoritarians differ from nonauthoritarians not so much in terms of a greater tendency toward ethnic or racial categorizations as in the extent to which authoritarians categorize and discriminate more sharply those who agree from those who disagree with their views.

6. OVERIDEALIZATION OF INGROUP AND VILIFICATION OF OUT-GROUPS. A sixth assumption about the nature of authoritarianism is that the authoritarian vilifies the outgroup but overidealizes the ingroup. If this assumption is correct, we should find, in a white population, that the greater the re-

jection of the Negro, the greater the acceptance of the white. In the research to which I have just referred, we were able to get independent measures of the extent to which each subject rejects Negroes and whites. We find, in our Northern sample, that the greater the rejection of the Negro, the greater also the rejection of the white. The correlation is .80. A similar finding is obtained for our Southern sample, with the exception that the correlation is lower—a +.43 correlation between rejection of the Negro and rejection of the white. In the study with Jewish children, those who express a dislike of Gentiles also express a dislike of Jews. These results, when considered alongside such other findings as those by Adorno *et al.* (1950), Campbell and McCandless (1951), Rokeach (1952), and Sullivan and Adelson (1954) would suggest that the authoritarian overidealizes the ingroup only when there is fear of retaliation. When given the opportunity, without fear of retaliation, the authoritarian seems quite capable of expressing his negative feelings toward the ingroup, no less than toward various outgroups.

Conformity to Authority

I turn now to the question which will concern us in the second part of this chapter. How are the formulations just presented to be related to the work of those who have concerned themselves with the general issue of conformity?

Prefatorily let me say that in my view the present formulations regarding the nature of authoritarianism are also formulations regarding the nature of conformity. Conformity is a state of mind, sometimes a momentary one induced by certain kinds of social pressure and sometimes a more enduring state built into the personality structure. It is a closed state of mind involving a certain kind of relation between a person and authority (individual or group). By virtue of effective reward and punishment imposed by authority, the person cannot distinguish, assess, or act on information except in a way desired by the source. It is a state of mind wherein the person is necessarily psychologically unaware that he cannot distinguish, assess, and act independently on information received from an authority. When in such a state of mind, the person will therefore *rationalize* his beliefs and actions in a way such that he will not expose, to himself or others, his dependency on authority, in order to maintain the illusion that he is an independent, reasonable, and thinking person. For conformity—like irresponsibility, bigotry, selfishness, and stupidity—is by its very nature threatening to the self-concept and must therefore be psychologically defended against at all costs, particularly through the processes of identification and internalization.[4] Thus, when we study conformity processes in a subject, we must guard against taking at face value the specific content of the information he gives us about his beliefs and actions and about the reasons for his beliefs and actions.

It is difficult to approach the question of how the present views differ from other contemporary conceptions of conformity because we typically employ a variety of different concepts when dealing with this social issue, such concepts as: acquiescence, authoritarianism, compliance, conformance, conformity, convergence, normative behavior, other-directedness, persuasibility, social influence, suggestibility, and yielding. To this list let me draw attention to several other concepts we all use which while more general in nature nevertheless also seem to involve conformity states and conformity processes, at least in part: acculturation and socialization, adaptive behavior and adjustment, the notions of average and normal, reference persons and reference groups, and the processes of identification and internalization. A formidable array of overlapping concepts!

In the interests of conceptual clarification and at the risk

---

[4] For a discussion of these processes leading to conformity see the stimulating paper by Kelman (1958).

of provoking controversy, let me make some observations from the vantage point of the position presented here about what in my opinion conformity is *not*.

1. CONFORMITY, SOCIAL INFLUENCE, AND DETERMINISM. Some conceptions of conformity seem to be so broadly defined that they are virtually synonymous with determinism. Conformity as a psychological concept is sometimes employed in the same sense in which a physical scientist might employ it when speaking of the behavior of the heavenly bodies as obeying or conforming to natural laws. I sense that some of us employ the concept of social influence in this way. Others define conformity as successful social influence. This too seems overly broad because it does not distinguish between successful social influence designed to lead to conformity (that is, to the inability to discriminate, evaluate, and act on information independent of source) from successful social influence designed to lead to its opposite, independence, as in the case of a wise parent or teacher who successfully influences his child or student to think for himself. Defined in these broad, deterministic ways we would all be incorrigible conformists, but this is nothing to get alarmed about because it isn't the issue we have in mind when we ordinarily think of social conformity.

2. CONFORMITY, SOCIALIZATION, AND ADJUSTMENT. Under the influence of cultural relativism in psychology and sociology such processes as socialization, acculturation, adaptation and adjustment are defined in terms of learning to conform to the norms and values of society. Thus, Talcott Parsons (1955; 1958) analyzes the processes of socialization and by implication, of adaptation and adjustment, in such a way that he would appear to be defending conformity as an integral and even necessary component of the socialization process. Such a view has been criticized by Mills (1959) as an

apology for the status quo. A similar criticism has been made by Lindner (1952) in his analysis of contemporary conceptions of personality adjustment and maladjustment.

Again it would appear that conformity defined as socialization is too broad and too crude. Socialization through the psychological processes of identification and internalization needs to be conceived as being not only in the service of conformity needs but also of independence needs. If a parent in middle class American society, for example, has really succeeded in socializing his child, that child by virtue of having become socialized, should exercise independence in his beliefs and actions, within the limits imposed and sanctioned by middle class society. For independence of thought and action may also be a dominant value in middle class society, at least in certain segments of it. One can, if one insists, call socialization toward independence also conformity, but to my mind, to do so would not serve the interests of conceptual clarity. Be that as it may, it would seem necessary to distinguish sharply between what we ordinarily call conformity, which implies a loss of independence of belief and action by virtue of the inability to distinguish information from source, and what we ordinarily refer to as socialization and adjustment, which need not necessarily imply such a loss of independence.

3. CONFORMITY, COMPLIANCE, AND COERCION. Compliance with authority may take place even if a person can psychologically discriminate, evaluate, and assess information independent of source. In such a case I would say that the compliance is a function of coercion and is not conformity. This is in contrast to the views of Kelman (1958) and Jahoda (1956) who tend to regard compliance as a form of conformity. For if compliance by coercion is conformity we would then have to say also that my being forced to hand over my wallet to a holdup man represents a class of behavior which may properly be regarded as conformity, or that the behavior

of prisoners in a concentration camp is an instance of conformity. To conceive of compliance as conformity is to miss the crucial point that conformity is a *state of mind*, not an action. It is a state of mind (or, if you don't like the word *mind*, substitute a state of the person, or an acquired behavioral disposition), arrived at through complex processes of identification and internalization, which enables the person to believe what he believes and act as he acts under the illusion that he does so of his own free will and without realizing that the pressures to do so really arise from without rather than from within. In other words, the conformist cannot know that he is conforming. If he does become aware that he is conforming and if he continues to believe and act as before, he is merely complying. Thus, there is all the world of difference between one professor who abhorred McCarthyism but nevertheless decided, consciously and shrewdly, to protect his job by complying in certain ways and another professor who also initially abhorred McCarthyism but more and more altered in his state of mind so that McCarthyite attitudes became internalized and assimilated into his own belief system. Similarly, we have an instance of conformity in the case of the Jewish concentration camp prisoners described by Bettleheim (1958) who, over and beyond the compliance demanded by their Nazi guards through coercion, "identified with the aggressor," and as a result took over (phenomenalogically speaking, willingly) the anti-Semitic attitudes of their captors.

4. CONFORMITY VIEWED FROM THE STANDPOINT OF GESTALT PSYCHOLOGY AND PHENOMENOLOGY. It is not possible to evaluate Gestalt and phenomenological approaches to the problem of conformity without also evaluating their systematic position in general. It will therefore be necessary to enter into a more extended discussion of Gestalt and phenomenological

psychology in order to clarify their approaches to conformity.

A major tenet of Gestalt psychology, which is also held in common with other versions of the phenomenological viewpoint (Krech & Crutchfield, 1948; Snygg & Combs, 1949), is that a person's behavior is a function of his "definition of the situation." According to this view it is the meaning a person attributes to a stimulus rather than the stimulus itself which determines his response. One and the same stimulus may be interpreted altogether differently depending on its role within the total stimulus configuration or the total social context. This view, first formulated by a Gestalt psychology concerned with the laws of perception, has been applied most systematically to the analysis of social behavior by Asch (1952). Thus, Asch has reinterpreted the results of the Lorge experiment on prestige suggestion in a way which denies that people react blindly or conformingly to prestige persons. The fact that a subject may react differently to a given political passage when it is attributed to different authors is not seen to be a result of prestige suggestion but of a restructurization or reinterpretation of the meaning of the passage. The meaning of the passage literally undergoes a transformation as authorship changes. Similar interpretations are made by Asch to account for the yielding behavior of subjects in his widely known experiments on the effect of group pressures on distortions in judgment.

It is of some interest to note that the term *conformity* is not used in describing or accounting for the behavior of the subjects—and for good reason. For what appears from the "outside" as conformity is from the "inside," readily understandable, reasonable, and even insightful. I am almost tempted to say that from the phenomenological standpoint conformity is no problem because there are no conformists. People behave in accord with their definition of the situation. When distortions in action, judgment, or perception do occur they are "a consequence of pressures from the social sphere, not of tendencies whose source is in the individual himself" (Asch, 1952, p. 495).

How does one go about obtaining information from the "inside"? Typically, it is obtained from the subject's own reports, often retrospective reports, concerning mental processes and behavior occuring earlier during an experimental session.

Herein, it seems to me, lies a major weakness of the phenomenological approach, not only with respect to the analysis of conformity but also more generally speaking. There is no way to distinguish between rational and rationalized reports within the framework of phenomenology. The content of such reports are typically taken at face value, which makes sense in the classical Gestalt studies of perception, wherein ego-defensiveness on the part of the subject is not an issue. But it makes less sense in social psychological investigations which are likely to arouse ego-defensiveness. If there were ever social situations which should bring out ego-defensive maneuvers it would be situations in which people are caught, or are in danger of catching themselves, red-handed in the act of yielding blindly to group pressures or to prestige persons. While there is no denying Asch's finding that subjects typically report meaningful, organized structurizations and restructurizations of social situations, it is impossible to tell whether conformity changes in attitude or perceptual judgment precede or are preceded by changes in meaning.

In a study by Rokeach and Eglash (1956) it was found that many subjects heartily endorsed such statements as the following:

The fallacy in Hitler's theories is shown by the fact that, after all, he lost the war.

The fact that God exists is proven by the fact that so many millions of people believe in Him.

The American economic and political system is preferable to the Russian, because the Soviet system means long hours at poor wages.

Negroes deserve equal treatment, because there is as yet no scientific evidence showing that there is any real difference in body odors.

No doubt, had the subjects who agreed with such statements been asked how they interpreted them, meaningful and understandable reports would have been obtained. Whatever they might have said, I think it reasonable to say that agreement with such statements are unreasonable and lacking in conviction.

The difficulty, it seems to me, lies in a conceptual confusion on the part of phenomenologists between the idea, on the one hand, that a person's phenomenal field is organized or meaningful or understandable and the idea, on the other hand, that it is therefore also reasonable or insightful or understanding. A psychotic's phenomenal field, to use an extreme example, is meaningful and understandable but may also be irrational and uninsightful. There is no contradiction between the two sets of ideas because one is made from the "inside" and the other from an objective standpoint "outside."[5]

Asch himself points out, correctly I think, that perhaps as a result of the impact of psychoanalysis, rationalization "has almost replaced thinking proper" and that it is "necessary to discriminate between rationalization and thinking" (Asch, 1952, p. 22). But, it would appear, the pendulum has swung to the opposite extreme and all I am suggesting is a revised

[5] Katz and Stotland (1959) arguing for the need of a "concept of appropriateness" take a similar view to the one taken here when they write: "The logical model of man is too simple to do justice to the complexities of social behavior in spite of its persuasive resurrection by the phenomenologists" (p. 447). And again: "Some Gestalt theorists have attempted to write the notion of stereotypes out of psychology because of the implications of blind or stupid behavior" (p. 448).

view of man, capable of both rational and rationalized behavior.

It's up to the psychological observer, not the person being observed, to specify what are the independent, objective, "outside" criteria on the basis of which it will be decided whether a person is conformist, stereotyped, blind, stupid, or whatever. This is not to say that the hard-won gains of phenomenology are to be discarded. It is only to say that the phenomenological approach is indispensable only up to a certain point, at the point where it is necessary to check phenomenal reality against objective reality. For there are many things the person we are studying cannot tell us, or will not tell us, or for dynamic reasons will distort in the telling. One way to get a better "outside" picture of the "inside," is to pay closer attention to the structure than to the content of the "inside." This is on the assumption that structure, being more genotypic, is less subject to disguise than content, which is more phenotypic. In this way, it is hoped, vital information about the phenomenal field can be extracted without necessarily having the subject's permission or cooperation. Of course, the structural attributes of the phenomenal field have to be sufficiently articulated so that they are operationally definable and measurable.

Summary

While authoritarianism has not been explicitly defined in a satisfactory conceptual way, one can discern many implicit assumptions about its nature which are widely accepted. I have had occasion here to consider six of these assumptions and to call for their reconsideration. First, the dichotomy between reliance on authority versus reliance on reason is suggested to be a false once since everyone has to rely on authority in order to know the world he lives in. Instead, I have proposed that we think in terms of open versus closed orientations to authority. Second, we should bear in mind the distinction between ideological content and ideological structure. A person may adhere to an ideology democratic in content but his mode of adherence may be authoritarian. Third, authoritarianism does not seem to imply an absolute rejection of negative authority. Instead, it seems more fruitful to conceive of a gradation of negative authority arranged on a continuum of similarity to positive authority, with rejection becoming increasingly greater as a function of dissimilarity. Fourth, the rejection of a particular outgroup is often traceable to the degree of cognitive similarity between outgroup and ingroup which is to a large extent independent of authoritarianism as such. Fifth, authoritarianism involves an exaggerated categorization of people in terms of belief congruence rather than in terms of racial or ethnic congruence. And, sixth, authoritarianism seems to involve a fear of the ingroup no less than a fear of the outgroup.

An attempt has been made to relate the formulations concerning the nature of authoritarianism to other contemporary conceptions of conformity behavior. I have suggested that certain conceptions of conformity behavior are too broad either because they are roughly synonymous with the notion of determinism, or too broad because they are roughly synonymous with such proesses as socialization and adjustment. I then have suggested that the states and processes associated with conformity are qualitatively different from those associated with compliance, which is based on coercion. Finally, I presented a brief analysis of the Gestalt and more generally, the phenomenological approaches to conformity and made an attempt to point out the basis of their shortcomings.

REFERENCES

Adorno, T. W., Frenkel-Brunswik, Else, Levison, D. J., & Sanford, R. N. *The authoritarian personality*. New York: Harper, 1950.
Arendt, Hannah. What was authority? In C. J. Friedrich (Ed.),

Authority. Cambridge: Harvard Univer. Press, 1958.

Asch, S. E.   *Social psychology*. New York: Prentice-Hall, 1952.

Bettleheim, B.   Individual and mass behavior in extreme situations. In Eleanor E. Maccoby, T. M. Newcomb, & E. L. Hartley (Eds.), *Readings in social psychology*. New York: Holt, 1958.

Burwen, L. S., & Campbell, D. T.   The generality of attitudes toward authority and non-authority figures. *J. abnorm. soc. Psychol.*, 1957, **54**, 24–31.

Campbell, D. T., & McCandless, B.   Ethnocentrism, xenophobia, and personality. *Hum. Relat.*, 1951, **4**, 185–192.

Catlin, G. E. G.   Authority and its critics. In C. J. Friedrich (Ed.), *Authority*. Cambridge: Harvard Univer. Press, 1958.

Christie, R., & Cook, Peggy.   A guide to published literature relation to the authoritarian personality through 1956. *J. psychol.*, 1958, **45**, 171–199.

Friedrich, C. J.   Authority, reason, and discretion. In C. J. Friedrich (Ed.), *Authority*. Cambridge: Harvard Univer. Press, 1958.

Fromm, E.   *Escape from freedom*. New York: Farrar & Rinehart, 1941.

Fruchter, B., Rokeach, M., & Novak, E. G.   A factorial study of dogmatism, opinionation, and related scales. *Psychol. Reports*, 1958, **4**, 19–22.

Hendel, C.   An exploration of the nature of authority. In C. J. Friedrich (Ed.), *Authority*. Cambridge: Harvard Univer. Press, 1958.

Jahoda, Marie.   Psychological issues in civil liberties. *Amer. Psychologist*, 1956, **11**, 234–240.

Katz, D., & Stotland, E.   A preliminary statement to a theory of attitude structure and change. In S. Koch (Ed.), *Psychology: A study of science*. Vol. 3. New York: McGraw-Hill, 1959.

Kelman, H. C.   Compliance, identification, and internalization: three processes of attitude change. *Conflict Resolution*, 1958, **2**, 51–60.

Kohler, W.   *The place of value in a world of facts*. New York: Liveright, 1938.

Krech, D., & Crutchfield, R. S.   *Theory and problems of social psychology.* New York: McGraw-Hill, 1948.

Krech, D. Notes toward a psychological theory. *J. Pers.,* 1949, 18, 66–87.

Lewin, K. *Field theory in social science.* New York: Harper, 1951.

Lindner, R. M. *Prescription for rebellion.* New York: Rinehart, 1952.

Mills, C. W. *The sociological imagination.* New York: Oxford Univer. Press, 1959.

Parsons, T. Social structure and the development of personality. *Psychiatry,* 1958, 21, 321–340.

Parsons, T., & Bales, R. F. *Family socialization and interaction processes.* Glencoe, Ill.: Free Press, 1955.

Rokeach, M. Attitude as a determinant of distortion in recall. *J. abnorm. soc. Psychol.,* 1952, 47, 482–488.

Rokeach, M. Political and religious dogmatism: An alternative to the authoritarian personality. *Psychol. Monogr.,* 1956, 70, No. 18 (Whole No. 425).

Rokeach, M. *The open and closed mind: Investigations into the nature of belief systems and personality systems.* New York: Basic Books, 1960.

Rokeach, M., & Eglash, A. A scale for measuring intellectual conviction. *J. soc. Psychol.,* 1956, 44, 135–141.

Rokeach, M., & Fruchter, B. A factorial study of dogmatism and related concepts. *J. abnorm. soc. Psychol.,* 1956, 53, 356–360.

Snygg, D., & Combs, A. W. *Individual behavior.* New York: Harper, 1949.

Sullivan, P. L., & Adelson, J. Ethnocentrism and misanthropy. *J. abnorm. soc. Psychol.,* 1954, 49, 246–250.

Tolman, E. C. Cognitive maps in rats and men. *Psychol. Rev.,* 1948, 55, 189–208.

Trueblood, D. E. *The logic of belief.* New York: Harper, 1942.

CHAPTER 8

Group Reinforcement of Individual Response Experiments in Verbal Behavior[1]

ARTHUR J. BACHRACH, DOUGLAS K. CANDLAND, and JANICE T. GIBSON

University of Virginia

Reduced to their essential characteristics, the responses of conformity and deviation represent a single response class—the behavior of an individual in relation to the behavior of other individuals who are functioning mutually as a group. This group, varying in cohesiveness, may be referred to by such terms as *community, culture,* or *society.* Our definition of group is, simply, a cohesion of three or more individuals whose response patterns are associated in some activity. Accepting conformity to or deviation from the group's response pattern as behavior produced and maintained in group-individual interaction, it is suggested that such behavior might best be approached within the framework of reinforcement theory. It is with the methodology of such an analysis that much of the present chapter will deal.

The starting point might well be an assumption that be-

[1] The support of the Group Psychology Branch, Office of Naval Research, and especially that of Luigi Petrullo and Joan Criswell of that Branch is warmly appreciated. The authors wish to thank Mrs. Katherine Tiffany for her thoughtful preparation of the manuscript and also for her help in the administration of the experiment; and Mrs. Mary Candland for preparation of the charts. The symbols were prepared by the senior author.

havior is a result of its consequences in which the model of Response $\longrightarrow$ Reinforcement is invoked. Reinforcement is inferred from the behavior of the individual; a reinforcement is any event which increases or decreases the probability of a given response. In individual-group interaction we assume the individual's behavior (his response $[R_1]$ will be reinforced by the group (R_G); or to be more precise, by the individuals who comprise the group $(R_{GI_{1,2,3,\ldots n}})$. The reinforcement will be either positive or negative depending on whether the probability of a response is increased or decreased. It is assumed further that the response of the individual will be reinforcing (again positively or negatively) to the group.

Conformity may be defined as a situation in which the group's reinforcement is adequate to produce and maintain behavior by the individual, and in which the behavior is, in turn, positively reinforcing to the group.

$$R_I \xrightarrow{\hspace{3cm}} R_G$$
$$\xleftarrow{\hspace{3cm}}$$

Deviation, on the other hand, represents a situation in which the group's reinforcement is not adequate to produce and maintain the same behavior by the individual which would in turn be reinforcing to the group:

$$R_I \longleftarrow\!\!-\!\!/\!\!-\!\!\longrightarrow R_G$$
$$-\!\!/\!\!\longrightarrow$$

An alternative possibility is that another group, G_2 is providing the reinforcements for the individual behavior:

$$R_I \longleftarrow\!\!-\!\!/\!\!-\!\!\longrightarrow R_G$$
$$\uparrow\downarrow -\!\!/\!\!\longrightarrow$$
$$RG_2$$

so that deviation from G_1 may be a facet of conformity to G_2. Other possible differential aspects of such reinforcement may be that a segment, or subculture, of G_1 may be positively reinforcing while the remainder of the group is not. For example, the adolescent segment of a middle class culture may reinforce the behavior of individuals considered deviant and not reinforced by the adult group members. It is also possible that G_1, or members of it, may reinforce putative deviant behavior by the individual as another aspect of its own reinforcement: "As the only extreme nonconformist of his generation, he [the hipster] exercises a powerful if underground appeal for conformists, through newspaper accounts of his delinquencies, his structureless jazz, and his emotive grunt words" (Bird, 1957).

We may derive certain ideas from these observations:

1. Reinforcement will be differential by members of a group; i.e., individuals within a group structure will differentially reinforce the behavior of another group or individual. For an effective analysis of group reinforcement the response pattern of each individual in the group should be studied.

2. With individual variation in view, group pressure to conform to behavior reinforcing to the group represents a situation in which a consistency of reinforcement among the group members exists.

3. Again with individual variation in view, the leader-follower relationships may be studied in reinforcement terms.

4. Conformity to one group (e.g., 'hipsters') may be a facet of deviation from another (e.g., conformists or 'squares'), allowing an examination of reinforcement contingencies in each group.

Background of the Present Study

A psychologist interested in studying conformity and deviation would be well rewarded by approaching the world of the hipster, truly a natural situation which may well offer what Egon Brunswik (1955) called a "representative design." The problem of investigation would be one which faces any naturalist-observer; he would be forced to take nature as it is and to minimize experimental manipulation. However, in order to isolate those variables which cannot be identified functionally with the field-study approach, we were seeking a representative design, a minimax if you will—a research design which would provide the minimum of artificiality and the maximum of control; a group-individual behavioral situation in which natural responses and natural reinforcements could be manipulated. And so we turned, naturally, to verbal behavior. It is likely that verbal behavior is the only type of learning in which the experimenter can feel reasonably certain that social factors predominate and that biochemical, physiological, constitutional, and genetic factors are noncontributory or minimal. Since group-individual interaction is mediated by verbal behavior, the major objective of this program was to examine verbal behavior in social situations as a function of the verbal reinforcement offered by other persons in the social situation. Skinner's definition of verbal behavior, in fact, emphasizes the social aspect: it is, he says, "behavior reinforced through the mediation of other persons" (1957).

Aside from its natural social aspect, the study of verbal behavior has other experimental advantages, as suggested by Skinner:

1. It is usually observed quite easily. (As Skinner notes, if it weren't it would be ineffective verbal behavior.)
2. There has never been any shortage of material.
3. The facts are substantial (careful observers will agree on what has been said and, of course, tape recording provides a true account as well).

4. A ready-made system of notation is available through writing (or as noted above, in tape recording, or in phonetic reproduction).

Verbal behavior is, then, a natural response with which to work. Moreover, it allows for specification of different subclasses. For example, one of Verplanck's studies (1955) illustrates a subclass of verbal behavior of interest to social psychologists. He chose to treat "stating an opinion" as a class of behavior representing a response and assumed that agreement with the speaker's stated opinion (or with paraphrases of it) would positively reinforce the speaker, an hypothesis which was confirmed experimentally.

In recent years the literature on verbal behavior has grown significantly. While there have been verbal conditioning studies for many years, the recent upsurge owes at least part of its impetus to a study by Greenspoon (1955) in which principles of reinforcement theory were applied to verbal behavior. His reinforcing stimuli were "mm-hmm" or "huh-uh" following one of two responses—plural noun or any word not a plural noun. The subject was asked to say, one at a time, all the words (exclusive of sentences, phrases, or numbers) he could think of for 50 minutes. For the first 25 minutes the reinforcing stimulus was delivered following each response; it was omitted during the last 25-minute extinction period. Greenspoon's finding, that "mmm-hmm" increased the frequency of plural noun responses and "huh-uh" decreased them, coupled with other results, indicated that verbal responses could be influenced by the experimenter and, moreover, without the subject's awareness of the relationship between their verbal behavior and that of the experimenter.

In a similar study, Mandler and Kaplan (1956) were concerned with the subjective evaluation of the reinforcing stimulus. Using "mm-hmm" immediately after every plural noun response they found that the subjects were generally aware of the stimulus. They also found that the subjects were divisible into two groups, the positive group consisting of those subjects who thought the "mm-hmm" had positive aspects—"that it meant they were doing all right, that it was encouraging them to go on"—and the negative group who thought the reinforcer had negative aspects, telling them that "they were going too fast, giving the wrong kinds of words." None of the subjects were able to state specifically the relationship between the occurrence of the reinforcing stimulus and their own behavior; i.e., the contingency existing between plural nouns and the "mm-hmm." The results indicated that the subjective evaluation of the reinforcing effect of the experimenter's behavior, the verbal stimulus, influenced the verbal behavior of the subjects; those who thought it positive responded appropriately, as did the group who thought it negative.

This finding adds a further dimension to Greenspoon's research, indicating that the reinforcement history of the individual is critical in the establishment of a reinforcing effect. Related to this, of course, is the evaluation of who would be a reinforcing figure—to be sure, even the clear interpretation of approval from a group or person whose approval is poorly valued might not be positively reinforcing.

Other studies, such as those of Kanfer (1958) and Salzinger (1957) have contributed much to the formation of an experimental analysis of verbal behavior. Krasner (1958) and Salzinger (1959) in two separate reviews have covered the literature (up to 1958) and should be consulted for background. Recent studies have generally confirmed the conditionability of verbal behavior while pointing out its multivariate nature.

The Units of Verbal Behavior

Following is a brief formulation of the possible units involved in verbal behavior which permit experimental manipulation.

A. *The reinforcement history of the group and of the individual.* Perhaps the most difficult single datum to obtain is the prior experience of the individual and the group (Kanfer & Karas, 1959). Such factors as sex of experimenters, authority of peer group members, attitudes toward certain figures, and a host of other factors may be in operation. All one can say is that these determining factors should be isolated. It is likely, however, that they will be inferred from behavior and emerge from the data.

B. *The reinforcement contingencies.*

1. *Nature of reinforcement.*

   a. Positive. Those consequences of the subject's response which are interpreted as "rewarding," i.e., likely to increase the probability of the response recurring.

   b. Negative. Those consequences of the subject's response which are interpreted as "punishing," i.e., likely to decrease the probability of the response recurring. It is differentiated from *withdrawal of positive reinforcement* (below) as follows: negative punishing would be exemplified by a verbal stimulus such as, "You're wrong, it doesn't look anything like that" or "I think that's a silly suggestion." Withdrawal of positive reinforcement is also an extinction technique but consists in such actions as ignoring subject's verbalizations after he has received positive reinforcement from them during the conditioning period.

   c. Withdrawal of positive reinforcement. See b above; this is now generally referred to as "time-out" (see Ferster, 1958).

   d. Type of reinforcement (e.g., money, candy, approval).

2. *Amount of reinforcement.* It is known that too little reinforcement may be insufficient to maintain behavior,

too much may produce satiation. This is another variable that can be studied.

   3. *Schedule of delivery* (examples, cf. Ferster & Skinner,
     1957).
     a. Continuous (crf). Each response reinforced.
     b. Fixed interval (fi). Response reinforced only after
      specific interval has elapsed.
     c. Fixed ratio (fr). Response reinforced only after
      specific number of responses has been completed.

C. *Discriminative stimuli* (S_D).
   1. *Stimuli to which response is contingent;* e.g., frowns,
    nods, smiles or S_Ds in experimental situation other than
    human, e.g., flashing light, buzzer.

D. *Response of individual.*
   1. *Behavior.* Verbal response of individual measured in
    terms of frequency (or rate) of response.

The frequency of response by the subject is perhaps the
most useful measure because of its relative clarity. Other possibilities for response classes include the pitch, stress, or in-
tonation level, as for example, the change in relative loudness
in talking when verbally told "Shh!" by another person in
combination with the S_Ds of head-shaking and finger pressed
to lips. Relative loudness is a variable which can be measured
but is not so clear nor so broad a response class as the frequency with which verbal responses are emitted—i.e., how
much a person talks in a situation in which other persons are
trying to influence rate.

Technique of the Present Study

The most serious limitation and, consequently, the most
difficult procedural problem in the analysis of verbal behavior
is that of the stipulation and identification of response classes
of verbal material, and the loss of precision which results
from the use of a human experimenter in place of an automatic reinforcement programmer.

In the early stages of this work an attempt was made to use specific words or phrases as response classes. However, it was found that the experimenters' performance was unreliable in identifying response classes with sufficient rapidity to offer reinforcement according to schedule. Accordingly, a rather gross response class was used: namely, the amount of time that the subject spoke. Although the use of this response class simplifies the work of the experimenters, and although it decreases greatly the number of procedural errors made by the experimenters, it creates several difficulties in the interpretation of the results. The results are fairly clear when considered in general, but the identification of particular effects is a perilous task.

An additional problem concerns the determination of whether the experimenters—the human programmers—affected the response rate of the subject by some method other than that of the reinforcement schedule under examination. Although in these studies the verbal responses of the experimenters were limited by their not being permitted to ask questions or to interrupt the subject so that these modes of response would not alter the subject's response rate artificially the possibility remains that the response rate had been altered by some other technique incidental in the behavior of the experimenters. Accordingly, it was decided to test the data of each subject from each session to determine whether or not the experimenters had maintained a constant rate of speech during the session. In all cases, a Friedman two-way analysis of variance (Siegel, 1956) was used, with successive minutes forming the rows in the analysis, and experimental periods forming columns. Although a test of this type is almost certain to eliminate from consideration any data on which the experimenters have shown variable verbal performance, the technique has the disadvantage that in order to use the results of a session, the experimenters must talk at a constant rate, regardless of the behavior of the subject. That is, even though a subject gives every indication of continuing to talk for the length of an acquisition period, it is necessary for the experimenter to maintain a rate of speech comparable to that which he had maintained during the operant period. Similarly, if the subject shows no sign of speaking during the extinction period, the experimenters are required to talk, for, say 20 seconds of every minute, after which they are required to remain silent. Although the decision that acceptable data must show that the experimenters did not vary their rate over the session probably eliminates some data which is actually relevant, it was felt that this severe test is necessary to eliminate artificial findings.

The technique used in these studies is, then, essentially a *post hoc* one: The session is completed, but one does not know until after the data have been examined to determine the verbal behavior of the experimenters whether or not the session was acceptable procedurally. This procedure is, of course, similar to the use of autopsy in studies of brain stimulation, and although it is wasteful in the sense that many hours are spent gathering unacceptable data, it is also a necessary procedure for the elimination of untrustworthy data.

Since the purpose of this work was to identify some of the variables associated with the conditioning of verbal behavior in small-group, social situations, the *post hoc* technique is unavoidable. When these variables are identified and their parameters known, it is reasonable to suppose that techniques can be devised without this encumbrance. However, in the present state of knowledge concerning verbal behavior in group situations, there is little choice but to probe with the hope of discovering a sensitive area.

Although the technique of using two experimenters in a three-person, social situation permits the investigation of verbal behavior under various schedule and reinforcement conditions, several difficulties in experimental procedure arise. Firstly, during the session, the task of the experimenters is to maintain a smooth discussion while speaking at a constant rate over the session and following the preestablished reinforcement program. Since the experimenters must cooperate with one another in eliciting and rewarding the responses of the subject, considerable practice is necessary in order for them to achieve this cooperation. For example, the subject offers verbal reinforcement to the experimenters in normal speech, and practice is necessary on the part of the experimenters in order for their verbal behavior to be insensitive to this.

Secondly, the subject usually shows an initial preference for reinforcement from one experimenter rather than another. Thirdly, the experimenters must develop certain acting skills: they are expected to talk about the same stimulus-cards for session after session, and it becomes increasingly difficult for them to talk about the cards with the spontaneity expected of a naive subject. Finally, because the verbal task is unstructured, the experimenter has considerable difficulty as a programmer during the test session in (1) determining the form of the reinforcement—"Mmm" or "Yes"—and in (2) judging the appropriate point at which to offer reinforcement so that the reinforcement is not incongruous with the preceding comment.

Although these difficulties produce high variability and consequent difficulty in the interpretation of data, the difficulties are not different from those found in any other attempt to design equipment adequate for stimulation and measurement. A new apparatus, whether human, electrical, or mechanical always has "bugs" in the system, and some time must be spent in the elimination of those features which are sources of variation in the data. When the apparatus is a human experimenter, the task of correcting the apparatus so that it follows its assigned program faithfully is impossible. The drawbacks in the present problem are that the basic equipment is a human which must serve as a programmer, and that this apparatus comes fully programmed with a set of verbal responses.

It is possible, of course, to examine the effects of verbal reinforcement without the introduction of a human experimenter. However, in order to do this, one must know what it is that he wishes to program. Until the relevant variables associated with verbal behavior are identified more clearly, the human programmer will be the only apparatus available.

FIGURE 8.1.   Examples of Chinese ideograms used as stimulus material. A *kuo* (kingdom). B (left), *Nu* (Woman) and (right), *tzu* (child).

PROCEDURE.   Stimulus materials were selected which would keep people talking naturally, with sustained interest and with minimal satiation. Simple free discussion was not effective. Chinese ideograms and American Indian symbols were selected because they provided material which was interesting to discuss because they sustained interest for long periods, and because they were relatively insoluble. (See Figures 8.1 and 8.2).

The procedure in these studies was essentially invariant. The subjects were either graduate students in the school of education of the University of Virginia, or nurses in training from the same school. An appointment was made with the subject by the departmental secretary. The subject was told that three subjects were needed for a study concerned with the ability of humans to translate symbols from foreign languages into English. When the subject arrived at the appointed time, one, or sometimes both, experimenters were present. When all three participants had arrived, they were introduced to one another and taken to a private office.

FIGURE 8.2. Examples of American Indian symbols used as stimulus material. A, butterfly. B, bird. C, deer tracks. X, ceremonial headdress. Y, enclosure for ceremonial dances. Z, medicine man's eye.

All three participants were seated around a desk on which a tape recorder and microphone were placed. The administrator announced that since the problem involved the finding of a solution by the three participants, the session would be tape-recorded for further use, and that he would be in the next office if he were needed. The administrator then read the following statement:

The purpose of this experiment is to investigate the cultural effects of problem solving. It is believed that there are certain aspects of symbolic problem solving that have no cultural boundaries; that is, that can be solved equally well by people of all backgrounds.

Your task in this experiment will be to examine the ideograms that will be shown to you and to decide as a group what they mean.

When any questions had been answered, the administrator started the tape recorder, turned up the first stimulus card, and left the room. Subsequent placement of the stimulus cards was accomplished in one of two ways, depending upon the experimental design for the particular session. When the changing of stimulus cards was used as a signal for the experimenters to change the reinforcement schedule, the administrator would reenter the room, place another card face up, and say, "Now try this one." When the reinforcement schedule was predetermined, the administrator would ask the group to turn over a new card whenever they had reached agreement on a solution to the previous card.

At the end of a session, the administrator thanked the participants, translated the symbols for them if they desired, and all three subjects were excused. Since a subject often proved to be more conditionable after several sessions (presumably because some rapport had been established by that time between the participants) it was found advantageous to employ the same subject several times when possible, although this was always done with different schedules and different stimulus cards.

The Acquisition and Extinction of Verbal Responses

Since one of the objectives of this work was to examine whether the effects of verbal conditioning in a small-group situation are identical to those effects found in the conditioning of the verbal behavior of a single individual, the first series of subjects was examined under the following four conditions (each condition lasted for a ten-minute period, the conditions were run in the order listed below, and each condition involved the discussion of a different stimulus card):

1. *Operant Level.* The experimenters attempted to maintain a normal rate of speech during this condition. No attempt was made to offer either reinforcement or punishment. (Throughout this report, the term *reinforcement* refers to positive verbal reinforcement [e.g., "Yes," "Good," "Mmm,"]: negative reinforcement or punishment refers to comments such as "No," or a horizontal shaking of the head; neutral reinforcement refers to the absence of either kind of reinforcement.)

2. *Acquisition.* Whenever the subject spoke, one, or both experimenters gave positive reinforcement by agreeing. Sometimes the reinforcements were extended to phrases such as "That's a good idea," "I think you're right," or "I can see that." At no time, however, did the experimenters ask a direct or indirect question of the subject. This limitation was imposed to prevent the experimenters from increasing the subject's response rate artificially.

3. *Extinction.* The experimenters did not comment on any remark made by the subject. They refrained from punishing responses (with remarks such as, "You're wrong!") and merely changed the topic of conversation once the subject had finished speaking. At no time was the subject interrupted by the experimenters. Since this procedure amounted to an ignoring of the subject, the procedure was undoubtedly perceived as punishing to some, if not all, of the subjects. Extreme individual differences were found among subjects during the extinction procedure: some subjects extinguished immediately and refused to speak during the remainder of the session; other subjects made periodic comments. When plotted, these periodic comments appear as "bursts," i.e., a long period of no responding, followed by a sudden burst of responding, followed by no responding again. Since such

differences probably reflect individual differences in tolerance to verbal statements (i.e., some subjects might perceive
the fact that the experimenters ignored their statements as
punishing) and individual differences as to what constitutes
verbal reinforcement and punishment, this finding suggests
that behavior during extinction might very well relate to
other personality varia-
bles. Although it is vital
to an understanding of
the effects of verbal conditioning to determine
what constitutes verbal reinforcement, punishment,
neutrality, or withdrawal,
for particular subjects,
such determinations were
not part of this program.

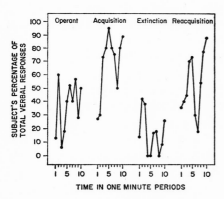

FIGURE 8.3.   Acquisition and extinction
of verbal response.

4. *Reacquisition.* The
procedure for the reac-
quisition condition was
identical to that for acquisition.

RESULTS.   Figure 8.3 shows the results of one subject
(male) during the conditions described above. The results
are plotted in terms of the percentage of the total speaking
time (experimenters and subject combined) consumed by
the subject. The conversion to percentage was used for several
reasons: (1) in order to compare the performance of subjects
with that of the experimenters, and (2) to eliminate artificial
differences arising from the fact that different stimulus cards
maintained different operant levels. The use of percentage
would not be justified, of course, if there were reason to
suppose that the responses of the experimenters were not
dispersed evenly over the session.

Although the variability is high, the effects of the different experimental conditions are clear. The subject's response rate during the operant period varied around 35 percent of the total talking time (for convenience, one might remember that were talking time divided equally among the three participants, one would expect the subject, and each experimenter, to consume 33 percent of the total talking time). There appears to be a tendency for the response rate during the operant period to rise during the last half of the operant period. This result probably reflects a "warming-up" effect on the part of the subject, and may indicate that any verbal response, even an apparently neutral response on the part of the experimenter, may be reinforcing to the subject. A longer operant period might have clarified this finding by indicating the point at which the subject's response percentage becomes stable.

During the acquisition period the subject's response rate climbed rapidly, until the subject was consuming 95 percent of the total talking time during the fifth minute. A slow decrease in talking time occurred after that point, but the response rate climbed to the 80 percent level again during the last two minutes. This "dip" probably reflects previous conditioning on the part of the subject: since the subject had monopolized the conversation for several minutes, there was a strong social tendency to relinquish the conversation in order to allow the other parties to speak. Since this tendency is so well built into most (but, unfortunately, not all) adult humans, a short, ten-minute session could not expect to overcome it. This depression effect during acquisition was characteristic of all subjects.

During the extinction procedure the subject showed three distinct bursts of talking—the second and third minutes, the sixth and seventh minutes, and the ninth and tenth minutes. The highest of these was only slightly over 40 percent of the total talking time and is only a little above the expected talking time estimate of 33 percent. On the other hand, at three points during extinction, the subject consumed none of the talking time. When it is remembered that the experimenters were forced, by the design, to talk only a portion of the time, this finding is striking. It means that during the extinction condition, fairly long periods of time passed without talking by any of the participants.

Although it is uneconomical to present complete data here on all subjects run in this series of tests, one of the most striking findings was that the extinction session produced consistent individual differences among subjects. Although the experimenters were careful not to use any negative reinforcement during this condition, but only ignored the comments of the subject, one male subject developed a strong dislike toward the male experimenter. (When the two met accidentally at a social gathering sometime later, the subject felt called upon to apologize for his behavior!) Since reaction to punishment and to authority has been a major area of research in the field of personality in recent years, an analysis of verbal behavior under conditions of verbal punishment may be helpful in identification of distinctive personality characteristics. These results indicate that individual differences to extinction are consistent with the subject.

The reacquisition period showed the same dip as was noted during the acquisition session. The subject's response percentage rose to 70 percent of the total talking time after the first five minutes, then declined to a lower performance in the seventh minute, and reached 90 percent by the conclusion of the test. That the initial rise in response percentage was not so rapid as that of the acquisition period may indicate the effects of recovery from extinction.

Extinction as a Function of the Sex of the Experimenter

The striking findings in regard to the extinction session during the first series of tests encouraged a consideration of extinction as a function of the sex of the experimenter. The influence of the sex of the tester in projective testing is well known, and it seemed likely that verbal behavior would show similar differences as a function of the sex of the experimenter. The general plan of this series of tests was to place the subject in a situation in which one experimenter gave positive reinforcement, while the other opposite-sexed experimenter gave negative reinforcement. It was expected that extinction and acquisition rates might change as a function of the sex of the experimenter giving positive or negative reinforcement.

Unfortunately, such an hypothesis requires a counterbalanced experimental design that was impractical. Accordingly, a design which was imperfect for comparison of results across subjects, but which was adequate for comparison of changes in the verbal behavior of one individual subject was adopted. The procedure was as follows:

1. *Acquisition.* The subject was positively reinforced for speaking by both experimenters, as in the series of studies described above.

2. *Neutral.* This procedure was identical to the procedure for determining the operant level described above. The experimenters attempted to maintain a normal amount of speaking time, with neither positive reinforcement nor negative reinforcement. As will be seen, the results were very far from that expectation. Although it seems obvious in retrospect, the supposedly neutral period yielded typical extinction results for all of the subjects. In short, neutral speech following a period in which verbal responding has been reinforced serves to extinguish the subject's responding.

3. *Positive and negative reinforcement.* One experimenter (the male, for example) gave positive reinforcement to the speech of the subject; the other (female) experimenter gave negative reinforcement. During negative reinforcement the

experimenter used such comments as "I think you're wrong," or "I don't see that at all."

4. *A second neutral period.*

5. *Reversed positive and negative reinforcement.* The procedure was identical to that of 3 above, except that the experimenters reversed roles. If the male experimenter gave positive reinforcement during the previous session, he gave negative reinforcement under this condition.

The complete session lasted for 50 minutes, and each reinforcement condition was ten minutes long.

RESULTS. Evidently a neutral period of speech following a period of positive reinforcement rapidly extinguishes the subject. Curiously, extinction appeared to be far more rapid when an acquisition period was followed by a neutral period than when an extinction period followed an acquisition period, as in the first series of tests. Since the major difference between the two series up to this point in the procedure was that the first set of subjects had been tested on an operant period, it seems likely that the operant period gave the subject an "anchor point" from which to operate. Accordingly, it seems plausible that the effect of a period of neutral reinforcement (that is, neither positive nor negative reinforcement) is dependent upon the preceding conditions. If the subject has experienced a neutral period, in the form of the ascertaining of an operant level, and then receives extinction, the extinction process is less rapid than when the anchor point has been determined by the acquisition period, as in the second series of tests.

Although the ideal design would have called for measuring the response of the subject to reinforcement from the different experimenters independently, this could not be done with a single subject. To attempt to counterbalance this contamination by the use of many subjects was not feasible, and, accordingly, it may be that the second reinforcement period was altered as a function of the preceding reinforcement period. Although the results cannot be independently examined in this design, the results do point up several encouraging modes of inquiry.

Figure 8.4 shows the performance of one male subject on the schedule described above. The data are plotted in two-minute-period blocks, and again the percentage of total talking time of the subject has been taken as the measure of verbal response rate, since statistical tests indicated that the experimenters spoke at a constant rate during the session.

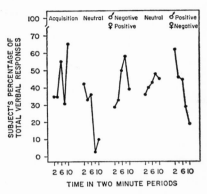

FIGURE 8.4. Effect of differential reinforcement of verbal response.

The acquisition results are not totally satisfactory. The subject showed two distinct jumps in percentage talking time, one in the fifth and sixth minute, and another in the last two minutes. Again the characteristic dip in response rate following a period of high responding is noted. During the supposedly neutral period, the subject showed rapid extinction. No identifiable burst effect is noted, and although the subject was consuming slightly over 40 percent of the total talking time at the beginning of the session, by the end of the session the response percentage was consistently under 10 percent.

During the first reinforcement period, the male experimenter gave negative reinforcement and the female experimenter gave positive reinforcement. This subject (a male) showed a consistent rise in response rate under these conditions until the last two minutes of the session. His response percentage rose from slightly under 30 percent at the beginning of the session to slightly under 60 percent up to the eighth minute of the session. Apparently, approval from the female experimenter outweighed disapproval from the male experimenter. That this effect persisted is seen during the following neutral period. Here the subject did not show the rapid deline evidenced in the first neutral period; rather, there is a slow rise from 33 percent to 44 percent over the ten-minute period.

The assumption that the female experimenter was far more effective in altering the verbal behavior of this male subject than the male experimenter was borne out in the final reinforcement session. During this session the male experimenter was giving positive reinforcement, and the female experimenter negative reinforcement. A rapid extinction curve results, with the subject dropping from over 60 percent of total verbal responses in the first two minutes to less than 20 percent in the final two minutes. No burst effect is noted.

Even though the final session was probably influenced by the distribution of reinforcement in the preceding reinforcement period, the subject's behavior with regard to the different experimenters was consistent. If the female experimenter gave positive reinforcement, the subject's percentage of total talking time increased; if she gave negative reinforcement, the response rate declined rapidly.

Figure 8.5, however, shows the results of another male subject who was given the same procedure. It is doubtful that acquisition can be said to have occurred with this subject; his percentage response showed a small increase to just above 40 percent, but then it dropped quickly to below 10 percent. Again, the neutral period had the effect of extinguishing the subject: in this case, the percentage response dropped to zero in the last two minutes.

During the first reinforcement period, the female experimenter gave positive reinforcement, and the male experimenter negative reinforcement. Under these conditions, the subject responded at the expected level (33 percent) at the beginning of the experimental session, but quickly dropped to below 10 percent from the fifth minute until the end of the session. The negative reinforcement offered by the male experimenter rapidly extinguished verbal responses of this subject, and the positive reinforcement offered by the female experimenter was not sufficient to overcome the effectiveness of the male experimenter.

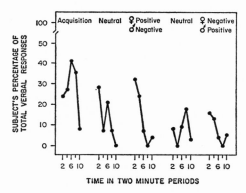

FIGURE 8.5. Effect of differential reinforcement of verbal response.

During the second neutral condition there was some indication that the subject might regain an expected level of performance, and his percentage response rate slowly rose to just under 20 percent at the end of the eighth minute of the condition. However, during the last two minutes, the response rate fell to 4 percent. When the reinforcement conditions were reversed in the final session, so that the male experimenter was giving positive reinforcement and the female experimenter negative reinforcement, the subject again showed extinction. Although these results are not so clear as those of Figure 8.4, the results indicate that this subject was sensitive to criticism per se, regardless of its origin. (Observationally, this subject was intensely interested in the problem during the acquisition and first neutral periods, but with the beginning of negative reinforcement from the male experimenter during the first reinforcement procedure, the subject became not only quiet, but surly as well. By the end of the test period, he was clearly anxious and distressed.)

Although it is impossible to form clear hypotheses from these results, both because of the problems in verbal conditioning which produce high variability, and because of the inadequacy of this particular experimental design for comparisons across subjects, the results are extremely suggestive. That subjects undergoing verbal conditioning show consistent response patterns to reinforcement as a function of individuals of different sexes offering reinforcement, points to an examination of the personality variables associated with these individual differences. It is unfortunate that the state of knowledge concerning the relevant variables which influence verbal behavior is so limited that it is impossible to attempt to make comparisons across subjects. With better control of the procedure, made possible by a better understanding of what must be controlled in such studies, it seems reasonable to suppose that such comparisons could be made, and that some fruitful hypotheses could be advanced concerning the role of personality in the determination of verbal behavior—or, perhaps more realistically, the role of verbal conditioning in determining personality.

A Pseudofixed-Interval Schedule[2]

In order to discover how well schedules of reinforcement could be controlled under conditions of social verbal reinforcement, an attempt was made to use a pseudofixed-interval schedule. The procedure for these subjects was the usual procedure used above; however, the subject was reinforced

[2] This works out actually to be a mixed extinction-crf schedule.

only during the last 30 seconds of each successive one-minute period. During the first 30 seconds the subject received neutral reinforcement. This procedure persisted throughout the entire session: no change in reinforcement schedule was made. The microphone and tape recorder were placed on a desk which also contained papers, books, etc. A desk clock was in view so that the experimenters could determine schedules. It was found after a few sessions that the experimenters used the clock only as a check (their own time-clock mechanisms, conditioned or otherwise, could predict the elapsed time interval with precision).

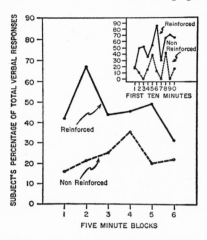

FIGURE 8.6.   Verbal behavior under pseudo-fixed-interval schedule of reinforcement.

Figure 8.6 shows the results of one subject in this group. Again the subject's response time is evaluated as the percentage of total speaking time consumed by the subject. During the first 30 seconds of neutral reinforcement, the subject's response percentage ranged between 16 and 35 percent of the total time: during the last 30 seconds of each minute when the subject's responses were reinforced, the subject's percentage of speaking time ranged between 31 and 67 percent. The subject's response percentage for the reinforced period was consistently above the percentage for the nonreinforced period; however, the percentage during the reinforced period did not show an increase over time, as one might expect from the pseudofixed-interval schedule: rather, the percentage hovers around 45 percent except for the last block.

Figure 8.7 shows the results of another subject. This subject received reinforcement during the last 15 seconds of each minute, and was not reinforced during the first 45 seconds. This figure shows successive nonreinforced periods in five-minute blocks as well as the mean percentage of non-reinforced periods in five-minute blocks. Under the pseudo-fixed-interval schedule one would expect the subject to show an increase in percentage talking time during the nonreinforced period preceding the reinforced period. Although this does occur in blocks 2-4, it was not true of the other blocks. It is possible, of course, that this expected effect would have occurred with continued testing. The results do show, however, that the subject's response rate increased during the reinforced period.

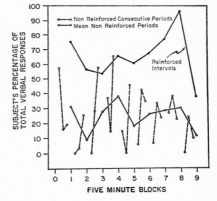

FIGURE 8.7. Verbal behavior under pseudo-fixed-interval schedule of reinforcement.

That social behavior may be examined as a function of the schedule of reinforcement seems clear; however, the difficulties encountered by the experimenters in producing such schedules, and the errors in the reinforcement program which result from this difficulty, suggest either that a great deal of practice on the part of the experimenter is necessary, or that some other design—perhaps a mechanical reinforcer—is necessary to insure accurate programming.

Summary

This chapter reports several attempts to control verbal behavior in small-group situations. Three participants, two of whom were actually experimenters, were asked to attempt to translate Chinese and American Indian ideograms into English. During the discussion the experimenters attempted to alter the response rate of the subject with different types of reinforcement and with different schedules.

The findings indicate that verbal behavior in a small-group situation is subject to the same laws of conditioning that have been found to hold for single individuals and for subhumans. The findings also suggest hypotheses concerning the influence of the verbal behavior of different participants in a small-group situation on the verbal behavior, both in terms of conformity and deviation, of an individual participant.

REFERENCES

Bachrach, A. J. The experimental analysis of behavior. In H. Lief, N. Lief, and V. Lief (Eds.), *The Psychological Basis of Medical Practice*. New York: Hoeber-Harper, in press.

Bird, C. Born 1930: The unlost generation, *Harper's Bazaar*, February, 1957.

Brunswik, E. The conceptual framework of psychology. In *International Encyclopedia of Unified Science*. Chicago: Univer. of Chicago Press, 1955. Vol. 1, part 2.

Ferster, C. B. Control of behavior in chimpanzees and pigeons by time-out from positive reinforcement. *Psychol. Monogr.*, 1958, **72** (Whole No. 461), 1–38.

Ferster, C. B., & Skinner, B. F. *Schedules of reinforcement*. New York: Appleton-Century-Crofts, 1957.

Greenspoon, J. The reinforcing effect of two spoken sounds on the frequency of two responses. *Amer. J. Psychol.*, 1955, **68**, 409–417.

Kanfer, F. H. Verbal conditioning: reinforcement schedules and experimenter influence. *Pyschol. Reports*, 1958, **4**, 443–452.

Kanfer, F. H., & Karas, S. Prior experimenter-subject interaction and verbal conditioning. *Psychol, Reports*, 1959, **5**, 345–353.

Krasner, L. Studies of the conditioning of verbal behavior. *Psychol. Bull.*, 1958, **55**, 148–171.

Mandler, G., & Kaplan, W. K. Subjective evaluation and reinforcing effect of a verbal stimulus. *Science*, 1956, **124**, 582–583.

Salzinger, K. An experimental approach to the interview. Paper read at the International Congress of Psychology, Brussels. 1957.

Salzinger, K. Experimental manipulation of verbal behavior: a review. *J. gen. Psychol.*, 1959, **61**, 65–95.

Siegel, S. *Nonparametric statistics*. New York: Mc-Graw-Hill, 1956.

Skinner, B. F. *Verbal behavior*. New York: Appleton-Century-Crofts, 1957.

Verplanck, W. S. The control of the content of conversation: reinforcement of statements of opinion. *J. abnorm. soc. Psychol.*, 1955, **51**, 668–676.

CHAPTER 9

Difference in Interview Interaction Behavior Among Normal and Deviant Groups[1]

JOSEPH D. MATARAZZO and GEORGE SASLOW
University of Oregon Medical School

Despite the importance of the topic to laymen and behavioral scientists, it is probably fair to say that students of human behavior are as uncertain today as they have always been regarding the question "what is 'normal' behavior?" One of the major reasons for the uncertainty is the difficulty in defining normal behavior (Green, 1948; Hacker, 1945; Mowrer, 1954; Shoben, 1957). Considerations which have been applied in attempted definitions are: conformity to or deviation from accepted group or cultural standards of behavior; the statistical "average"; an "ideal" norm; personal "consistency"; an absolute standard of "right and wrong" or "good and bad"; and others. Another considerations which some writers believe is relevant to this question is the role of *situational* factors. That is, can normality or abnormality be defined independently of the context in which the behavior occurs? The data to be presented below, derived from two-person interactions in which, to some degree, the situa-

[1] This investigation was supported by a research grant (M-1938) from the National Institute of Mental Health, of the National Institutes of Health, U.S. Public Health Service.

tional variable (the interviewer's behavior) has been standardized, bear upon this question.

Background of the Present Study: Previous Research on Interview Interaction Patterns

A research psychiatric interview (Chapple, 1949; Matarazzo, Saslow, & Matarazzo, 1956) similar in all respects to a typical initial interview, despite its being standardized along certain minimal dimensions, has allowed us in previous studies to investigate a number of characteristics of the overt interview interaction behavior of hundreds of patient-subjects. Standardization of this otherwise typical initial psychiatric interview has consisted of: (1) having the interviewer confine each of his comments to a duration of approximately five seconds; and (2) having him vary his behavior sequentially throughout the interview so that in three periods of the interview he carries out a free-give-and-take, nondirective type of interview, and in two other periods he places the patient in a mildly stressful situation (by remaining silent in one period and by interrupting the patient in a second stress period).

Experience with hundreds of different subjects and six different interviewers has made it clear to us that: (1) very experienced visiting psychiatrists and psychologists watching the interviews through a one-way mirror, when told nothing of the minimal standardization, cannot differentiate these interviews from the typical initial interview (that is, when the research interviewer's silence and interrupting behavior occur in their predetermined sequence, uninitiated but experienced therapists are unaware of these otherwise striking changes in the interviewer's behavior); (2) no restrictions of any kind are placed upon the *content* of the interview by the slight standardization and thus, as with other initial interviews, the interviewer follows the leads of the patient as to what is discussed in the interview, thereby placing no restriction on either patient or interviewer as to what can be discussed during the minimally standardized research interview; (3) out of hundreds studied, with one exception, no patient or normal subject has ever reported, before being told at the end of the interview, that behavioral observations were being made on him and the interviewer through a one-way mirror, or that the interview was artificial in any way; (4) contrary to what one might at first suppose, interviewers of varying levels of experience (from highly experienced psychiatrists, psychologists, and internists, on the one hand, to beginning clinical psychology fellows or psychiatric residents, and relatively inexperienced department store personnel office interviewers, on the other hand) can with minimal practice (about ten interviews) learn both to speak only in utterances of approximately five seconds throughout the whole interview and to remain silent or interrupt (again with five-second utterances) in two of the periods of the interview.

CURRENT FINDINGS.   Our results to date with the partially standardized research interview suggest that interviewee interaction patterns have the following characteristics. First, there are wide *individual differences* in interaction patterns among subjects. Second, the interviewee interaction characteristics for any given subject are highly *stable* (reliable) across two different interviewers when the latter standardize their interviewing behavior along the predefined dimensions of our standardized method. At the same time, the interviewee characteristics are highly *modifiable* by planned changes in the intrainterview behavior of either interviewer (Matarazzo, Saslow, Matarazzo, & Phillips, 1958). Third, the marked stability and reproducible modifiability of an individual's interaction patterns, found for our first sample of subjects (Saslow, Matarazzo, & Guze, 1955) could be cross-validated in a second sample (Matarazzo, Saslow, & Guze, 1956). Both these studies utilized two interviewers, each independently interviewing the same patient; and employed a test-retest interval of only a few minutes between the first and second interview. Fourth, the stability and modifiability were equally striking when only a single interviewer was used and the test-retest interval between his two interviews with the same patient was extended to seven days (Saslow, Matarazzo, Phillips, & Matarazzo, 1957); five weeks (Saslow & Matarazzo, 1959); and eight months (Saslow & Matarazzo, 1959). In addition, these various studies established high reliability for the following aspects of interview interaction behavior: the reliability of the *interviewer* who serves as the independent variable by conducting the standardized interview (Saslow & Matarazzo, 1959, pp. 135-139); the reliability of the *interviewee* interaction patterns, the dependent variables (pp. 139-148); the reliability of the *observer* who observes the interviewer-interviewee interaction and records his observations by pressing separate keys for each participant (Phillips, Matarazzo, Matarazzo, & Saslow, 1957); and, finally, the reliability of the *scorer* who scores the final Interaction Chronograph record (Saslow, Matarazzo, & Guze, 1955, p. 429).

VALIDITY STUDIES.   Having established unusually high reliabilities for these interview interaction behaviors, we have thus far approached the question of their validity from a number of points of view; amounting largely to what Cronbach and Meehl (1955, pp. 286–287) call the "bootstraps" method. The first of these studies (Matarazzo, Saslow, & Hare, 1958), a factor analysis of 12 of the interview interaction variables, revealed that the standardized interview was made up of two stable and independent factors: *silence* behavior and *action* behavior (i.e., duration of the interactee's habitual silence, or latency, before speaking; and the average duration of each of his utterances, or actions). Two weaker factors also emerged: *initiative* behavior and *adjustment* behavior (the frequency with which a subject initiates or starts again with another communication of his own when his partner has not answered him; and the efficiency with which a member of the communicating pair adjusts or maladjusts to his partner by waiting too long and by interrupting).

A second validity study reported a number of interesting psychological test and organismic correlates of interview interaction patterns (Matarazzo, Matarazzo, Saslow, & Philips, 1958). The third study, now being replicated, investigated the relationship between some aspects of the verbal content of the interview and the formal (temporal) overt interviewee interaction patterns (Phillips, 1957). Our fourth approach to the validity problem (Hare, Waxler, Saslow, & Matarazzo, 1960) involved the simultaneous recording of Bales Interaction Process scores and our own interview interaction measures in 24 interviews, and a comparison of the relationships between the two sets of independently determined interview measures.

The first of the validity studies (factor analysis) was an attempt to establish what Cronbach and Meehl (1955, p. 287) call construct validity, while the last three are more properly attempts to demonstrate concurrent validity (American Psychological Association, 1954).

Another validity study (of concurrent validity) furnished the data for the present discussion. This study was designed to investigate the differences, if any, between the interviewee interaction behaviors of subjects in five different diagnostic *groups,* all of whom were interviewed by use of the minimally standardized interview method. It is thus a follow-up of some interesting observations made in 1942 by Chapple and Lindemann (Chapple, 1942; Chapple & Lindemann, 1942) that the interview behavior of different psychiatric patients might show such large differences as to be singularly important in the differential diagnosis of one type of psychiatric patient from another type. Since Chapple and Lindemann, in their

two preliminary communications, presented interview interaction curves for only one or two patient-subjects in each of
nine diagnostic subgroups, we felt it important to study the
interview behavior of larger samples of subjects. In addition,
since 1942, several new interview variables (Chapple, 1949)
have been added by Chapple to his interview recording device, the Interaction Chronograph. These additions permitted us to investigate a greater number of interviewee
characteristics.

LIMITATIONS. We would have liked, in the present study,
to investigate the interview behavior of a variety of well-
defined specific psychiatric groups. However, in view of the
commonly recognized, notoriously low reliability of specific
psychiatric differential diagnoses (Ash, 1949; Gleser, Haddock, Starr, & Ulett, 1954; Hunt, Wittson, & Hunt, 1953;
Raines & Rohrer, 1955), we limited ourselves, in our first
approach to the problem, to a study of differences, if any,
in broadly defined psychiatric groups. The above investigators have shown that while one typically finds low interjudge agreement among psychatric specialists on such specific
diagnoses as "anxiety neurosis" or "manic-depressive psy-
chosis," one finds very high interjudge reliability for such
broad diagnostic categories as "neurotic" versus "psychotic."
This study is therefore limited to an investigation of differences, if any, among the following broad groups of subjects:
normals (two groups); a group of outpatient neurotics; a
group of mixed outpatient and inpatient neurotics and psychotics; and a group of chronic, hospitalized psychotics (a
very carefully selected group of chronic schizophrenics who
were being studied by a variety of biochemical and other research methods).

Procedure

Specifically, the five groups consisted of: (1) 19 highly
selected, chronic (all hospitalized uninterruptedly for a mean

of 8.3 years, range 3 to 18 years), white, male, schizophrenic patients (diagnosis agreed upon by two experienced psychiatrists in each case), ranging in age from 27 to 42 (mean, 33), who were interviewed by us at the Research Facility of the (New York) Rockland State Hospital;[2] (2) 40 unselected mixed acute psychotic and neurotic patients, 14 inpatients and 26 outpatients, 25 females and 15 males, all white, and ranging in age from 15 to 80 (mean, 40) from the Massachusetts General Hospital in Boston; (3) 60 unselected, primarily neurotic outpatients, all white, 32 female, 28 male, ranging in age from 16 to 62 (mean, 33), from the Washington University School of Medicine (St. Louis) Department of Psychiatry Outpatient Clinic; (4) 40 unselected normals, who were applicants for sales jobs, 20 female, 20 male, all white, from Gilchrist's Department Store in Boston; and (5) 17 unselected normals, who also were applicants for sales jobs, 14 female, 3 male, all of whom were white, from Carson-Pirie-Scott Department Store in Chicago.

RECORDING INTERVIEW INTERACTION BEHAVIOR. The recording of interview observations for all five groups was by Chapple's Interaction Chronograph (Matarazzo, Saslow, & Matarazzo, 1956). This instrument, a large computer which is activated by an observer from the other side of a one-way mirror while the interviewer is conducting the previously described minimally standardized interview, with a single interviewee, permits the continuous and simultaneous measurement and recording of such interviewee and interviewer interaction variables as: the number of *units* of each person's interaction; duration of each of these *actions;* the duration of each *silence;* the frequency with which the interviewee takes the *initiative* during a subperiod in which the interviewer

[2] We would like to thank Alfred M. Stanley, M.D., Nathan S. Kline, M.D., and other members of the medical, nursing, and research staff for the considerable time and effort they contributed on our behalf in the execution of this study.

TABLE 9.1.   Definitions of the Interaction Variables Studied

1. S's Units:	The number of times the subject acted.
2. S's Action:[a]	The average duration of the subject's actions.
3. S's Silence:[a]	The average duration of the subject's silences.
4. S's Tempo:[a]	The average duration of each action plus its following inaction as a single measure.
5. S's Activity:[a]	The average duration of each action minus its following inaction, as a single measure.
6. S's Adjustment:[a]	The durations of the subject's interruptions minus the durations of his failures to respond, divided by S's Units.
7. Interviewer's Adjustment:[a]	The durations of the interviewer's interruptions minus the durations of his failures to respond, divided by S's Units.
8. S's Synchronization:	The number of times the subject either interrupted or failed to respond to the interviewer, divided by the number of S's Units.
9. Interviewer's Units:	The number of times the interviewer acted.
10. S's Initiative:	The percent of times, out of the available number of opportunities (usually 12) in Period 2, in which the subject acted again (within a 15-second limit) following his own last action.
11. S's Quickness:[a]	The average length of time in Period 2 that the subject waited before taking the initiative following his own last action.
12. S's Dominance:	The number of times (out of 12) in Period 4 that the subject talked down the interviewer minus the number of times the interviewer talked down the subject, divided by the number of S's Units in the Period.

[a] Values for these variables are recorded in hundredths of a minute. To convert to seconds multiply the given value by 0.6.

purposely reacts with silence by failing to respond to the interviewee's last utterance; the frequency of each participant's *interruptions* and the resulting dominances and submissions; and several other variables.

Definitions of the 12 interview interaction variables studied in the five groups comprising the present study are given in Table 9.1. Chapple's own early experiences with interviewers, each of whom used his own individual interviewing style (Chapple, 1940; 1949; 1953; and Chapple & Arensberg, 1949), and the results of the recent studies on verbal conditioning (Krasner, 1958), all indicate the need for some minimal control or standardization of the interviewer's behavior if the clinical interview is to be used as a research tool. To this end, Chapple suggested some simple rules to guide the interviewer's behavior. In addition, prescribing that the interviewer behave in a number of different specified ways as the interview proceeds, standardizes the interview so that it is possible to sample a larger portion of the interviewee's repertoire of interaction responses. Therefore, unknown to the interviewee, the standardized interview is divided into five periods, with Periods 1, 3, and 5 as free (essentially nondirective interviewing) give-and-take periods, and Period 2 (silence) and Period 4 (interruption) as stress phases of the interview.

The characteristics of such a partially standardized interview are shown in Table 9.2, whereas the "rules" governing the interviewer's behavior have been standardized by (Matarazzo, Saslow & Guze, 1956) and are given in Table 9.3. Essentially these rules require that the interviewer: (1) speak in utterances of approximately five seconds each time he speaks, (2) verbally respond to the interviewee's last remark quickly (with a latency of one second or less) in the three free periods, (3) fail to respond to the interviewee's last remark 12 times in Period 2 (our interviewers inconspicuously count these and the interruptions in Period 4 by using a heavy string

with 12 knots on it), and (4) verbally interrupt the interviewee each time he speaks, for a total of 12 times in
Period 4.

As can be seen in Table 9.2, with its two stress periods and
three nonstress periods, the standardized interview provides
a means for eliciting a sample of interviewees' behaviors (dependent variables) in a complex, but miniature interpersonal
situation, the characteristics of which (the time dimension of

TABLE 9.2.   Characteristics of the Standardized Interview

Period	Type of Inter-viewing	Duration of Period Fixed Duration	Variable Duration
1	Free	10 minutes	
2	Stress (Silence)		12 failures to re-spond, or 15 min-utes, whichever is shorter
3	Free	5 minutes	
4	Stress (Interruption)		12 interruptions, or 15 minutes, whichever is shorter
5	Free	5 minutes	
Total		20 minutes	plus a maximum of 30 more min-utes

the interviewer's behavior) to a certain degree are objective
and predefined (independent variables). Because of the variable duration of the two stress periods, the standardized
interview can vary in length from approximately 25 minutes
to 50 minutes (in practice, the mean length turns out to be
about 32 minutes and the entire range is utilized).

In the present study three different interviewers were used.
One, an experienced male psychiatrist, interviewed each of
the subjects in the three patient groups. The second and third
interviewers, both female, were experienced interviewers

TABLE 9.3. Rules for Interviewer

Periods 1 to 5 (all periods):
  a. Interviewer introduces each period by a 5-second utterance (following his signal to the observer).
  b. All interviewing must be *nondirective*. No direct questions, no probing or depth interviewing. Interviewer can reflect, ask for clarification, ask for more information, introduce a new topic area, etc. In general, interviewer's comments should be nonchallenging and open-ended and related to the subject's past comments or to some new, general topic.
  c. All interactions must be verbal only, or verbal and gestural at the same time; i.e., interviewer cannot use head nods and other gestures alone. This rule simplifies the observer's task.
  d. All of interviewer's utterances must be of approximately *5-seconds'* duration.
  e. After subject finishes a comment or other interaction, interviewer must respond in less than 1 *second,* except as otherwise noted in Period 2.
  f. Each time subject interrupts interviewer, the latter must continue to talk for 2 more seconds. This rule insures more explicit definition of a subject's ascendance-submission pattern than would be possible if interviewer "submitted" immediately.

Periods 1, 3, and 5:
  a. Interviewer must never interrupt subject.
  b. If, after interviewer makes a comment, subject does not respond, interviewer must wait 15 *seconds* and then speak again for 5 seconds.

Period 2 only:
  a. Interviewer must "fail to respond" to last interaction of subject a total of 12 times (or for 15 minutes, whichever is shorter).
  b. After interviewer has been silent for 15 seconds (and subject has not taken initiative) interviewer makes another 5-second comment.

Period 4 only:
  a. Each time subject acts, interviewer must interrupt subject for 5 seconds for a total of 12 times.
  b. Interviewer's interruption should begin about 3 seconds after subject has begun his action.
  c. After having interrupted subject, if the subject continues through the interruption (does not submit), interviewer will not interrupt again until subject has finished his utterance, i.e., interviewer will interrupt subject only once during each utterance of the latter if subject does not "yield."
  d. The period is ended after 12 interruptions or 15 minutes of attempting to obtain these.

from the personnel departments of their respective department stores. Earlier research with different interviewers (Saslow & Matarazzo, 1959) has shown that the reliability across different *interviewers* is very high for the interview interaction variables investigated in the present study. Thus, there is every reason to assume that, for all practical purposes, any differences found in the five subject-groups are probably not a function of interviewer differences. Evidence supporting this assumption is to be found in the present study. The many similarities between the interview behaviors of the two normal groups, who were interviewed in two different cities by two different interviewers, and the many differences among the three different patient samples, all of whom were interviewed by the *same* interviewer, provide suggestive evidence that the variance contributed by different interviewers is probably much less important than is the variance due to differences in subjects. Thus our three interviewers in this study, all following the rules of the standardized interview, could be thought of as essentially one interviewer.

The subjects, however, cannot all be said to have had the same "set." The three patient groups obviously were being interviewed by a psychiatrist in a psychiatric setting. The two groups of normal subjects were in a personnel department being interviewed for a sales job. Nevertheless, it is our opinion, based on interviewing both job applicants and patient groups, that the "set" of the subject as to the purpose of the interview probably is a less important variable than is his broadly defined mental health status (namely, normal, neurotic, and psychotic). We are currently exploring ways of experimentally manipulating "set" as an independent varible and, thus, hope soon to be better able to examine our guess that this variable probably contaminated the present study only minimally, if at all. Normal groups such as the ones we have used here have been employed by other investigators successfully as comparison groups for patient populations, despite the fact that, in other studies, as well as our own, normal Ss understandably have a different "set" than do psychiatric patients.

RESULTS.   Table 9.4 presents, for each of the five groups, means and standard deviations for the 12 interview inter-action variables recorded during the partially standardized interview. The first nine of these variables show the mean scores obtained for each group on the basis of the total inter-view (i.e., means based on the total of all five periods), while the last three variables are means from the scores of only one period (Period 2 or Period 4) of the interview.

Several findings are immediately apparent from the results presented in Table 9.4: (1) the large number of significant differences present in the interview behavior of each of the three patient groups, comparing each group with every other, and each of these with each of the two normal groups; and (2) the fact that these differences among means reach an un-usually high degree of statistical significance (see second column from the right in Table 9.4) despite the very consider-able individual differences *within* each of the five broad diag-nostic groups (as shown by the large standard deviations) for all of the 12 variables.

Statistical analysis of the data presented in Table 9.4 con-sisted of a standard analysis of variance of independent groups by F-test (McNemar, 1955) of the differences across the means of the five groups. Table 9.4 shows that the differences in means across the five groups reached the .001 level of prob-ability for 10 of the 12 variables, and the .05 level of probabil-ity for one variable, *S's Initiative*. Only one variable, *S's Quickness* in Period 2, failed to discriminate the means of the five groups.

It is clear from Table 9.4 that the standard deviations ob-tained for each of the 12 interview variables differ widely from group to group, thus suggesting nonhomogeneity of variance among these five populations. Statistical confirmation of this suggestion is given in the last column on the right in Table 9.4, where are shown the probability levels of Bartlett's F-test for the homogeneity of variances (McNemar, 1955, p. 247). Having thus demonstrated nonhomogeneity of variance some investigators would not have employed the previously discussed F-test across means. However, inspection and comparison of the frequency distributions of individual subjects in each of the five groups; the obtaining of *identical*[3] significance levels by the use of a nonparametric statistic, the Kruskal-Wallis One Way Analysis of Variance by Ranks (Siegel, 1956, p. 184); and knowledge of the results of Norton's study (quoted in Lindquist, 1953, pp. 78–86), which showed that analysis of variance is still appropriate with distributions like those reported here—all combined to justify the use of conventional analysis of variance.

Table 9.5 presents the significance levels of differences in means between pairs of the diagnostic groups shown in Table 9.4. Similar data for the standard deviations shown in Table 9.4 are given in Table 9.6. Table 9.5 shows that whereas the two normal groups differ from each other on only several interview variables, and whereas the three patient groups differ from each other only a little more, the normal groups clearly differ from each of the three patient groups on most of the interview interaction variables.

The data in Tables 9.4, 9.5, and 9.6 are presented primarily as an overall summary of the results. Because of the many interesting differences found, and because frequency distributions for individual interview variables have not previously been published, we feel it useful to present for each of the 12 variables the frequency distributions of the actual mean score for the total interview *of each subject* in each of the

[3] The only difference from the probability levels shown in the second column from the right in Table 9.4 was that the significance level of *S's Initiative* now attained a probability value of .02 instead of the previous .05 value.

TABLE 9.4. Total Interview Interaction Scores: Means, Standard Deviations, and F-Tests Over Five Samples

Interview Variable		Chronic Psychotics (N=19)	Mixed Psychotics and Neurotics (N=40)	Neurotics (N=60)	Normals Gilchrist's (N=40)	Normals Carson's (N=17)	P Level of F-Test	P Level of Bartlett's
1. S's Units	M	80.95	87.22	72.00	46.82	45.24	.001	.001
	SD	34.93	29.02	23.34	13.52	17.56		
2. S's Action	M	51.63	32.12	40.77	88.72	101.24	.001	.001
	SD	67.65	22.24	25.64	48.53	62.23		
3. S's Silence	M	10.53	9.00	9.08	11.15	8.43	.001	.001
	SD	4.93	1.85	3.16	2.26	2.03		
4. S's Tempo	M	62.68	41.52	50.82	100.30	109.47	.001	.001
	SD	65.24	22.51	24.26	49.16	62.25		
5. S's Activity	M	40.95	23.42	32.92	78.05	92.53	.001	.001
	SD	70.39	22.40	26.15	47.75	62.07		
6. S's Adjustment	M	−3.36	−.46	−1.12	−.06	−.01	.001	.001
	SD	3.44	.79	1.26	.49	.32		
7. Int.s' Adjustment	M	−1.46	−2.12	−1.92	−2.92	−1.65	.001	.001
	SD	1.27	.80	.95	1.49	1.44		
Int.'s Adjustment (1, 3, 5 only)	M	−.64	−.71	−.56	−.90	−.76	.05	.001
	SD	.21	.24	.40	.94	.40		
8. S's Synchron	M	.97	.88	.84	.67	.82	.001	.001
	SD	.10	.06	.07	.17	.08		
9. Int.'s Units	M	73.53	70.60	60.56	39.00	42.00	.001	.001
	SD	35.64	26.86	21.23	12.96	15.54		
10. S's Initiative[a]	M	.59	.72	.72	.62	.69	.05	
	SD	.28	.20	.20	.20	.14		
11. S's Quickness[a]	M	−11.50	−11.75	−10.35	−12.59	−11.22		.02
	SD	7.66	4.45	4.48	4.19	4.61		
12. S's Dominance[a]	M	−.67	−.55	−.40	−.10	.28	.001	.001
	SD	.24	.24	.27	.50	.54		

[a] Two of these variables (10 and 11 are recorded only in Period 2, whereas one variable (12) is recorded only in Period 4.

TABLE 9.5. Significance Levels of t-Tests[a] of Differences Between Means of Pairs of Diagnostic Groups

Interview Variable	Pairs of Diagnostic Groups[b] Being Compared									
	S—M[a]	S—O	S—N1	S—N2	M—O	M—N1	M—N2	O—N1	O—N2	N1—N2
1. S's Units			.001	.001	.01	.001	.001	.001	.001	
2. S's Action			.01	.001		.001	.001	.001	.001	
3. S's Silence				.05		.001		.001		.01
4. S's Tempo			.001	.001		.001	.001	.001	.001	
5. S's Activity			.01	.001		.001	.001	.001	.001	
6. S's Adjust.	.001	.001	.001	.001	.05			.001	.01	
7. Int.'s Adjust	.05		.001			.01		.001		.001
8. S's Synchron.	.001	.001	.001	.001	.05	.001	.05	.001		.001
9. Int.'s Units		.05	.001	.001	.05	.001	.001	.001	.01	
10. S's Initiative	.02	.01				.05		.02		
11. S's Quickness								.05		
12. S's Dominance		.01	.001	.001	.05	.001	.001	.001	.001	.001

[a] See McNemar (1955, p. 259) for a description of the t-test used.
[b] S is Schizophrenics; M is mixed MGH in- and outpatients; O is WU outpatients; N1 is Gilchrist's normals; and N2 is Carson's normals.

TABLE 9.6. Significance Levels of t-Tests[a] of Differences Beween Variances of Pairs of Diagnostic Groups

Interview Variable	Pairs of Diagnostic Groups[b] Being Compared									
	S–M[a]	S–O	S–N1	S–N2	M–O	M–N1	M–N2	O–N1	O–N2	N1–N2
1. S's Units		.02	.002	.02		.002	.02	.002		
2. S's Action	.002	.002	.002			.002	.002	.002	.002	
3. S's Silence	.002	.02	.002	.002	.002			.02		
4. S's Tempo	.002	.002				.002	.002	.002	.002	
5. S's Activity	.002	.002	.02			.002	.002	.002	.002	
6. S's Adjust.	.002	.002	.002	.002	.002	.002	.002	.002	.002	
7 Int.'s Adjust.	.02					.002	.02	.002		
8. S's Synchron.	.002		.02			.002		.002		.002
9. Int.'s Units		.02	.002	.002	.02	.002	.02	.002		
10. S's Initiative		.02		.02						
11. S's Quickness	.02	.002	.002							
12. S's Dominance			.002	.02		.002	.002	.002	.002	

[a] See McNemar (1955, p. 259) for a description of the t-test used.

[b] S is Schizophrenics; M is mixed MGH in- and outpatients; O is WU outpatients; N1 is Gilchrist's normals; and N2 is Carson's normals.

five groups. These are presented in Figures 9.1 through 9.12. For nine of the interaction variables, the mean score for the total interview was obtained for every individual, and this mean score for each individual S is shown as a single square in nine of the figures. For the remaining three variables, similar data are shown for the appropriate single period of the interview. The frequency distributions thus obtained allow one to gain a picture of the range of individual differences *within* each of the five diagnostic groups, as well as differences in means *between* diagnostic groups.

The results for several of these variables will now be described in greater detail. From Figure 9.1 it is clear that with the interviewer's behavior minimally standardized as shown in Tables 9.2 and 9.3, normals, as a group, interact only about half as often (medians of 41.0 and 44.0) during the interview as do the schizophrenics of this study (median of 85); with the neurotic group (median of 66.7) and mixed neurotic-psychotic group (median of 80.0) falling in between. Figure 9.1 also clearly shows the considerable differences among individual subjects *within* each of the five groups. Thus, during the same standardized (total) interview, one normal had 15 interaction units, while another had 81. Despite these individual differences, however, *not a single normal subject earned an S's Units score above the median of both the mixed (neurotic-psychotic) group and the schizophrenic group.* Since each of the subjects in the three patient groups was reinterviewed in a subsequent reliability check on the interviewee scores (Saslow & Matarazzo, 1959), and the results for all individuals were strikingly similar to those obtained in the first interview and shown in Figures 9.1 through 9.12 (test-retest coefficients of correlation for all of the data shown in Figures 9.1 through 9.12 were typically of the order of .75 or larger); and since the surprisingly similar results of either of the normal groups shown in Table 9.4 and Figures 9.1 through 9.12 could be used for inferring the reliability of the findings in the other normal group, one can assume that the results presented in Tables 9.4, 9.5, and 9.6, and Figures 9.11 through 9.12 represent *highly stable behavioral characteristics* which appear to be *unique and reproducible* for any given subject. For this reason, the differences demonstrated *among the*

FREQUENCY DISTRIBUTIONS: S's UNITS

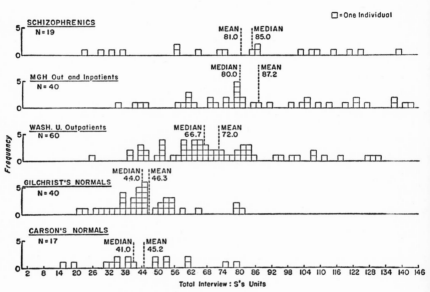

FIGURE 9.1.   Frequency distributions: S's units.

different groups are more reliable than is often the case in research of the type here reported.

Using a somewhat different interaction measure—Bales Interaction Process Analysis (based on content)—Roberts and Strodtbeck (1953) were able to demonstrate certain differences in interactional characteristics between psychiatric groups. One of their findings was that, in group therapy sessions, paranoid schizophrenics had a significantly higher *rate* of interaction than did depressed patients. This finding was consistent with expectations based on reported clinical differences between these two groups. Thus, the data in our Figure 9.1, showing clear differences in the interaction rate (frequency) of our five groups, is consistent with the findings of Roberts and Strodtbeck.

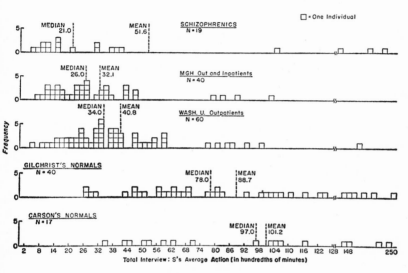

FIGURE 9.2. Frequency distributions: S's action.

Figure 9.2 adds another dimension to the results shown in Figure 9.1. From the former it is clear that, although normals speak less often than do neurotics, mixed neurotics-psychotics, and psychotics, in that order (Figure 9.1), they speak in utterances (Actions) two to four times as long, on the average, as those of the three patient groups (medians of 97.0 and 78.0 versus 34.0, 26.0, and 21.0, respectively). The results shown in Figure 9.2 are not surprising after knowledge of the results of Figure 9.1 since, in a previous study (Matarazzo, Saslow,

& Hare, 1958), we have reported a highly significant cross-validated correlation of (minus) .73 between number of S's Units and average duration of each of these units (S's Action).

Like Figure 9.1, Figure 9.2 reveals considerable variation

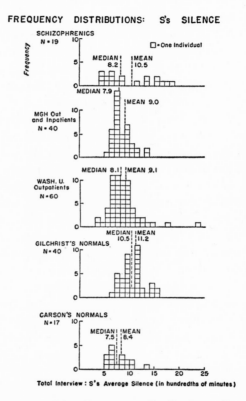

FIGURE 9.3. Frequency distributions: S's silence.

among individuals within each of the five groups. Again *not one* normal subject (out of the 57 Ss in the two normal groups) earned an average duration of action score below the median (21.0) of the schizophrenic group or the mixed group

(26.0); while only four of them (7 percent) earned a score below the median (34.0) of the neurotic group.

INTERPRETATIONS.   From Figures 9.1 and 9.2 it can be concluded that, on the average, compared to our schizophrenics (and two remaining patient groups), normals speak significantly less often in interviews but with longer (average) utterances per communication unit. That not all normals (or all schizophrenics, neurotics, etc.) are alike on either of these two interview interactions variables, or any of the other variables, is also strikingly clear from the results obtained. In fact, the results obtained strongly suggest that the differences *within* any group are probably just as important as the differences between groups. For example, from Figure 9.2 it can be hypothesized that the four schizophrenics with the longest duration of action scores (extreme right at top of Figure 9.2) might conceivably constitute one subtype (e.g., schizo-affective while those at the extreme left might constitute another subtype (e.g., catatonia). Thus the method of measurement herein described conceivably may be useful in providing helpful objective information for use in differential diagnosis within patient groups, as well as between broad patient and normal groups. To accomplish this will, of course, require adequate consideration of differences in base rates of such diagnostic groups. Since in this study we were more interested in the results as they apply to personality theory rather than to diagnosis per se, we have not pursued in detail the implications of the results for individual diagnosis. Application of the Interaction Chronograph method to individual diagnosis will require further refinements in the measurement and definitions of the interaction variables.

Another implication in the data shown in Figure 9.2 (or, for that matter in the whole of Table 9.4 and each of the 11 remaining figures) is worth mentioning. One can assume for heuristic purposes that the five groups presented in Figure

9.2 are arranged according to a crude scale of *degree of mental health;* i.e., from normal, through mildly disturbed (neurotic), through more disturbed (mixed neurotic-psychotic), through very disturbed (chronic schizophrenics). If this can be accepted as a rough index of severity of behavioral disorder or, in retrospective operational terms, the degree of likelihood that one will be a normal, an outpatient, or a

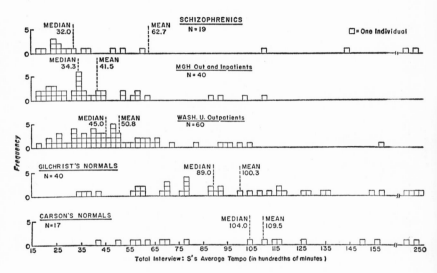

FIGURE 9.4.   Frequency distributions: S's tempo.

chronic inpatient, then the data in Figure 9.2 suggest that the longer a person's interview actions the higher the probability that he is healthy. This hypothesis could be checked in a variety of ways. For example, normals could be rated as to degree of emotional health by use of any of the available objective anxiety scales. It could be hypothesized from Table 9.2 that subjects with the higher anxiety scores will have the shorter interview action scores. Similarly, neurotic outpatients judged to be improved (by suitable criteria) might be expected to be speaking in longer average interview utterances at the end of psychotherapy than at the beginning; i.e., be more like the normals in Figure 9.2 at the end of therapy than like the neurotics.

An indirect finding in a study by Phillips (1957) suggests that this method of reasoning may have some merit. Con-

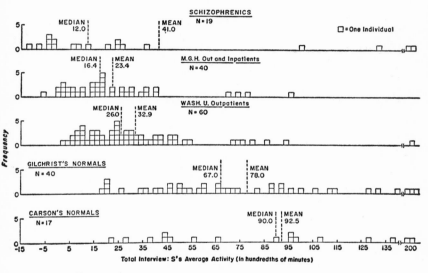

FIGURE 9.5.   Frequency distributions: S's activity.

sistent with the findings shown in Figure 9.2, Phillips found that the more highly introspective, self-centered (schizoid) individuals, as determined from a subject's interview *content,* tended to have shorter average interview actions. Persons who spoke significantly more often per unit time about other people and other aspects of interpersonal behavior (i.e., were not therefore judged "schizoid") tended to speak in longer interview actions.

Phillips' data also showed that her schizoid subjects had longer average negative adjustment scores when compared to all other patients. Figure 9.6 of the present study shows that the maladjustment variable may be one of the most effective for discriminating our schizophrenic group from each of the four other groups. This variable, an algebraic measure of a subject's durations of interruptions of the interviewer minus

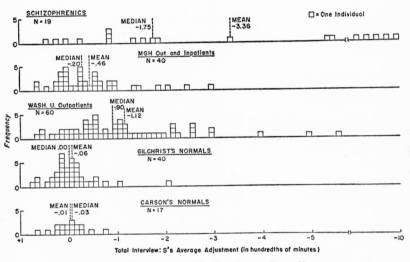

FIGURE 9.6. Frequency distributions: S's adjustment.

his durations of failures to respond to the interviewer (i.e., an algebraic sum of his two types of maladjustments), yields scores of essentially zero for our two normal groups (medians of .00 and −.03 hundredths of a minute, respectively). This means that, in terms of duration measures, our normal Ss may have tended to interrupt and fail to respond about an equal amount. Inspection of the raw data from which the scores shown in Figure 9.6 were obtained reveals that, in fact, these normals did little interrupting and failing to respond. Thus, for normals, the differences between these two measures, interruptions minus failures to respond, or S's Adjustment, distribute themselves around a mean and median of 0.00 (see Figure 9.6), with failures to respond contributing most of the relatively small variance which is present. (In a

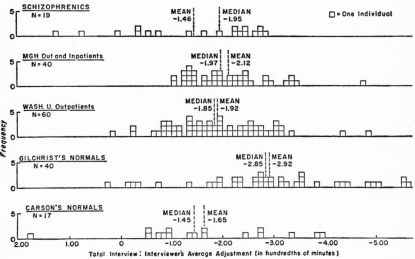

FIGURE 9.7. Frequency distributions: Interviewer's adjustment.

recently completed new sample of 40 normal Ss, 20 policeman and 20 fireman applicants, an r of .992 was found between *S's Adjustment* and *S's Latency,* or failure to respond; thus indicating that, for this new group of normals, Chapple's *S's Adjustment* variable is exclusively a measure of durations of failures to respond, rather than durations of interruptions.)

For schizophrenics, however, it does *not* appear that the algebraic sums of durations of failures to respond and durations of interruptions distribute themselves around a mean and median of 0.00 or that the distributions of each of these two subparts deviate from zero very little. The data in Figure 9.6, as well as inspection of the raw data, show that few, if any, of the normals but two thirds of the schizophrenics had relatively long latencies: median and mean for the algebraically determined adjustment score for the schizophrenics was −1.75 and −3.36 hundredths of a minute, respectively. That

FREQUENCY DISTRIBUTIONS: S's SYNCHRONIZATION

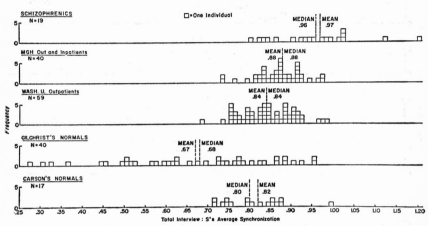

FIGURE 9.8. Frequency distributions: S's synchronization.

is, since the Interaction Chronograph does not yield separate interruption and latency scores but, rather, gives one algebraic sum of the two, these data reveal that the average schizophrenic failed to respond to the interviewer longer than he interrupted: with a *median* duration of (1.75 times 0.6), or 1.05 seconds; and a *mean* of (3.36 times 0.6) or 2.02 seconds. Thus, relative to his own durations of interruptions, the typical schizophrenic subject often waited longer (by an average of one to two seconds) before responding to the interviewer's last comment. Clinicians have long considered long latencies as almost pathognomonic of schizophrenia. Phillips' results with schizoid neurotics, and our own results shown in Figure 9.6, are an objective demonstration of the usefulness of "long latency" as a clinical sign. Thus, the results in Figure 9.6, in our group of 19 schizophrenic subjects, bear out the report by Chapple and Lindemann (1942, p. 6) based on just a few cases that "one of the most characteristic diagnostic factors (seen in the Interaction Chronograph behavior) in schizophrenia is the so-called blocking and latency of response"; i.e., high negative adjustment scores.

The values for *S's Adjustment* in Figure 9.6 and Table 9.4 are shown in *hundredths of a minute*. Conversion of the *means* for this variable into *seconds* yields the following average *S's Adjustment* for the values shown in Table 9.4; schizophrenics, −2.02 seconds; mixed neurotics-psychotics, −.28 seconds; neurotics, −.67 seconds; Gilchrist normals, 0.04 (.036) seconds; and Carson normals, .01 (.006) seconds. The range, therefore, is from .01 seconds or less, for normals, to 2.02 seconds for the schizophrenic group: a two-hundred-fold range. Statistical analysis bears out these striking differences, since Table 9.5 shows that, for the S's Adjustment variable, each of the patient groups differ at a high level of probability from each other, and from each of the normal groups, while the normal groups do *not* differ from each other.

The *mean values for the Interviewer Adjustment* score shown in Table 9.4 and Figure 9.7 range from −1.46 to −2.92 *hundredths* of a minute; or from −.88 to −1.75 seconds. The adjustment behavior of the three interviewers with these five groups was thus from approximately .9 seconds to 1.8 seconds; a two-fold range. However, since the standardized interview (Tables 9.2 and 9.3) calls for the interviewer to "maladjust" in two periods (i.e., by failing to respond up to 15 seconds for each of 12 times in Period 2, and by interrupting the subject 12 times in Period 4), the values for *Interviewer Adjustment* in Table 9.4 and Figure 9.7 contain a built-in artifact.

A better (but due to some machine measurement short-comings, by no means perfect) measure of interviewer's adjustment can be derived from the three free give-and-take, nonstress periods. Values in hundredths of a minute for

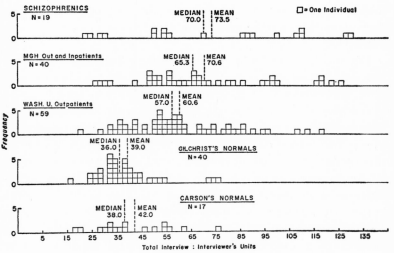

FIGURE 9.9.   Frequency distributions: Interviewer's units.

mean *Interviewer's Adjustment* for these three periods are also shown under variable number 7 in Table 9.4. They range from −.56 to −.90 hundredths of a minute. Converted into seconds the five interviewer values, from left to right in Table 9.4 are −.38, −.43, −.34, −.54, and −.46 seconds, respectively. Thus, as they followed the rule to "respond within one second" in these three periods, our interviewers, themselves, had a range of adjustment to different subject groups from .34 to .54 seconds. As shown in Table 9.4 these differences still reach the .05 level of probability. However, despite this statistically demonstrable difference among our interviewers, the difference between responding to an interviewee within a third of a second (.34) and within a half second (.54), may be unimportant, for all practical purposes. When one takes into account the reaction time of the observer, a difference of .20 seconds is certainly an acceptable error. Whether or not it is, however, is still not as important as the fact that the five groups themselves had a two-hundred-fold range (.01 to 2.02 seconds) in adjustment compared to the interviewer's one-and-one-half-fold range (.34 to .54 seconds).[4]

For interviewees, it is clear from the results shown in Figure 9.6 that, as suggested by Chapple and Lindemann (1942, p. 6), a negative S's Adjustment score may very well be "one of the most characteristic diagnostic factors in schizophrenia." However, despite the strong confirmation of this suggestion in our own results, it is also clear to us that measurement of this variable will have to include *individual* recording of *both* its components, as well as their algebraic sum. That is, modifications will have to be made in the Interaction Chronograph, or similar recording devices, in order to permit *separate* measurement of S's durations of interruptions and failures to respond. These separate scores could then be algebraically added, thus yielding the present S's Adjustment score as well as its two individual components. In this way an analysis is possible of the proportion of each of these two types of maladjustment in each S's Adjustment score. It may very well be that normals as well as different patient groups

[4] As previously mentioned, when converted to hundredths of a minute, these interviewer adjustment scores (derived from Periods 1, 3, and 5) range from .56 to .90 hundredths of a minute. As can be seen in Figure 9.6, these two interviewer values are well within the range of scores obtained by the Ss in the two normal groups. Thus, the adjustment scores of our interviewers, themselves, are more like those of all our normal Ss than they are like those of many of our patient Ss.

differ in the extent to which they display each of the two types of maladjustments.

As shown in Table 9.4 and Figure 9.12, another interaction variable which shows considerable differences between the normal and patient groups is *S's Dominance*. This variable is recorded only in Period 4 where the interviewer in a standardized manner interrupts the interviewee 12 times. (Because of unusually long durations of responses for some Ss, and following standardized procedure as shown in Table 9.2, the actual interruption units in Period 4 have occasionally, but not often, numbered only 10. Likewise, at the other end of the range, due to observer or interviewer error, they have sometimes numbered 13 or 14.) Following Chapple, the formula for obtaining S's Dominance in Period 4 which we have used to date is as follows:

S's Dominance =

$$\frac{\text{No. of S's Dominances} - \text{No. of Int's. Dominances}}{\text{No. of S's Units in Period 4}}$$

Thus, if the interviewer interrupts 12 times, and S each time continues to talk (i.e., thereby dominating the interviewer in each of the 12 interviewer interruptions), S's Dominance score would be 12 − 0 divided by 12, or + 1.00. If, on the other hand, S quickly quit talking each time the interviewer interrupted, thus permitting the interviewer (who talks for 5 seconds each time he interrupts) to dominate each unit, S's Dominance score would be 0 − 12 divided by 12, or − 1.00. Thus, S's Dominance score can range from − 1.00 for the S who submits to each of 12 interviewer interruptions to + 1.00 for the S who continues to talk through each interviewer interruption. An S who dominates 6 times and submits 6 times would earn a score of 0.00.

As can be seen in Figure 9.12, only four patients (3 percent) out of the 119 in the 3 patient groups earned plus scores (i.e., greater than 0.00). On the other hand, 28 (49 percent) out of the 57 normal Ss earned such plus Dominance scores (shown to the left of o.oo in Figure 9.12). It is clear then, that during the 12 prearranged interviewer interruptions, one out of every two of the normal Ss in this study, versus one out of every 33 patients, dominated the interviewer more often (or at least as often) as he dominated them. In the group of Carson's normals 13 out of 17 (76 percent) had plus Dominance scores whereas only 4 (24 percent) had minus Dominance scores; the actual mean and median Dominance score being +.28 and +.39, respectively. As also shown in Figure 9.12 the Gilchrist normals, on the other hand, contained more Ss with minus Dominance scores, thus yielding a mean and median of −.10 and −.14. Despite this relatively greater frequency of minus Dominance scores, the Gilchrist group still contained 15 Ss out of 40 (38 percent) who earned plus Dominance scores. The comparable percentages of plus Dominance scores for the three patient groups is 5 percent, 2.5 percent, and zero percent for the neurotic, mixed psychotic-neurotic, and psychotic (chronic schizophrenic) groups, respectively. Thus 76 percent of one group of normals and 38 percent of a second group had plus Dominance scores compared to a value under 5 percent in each of three patient groups.

Normal Behavior and Specific Situations

Tables 9.4, 9.5, and 9.6, and Figures 9.1 through 9.12 show that many differences exist between our normal groups and each of the patient groups. Also, there are slight but, nevertheless, statistically demonstrable differences between our two normal groups.[5] These differences are demonstrable

[5] In this sense, it is important to recognize that although the two normal groups used in our present study were applying for a *wide variety* of department store jobs, and thus constitute a crude representation of all normals, they nevertheless were homogeneous in that they were all department store applicants. Current research with other relatively homogeneous groups of normals (policeman and fireman applicants; experienced nurses; student nurses; etc.) suggests that, on some dimensions, normal groups will be found to differ from other normal groups. This seems to bear out Chapple's hypothe-

despite the existence of large individual differences *within* any one group. The obtained differences in interview behavior have thus been shown to be related to criteria (clinical diagnoses) external to the standardized interview itself. It is worth examining this relationship a little more closely.

Consider first the two normal groups. In the sense that they were both given the same criterion or clinical classifica-

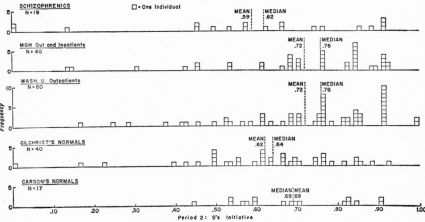

FIGURE 9.10. Frequency distributions: S's initiative.

tion ("normal"), it was assumed that the two groups were identical along a number of relevant behavioral dimensions. Yet, objective measures of actual interview behavior in a standardized situation revealed them to be different in several ways. What can be the meaning of the fact that one group of "normals," which consisted of consecutive applicants for jobs (not specified in advance) in a department store in one city

sis that, since the pattern of interactional characteristics even of normals will differ, from one person to the next, job placement ought to keep clearly in mind the degree to which any individual's interactional repertoire will mesh with the specific job requirements.

(Chicago), is found to differ in several ways from another group of "normals" consisting of consecutive applicants for jobs in a department store in a second city (Boston)? It is clear that they were drawn from two slightly different samples of "normals." That is, one possibility may be that the term *normal* as applied to a given individual, without adequate definition of his situational context (in this case the specific

FREQUENCY DISTRIBUTIONS: S's QUICKNESS

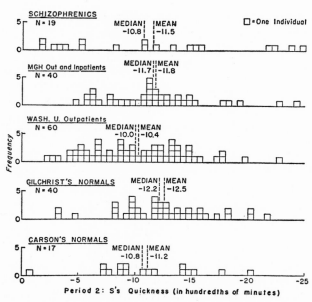

FIGURE 9.11. Frequency distributions: S's quickness.

kind of sales job he is applying for), is inadequate. Thus, even such a situational context as "department store" is evidently not sufficiently definitive. The reason for this is that a department store, like other human organizational groups, consists of a multitude of subsituational contexts. Therefore, a person may function well in one of these subsituational contexts (i.e., be normal and adequately productive) but not in another (in which he would be a poor worker, in trouble with his work associates, or otherwise be abnormal). The relevance of such considerations to a clearer understanding of the concept of normality is stated in a recent article by Chapple and Sayles:

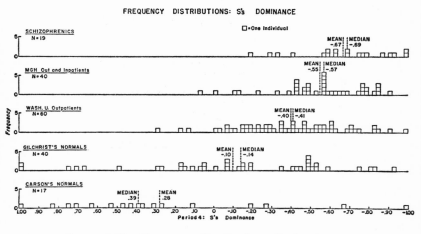

FIGURE 9.12. Frequency distributions: S's dominance.

Just as each person is (interactionally) different, so each job differs in its behavioral requirements. The salesman obviously has to have a high degree of activity and drive and initiate a high proportion of contacts; since he meets a wide variety of people, he has to be flexible in his adaptation to them; a machine operator or a bookkeeper, on the other hand, shows little need of these characteristics. How much you listen, how dominant you are, how much initiative you show, whether you are quick or slow to act, are all characteristics which vary in their importance from job to job.

Not only do jobs differ in their inherent interactional dimensions; they also differ according to the personalities who fill the surrounding organizational positions. The personality of the supervisor, whom the man we promote will have to report to, is of substantial significance in making our choice. Similarly, when the organizational structure necessitates two or more executives working closely together, the personality of "the other" is one of the most important elements in each man's job description [Chapple & Sayles, 1958].

It is clear from the above argument that an individual called "normal" in one subsituational context may very well be called "deviant" in another apparently not too different subsituational context (e.g., selling two kinds of articles within the same department store). On a larger scale, an individual may be normal, in the sense of adequate, in one profession but not another; in the case of his adjustment with one roommate, spouse, or teacher, but not another roommate, etc.

How far can one extend this way of regarding normality and abnormality as context-bound? Carried to its logical conclusion, this idea implies that no matter how deviant an individual is (by clinical criteria) one may be able to find a situational context in which he functions adequately. The limit to this argument in practice appears to be that at some point society, noting that an individual has failed to find suitable contexts (in a sufficient number of society's institutions; i.e., family, secondary groups, job, etc.), labels him "abnormal." Or, coming to similar conclusions, the individual defines himself as requiring the help of a psychiatrist or a psychiatric hospital.

By whom, and how, should decisions regarding this cutoff point be made? The difficulty experienced when one culture (American) attempted to make this decision for another (Navajo), in the case of so apparently uncomplicated a disorder as congenital hip disease, is impressively described in a recent article by McDermott, Deuschle, Adair, Fulmer, and Loughlin (1960). An American research team of physicians and anthropologists found that the treatment recommended by American physicians for congenital hip disease among the

Navajo (in terms of our modern understanding of the nature of this condition), would have transformed "something that was no real handicap, and was almost a blessing, into something that represented a very serious handicap indeed" (p. 281).

Recent work on mental illness (Hollingshead & Redlich, 1958) suggests that, in our own society, we may act with as little effectiveness when members of one socio-economic group attempt to make this decision for members of another (lower) group in the matter of the abnormality called mental illness. In addition, recent changes in the pattern of dealing with the mentally ill have demonstrated that with the appropriate use of more of society's resources (new drugs, psychotherapy, therapeutic community-oriented hospital units, etc.), changes can be produced in the individual's interactional pattern so that he can now function in more of the available situational contexts. We must conclude, therefore, that the definition of a sharp boundary between normal and abnormal requires consideration of questions such as those posed above.

The large individual differences shown in Figures 9.1 through 9.12 also raise a question of a rather different kind in relation to the topic of normality and abnormality. In Figure 9.1, four of the 19 schizophrenics had values for *S's Units* within the range of the two normal groups. Does this fact mean that these four schizophrenics were more like the normal subjects in some other interactional respects as well? To answer such a question will require a method which characterizes a single individual's interactional *pattern* in a manner which permits effective comparison with another individual. Two possible methods of doing this have occurred to us. One, the method of *multiple discriminant analysis,* recently utilized by Thorndike and Hagen (1959, pp. 314-323) appears to permit the translation of any given individual's 12 Interaction Chronograph scores into a *single* point in n-dimensional space for comparison with other similar points.

Thus, the *total* interaction pattern of one individual can be compared with the *total* interaction pattern of a second individual. The other, a method of analysis of carefully defined units of behavior occurring in *different sequential patterns* (e.g., a pattern consisting of a long action followed by a short action followed by a long action, versus a pattern consisting of three long actions; or the pattern provided by a long action followed by a short action versus the different pattern provided by a short action followed by a long action) may be as useful in the study of human interaction as it was found by Hebb (1954, pp. 545–547) in his studies of the social behavior of the chimpanzee. One or the other of these approaches may allow us better to study larger patterns of behavior and thus to compare the behavior of a person called "deviant" with one called "normal," or two or more persons each of whom previously was considered normal. If either of these two approaches should yield clear differences between normal and deviant groups, one may feel that the need for understanding subsituational contexts in relation to adjustment is of less importance than is the variance contributed by the "normal-deviant" classification. However, even should this latter be true, analysis of the variance due to subsituational contexts, included along with the analysis of this broader classification (i.e., of individual differences), may further our understanding still more.

Summary

Data have been presented from a study on the differences between interview interaction behavior under partially standardized conditions of five groups of subjects: psychotics (chronic schizophrenics); mixed neurotics and psychotics; neurotics; and two groups of normals. The results reveal a number of statistically significant differences in the interview behavior of these different groups. The findings suggested a number of problems pertinent to the question "What is normal (or deviant) behavior?" In particular, the situational context (in contrast to personality or individual characteristics) was examined as one of the important ingredients necessary to our understanding of the concepts of normality and deviation. Thus, following a suggestion from Chapple, if we wish to understand why a person called "normal" can function well in one job, but be a deviate in a second job, possibly we must first understand the differences between the interactional requirements of these two jobs, or other situational contexts.

REFERENCES

Ash, P.   The reliability of psychiatric diagnosis. *J. abnorm. soc. Psychol.*, 1949, **44**, 272–276.

American Psychological Association.   Technical recommendations for psychological tests and diagnostic techniques. *Psychol. Bull.*, 1954, **51**, (2), 1–38.

Chapple, E. D.   Quantitative analysis of the interaction of individuals. *Proc. Nat. Acad. Sci.*, 1939, **25**, 58–67.

Chapple, E. D.   "Personality" differences as described by invariant properties of individuals in interaction. *Proc. Nat. Acad. Sci.*, 1940, **26**, 10–16.

Chapple, E. D.   The measurement of interpersonal behavior. *Transactions of the N. Y. Acad. of Sci.*, 1942, **4**, No. 7 (Whole No. (2), 213–233.

Chapple, E. D.   The Interaction Chronograph; its evolution and present application. *Personnel*, 1949, **25**, 295–307.

Chapple, E. D.   The standard experimental (stress) interview as used in Interaction Chronograph investigations. *Human Organiz.*, 1953, **12**, 23–32.

Chapple, E. D., & Arensberg, C. M.   Measuring human relations: An introduction to the study of the interaction of individuals. *Genet. Psychol. Monog.*, 1949, **22**, 3–147.

Chapple, E. D., Chapple, M. F., & Repp, J. A.   Behavioral definitions of personality and temperament characteristics. *Human Organiz.*, 1954, **13**, 34–39.

Chapple, E. D., & Donald, G., Jr. A method for evaluating supervisory personnel. *Harvard Bus. Rev.*, 1946, **24**, 197–214.

Chapple, E. D., & Lindemann, E. Clinical implications of measurements of interaction rates in psychiatric interviews. *Appl. Anthrop.*, 1942, **1**, 1–11.

Chapple, E. D., & Sayles, L. R. The man, the job, and the organization. *Personnel*, 1958, **34**, 8–20.

Cronbach, L. J., & Meehl P. E. Construct validity in psychological tests. *Psychol. Bull.*, 1955, **52**, 281–302.

Gleser, Goldine, Haddock, J. Starr, P., & Ulett, G. Psychiatric screening of flying personnel: Interrater agreement on the basis of psychiatric interviews. *USAF Sch. of Aviation Med., Rep. No. 10*, Project No. 21–0202–0007, 1954.

Green, A. W. Culture, normality, and personality conflict. *Amer. Anthropol.*, 1948, **50**, 225–237.

Hacker, F. H. The concept of normality and its practical significance. *Amer. J. Orthopsychiat.*, 1945, **15**, 47–64.

Hare, A. P., Waxler, Nancy, Saslow, G., & Matarazzo, J. D. Simultaneous recording of Bales and Chapple interaction measures during initial psychiatric interviews. *J. consult. Psychol.*, 1960, **24**, 193.

Hebb, D. O., & Thompson, W. R. The social significance of animal studies. In G. Lindzey (Ed.), *Handbook of social psychology*. Vol. 1, 1954. Pp. 532–561.

Hollingshead, A. B., & Redlich, F. C. *Social class and mental illness.* New York: Wiley, 1958.

Hunt, W. A., Wittson, C. L., & Hunt, Edna B. A theoretical and practical analysis of the diagnostic process. In P. H. Hoch & J. Zubin (Eds.), *Current problems in psychiatric diagnosis.* New York: Grune & Stratton, 1953. Pp. 53–65.

Krasner, L. Studies of the conditioning of verbal behavior. *Psychol. Bull.*, 1958, **55**, 148–170.

Lindquist, E. F. *Design and analysis of experiments in psychology and education.* Boston: Houghton Mifflin, 1953.

McDermott, W., Deuschle, K., Adair, J., Fulmer, H., & Loughlin,

Bernice. Introducing modern medicine in a Navajo community. *Science*, 1960, 131, 197–205, 280–287.

MacKinnon, D. W. The structure of personality. In J. McV. Hunt (Ed.), *Personality and the behavior disorders*. Vol 1. New York: Ronald Press, 1944. Pp. 3–48.

McNemar, Q. *Psychological statistics*. New York: Wiley, 1955.

Matarazzo, J. D., Saslow, G., & Guze, S. B. Stability of interaction patterns during interviews: a replication. *J. consult. Psychol.*, 1956, 20, 267–274.

Matarazzo, J. D., Saslow, G., & Hare, A. P. Factor analysis of interview interaction behavior. *J. consult. Psychol.*, 1958, 22, 419–429.

Matarazzo, J. D., Saslow, G., & Matarazzo, Ruth G. The Interaction Chronograph as an instrument for objective measurement of interaction patterns during interviews. *J. Psychol.*, 1956, 41, 347–367.

Matarazzo, J. D., Saslow, G., Matarazzo, Ruth G., & Phillips, Jeanne S. Stability and modifiability of personality patterns during a standardized interview. In P. A. Hoch and J. Zubin (Eds.), *Psychopathology of communication*. New York: Grune & Stratton, 1958.

Matarazzo, Ruth G., Matarazzo, J. D., Saslow, G., & Phillips, Jeanne S. Psychological test and organismic correlates of interview interaction behavior. *J. abnorm. soc. Psychol.*, 1958, 56, 329–338.

Mowrer, O. H. What is normal behavior? In L. A. Pennington and I. A. Berg (Eds.), *Introduction to clinical psychology*. New York: Ronald Press, 1954. Pp. 58–88.

Phillips, Jeanne S. The relationship between two features of interview behavior comparing verbal content and verbal temporal patterns of interaction. Unpublished doctoral dissertation, Washington Univer., St. Louis, 1957.

Phillips, Jeanne S., Matarazzo, J. D., Matarazzo, Ruth G., & Saslow, G. Observer reliability of interaction patterns during interviews. *J. consult. Psychol.*, 1957, 21, 269–275.

Raines, G. N., & Rohrer, J. H. The operational matrix of psychiatric practice: I. Consistency and variability in interview impressions of different psychiatrists. *Amer. J. Psychiat.*, 1955, 11, 721–733.

Roberts, B. H., & Strodtbeck, F. L. Interaction process differences between groups of paranoid schizophrenic and depressed patients. *Int. J. group Psychother.*, 1953, 3, 29–41.

Saslow, G., & Matarazzo, J. D. A technique for studying changes in interview behavior. In E. A. Rubenstein and M. B. Parloff (Eds.), *Research in psychotherapy.* Washington, D.C.: American Psychological Association, 1959. Pp. 125–159.

Saslow, G., Matarazzo, J. D., & Guze, S. B. The stability of Interaction Chronograph patterns in psychiatric interviews. *J. consult. Psychol.*, 1955, 19, 417–430.

Saslow, G., Matarazzo, J. D., Phillips, Jeanne S., & Matarazzo, Ruth G. Test-retest stability of interaction patterns during interviews conducted one week apart. *J. abnorm. soc. Psychol.*, 1957, 54, 295–302.

Shoben, E. J., Jr. Toward a concept of the normal personality. *Amer. Psychol.*, 1957, 12, 183–189.

Siegel, S., *Nonparametric statistics for the behavioral sciences.* New York: McGraw-Hill, 1956.

Thorndike, R. L., & Hagen, Elizabeth. *Ten thousand careers.* New York: Wiley, 1959.

CHAPTER 10

Measuring Deviant Behavior by Means of Deviant Response Sets[1]

IRWIN A. BERG

Louisiana State University

There are literally thousands of studies which seek, with varying degrees of success, to predict behavior in one area from the responses made in another area. The majority of these researches are concerned with predicting deviant behavior in the psychopathological sense by means of responses made to various items in psychological tests such as the *Minnesota Multiphasic Personality Inventory* (MMPI), the *Rorschach, Thematic Apperception Test* (TAT), etc. The present paper is concerned with a theoretical explanation of how such studies predict behavior and offers some empirical evidence in support of the theory. In order to present this explanation, it is necessary to review selectively two broad classes of research. One deals with the concept which has appeared in the literature under such terms as "set," *Einstellung,* "biased responses," "systematic error," or "response style." The other deals with the numerous studies of clinical predictions.

The Problem of Set

The problem of set is a rather old one in psychological

[1] Material from this chapter was presented at a Symposium on Experimental Clinical Psychology at the University of Virginia School of Medicine in 1959.

research (Gibson, 1941). It has long been known that in unstructured stimulus situations human responses often do not
follow normal probability distributions. Such biases are most
apparent in free choice situations where there is no reason to
choose one response over another. When a coin is flipped, for
example, 80 percent of the subjects will call "heads" on the
first toss instead of the 50 percent expected by chance (Goodfellow, 1940). Similarly in a "pick one number" type of situation, 3, 7, and 9 are chosen with significantly greater frequency than other numerals (Ross & Kohl, 1948). The same is
true of letters of the alphabet; for B is preferred in a choice
of A, B, C, D; and X in a choice between X and Y (Berg &
Rapaport, 1954). Such biases also appear in motor responses.
One may turn either right or left and reach the same point
in many museums or theater galleries; however as Robinson
(1933) observed, three people turn right for every person
who turns to the left. Skewed responses also occur where a
judgment is involved but where the issue is apparently unimportant to the subject. There is a significant tendency in
our culture to say "yes," "agree," "true," or "satisfied" as
opposed to "no," "disagree," etc. (Berg & Rapaport, 1954;
Cronbach, 1946; Gaier & Bass, 1959; Hathaway, 1948; Lorge,
1937; Singer & Young, 1941.

The general significance of the problem has been carefully
reviewed by Jackson and Messick (1958) in a lucid analysis
of the differences between *content* and *style* in personality
assessment. Content, of course, is cognitive and represents
what a person does or says while style is *how* he does or says
it—his manner of responding. Accordingly, Jackson and Messick recommend the term *style* as being more accurate than
the term *response set* when referring to the "how" characteristics of a response. Campbell (1958) has considered such response biases as imperfections in the human links of communication systems. While he does not examine systematic

error specifically in relation to personality characteristics, Campbell's appraisal is unusually complete in describing the various forms and conditions of response bias.

STABILITY OF DEVIANT RESPONSE SETS.   These response biases are quite stable, and since they occur in many psychological tests, they often affect test validity and reliability. Cronbach (1946; 1950) has described a large number of response sets in tests and given them names such as *acquiescence, evasiveness, caution-incaution,* etc. Frederiksen and Messick (1958) have described sets which they label *criticalness.* At times, response sets can render a test invalid and, because of them, reliability may be spuriously high. The F or fascism scale of the *Authoritarian Personality* (Adorno, Frenkel-Brunswik, Levinson, & Sanford, 1950), for example, appears to measure acquiescence rather than fascistic tendencies (Bass, 1955; Chapman & Campbell, 1957; Cohn, 1952; Jackson, Messick, & Solley, 1957). Shelley (1956) found acquiescence to be a factor which affected the validity of the *California Attitude Scale.* There does appear to be a relationship between such response biases and personality characteristics; however this relationship is not close. Guilford (1954) used the number of "?" responses made on three of his tests by a group of foremen. This "indecision score" was related to the foremen's proficiency, but the correlations were low. With a similar line of thought, Rubin-Rabson (1954) correlated the number of noncommital responses on a social attitudes test with the Bernreuter self-sufficiency scores made by the same subjects. The correlation was $-.43$ which is about as high as a degree of relationship as may be obtained when the direct expression of set is used for predicting facets of personality. As will be seen later, when responses which go counter to the direct expression of bias are used, the relationship to personality traits is much stronger.

Clinical Prediction Research

Thus it appears that biased responses appear in a wide range of settings and they bear a tantalizing relationship to personality traits. The relationship is not strong enough to use them directly as personality measures nor weak enough to ignore them. These studies of set represent one of the two broad areas of research mentioned earlier as essential for a proposed theoretical explanation of deviant behavior assessment. The other area is that of clinical prediction research. These clinical studies usually use responses obtained in one stimulus situation in an effort to predict aberrant behavior in another situation. Typically, a psychological test is used to forecast emotional and intellectual deviations; however the same technique has been used to measure vocational interests, social attitudes, and the like.

PRODUCTION OF DEVIANT RESPONSE SETS BY MANY STIMULUS PATTERNS. The degree to which standard tests like the Rorschach, TAT, etc., can identify personality characteristics is well known; therefore little need be said of them. More important for our purposes is the evidence which shows that a very wide range of stimulus patterns can be used to produce responses which serve to identify various clinical groups. For example, Voth (1947) used the autokinetic phenomenon to differentiate categories of mental hospital patients. This technique requires only a stationary light in a dark room. The light seems to move under such conditions, and Voth used the degree of apparent movement to separate significantly the various classifications of patients. He tested 845 patients and 423 normal subjects and found that some patient groups, such as schizophrenics and epileptics, experienced more extensive apparent movement compared to the normal subjects while manic-depressive and involutional patients revealed little or none. Rechtshaffen and Mednick (1955) also used the autokinetic phenomenon. However, instead of using the degree of apparent motion as a measure, they informed the subjects that the "moving" light would write words. The subjects were then instructed to report what words were written by the light. They found that responses ranged from impersonal to highly personal words of possible diagnostic significance. A somewhat similar perceptual phenomenon is the Archimedes spiral aftereffect in which a rotated spiral appears to expand or contract depending upon the direction of rotation. Freeman and Josey (1949) and Price and Deabler (1955) have reported that this technique can validly distinguish patients suffering from organic brain damage from nonorganic cases. Recent studies have suggested that the interpretation of the earlier spiral aftereffects research was perhaps overly optimistic (Johnson, Bauer, & Brown, 1959; Philbrick, 1959) however until the issue is finally settled we may consider it as an interesting departure from the usual diagnostic methods.

Berg and Collier (1953) used extreme response sets (i.e., tendency to choose options *Like Much* or *Dislike Much*) as they appeared on the *Perceptual Reaction Test,* a test composed of 60 abstract designs, to distinguish significantly various groups such as high and low anxiety subjects. Lewis and Taylor (1955) repeated this study with a systematic variation of the option positions and showed that the extreme preference was not for the extreme position, as Berg and Collier had thought, but rather for the extreme option content. Possibly the most extensive series of investigations concerning relationship of perception to personality is that of Witkin (1959) and his associates (Witkin, Lewis, Hertzman, Machover, Meissner & Wapner, 1954). Using various techniques such as embedded figures and tilting room apparatus, these investigators found significant differences in the perceptual responses of males and females and among various groups of normal and maladjusted children. A somewhat different approach was used by Eysenck (1947), who measured general neuroticism by the amount of body sway which occurred in response to spoken suggestions that the subject was falling forward or backward. Another unusual technique is the use of food aversions for diagnostic purposes. Wallen (1945) and Gough (1946) found that neurotic males disliked significantly more foods than normal subjects. Altus (1949) found a correlation of .497 between number of food aversions and a test of adjustment used with Army illiterates. Smith, Powell, and Ross (1955) showed that high-anxiety subjects disliked significantly more foods as compared to low-anxiety subjects. Wallen (1948), in another study, found a significantly larger number of food aversions for intracranial injury patients, epileptics, neurotics, etc., when compared to normal subjects.

OTHER RESPONSE PATTERNS. Many other response patterns might be cited to illustrate the diversity of diagnostic techniques which have been used. Hand preference, for example, has been periodically studied as a diagnostic tool for more than 50 years. Goddard (1902) and Doll (1916) found a preponderance of left-handedness among mental retardates while Burt (1921) and Wile (1932) found a significantly larger number of sinistrals among neurotics. Word choice in written and spoken language has also been utilized as a measure of personality and adjustment, as shown in the studies of Berg (1958), Chodorkoff and Mussen (1952), Fairbanks (1944), Lorenz and Cobb (1952, 1953), Mann (1944), and Roshal (1953). Preferences for various sounds have also been used in personality diagnosis. Cattell and Anderson (1953) and Simon, Holtzberg, Alessi, and Garrity (1951) have used musical excerpts for this purpose while Grings (1942) and Adams (1959, 1960a) have used meaningless sounds to identify schizophrenic and other patient groups. The list of such studies in a wide variety of areas could be extended at great length. Indeed, it could be shown also that a similar variety of techniques have been used in studying creativeness, personality factors in physical disease, vocational choice, etc. However, the important point is that particular stimulus content does not appear to be important for eliciting responses which have considerable value for personality appraisal. In a chapter on "The Unimportance of Test Item Content" Berg (1959) has reviewed a large number of researches which bear upon this point.

DEVIANT BEHAVIOR OTHER THAN PSYCHOPATHOLOGY. One may employ stimuli of virtually any kind to assess deviant behavior. In addition to the standardized personality tests, one may use the apparent movement of a stationary light, embedded figures, food aversions, sounds, choice of words, and myriad other stimulus patterns. It seems highly probable that odor, taste, and skin sensations could also be used, although they have not actually been tried, as well as vision and audition. In any case, the deviant behavior which may be appraised in this way is immensely broad. Not merely the behavior deviations such as schizophrenia are included but any abnormal behavior, that is, *ab-normal* in the literal sense of being away from the normal. Hence any externally identifiable atypicalities such as genius, academic over- or under-achievement, accident proneness, vocational success, etc., should be distinguishable by employing any of a wide range of stimuli and in several sense modalities if desired. This leaves us with two questions: (1) Why is it possible to assess a wide variety of deviant states with such a wide variety of stimulus conditions? (2) What is the evidence and what is a suitable research model for gathering such evidence?

The Deviation Hypothesis

The reason why a wide variety of atypical behavior patterns can be measured by means of responses made to many stimulus conditions is that deviant responses are general; and if they occur in an important area of behavior (i.e., mental deficiency, psychotic reactions, etc.), they will also occur in areas of behavior which are not regarded as important (i.e., food aversions, word choice, etc.). This notion has been formulated by Berg (1955, 1957) as the *Deviation Hypothesis,* as follows: "Deviant response patterns tend to be general; hence those deviant behavior patterns which are significant for abnormality (atypicalness) and thus regarded as symptoms (earmarks or signs) are associated with other deviant response patterns which are in noncritical areas of behavior and which are not regarded as symptoms of personality aberration (nor as symptoms, signs, earmarks)" (Berg, 1957, p. 159). Accordingly, the very large number of studies which have met with some success in identifying personality disturbances, vocational choice, and the like are able to do so because deviant responses are general. That is the common thread running through all such studies. Deviant response patterns in a noncritical area of behavior are used to identify deviant response patterns in a critical area.

Many clinical techniques predict behavior. There are many studies, thousands of them, which predict deviant behavior at least sufficiently well for the authors to get their researches published. These studies have met with at least some success by employing a surprisingly wide variety of techniques and using a broad range of stimuli to evoke responses. Such are the facts and they are well known and well established. What the Deviation Hypothesis has to contribute is not the patently naive assertion that deviant behavior can be measured by a variety of methods; for obviously this has been done for many years and is still being done. *The Deviation Hypothesis offers an explanatory and unifying principle which is considered to account for the findings of huge numbers of disparate researches.* In brief, some of the specific things offered by the Hypothesis are:

1. A definition of deviant responses in simple and operational statistical terms—No hunches, clinical intuition, judgments, ratings, or other subjective appraisals are involved. A deviant response can be defined precisely at any given level of statistical significance. The definition will be straightforward, operationally clean, and easily replicable.

2. A deduction drawn from a vast array of evidence that virtually any relatively unstructured stimulus content can be used to elicit deviant responses. This is not, of course, central to the Hypothesis proper. However, it points up the fact that the concern over phraseology in verbal test items, the categories of item classification, the explorations with new forms of stimuli like autokinetic phenomena were of quite minor significance since almost anything could have been used to produce the same results. This is not saying, it should be emphasized, that any item is as good as any other for a particular purpose. Such an assertion would be absurd. But it is saying that for a given verbal item, for example, one would find a design or a sound that would do as well. At least, all the evidence we have thus far garnered forces us to that conclusion.

3. A statement of the pervasiveness of deviant responses and how they are found in critical as well as noncritical areas of behavior.—The important thing in this connection, of course, is how deviant responses may accordingly be used for assessment purposes. Everyone shows a number of deviant responses which are the product of past learning, inherited structure, and physiological, etc., factors. In most areas of behavior, such responses are usually few and inconsequential for the normal person. In particular areas of behavior these responses somehow hang together, forming a pattern which can be identified by simple methods of statistical analysis. They may be said to become meaningful in a particular behavioral area in terms of the past history of the organism. Thus, an engineer, a schizophrenic, or a genius should each

reveal atypical responses which form a pattern peculiar to his special class. The pattern would be largely shared by other members of the same class—i.e., other engineers or schizophrenics or geniuses.

4. A conceptual framework is offered which shows how a great variety of problems may be attacked. This is not restricted to psychopathology but would include any class of behavior which is identifiable by valid external criteria. Thus there is believed to be a heuristic quality inherent in applications of the concept.

5. As noted earlier, the Hypothesis lays bare the common element in a very large number of independent studies. Assuming the Deviation Hypothesis continues to hold up in the face of further empirical evidence, real benefit will accrue from the unifying principle. As a minimum, the behavioral scientist would have an explanation of why varied studies predict behavior as they do.

THE SOCIAL DESIRABILITY VARIABLE. In this context, it is pertinent to call attention to the work of Edwards (1957, 1959) with the social desirability variable in personality assessment. Edwards has indicated that the predictive value of verbal personality tests of the inventory, Q-sort, or adjective check-list format can be largely accounted for (correlations around .87) by the values obtained on social desirability scale for the same test items. His social desirability set has explained a number of puzzling features concerning verbal personality test items, and he has an impressive array of evidence to back up his statements. The study by Wiggins and Rumrill (1959), however, suggests that the purity of the social desirability dimension may be seriously questioned, at least as Edwards identifies it. It is believed that Edwards' social desirability variable may be viewed, in Deviation Hypothesis terms, simply as one class of deviant responses. Edwards seems to be aware of the possible relationship, although he perhaps would not accept with alacrity such bland incorporation of his concept into the Deviation Hypothesis framework. Edwards remarks, in a footnote, "According to Berg's deviant set hypothesis, if a subject tends to make responses *avoided* by the majority of a group of subjects, this tendency may be related to other forms of deviancy from normative standards. On the SD (Social Desirability) scale, then, deviancy would be more or less synonymous with 'social undesirability' which, in turn, has been shown to be related to 'abnormality' as measured by the clinical scales of the MMPI" (1959, fn., p. 111). He seems to have misunderstood how deviant responses are identified. The *majority* of a group of subjects is not required to respond in a given direction. All that is needed is that significantly more subjects in either of the groups compared select a particular option. In other words, deviant responses are not only those responses which are avoided by the majority of a group of subjects, as Edwards says, but also those which avoid those responses which a significant number of subjects in one group prefer. Thus, if only 30 subjects in a group of a thousand preferred option X, the response in a comparison group of similar size would be deviant if no subjects chose X. The important thing is that the responses of the criterion group differ from the deviant group at a given level of statistical significance, i.e., the 1 percent level. In any case, Edwards does have a provocative explanation for the predictive usefulness of verbal personality measures. Wiggins (1958) has presented a carefully thought-out review of Edwards's book on the SD variable.

Critical and Noncritical Areas of Behavior

Some elaboration of critical and noncritical areas of behavior is perhaps necessary before proceeding further. How a person parts his hair, for example, whether he likes or dislikes abstract designs, whether he responds *true* or *false* to a question such as "I sometimes feel lonely" are instances of noncritical areas of behavior. That is, such behavior is unimportant in our culture in the sense that it will not send us to a schizophrenic ward or a jail nor will it label us directly as a genius, a successful lawyer, or a scholastic underachiever. By contrast, if a person reports that astral voices urge him to kill somebody, if he talks in word salad, or if he forges checks, his responses are in a critical area of behavior.

Putting it another way, response patterns in critical areas of behavior have *value* attached to them in a particular culture and they usually bear classificatory labels. The value may be positive or negative; the same is true of the denotative or connotative significance of the label. Slicing into living human flesh, for example, requires responses which are obviously in a critical area of behavior. Yet the responses will be positively valued if performed by one of the Mayo brothers with the label *surgeon* and negatively valued if performed by Jack the Ripper with the label *murderer*. Both surgeons and murderers who work with knives exhibit deviant responses in a critical area. Therefore, according to the Deviation Hypothesis, both groups should also reveal deviant responses in noncritical areas. Undoubtedly, they will have some deviant responses in common; but the important thing is that they exhibit deviant response patterns which distinguish each group from the general population and which also distinguish each group from the other. This does *not* mean that all noncritical area responses will be deviant for persons who are deviant in a critical area of behavior. It does mean that *some* of the noncritical responses are deviant and occur in sufficient number to form a pattern.

In noncritical areas of behavior most deviant response patterns bear no label and have no particular value associated with them. Indeed, the public at large remains unaware of such responses. Who knows whether a given person would strongly dislike a particular chord of music or would like a certain abstract drawing? Even with such knowledge, who

could tell whether such likes or dislikes would be two indicators, among many others, that the person was a psychopath,
an engineer, a victim of tuberculosis, or something else? A
few noncritical deviant responses, of course, may draw public
attention and the responses may be assigned a vague label.
Thus a man may wear only flowing Windsor ties, high button
shoes, and carry a rolled umbrella, rain or shine. Another
may speak in a hollow voice and utter disconcerting remarks
at social gatherings. Still another may be enthusiastically cooperative in any social activity. The first person may be
labeled a *screwball,* the second a *creep,* the third a *good egg*
or some similar term. But the labels are ill defined and no
definite status is associated with such noncritical deviant
responses. One does not go to Alcatraz nor to Harvard, to
Bedlam nor to Congress because of them. They are deviant
responses but noncritical.

A few areas of apparent critical behavior are misleading
since they are not really identifiable by external criteria. For
example, criminals may at first glance appear to be a group
with externally identifiable behavior in a critical area. However, as a moment's reflection will reveal, criminals as a group
have really nothing in common except that they did something the law proscribed. They may have peddled narcotics
or moonshine, stolen something, or murdered someone.
There is no valid class of responses for them. Nevertheless,
it seems feasible that particular types of criminal behavior,
such as forgery or burglary, would be associated with certain
deviant personality and skill variables. Thus those deviant responses which determined the critical area of the particular
offense should be accompanied by other deviant responses in
a noncritical area. The same line of thought probably applies
to executives and supervisors. There do not seem to be any
external criteria which distinguish all executives or supervisors. A supervisor of longshoremen may roar in lurid

obscenity while the supervisor of bank tellers may whisper when giving his orders. But if successful supervisors or executives were carefully classed in terms of specific supervisory situations, there should then be a useful commonality of external behavioral criteria and the Deviation Hypothesis would be applicable to each situational category.

SET AND EXTERNAL CRITERIA. Thus, any group which is identifiable by valid external criteria should reveal sets which are manifested in both critical and noncritical areas by deviant response patterns. The present writer at one time had labeled responses which departed significantly from the normal probability distribution as *biased responses,* i.e., 80 percent of a group of subjects calling "heads" when a coin is tossed although the statistical probability of "heads" is only 50 percent. Deviant responses were thought of as those responses which departed from some criterion group distribution, i.e., 60 percent of normal subjects like a particular abstract design while 85 percent of a group of neurotic subjects dislike it. However, this use of *bias* and *deviant* appears to have caused some confusion. Therefore the terms *absolute* and *relative response sets* proposed by Rettig, Jacobson, Despres, and Pasamanick (1958) are to be preferred. Absolute response sets are those responses which significantly depart from chance or normal distribution curve expectancy. Relative response sets are those which deviate significantly from the responses of a criterion group. This is a straightforward way of defining the two kinds of set. Either type of response set can be employed for assessment purposes. However, the present writer and his students have used criterion groups, rather than normal probability distributions, as the basis for comparisons and this means that relative response sets alone will be isolated here.

Research Framework of the Deviation Hypothesis

Thus far, a variety of empirical studies have been cited with the aim of demonstrating that the Deviation Hypothesis is a unifying principle which can account for the predictive value of a great number of clinical and other researches. For the most part, these studies were published before the Deviation Hypothesis was formulated; and in any case they were not intended to be specific tests of the Hypothesis. There have been specific tests of the Hypothesis and evidence from such studies will be offered later. At this time, however, it seems appropriate to describe the general research framework in which our data have been gathered. Other approaches could easily be used but ours has the twin virtues of familiarity and simplicity. Those of us who have studied particular aspects of the Hypothesis have used largely one research design. This is what Edwards (1959) has called the criterion group method. It is also essentially the method used by Hathaway and McKinley (1943) and Strong (1935) in constructing respectively the MMPI and the Vocational Interest Blank (VIB).

CRITERION GROUP METHOD.   Two groups are required when using the criterion group method—a criterion group and a deviant group. The criterion group is usually people in general or a random sample of the normal population. However, any group which serves as the basis for comparison may be used for criterion purposes. Thus, a group of neurotics could be compared with a group of schizophrenics and the neurotics could be considered the criterion group if desired. Barnes (1955), for example, used groups of psychotic and character disorder subjects in constructing a differential diagnosis scale based upon deviant responses. The deviant group is always a special segment of the general population which is identifiable by external criteria along the lines described earlier. This group could be a group of schizophrenics identified by their symptomatology, a group of accident-prone subjects identified by their safety record, chronic heart disease patients as determined by EKG findings, geniuses as measured by IQ levels, a group of successful orthodonists identified on the basis of training and experience, and the like. Any group which similarly exhibits a special pattern of responses in a critical area could serve as the deviant group. It does not matter whether these special responses are the product, singly or in combination, of past learning, inherited structure, or of organic and physiological state. The important thing is that the group has some validly ascertainable characteristics of attitude, training, dysfunction, etc., in a critical area which the group members share and which sets them apart behaviorally from other groups or people in general. Thus they are deviant in the sense of being apart, not necessarily in the sense of being pathological in behavior. The area must, of course, have some critical meaning in our culture. People who wear brown shoes are apart from people who wear black shoes but this has no particular significance.

OBTAINING A SERIES OF RESPONSES.   After the criterion and deviant groups have been determined, the next step is to have the subjects in both groups respond to a series of relatively unstructured stimulus patterns. The stimuli, as outlined earlier, may be a stationary light, a tilting room, sentences from the MMPI or VIB, lists of foods, abstract designs, and so on. The particular stimulus content is unimportant. It *is* important that the stimuli possess little structure in the sense that there be no obviously correct answer or that a particular response is desirable. For example, a stimulus pattern in the form of a test item such as, "The Declaration of Independence was signed in: (1670) (1776) (1898)" has a great deal of structure and would not be likely to produce deviant responses because nearly every American would know the right answer. A series of stimulus patterns, rather than a single stimulus, is also important because a larger number of responses are produced. It seems highly probable that the use of the Archimedes spiral aftereffect or hand preference as diagnostic indicators have low predictive efficiency because they are essentially one or two item tests and, as a result, only a few deviant responses are possible. By contrast, the MMPI has 550 items and does a rather good job of diagnosis. In our studies, we have used the Perceptual Reaction Test (PRT) by Berg, Hunt, and Barnes (1949). This test is composed of 60 abstract designs drawn with ruler and compass. The subject is required to mark one of the following four options for each design: *Like Much, Like Slightly, Dislike Slightly, Dislike Much.* This makes a total of 240 possible responses; and, since failure to respond to any of the 60 items has been found to be significant, a total of 300 responses are considered to be available. Only about seven minutes are required for normal subjects to complete the test.

FIGURE 10.1. Examples of two designs used in the Perceptual Reaction Test.

TABULATION OF RESPONSES. When the criterion and the deviant groups have responded to the series of stimulus patterns, the responses are separately tabulated for each group and separately for each item and each option. This is quite essential, for if either options or items are combined, deviant responses will be masked.[2] Then, the level of statistical sig-

---

[2] Lest it be assumed that undue emphasis be given to this point, it may be noted that one student with a faulty understanding of criterion group procedures thought to save time by totaling the PRT *Like Much, Like Slightly,* etc., options and obtaining a Chi-square value. This is akin to studying the accuracy of cashiers in making change by averaging their weekly receipts. The overpayments of one day will be masked by the shortchanges for another day, and no accurate picture of their deviant change-making behavior will be obtained.

nificance for each option of every PRT item is individually determined. Usually, we employ a differentiation at the 1 percent level and occasionally the 5 percent level of confidence as our definition of a deviant response. At first glance this appears to involve a great deal of work. If five groups are compared separately by males and females, for example, the significance level of 300 responses for each of the ten comparisons, a total of 3,000 significance level determinations, will have to be made.[3] There is a fair amount of drudgery involved but not nearly so much as it may seem. IBM cards make for speedy data tabulation and simple nomographs may be quickly constructed for testing the significance of differences for proportions. Often existing nomographs can be used, such as the one by Mainland and Murray (1952). Also, a number of response frequencies are so obviously similar that no significant differences exist and, accordingly, no test need be made.

IDENTIFICATION OF DEVIANT RESPONSE SETS. If the responses of operationally clean criterion and deviant groups are analyzed in this way, a sizeable number of deviant responses will be identified which distinguish the two groups. With deviant responses defined at the 1 percent level of confidence, three responses will, of course, be significant on the basis of chance when all of the 300 possible PRT responses are used. With various groups of neurotics, psychotics, mental retardates, etc.,

[3] Males and females usually differ in their responses to unstructured stimuli. A reasonably valid and reliable scale for MF of interest, for example, has been constructed by using the criterion group method for isolating relative response sets when males and females were compared solely with respect to Perceptual Reaction Test option preferences. Therefore, any research on deviant responses should treat data for males and females separately until it has been clearly demonstrated that differential response tendencies do not exist. In this connection it may be noted that racial and cultural differences in response patterns are also present. While these are probably due to different learning experiences, it is important to take them into account when tabulating data obtained from subjects of markedly different cultural backgrounds.

we have found from 50 to 200 of the 300 PRT options capable of producing 1 percent level deviant responses. Such deviant response frequency means that it is a relatively simple matter to construct a scale, making it possible to assess a single person on the trait or characteristic involved. Barnes (1955) has done this for eight clinical scales developed from PRT deviant responses—really 16 scales since he used the Katzell (1951) item cross-validation technique. However, since we use the PRT only as a research tool and have not released it as a clinical test nor for public circulation, we have seldom bothered to prepare appropriately simple scoring keys for our scales. The only important thing for us currently is that useful scales can and have been constructed. We continue to use the PRT because we have about 5000 cases on IBM cards and know how the PRT stimulus patterns function for various groups and under various conditions. The PRT is undoubtedly a useful test but other stimulus patterns could be used just as well. Our current interest is in the Deviation Hypothesis, not the test.

It should be noted that when the significance level of each option in every item has been determined, some of the options will be significant in the direction of the criterion group and some will be significant in the direction of the deviant group. Both types of responses differentiate the two groups, and therefore, are deviant responses. If a scale is to be constructed, both types of responses would be used. Let us examine an actual case in point. Table 10.1 was prepared by summarizing the raw data obtained from Barnes (1955) for item 56 of the PRT. This item is a drawing of a triangle with a bar balanced across the top. The criterion group was 850 normal subjects (500 males, 350 females) and the deviant group was 167 hospitalized schizophrenic patients (99 males, 68 females). As is our practice, the males and females in each of the groups are compared separately although the male-female response differences within each group in this par-

TABLE 10.1. Comparison of Normal and Schizophrenic Responses to One PRT Test Item

| Option | Schizophrenic (N=167) | | | | Normal (N=850) | | | |
| | Male (99) | | Female (68) | | Male (500) | | Female (350) | |
	N	%	N	%	N	%	N	%
0. No Response	2	2.0	4	5.9	0	0.0	0	0.0
1. Like Much	33	33.4	21	30.9	36	7.2	22	6.3
2. Like Slightly	31	31.3	24	35.3	117	23.4	70	20.0
3. Dislike Slightly	17	17.2	9	13.2	190	38.0	114	32.6
4. Dislike Much	16	16.1	10	14.7	157	31.4	144	41.1
Total	99	100.0	68	100.0	500	100.0	350	100.0

SOURCE: I. A. Berg. *J. Psychol.*, 1955, **40**, 63.

ticular case are not so pronounced as they usually are. The first three options *No Response, Like Much,* and *Like Slightly* were favored by the schizophrenic males and females when compared to normal males and females. The differences, while not immense, are beyond the 1 percent level of statistical significance. The last two options, *Dislike Slightly* and *Dislike Much,* were favored by the normal or criterion male and female groups. These options also distinguish the schizophrenic and normal groups at the 1 percent level of significance but in the opposite direction. Thus, while all five of the options in our example are deviant responses at the 1 percent level, the first three of the responses are in the direction of schizophrenia and the last two are in the direction of normality. In making up a scale we would assign one point for "schizophrenia" (plus) if one of the first three options were chosen or one point for "normality" if one of the last two options (minus) were marked.[4] In scoring, the plus points and the minus points are totalled separately and then added together for the final score. A final score which is a negative or minus number would then be in the direction of the criterion group (the normal population in Table 10.1) and a plus or positive number would be in the direction of the deviant group (schizophrenics in the present example). Undoubtedly, a simpler scoring system could be worked out; however as noted earlier, our present focus of interest is on

[4] The level of significant differences sometimes just barely reaches the .01 level and in other cases may be extremely high, such as the .00001 level. At times, the question has been raised whether it would not be highly desirable to assign a much heavier scoring weight to such items which are ultra significant. We have not done so for several reasons. When a study is cross-validated by using deviant groups in another section of the country, the ultra significant deviant responses rarely maintain their extreme discriminative power although they remain comfortably beyond the 1 percent level. The ordinary 1 percent level deviant responses, however, usually do hold up quite well under cross-validation. Also, the nuisance of assigning differential weights to various responses is hardly worth the effort since the gain in discriminative power is actually very small. In this context, Guilford (1936, p. 448) observes that the correlation of weighted and unweighted scores is almost perfect.

a series of empirical tests of the Deviation Hypothesis and not upon a convenient clinical tool. It seems necessary to stress this, for a number of our colleagues of practical orientation have expressed perplexity at our concern with what they regard as a peripheral problem at the expense of an obviously utilitarian application.

Specific Tests of the Deviation Hypothesis

This, then, is the general research design we have commonly used. There have been occasional excursions along other research pathways, as we shall note, but inevitably we have returned to the criterion group method as a more convenient research framework. With this in mind, we may now review some of the data obtained from studies which were specific tests of the Deviation Hypothesis. The work of Barnes has been referred to several times; so his research may suitably be the first to be considered. In his first study Barnes (1955) administered the PRT to 546 patients (360 males and 186 females) suffering from various psychiatric disorders. These patients made up his various deviant groups. For his criterion group he used 1700 normal subjects (1000 males and 700 females). The deviant and criterion groups were divided in half into A and B groups on a random basis and each group was treated independently as outlined by Katzell (1951) in his cross-validation method. This technique permits a double cross-validation since the options found to be significant in group A are cross-validated on group B while the items found to be significant in group B are cross-validated on group A. The actual identification of deviant responses was the same as that described earlier.

SCALES DEVELOPED FROM DEVIANT RESPONSE SETS. Barnes developed the following scales: *Delta* (male and female scales) —The deviant group was a heterogeneous population of 546 patients who had various psychiatric diagnoses. The one

thing this group had in common was that they were hospitalized because of some behavioral disturbances. *Psi* (male
and female scales)—The deviant group was composed of those
patients who were diagnosed as being afflicted with some form
of psychotic reaction. *Sigma* (male and female scales)—The
deviant group was made up of patients who had been diagnosed as schizophrenic. *Chi* (male scale only)—The deviant
group was a group of male character disorder patients.

All of the foregoing scales were developed with a normal
population as the criterion group. Barnes developed one additional scale as a "diagnostic sharpener" scale in which he
followed the same technique but used the group of psychotics
as the criterion group and the character disorder group as his
deviant group. This *Psi-Chi* scale permitted determining
whether subjects who scored high on both the psychotic and
character disorder scales revealed response patterns which
more closely resembled one group or the other.

The scales had four-day interval test-retest reliabilities
ranging from .55 for *Chi* to .75 for *Sigma*. Stepped-up
split-half reliabilities, of course, are usually higher; however
the test-retest reliability determination is more meaningful
in terms of how such scales could be used clinically. The
validity of Barnes' scales was determined by two separate
cross-validations. In this connection it is interesting to note
that, while Barnes used deviant groups composed of patients
obtained from hospitals in the far West and the Midwest, a
group of schizophrenics in a Louisiana hospital yielded *Sigma*
scale results which were very close to Barnes' original data
(Harris, 1958).

The findings from Barnes' study are given at some length
because they show what can be done with a specific application of the Deviation Hypothesis. Attention is called to the
fact that the instrument Barnes used for eliciting relative
deviant response sets, the PRT, takes only about seven
minutes to administer—a minuscule sample of behavior. Also,

the PRT has no particular content. It is merely 60 abstract designs of no special meaning. Then, to prepare his scales, Barnes used only deviant responses defined statistically as described earlier. Once he obtained his criterion and deviant groups, no ratings, judgments, opinions, or similar subjective procedures were used. He employed only simple statistical methods with a simple research design. Yet with a seven-minute sample of behavior he was able to obtain a reasonably valid and reliable series of clinical scales by the use of relative deviant response sets.

IMMATURITY AND SCHIZOPHRENIA MEASURED BY DEVIANT RE-SPONSES. In another test of the Deviation Hypothesis, Hesterly and Berg (1958) hypothesized that normal, young children should be significantly differentiated from normal adults on the basis of deviant response frequency as elicited by the PRT. Then, since adult schizophrenics are commonly regarded as exhibiting immature behavior, they also hypothe-sized that the deviant response patterns of adult schizo-phrenics should approximate the deviant response patterns of normal children when both groups were separately com-pared with normal adults. Three groups of 100 children ap-proximately aged 8, 10, and 12 years (150 males and 150 females) and the data for schizophrenic adults obtained by Barnes were used in the study. It was found that the youngest group of children had the largest number of deviant re-sponses which distinguished them from normal adults. With increasing age, the groups of children revealed a decreasing number of deviant responses. When the deviant response pat-terns of the normal young children were compared with the group of adult schizophrenics, it was found that the schizo-phrenics and youngest group of children had deviant response patterns which were quite similar. As hypothesized, the de-gree of similarity decreased when comparisons were made with older children. The results are considered to support the Deviation Hypothesis and also to support the notion that schizophrenic responses are characterized by immaturity.

DEVIANT RESPONSES AND CHRONOLOGICAL AGE. With the data from the above study in mind, Hesterly (1960) felt that it should be possible to construct a maturity scale based upon PRT deviant responses which occurred at different chronological age levels. He used 2253 subjects ranging in age from 6 to 83 years. Separate analyses were made for males and females and the Katzell (1951) double cross-validation technique was employed to identify deviant responses at the .0025 level of significance. As hypothesized, he found that the frequency of deviant responses decreased with increasing chronological age up to approximately age 19. From age 20 to about age 60 the deviant response patterns were relatively stable. After age 60, Hesterly found systematic pattern and deviant response frequency changes with increasing chronological age. Significantly, the deviant response pattern of the elderly adults resembled the pattern for normal children. This is not to say that the deviant response patterns of young children and elderly adults were identical. But, while there were certain differences, there were very definite similarities. Furthermore, the deviant response patterns for young children and the aged adults resembled each other much more closely than either resembled the pattern for normal adults in the age 20–60 range. These findings are in harmony with the generally held idea that elderly persons often enter a "second childhood."

In appraising Hesterly's findings, it should be emphasized that he employed an extremely rigorous criterion in identifying deviant responses. He used two cross-validations in preparing his chronological age maturity scale and he included only those deviant responses which were beyond the .0025 level of significance (ordinarily the .01 level is used). Despite this stringent criterion, to take an admittedly favorable example, he found 176 deviant responses out of a possible 300 which differentiated 6-year-old children from normal adults aged 20–60.

A SCALE FOR EMOTIONAL DISTURBANCE IN CHILDREN. Children whose behavior is sufficiently aberrant that it is deemed necessary to place them under psychiatric treatment meet many of the criteria for identifying deviant groups. While the criteria are not as objectively sanitary, for example, as chronological age, children who require psychiatric care because of emotional disturbance are behaviorally different from children who do not. On this basis, House (1960) used the criterion group method to compare the PRT responses of 240 disturbed children aged 7–15 years with the responses of 400 normal children matched for age, sex, intelligence level, and approximate socioeconomic status. He found that 94 to 112 of the 240 possible responses were deviant as defined by the .01 level of statistical significance. With these data, House successfully constructed scales for emotionally disturbed male and female children.

DEVIANT RESPONSES AMONG MENTAL RETARDATES. Mental defectives commonly reveal a wide variety of responses which are atypical; hence this group should be quite suitable for an empirical test of the Deviation Hypothesis. Cieutat (1960) administered the PRT to 433 mental retardates (240 males, 193 females) aged 16–67 and compared their responses to 850 normal adults (500 males, 350 females). At the .01 significance level, 187 responses of a possible 240 for the male defectives were deviant and 164 for the females. By means of this large number of deviant responses, Cieutat was able to construct an *Iota* scale, as she termed it, which measured mental retardation. She then examined Berg's (1955) assertion that with increasing severity of a disorder the deviant response frequency should increase. She reasoned that the more severely retarded subjects should exhibit a larger number of deviant responses when compared to those subjects who were less retarded as defined by IQ level. As predicted, she found a regularly increasing deviant response frequency as the degree of retardation increased. Cieutat next considered the question of whether mental retardates differed from schizophrenics in their deviant response pattern. It had been established by Barnes (1955), Harris (1958), and Adams (1959) that schizophrenics differed from normal subjects in this respect and Cieutat's own work demonstrated that mental retardates also differed from normal subjects in terms of deviant responses. But the question remained as to whether the two deviant groups differed from each other in response pattern. Therefore she compared schizophrenics with mental retardates, using the criterion group method with the PRT, and found 98 responses for males and 76 for females distinguished the two conditions at the .01 level. Thus, while the frequency of deviant responses of both schizophrenics and mental retardates is high, the two deviant groups are readily differentiated on the basis of response pattern. Indeed, a diagnostic sharpener scale could undoubtedly be constructed if desired, much as Barnes' (1955) *Psi-Chi* scale intensified the deviant response pattern differences between psychotic and character disorder groups.

THE PROBLEM OF SENESCENCE.   The physical and behavioral differences between an atypical child of 5 and one 10 years older is apparent, even to the unpracticed eye. But at the other end of the human life span, such physical and behavioral characteristics related to age are often mystifying. An age difference of 10 or even 20 years may mean little, for a person of 70 may look and act as if he were 50 and vice versa. Aware of such factors, Hawkins (1960) took a carefully selected group of 32 males aged 50 to 79 and compared them with a group of 32 males aged 19 to 24, matched for education and approximate socioeconomic background. The oldsters were in no sense typical of the general population in their age range. They averaged three years of college (as did the young males) and they held important positions such as school board presidents, bank officers, clergymen, merchants, etc. Both young and old groups were given the PRT, the *Wonderlic Personnel Test,* and a medium difficulty level paired-associate learning task. The PRT deviant response frequency when the two groups were compared was at a purely chance level. In other words, older men who were still capable of energetically pursuing their careers revealed no deviant responses, on the PRT, which distinguished them from much younger men. Further, the two groups did not differ significantly on a measure of PRT response variability-rigidity developed by Adams (1960a). This measure of variability-rigidity, incidentally, predicted performance on the learning task better than the intelligence test scores.

Hawkins, of course, had an unusual group of older persons. They were active in their business or profession and whether their activities kept them young, so to speak, or whether they would have remained young anyway is moot. As a guess, they would have exhibited similar zest in any situation. By contrast, Boozer (1961) used elderly subjects who were much more typical of the general, aged population. She administered the PRT to 2056 subjects, of whom 602 were aged 60 to 97. The others were schizophrenic adults and normal adult controls. Her elderly subjects were divided into normal, aged persons who were members of Golden Age Clubs, and Senior Citizens Groups. These subjects were old but still managing their own affairs competently. Some were retired and some were still employed. A second group was composed of aged subjects who were resident patients in a state mental hospital. Some of these patients exhibited a few symptoms of senility and were not fully capable of managing their own affairs. The third group of subjects was made up of persons who were living in public or private homes for the aged. Some of these persons were infirm and required nursing care while others lived there because they had no other place to go. When the PRT options for the aged but otherwise normal subjects were compared with normal adults aged 20–60, Boozer found that 175 to 189 of a possible 300 responses were deviant at the .01 level of significance. Using Katzell's (1951) technique, she constructed a scale for aging or normal senescence. This method requires two cross-validations and permits a combined final scale in which deviant responses may be defined statistically at the rigorous .0025 level. As a check on the possible influence of residing in homes for the aged, she compared the 60 elderly persons who lived in such homes with the 240 normal aged persons who were members of Golden Age, etc., groups. Only two deviant responses were obtained, a purely chance level, which indicated that the two groups were much the same in terms of deviant response characteristics. A similar dearth of deviant responses was found when the aged hospitalized subjects were compared with the normal aged groups. Definitely senile patients were not represented in the hospitalized group since they were unable to take the test. Thus hospitalization or residence in a home for the aged was not reflected in deviant response frequency, but numerous deviant responses were obtained when persons aged 60 to 97 were compared with others aged 20–60. The aging scale based upon these deviant responses, called *Alpha* by Boozer, was checked for similarity to the schizophrenia (*Sigma*) and hospitalized mental patient (*Delta*) scales prepared by Barnes (1955) and it was found to be distinctly different in pattern from the Barnes scales.

CHRONIC PHYSICAL DISEASE AND DEVIANT RESPONSE PATTERNS. It seems feasible that when a person has been chronically ill with a serious disease certain personality characteristics should change. The victim of tuberculosis, cardiac disorder,

cancer, diabetes, etc., must alter many of his previous response patterns after he comes down with the particular disorder. Long established habits of eating, of activity level, of
sleep, and the like often must be modified as part of the treatment process. If so, many other responses should also be
changed and according to the Deviation Hypothesis, they
should form a unique pattern. There are problems, of course,
in satisfactorily identifying such groups but it can be done.
The problems are not those of clinical diagnosis; for operationally sound identification is clearly possible for diseases
of the kind mentioned above. Rather the problem lies in the
victim's awareness of the significance of the disorder and his
willingness to follow the medically prescribed changes in his
way of life. Nearly everyone has heard of heart disease and
diabetes sufferers who, because of ignorance, did not follow
the regimen essential for treatment. Such persons changed
no responses as a result of their disease and, hence, the Deviation Hypothesis would probably not be applicable. But with
appropriate care, subjects who have not changed their living
habits after such illness can be eliminated from a study.

Tuberculosis is objectively identifiable by sputum and
X-ray evidence and successful treatment requires behavioral
changes of a critical nature. With such factors in mind, Engen
(1959) administered the PRT to 200 hospitalized tuberculosis
patients who had been positively diagnosed. He found 73
of the 300 PRT option choices were deviant at the .01 level
of significance for males and 31 for females when compared
to normal persons, a number sufficient to prepare a scale for
deviant responses associated with tuberculosis. Male patients
diagnosed as "far advanced" in tuberculosis revealed a significantly larger number of deviant responses when compared to moderate cases. However, no similar differences
were found for the female patients when the same comparison was made. When the PRT deviant response pattern
was checked against the pattern found for schizophrenics,

Engen found the patterns to be unlike one another.

Employing a design similar to that of Engen, Berg (1961) administered the PRT to 125 cardiac patients (45 males, 80 females) and compared their responses to those obtained from normal subjects. When compared to an unselected, census-type group of normal persons, the cardiac males revealed 86 and the females 65 deviant responses at the .01 level of significance. The cardiac patients were older and of somewhat lower socioeconomic status than the normal group; therefore each cardiac patient was matched for age, sex, general intelligence, educational level, and socioeconomic background with the appropriate control group member. When the matched groups were compared, it was found that 23 responses for the cardiac males and 25 for the females were deviant at the .01 level, a number quite adequate for scaling. Berg also checked the cardiac groups against the deviant response patterns of schizophrenics and found the cardiac patients to be distinct from schizophrenia. The cardiac patients were then scored on the PRT M-F scale with the result that the cardiac males scored at the same level as normal males; however the cardiac females scored significantly in the masculine direction. This latter finding is intriguing since one is led to speculate that females who exhibit M-F response patterns which are more characteristic of males than of females may possibly be more prone to heart disease. This is running far in advance of the evidence, of course, and much more data are required before such conjecture becomes fact.

NEUROTICS AND DEVIANT RESPONSE SETS. The criterion-groups design was also used by Roitzsch and Berg (1959) in a study of adult neurotics. They hypothesized that neurotics were also immature but to a lesser degree than schizophrenics. Therefore, the adult neurotics should exhibit a deviant response frequency which was similar to that of older normal children. They also hypothesized that normal children should be differentiated from normal adults on the basis of deviant responses obtained with the PRT. Similarly, adult neurotics should be distinguishable from normal adults on the basis of PRT deviant responses. However, the normal children and the adult neurotics should exhibit a similar deviant response frequency. Three groups of 100 normal children aged 13, 14, and 16 years (150 males and 150 females) and 45 neurotic adults (20 males and 25 females) were used in the study. It was found that 74 to 144 of 240 available PRT options differentiated the groups of normal children from the group of normal adults. The neurotic adults were distinguished from normal adults by 132 deviant responses for the group of males and 120 for the group of females when 240 was the possible maximum. When the deviant response frequency of the children and the neurotics were compared, there was no significant difference. Thus the evidence of the present and of previous studies indicated that schizophrenics could be differentiated from normal subjects and neurotics could be differentiated from normal subjects on the basis of deviant responses obtained with the PRT. However, the question then arose as to whether the schizophrenics and neurotics were different from each other on the basis of deviant responses. Accordingly, the PRT responses of the neurotic groups were scored with Barnes' schizophrenia or *Sigma* scale. It was found that the neurotic males and females were distinguished from the schizophrenics at the 1 percent level of confidence. Thus, while both groups are different from normal groups in terms of deviant response frequency and pattern, they are also different from each other on the same basis.

Other Studies in the Deviation Hypothesis Frame of Reference

The foregoing studies either constructed scales based upon deviant responses or presented sufficient data to show that other scales could be constructed if desired. In this connection it may be recalled that an additional scale for M-F of interest was earlier mentioned as having been developed by the present writer. Gunderson (1953) has validated this scale in a study of counselors, policemen, musicians, librarians, teachers, and housewives. In terms of PRT M-F scores, female occupational groups were not differentiated significantly from each other nor from housewives. Male musicians, policemen, and teachers were differentiated from each other at the 1 percent level of confidence.

NEUROTIC REJECTION AND PSYCHOTIC ACCEPTANCE OF STIMULI. Besides the studies showing the feasibility of constructing valid scales based solely upon deviant responses, the Deviation Hypothesis has been applied to other psyschological test phenomenon (cf. Adams & Berg, 1961). Various studies have indicated that neurotics tend to reject a high proportion of stimulus patterns and psychotics tend to accept them. There seems to be a neurotic and a psychotic response set which, as Berg (1955) noted, seem to be in opposite directions. Wallen's (1945) finding that neurotics tend to dislike many foods is a case in point. The same may be said of Eysenck's (1955) identification of separate dimensions for neurotics and psychotics. Similarly, Cottle and Powell (1951) found that marking all MMPI items "true" produced high scores on the psychotic triad scales and marking all items "false" resulted in high scores on the MMPI neurotic triad scales. With such findings in mind, Barnes (1956a) recalled that the individual record form of the MMPI provides that only those items which are answered in the infrequent direction are recorded. Such items are deviant responses in terms of the Deviation Hypothesis definition. Therefore, Barnes reasoned, atypical "true" answers on the MMPI should correlate highly with the psychotic triad, and atypical "false" answers should correlate highly with the neurotic triad. His results were in the expected direction. The Ss or schizophrenia scale correlated .90 with the simple count of atypical "true" responses and the D or depression scale correlated .73 with the total of atypical "false" responses. Accordingly, it seems that the carefully described 26 categories of test item content employed by the MMPI are probably irrelevant for clinical measurement purposes. The important thing seems to be the deviant responses.

Barnes (1956b) performed a similar analysis in another study. Wheeler, Little, and Lehner (1951) factor analyzed the MMPI scales and found a psychotic and a neurotic factor. Since their factor loadings were similar to the correlations he had reported in an earlier study, Barnes (1956a), believed that the vector representing atypical "true" answers should be approximately collinear with the Wheeler, Little, and Lehner psychotic factor and the vector representing atypical "false" answers would be approximately collinear with their neurotic factor. Such a deduction appeared reasonable to him in terms of the Deviation Hypothesis conceptual framework. By using an indirect test of his hypothesis, Barnes concluded that the number of atypical "true" answers was a pure factor test of the MMPI psychotic factor and that the number of atypical "false" answers had a heavy loading on the neurotic factor.

AUDITION AND DEVIANT RESPONSE SETS. Adams (1959) administered the PRT and a specially constructed "audition test" to 164 (88 males and 76 females) schizophrenic patients. The audition test was composed of 50 tape-recorded meaningless sounds to which the subjects responded by checking either *Like Much, Like Slightly, Dislike Slightly,* or *Dislike Much* for each sound. Using the criterion group method, he found that one out of every three of the possible responses to his series of auditory stimuli was deviant at either the 1 or 5 percent level of significance when the schizophrenics were compared to normal adults. The frequency of deviant responses on the PRT was somewhat greater. Thus, it appears that, while cumbersome to use, auditory as well as visual stimuli can be employed to measure personality characteristics.

In this connection it is perhaps worth noting that Berg (1955, pp. 69 f.) observed that both Strong's Vocational Interest Bank (VIB) and Hathaway's MMPI were successful inventories, not because of their item content, but because they both used deviant responses. On this basis, Berg asserted that the MMPI scales should be capable of reconstruction from the VIB items and the VIB scales from the MMPI items. Garman and Uhr (1958) have done something along such lines by preparing an anxiety scale derived from VIB items. Somewhat similarly, Holland (1958) used a list of 300 occupational titles to produce a series of personality scales by employing what appears to be a deviant response technique. These writers were not engaged, of course, in a test of the Deviation Hypothesis; however their results seem to confirm in part what had earlier been predicted. A study which did directly test one facet of the Hypothesis is that of Asch (1958) in which he used negative response bias (tendency to respond *disagree* when in doubt) to study neuroticism. Asch found that relative freedom from negative response bias was associated with better adjustment and that there was a significant relationship between negative responses and neurotic reactions.

OTHER RESEARCH DESIGNS.　Several other researches have tested specific facets of the Deviation Hypothesis without utilizing the criterion group method. Grigg and Thorpe (1960), for example, used the Gough Adjective Check List in a very carefully executed study of deviant responses in college adjustment clients. From the Gough list of 300 items, Grigg and Thorpe prepared a list of 72 of the most commonly (84 percent or more) and uncommonly (16 percent or less) selected adjectives. This revised check list was then given to

1400 entering freshmen at the University of Texas. Deviant response scores were determined for each subject by counting the number of times a commonly selected adjective was *not* checked and the number of times an uncommonly selected adjective *was* checked by the subjects. At the close of the academic year, the deviant response scores for those students who had reported to the Student Health Center or to the University Counseling Bureau for psychiatric help, for personal adjustment or vocational counseling, 247 in all, were compared with 150 randomly selected, nonclient controls. The hypothesis was that the nonclient and the vocational counseling group would have a significantly lower frequency of deviant responses than the psychiatric treatment and personal adjustment counseling groups. Such was found to be the case, and the authors concluded that the Deviation Hypothesis was supported by their findings. The Grigg-Thorpe design has many advantages; for their approach would permit them to dip repeatedly into the original pool of subjects for other operationally identifiable deviant groups. Very brilliant students, for example, should have a significantly high frequency of deviant responses, so should scholastic underachievers as well as others. The only essential precaution is to make certain that any groups designated as deviant be determined on the basis of valid behavioral criteria.

Another novel situation was that used by Bullock (1960) in a study of the performance of psychiatric patients for a brief operant discrimination test. Compared to normal subjects, the patients were significantly less likely to reach established performance criteria. In mulling over these differences in operant conditioning performance, Bullock recalled that the present writer had observed that conditioned responses could probably also be used as noncritical area responses, although they had never actually been utilized for such purposes. Using the criterion group method, Bullock was able to identify a number of significant performance deviations between the normal and psychiatric groups, and he concluded (p. 91) that his investigation ". . . provides preliminary support for Berg's contention that the Deviation Hypothesis can be extended to 'conditioned responses.' "

As a final example of a specific test of the Deviation Hypothesis which did not use the criterion group method, the important study by Adams (1960b) may be considered. He used five groups of 100 subjects each, 50 males and 50 females, as follows: normal children, normal adolescents, normal adults, schizophrenic adults, and neurotic adults. The PRT was administered to all subjects and scored in terms of the following operationally defined variables:

1. *Statistical rigidity,* based upon the variance in selection of option choice. Choosing the same option for every PRT item would yield a maximum rigidity score while changing the option choice for every item would provide a minimum rigidity score.

2. *Acquiescence,* based upon the frequency with which the option "like much" was selected in responding to the test items. This was the tendency to respond in a positive direction.

3. *Negativism,* based upon the frequency with which "dislike much" was chosen. This was the tendency to respond in a negative direction.

4. *Perseveration,* based upon the tendency to repeat the previous option choice. The score was the number of runs where the same response was repeated for successive option.

5. *Affect constancy,* based upon the maintenance of a particular emotional tone in selecting options. The measure was the highest frequency of a given option class, i.e., "like slightly."

6. *Affect shifts,* based upon shifts from one extreme of option choice to the other, i.e., changing from "dislike much" on one option to "like much" on the next.

7. *Affect ratio,* based upon the square root of the ratio of acquiescence to negativism.

Adams then determined that his various groups differed in the patterns of bias they exhibited. The neurotic and normal adults, for example, differed significantly on all variables except those of *acquiescence* and *negativism.* The adolescent and adult neurotic groups were similar in terms of *acquiescence* and *perseveration.* These data were factor analyzed and four factors emerged: *general variability, acquiescence, negativism,* and *hostility expression.* Thus Adams began with deviant response classes and showed that operationally identified deviant groups revealed characteristic patterns which were derived from these response classes. It appears, therefore, that Adams' findings lend strong support to the idea of utilizing deviant responses for the measurement of personality charateristics.

Some Negative Results

A good deal of evidence has been presented to show that the predictions made from the Deviation Hypothesis have been confirmed rather well when put to empirical test. Lest it be assumed that our predictions have been uniformly, even routinely, upheld, it may be instructive to examine three instances where our results were not positive, together with the reasons for such failures. Berg (1957) had indicated that with increasing deviation in a critical area of behavior there should be an increasing frequency of deviant responses in a noncritical area of behavior. Thus mild cases of schizophrenia would be expected to exhibit fewer deviant responses on the PRT, for example, than schizophrenics who were diagnosed as *moderate* or *severe.* Harris (1958) tested this subhypothesis with a group of 100 (50 males and 50 females) hospitalized schizophrenics. For the group as a whole he found a large number of deviant responses on the PRT—192 deviant responses for males and 166 for females out of 240 possible responses. But when he attempted to divide his subjects into subgroups of mild, moderate and severe degrees of schizophrenia, he ran into trouble. He tried psychiatric rating scales, length of hospitalization, chronicity versus acuteness of symptoms without being able to obtain valid differentiations for severity of the disorder. Apparently, one severe symptom, such as hallucinatory voices, may sometimes be regarded as indicative of more severe schizophrenicity than a dozen less dramatic symptoms such as apathy, occasional neologisms, etc. Whatever the reasons, Harris was unable to obtain useful categories for severity of schizophrenia. He did obtain a large number of deviant responses, thereby confirming Barnes' results, but he did not obtain differential deviant response frequencies for degrees of schizophrenicity.

DEGREE OF EMOTIONAL DISTURBANCE NOT REFLECTED BY DEVIANT RESPONSE FREQUENCY. House (1960) was able to construct a scale for emotional disturbance in children; however he was unable to obtain evidence for increased frequency of deviant responses with increased severity of emotional disturbance. He used the pooled clinical judgments of a professional staff for determining categories of *mild, moderate,* and *severe* degrees of disturbance. Like Harris, House felt that the source of difficulty probably lay in the problem of clinically rating the severity of the disorders. Whether such is the case or not, it is true that where relatively objective criteria are used, deviant response frequency is related to the degree with which a particular dimension or condition exists. For example, Hesterly (1960) found deviant responses increased with decreasing chronological age and Cieutat (1960) reported similar positive results for degree of mental retardation. But age level can be accurately determined from birth certificates and severity of mental retardation from intelligence tests. Hence, the problem seems to center in the fallibility of subjective clinical appraisals. In any event deviant response frequency does not relate to degree or severity when clinical estimates or rating scales based upon such estimates are used. But when severity or degree is determined by objective criteria, the relationship does appear, at least insofar as our present evidence indicates.

DELINQUENCY NOT A VALID CATEGORY OF BEHAVIOR. Another failure was an attempt to distinguish on the basis of PRT deviant responses, a group of juvenile delinquents from a group of nondelinquents matched for age, IQ, and similar variables. Apparently, delinquent behavior is not a valid behavioral category any more than criminal behavior is. Delinquents are sent to reformatories for offenses such as persistent theft, vandalism, sexual offenses, physical assaultiveness, etc. Some delinquents perhaps would have been continued on probation instead of being incarcerated except that their homes were considerably worse than the reform school. Thus, like the executive or criminal groupings, mentioned earlier in this article, delinquents are not identifiable by external criteria and, accordingly, are not a valid deviant group.

The Major Sources of Difficulty

Our experience would indicate that, among other possible factors, there are three major sources of difficulty which can, in varying degree, interfere with the use of deviant responses for predicting behavior in a critical area from responses which occur in a noncritical area of behavior. First, *there may be a lack of operationally clean criteria in identifying either the criterion or deviant groups or both.* Our attempt to use a group of delinquents as a deviant group is a case in point. The same is true of the previously described attempts to divide schizophrenics and emotionally disturbed children into mild, moderate, and severe categories. In this connection it may be noted that even where deviant responses occur with considerable frequency, their predictive usefulness could probably have been even better had the criterion and deviant groups been more rigorously defined. Barnes once remarked that, excellent as his findings were, he was convinced that he could have achieved even more striking results had he been able to avoid a dual contamination in his groups. That is, among his normal criterion group subjects was a small but definite number who were seriously maladjusted persons. They were normal only in the courtesy sense of not being hospitalized. Similarly, the deviant group had a small number of patients who really were ready for discharge; for they were about as normal as many subjects in the criterion group. But sometimes through oversight and sometimes because the patient had a previous history of assaultive behavior, hospitals occasionally do not release a patient even though the patient is reasonably normal. Be that as it may, such factors make for varying degrees of contamination in criterion and deviant groups.

A second source of interference in utilizing deviant response sets for prediction purposes occurs where too few items are available to evoke responses. The studies described earlier in which the Archimedes spiral aftereffect and the studies which used hand preference as diagnostic indicators for personality disturbance are probably cases in point. Such studies are essentially one-item tests in which only two or three responses are possible. Thus they really should not be expected to distinguish very well between groups; certainly not as well as the MMPI, for example, which has 550 items, not just one. This is not to say that a single-item test is useless, but rather that it will have a much larger number of false negative and false positive identifications than a series of items. A single item test may have some limited but highly practical value as illustrated by a spur-of-the-moment test concocted by an American Army private during the Battle of the Bulge. A number of German soldiers were known to be masquerading in American uniforms and the problem was to detect them. The Army private identified a number of the German infiltrators simply by asking them to spit on the ground. Americans, he said, expectorated with *oomph* and propelled the saliva away from them. Germans and most Europeans, the private asserted, sputtered in a frothy spray when expectorating. The private falsely identified some native-born but dribble-chin Americans but he correctly identified several German spies who had been undetected up to that time. Undoubtedly, he also missed some Germans who spat rather than sputtered when discharging saliva.

The third source of interference with the eliciting of deviant response set occurs where there is too pronounced structure in the stimulus content of the item. If an item has but one obvious answer for most persons, there can be no deviant response. The present writer, in an earlier article (1957), has described how he originally sought to use objective history and algebra tests to produce response sets which could be used to measure personality traits. These attempts did not work out very well, partly because the test items were rather definitely structured and partly because the multiple-choice item form often used in these tests was relatively free from response set influence as Cronbach (1946; 1950) and Rapaport and Berg (1955) have noted. For best results in eliciting deviant responses, the items should be relatively unstructured.

THE SOURCES OF INTERFERENCE RECAPITULATED. These factors, then, are the major sources of interference with the operation of deviant response sets. Reasonably careful planning can eliminate or, at least, markedly reduce the influence of such factors. There are other factors, by contrast, which presumably can increase the number of deviant responses if one cares to use them for this purpose. The word *presumably* is used because only one such factor has actually been utilized in this way. When taking a test designed to elicit deviant response sets, it often happens that peripheral deviant responses appear but for which no formal means of identifying them has been provided. For example, the PRT has 60 designs, each of which has four options or 240 total possible responses in all. The instructions emphasize that one option must be marked for every design and on every page the same instruction is repeated. Normal subjects virtually never fail to mark their preferences for every design; however, a number of subjects with severe emotional disturbances do omit certain designs. Such omissions are not entirely due to inattention to the task, for some subjects will volunteer, "I won't look at it" or "It's awful!" Accordingly, we have occasionally used such response omissions as a deviant response since they almost never occur among normal subjects. This increases the total possible number of deviant responses on the PRT from 240 to 300. While the "no response" category is the only peripheral set we have actually employed, there are others which seem likely to be equally useful. For example, normal subjects finish the PRT in six or seven minutes. Psychotic subjects often take much longer. Thus an inordinate time for completing the test could probably be used to increase the deviation score. Schizophrenic patients sometimes embellish the PRT designs or other parts of the test by writing in remarks or adding designs, a tendency not found among normal subjects (Adams & Berg, 1961c). A system of increasing the schizophrenia score by a point or so for each design or group of embellishments could undoubtedly be worked out. In his doctoral thesis but not in his published article, Barnes (1955) has photographs of several examples of such schizophrenic additions to PRT test booklets which he found in his research. When giving his audition test, Adams and Berg (1961b) found that some of the comments volunteered by both his normal and schizophrenic subjects were significant in the deviant response sense. Some normal subjects remarked that a particular sound used by Adams and Berg was "like a foghorn" while several schizophrenic subjects said of the same sound, "they are drowning a baby" or uttered something similarly macabre. The embellishments reported by Barnes and the failure to mark a test option are objectively ascertainable while the "drowning baby" type of responses noted by Adams and Berg are not. Yet, if desired, a frequency list of volunteered responses could be worked out along the lines used in word association tests and deviant responses could then be identified by references to the list. Be that as it may, it seems quite likely that a number of similar peripheral deviant responses could be found and put to use when distinguishing criterion and deviant groups.

Unresolved Problems

There are a number of unresolved problems concerning deviant response sets. For example, what causes them? As noted earlier in this chapter, past learning, hereditary structure, and physiological or organic state, either singly or in combination, are presumably involved. But how? A large amount of empirical data on the learning of deviant responses, on biochemical influences, including drugs, on constitutional and disease conditions, etc., is needed before even a partial answer can be forthcoming. While the task is indeed formidable, it seems eminently worthwhile; for it seems clear, to the present writer at least, that in the answer to this problem lies the explanation of the fundamental nature of personality. Another unresolved problem is that of measuring degree of structure in the stimulus patterns employed to elicit deviant responses. One could use ratings or some similar evaluative approach, of course; however, since research on the Deviation Hypothesis has adhered to objective criteria and statistical definitions, it seems highly undesirable to have recourse to ratings except as a last resort. Actually, no one has tackled the problem yet, as far as we know; and as a guess, it seems likely that the measurement of structure by objective means should not really be extremely difficult although it is likely to be laborious. If structure could be measured, it would be of considerable help in obtaining items of suitable stimulus content to produce deviant response sets of maximum usefulness. One more unresolved problem may be mentioned. This is the problem of measuring psychological distance between options on a test such as the PRT. For example, is the psychological distance in terms of degree of affect between options *Like Much* and *Like Slightly* the same as the psychological distance between *Dislike Much* and *Dislike Slightly*? It seems likely that it is not, but we have no objective means of determining the distance. Purely as a guess, this problem is likely to prove knotty if subjective rating-type approaches are avoided, as they should be.

Summary

Deviant responses tend to be general; thus if they occur in one area of behavior, they may be expected to occur in certain other areas of behavior. This is the essence of the Deviation Hypothesis, which seeks to explain why a large number of clinical prediction studies are able to forecast deviant behavior with at least some degree of success. This is true for a wide variety of stimulus conditions, response measures, and for various patient groups. The same statement may be applied to studies which are not concerned with psychopathological states, such as research on vocational interest, attitudes, and the like. There is considerable evidence which indicates that responses made in a noncritical area of behavior (such as preferences for abstract designs) can be used to predict behavior in critical areas (such as schizophrenia). The simplest way of eliciting such deviant responses is by the use of unstructured stimuli. The particular form of stimulus content is not important; for in various researches the stimuli employed have included lists of foods, the autokinetic phenomenon, abstract designs, meaningless sounds, etc. It is important, however, that the criterion and deviant groups be carefully identified by means of valid behavioral characteristics. Then, the deviant responses can be identified by purely statistical methods and, if desired, a scale developed from the responses. The work on the Deviation Hypothesis is an extension of the old studies of "set" or *Einstellung*. The Hypothesis is intended to be an explanatory and unifying principle which accounts for a broad range of disparate studies which seek to predict behavior in a variety of situations by many forms of stimulus conditions and a wide variety of response measures.

REFERENCES

Adams, H. E. Statistical rigidity in schizophrenic and normal groups measured with auditory and visual stimuli. *Psychol. Rep.*, 1960a, **7**, 119–122.

Adams, H. E. Deviant responses in the measurement of personality characteristics. Unpublished doctoral dissertation, Louisiana State Univer., 1960b.

Adams, H. E., & Berg, I. A. Affective tone of test option choice as a deviant response. *Psychol. Rep.*, 1961a, **8**, 79–85.

Adams, H. E., & Berg, I. A. Schizophrenia and deviant response sets produced by auditory and visual test content. *J. Psychol.*, 1961b, **51**, 393–398.

Adams, H. E., & Berg, I. A. Schizophrenia and the frequency of qualitative deviant responses. *Psychol. Rep.*, 1961c, **8**, 123–126.

Adorno, T. W., Frenkel-Brunswik, Else, Levinson, D. J., & Sanford, R. N. *The authoritarian personality.* New York: Harper, 1950.

Altus, W. D. Adjustment and food aversions among army illiterates. *J. consult. Psychol.*, 1949, **13**, 429–432.

Asch, M. J. Negative response bias and personality adjustment. *J. counsel. Psychol.*, 1958, **5**, 206–210.

Barnes, E. H.   The relationship of biased test responses to psychopathology. *J. abnorm. soc. Psychol.*, 1955, **51**, 286–290.

Barnes, E. H.   Factors, response bias, and the MMPI. *J. consult. Psychol.*, 1956a, **20**, 419–421.

Barnes, E. H.   Response bias and the MMPI. *J. consult. Psychol.*, 1956b, **20**, 371–374.

Bass, B. M.   Authoritarianism or acquiescence? *J. abnorm. soc. Psychol.*, 1955, **51**, 616-623.

Berg, I. A.   The reliability of extreme position response sets in two tests. *J. Psychol.*, 1953, **36**, 3–9.

Berg, I. A.   Response bias and personality: The Deviation Hypothesis. *J. Psychol.*, 1955, **40**, 61–71.

Berg, I. A.   Deviant responses and deviant people: the formulation of the Deviation Hypothesis. *J. counsel. Psychol.*, 1957, **4**, 154–161.

Berg, I. A.   Word choice in the interview and personal adjustment. *J. counsel. Psychol.*, 1958, **5**, 130–135.

Berg, I. A.   The unimportance of test item content. In B. M. Bass and I. A. Berg (Eds.), *Objective approaches to personality assessment.* New York: Van Nostrand, 1959, Pp. 83–99.

Berg, I. A.   The relationship of deviant responses to cardiac disease. *Psychol. Rep.*, 1961, submitted for publication.

Berg, I. A., & Collier, J. S.   Personality and group differences in extreme response sets. *Educ. psychol. Measmt.*, 1953, **13**, 164–169.

Berg, I. A., Hunt, W. A., & Barnes, E. H.   *The perceptual reaction test.* Evanston, Ill.: Irwin A. Berg, 1949.

Berg, I. A., & Rapaport, G. M.   Response bias in an unstructured questionnaire. *J. Psychol.*, 1954, **38**, 475–481.

Boozer, D. G.   Response sets as indicators of senescence and of psychopathology in old age. Unpublished doctoral dissertation, Louisiana State Univer., 1961.

Bullock, D. H.   Performances of psychiatric patients in a brief operant discrimination test. *Psychol. Record,* 1960, **10**, 83–93.

Burt, C.   *Mental and scholastic tests.* London: County Council, 1921.

Campbell, D. T.   Systematic error on the part of Human links in communication systems. *Inform. and Control,* 1958, **1**, 334–369.

Cattell, R. B., & Anderson, J. A.   The measurement of personality behavior disorders by the IPAT Music Preference Test. *J. appl. Psychol.,* 1953, **37**, 446-454.

Chapman, L. J., & Campbell, D. T.   Response set in the F scale. *J. abnorm. soc. Psychol.,* 1957, **54**, 129–132.

Chodorkoff, B., & Mussen, P. H.   Qualitative aspects of normals and schizophrenics. *J. consult. Psychol.,* 1952, **16**, 43–48.

Cieutat, L. G.   Deviant responses as a function of mental deficiency. Unpublished doctoral dissertation, Louisiana State Univer., 1960.

Cohn, T. S.   Is the F scale indirect? *J. abnorm. soc. Psychol.,* 1952, **47**, 185–192.

Cottle, W. C., & Powell, J. O.   The effect of random answers on the MMPI. *Educ. psycho. Measmt.,* 1951, **11**, 224–227.

Cronbach, L. J.   Response sets and test validity. *Educ. psychol. Measmt.,* 1946, **6**, 475–494.

Cronbach, L. J.   Further evidence on response sets and test designs. *Educ. psychol. Measmt.,* 1950, **10**, 3–31.

Doll, E. A.   Anthropometry as an aid to mental diagnosis. *Pub. New Jersey Trng. Sch.,* 1916, **8**, 1–7.

Edwards, A. L.   *The social desirability variable in personality assessment and research.* New York: Dryden, 1957.

Edwards, A. L.   Social desirability and personality test construction. In B. M. Bass and I. A. Berg (Eds.), *Objective approaches to personality assessment.* New York: Van Nostrand, 1959. Pp. 100–118.

Engen, E. P.   Response set of pulmonary tuberculosis patients. Unpublished doctoral dissertation, Louisiana State Univer., 1959.

Eysenck, H. J.   *Dimensions of personality.* London: Kegan Paul, 1947.

Eysenck, H. J.   Psychiatric diagnosis as a psychological and statistical problem. *Psychol. Rep.,* 1955, **1**, 3–17.

Fairbanks, H.   The quantitative differentiation of samples of spoken languages. *Psychol. Mongr.,* 1944, **56**, 19–38.

Frederiksen, N., & Messick, S.   Response set as a measure of personality. *Tech. Rept.,* Project NR 151–113. Contract NONR 694 (oo), Educational Testing Service, Princeton, N.J., 1958.

Freeman, E., & Josey, W. E.   Quantitative visual index to memory impairment. *Arch. neurol. Psychiat.,* 1949, **62,** 794–796.

Gaier, E. L., & Bass, B. M.   Regional differences in interrelations among authoritarianism, acquiescence, and ethnocentrism. *J. soc. Psychol.,* 1959, **49,** 47–51.

Garman, G. S., & Uhr, L.   An anxiety scale for the Strong Vocational Interest Inventory: Development, cross-validation, and subsequent tests of validity. *J. appl. Psychol.,* 1958, **42,** 241–246.

Gibson, J. J.   A critical review of the concept of set in contemporary psychology. *Psychol. Bull.,* 1941, **38,** 781–817.

Goddard, H. H.   The height and weight of feeble-minded children in American institutions. *J. nerv. ment. Dis.,* 1902, **39,** 217–235.

Goodfellow, L. D.   The human element in probability. *J. gen. Psychol.,* 1940, **33,** 201–205.

Gough, H. G.   An additional study of food aversions. *J. abnorm. soc. Psychol.,* 1946, **41,** 86–88.

Grigg, A. E., & Thorpe, J. S.   Deviant responses in college adjustment clients: a test of Berg's Deviation Hypothesis. *J. consult. Psychol.,* 1960, **24,** 92–94.

Grings, W. W.   The verbal summator technique and abnormal mental states. *J. abnorm. soc. Psychol.,* 1942, **37,** 529–545.

Guilford, J. P.   *Psychometric methods.* New York: McGraw-Hill, 1936.

Guilford, J. P.   The validation of an "indecision" score for predicting proficiency of foremen. *J. appl. Psychol.,* 1954, **38,** 224–226.

Gunderson, E. J.   A study of masculinity-femininity of interest in selected occupations. Unpublished master's thesis, Northwestern Univer., 1953.

Harris, J. L.   Deviant response frequency in relation to severity of schizophrenic reaction. Unpublished master's thesis, Louisiana State Univer., 1958.

Hathaway, S. R.   Some considerations relative to nondirective counseling as therapy. *J. clin. Psychol.,* 1948, **4,** 226–231.

Hathaway, S. R., & McKinley, J. C. *The Minnesota Multiphasic Personality Inventory* (Manual). New York: Psychology Corporation, 1943.

Hawkins, W. A. Deviant responses, response variability, and paired associate learning. Unpublished doctoral dissertation, Louisiana State Univer., 1960.

Hesterly, S. O. Deviant response patterns as a function of chronological age. Unpublished doctoral dissertation, Louisiana State Univer., 1960.

Hesterly, S. O., & Berg, I. A. Deviant responses as indicators of immaturity and schizophrenia. *J. consult. Psychol.,* 1958, **22,** 389–393.

Holland, J. L. A personality inventory employing occupational titles. *J. appl. Psychol.,* 1958, **42,** 336-342.

House, C. W. Response bias as a measure of emotional disturbance in children. Unpublished doctoral dissertation, Louisiana State Univer., 1960.

Jackson, D. E., & Messick, S. J. A note on "ethnocentrism" and acquiescent response sets. *J. abnorm. soc. Psychol.,* 1957, **54,** 132–134.

Jackson, D. E., & Messick, S. J. Content and style in personality assessment. *Psychol. Bull.,* 1958, **55,** 243–252.

Jackson, D. E., Messick, S. J., & Solley, C. M. How rigid is the "authoritarian"? *J. abnorm. soc. Psychol.,* 1957, **54,** 137–140.

Johnson, D. E., Bauer, R. W., & Brown, D. R. Visual afterphenomena in diagnosis. *J. consult. Psychol.,* 1959, **23,** 90.

Katzell, R. A. Cross-validation of item analyses. *Educ. psychol. Measmt.,* 1951, **11,** 16–22.

Lewis, N. A., & Taylor, J. A. Anxiety and extreme response preferences. *Educ. psychol. Measmt.,* 1955, **15,** 111–116.

Lorenz, M., & Cobb, S. Language behavior in psychoneurotic patients. *Arch. neurol. Psychiat.,* 1953, **69,** 684–694.

Lorenz, M., & Cobb, S. Language behavior in manic patients. *Arch. neurol. Psychiat.,* 1952, **67,** 763–770.

Lorge, I. Gen-like: halo or reality? *Psychol. Bull.,* 1937, **34,** 545–546.

Mainland, D., & Murray, I. M. Tables for use in fourfold contingency tests. *Science,* 1952, **116,** 591–595.

Mann, M. B. The quantitative differentiation of samples of written language. *Psychol. Monogr.*, 1944, **56**, 41–74.

Philbrick, E. B. The validity of the spiral aftereffect as a clinical tool for diagnosis of organic brain pathology. *J. consult. Psychol.*, 1959, **23**, 39–43.

Price, A. C., & Deabler, H. L. Diagnosis for organicity by means of spiral aftereffect. *J. consult. Psychol.*, 1955, **19**, 299–302.

Rapaport, G. M., & Berg, I. A. Response sets in a multiple-choice test. *Educ. psychol. Measmt.*, 1955, **15**, 58–62.

Rechtshaffen, A., & Mednick, S. A. The autokinetic word technique. *J. abnorm. soc. Psychol.*, 1955, **51**, 346.

Rettig, S., Jacobson, F. N., Despres, L., & Pasamanick, B. Rating response set as a function of objective status criteria. *Sociometry*, 1958, **21**, 281–291.

Robinson, E. S. The psychology of public education. *Am. J. Pub. Hlth.*, 1933, **23**, 1–125.

Roitzsch, J. C., & Berg, I. A. Deviant responses as indicators of immaturity and neuroticism. *J. clin. Psychol.*, 1959, **15**, 417–419.

Roshal, J. J. G. The type-token ratio as a measure of changes in behavior variability during psychotherapy. In W. U. Snyder (Ed.), *Group report of a program of research in psychotherapy.* University Park, Pa.: Pennsylvania State Univer. Press, 1953, 94–104.

Ross, S., & Kohl, D. M. Perceptual factors in number choices. *J. gen. Psychol.*, 1948, **39**, 39–47.

Rubin-Rabson, G. Correlates of the noncommittal test-item response. *J. clin. Psychol.*, 1954, **10**, 93–95.

Shelley, H. P. Response set and the California Attitude Scale. *Educ. psychol. Measmt.*, 1955, **16**, 63–67.

Simon, B., Holzberg, J. D., Alessi, S. L., & Garrity, D. A. The recognition and acceptance of mood in music by psychotic patients. *J. nerv. ment. Dis.*, 1951, **144**, 66–78.

Singer, W. B., & Young, P. T. Studies in affective reaction: III. The specificity of affective reactions. *J. genet. Psychol.*, 1941, **24**, 327–341.

Smith, W., Powell, E. K., & Ross, S. Manifest anxiety and food aversions. *J. abnorm. soc. Psychol.*, 1955, **50**, 101–104.

Strong, E. K., Jr. *Manual for Vocational Interest Blank for Men.*

Stanford: Stanford University Press, 1935.

Voth, A. C. An experimental study of mental patients through the autokinetic phenomenon. *Amer. J. Psychiat.,* 1947, **103,** 793–805.

Wallen, R. W. Food aversions of normal and neurotic males. *J. abnorm. soc. Psychol.,* 1945, **40,** 77–81.

Wallen, R. W. Food aversions and behavior disorders. *J. consult. Psychol.,* 1948, **12,** 310–312.

Wheeler, W. M., Little, K. B., & Lehner, G. F. The internal structure of the MMPI. *J. consult. Psychol.,* 1951, **15,** 134–141.

Wiggins, J. S. A review of Edwards, A. L. *The social desirability in personality assessment and research. Contemp. Psychol.,* 1958, **3,** 326–328.

Wiggins, J. S., & Rumrill, C. Social desirability in the MMPI and Welsh's factor scales A and R. *J. consult. Psychol.,* 1959, **23,** 100–106.

Wile, I. S. The relation of left-handedness to behavior disorders. *Am. J. Orthopsychiat.,* 1932, **2,** 44–57.

Witkin, H. A. The perception of the upright. *Scient. Amer.,* 1959, **200,** 50–56.

Witkin, H. A., Lewis, H. B., Hertzman, B., Machover, K., Meissner, P. B., & Wapner, S. *Personality through perception.* New York: Harper, 1954.

CHAPTER 11

Social Exceptions that Prove the Rule[1]

PAULINE NICHOLS PEPINSKY

The Ohio State University

This chapter is concerned with a study of productive non-conformity. It is a report on an attempt to identify some conditions under which nonconformity *can* mean, not a neurotic self preoccupation, nor a kind of conformity in reverse, but behavior that is socially constructive. Three phases of the work to date will be reviewed: (1) a preliminary search for hypotheses in three natural situations, (2) the inductive development of a general conceptual scheme, and (3) a series of laboratory experiments now underway.

This research takes place under the invisible, but pervasive auspices of the *Zeitgeist* and the *Ortgeist* of contemporary America. In our several fields, we share a major concern with man and his social predicament, and we have had professional reasons to be particularly interested in the recent and widespread viewing-with-alarm of our present state as an "age of

[1] This research is being conducted under Project NR 170-396, Contract NONR 495 (15), between The Ohio State University and the Office of Naval Research. Reproduction of this chapter, in whole or in part, is permitted for any purpose of the U.S. Government. The present paper borrows heavily from material contained in previous reports to ONR (Pauline & H. Pepinsky, 1958, 1959; Pauline Pepinsky, 1959) and from a previously prepared paper describing the campus field study (Pauline Pepinsky, 1960). H. B. Pepinsky, R. J. Campbell, and B. A. Norton all have made indispensable substantive and critical contributions to the work reported.

conformity." The prototypic "status seeker," the "exurban-ite," "organizational man," is seen as submerged in "together-ness," lost in "groupthink," victimized by "hidden per-suaders," and wandering lonely in a crowd.

At the same time we are reminded that we also live in an "age of anxiety," fraught with major change and awful un-certainty. We are admonished to "reconsider individualism," to develop "originality" and "creativity," to give recognition to the "uncommon man," and to strive toward a "maximum utilization of our human resources." If it is bad to be a "con-formist," it is no better to be a "beatnik" or an "outsider," and our clinical literature abounds with descriptions of non-productive deviations from accepted norms. The efforts of the behavioral scientist at clarification are not made easier by the semantic confusion with which the current hubbub is rife. But neither would he deny that the catch phrases just recited refer to a welter of problems as complex as they are fuzzily defined.

The present research has been launched under no delusion that these matters will submit readily to easy, all-encompass-ing solutions. The hope is at least to demonstrate one way of trying to ask answerable questions about the occurrence of productive nonconformity and to push the inquiry far enough to make an informed guess about how fruitful this particular approach is likely to be. It is an immediate obli-gation to make explicit the restricted character of the situ-ations and the behavior under study.

BASIC DEFINITIONS AND CONCEPTS. Because the terms *non-conformity* and *productivity* have been so variously and (in the popular literature) so ambiguously defined of late, it is important to make clear at once what is meant by them here. First of all, *nonconformity is defined as individual behavior that, when viewed over time, is in both observed statistical and inferred psychological senses independent of the pre-*

vailing social norms. By such norms are meant the generally accepted standards against which the behavior of given individuals in given situations is subject to assessment. Secondly, *productive nonconformity is independence that also can be shown to make a positive and significant contribution to either (1) the task accomplishment of a particular group, organization, or society; or (2) the task accomplishment of an individual in a particular social setting.*

These general and provisional definitions permit the investigator to examine either a series of N decisions reached or positions taken by the same actor in the context of work on a single complex task in a given group setting, or a series of N decisions reached or positions taken by the same actor in a set of N group situations. Present experimental interest is restricted to nonconforming behavior defined in the former sense. The notion of nonconformity as independent behavior means that theoretically the statistical association between the task-relevant behavior of an individual and the behavior specified by the relevant social norm approaches zero as a limit with a large N of behaviors sampled over time. Both consistently rebellious behavior ("negative conformity") and consistently compliant behavior ("positive conformity") are definitionally regarded as illustrations of conformity, since both types of habitual responses are statistically predictable with better than chance accuracy from knowledge of the group standards alone. (That is, a correlation of minus one permits as accurate a prediction as a correlation of plus one.) Instead, nonconforming behavior in the present sense is assumed to be predictable from knowledge of personal, task, and other situational variables.

Application of the *statistical* criterion of independence implies that a measure of individual behavior involves repeated sampling over time, that whether a single behavorial instance constitutes independence or conformity is indeterminate, and admits the possibility that an erroneous inference may be drawn about the direction or extent of conformity, if the sample of observations is small or biased. Application of the *psychological* criterion of independence demands inference from evidence other than such statistical association that the actor's behavior is determined, not by a group standard of performance but by such antecedents as his own personal standards or the requirements of the task he faces. The concept of independence or nonconformity should be understood as relative, both to the situation and in degree. Some individuals are to be regarded as more or less conforming than others in the sense that a greater or a smaller proportion of the variability in their observed behavior over time is to be accounted for by the stipulations of the relevant social norms. It should be emphasized that as an alternative to consistent agreement with a majority position, the behavior referred to is not that of the persistent "aginner." The concept of reaction formation provides one way to explain that kind of response to group influence.

The notion of productivity as an amount of task accomplishment presumes that an actor's and a group's performance can be meaningfully subjected to *contemporary* assessment either by an external observer or by the actor's peers or superiors within a given social system. The term *task* refers to the confrontation of an individual or a group with a stimulus situation in which the individual or the group is held accountable for some outcome such that his, or their behavior is subject to assessment against specifiable criteria. "Task" as defined by an observer may or may not correspond to an individual's or a group's "problem" as defined and responded to by the actor himself or by the group members (Pepinsky, Pepinsky, & Pavlik, 1958). It is not to be assumed without independent evidence that his task and his problem are phenomenally equivalent for the subject. The above definition of a task allows for as broad an example as, say, "getting a college education," and does *not* equate outcome with tangible products like shoes. A measurable outcome might be "number of original ideas."

An important restriction upon the present research is that it confines itself to questions about the contemporary assessment of independent behavior. It does not include the present assessment of remote, past events, nor can it preclude future revisions of present social judgments. Changing economic and social conditions in the American society at large can drastically modify negotiations within groups and organizations over time. But the general concept of productivity as task accomplishment is based upon an assumption that achievement orientation is a continuing and pervasive American characteristic (Parsons, 1951), although definitions of task and criteria of task accomplishment are expected to vary from situation to situation, from time to time, and from person to person.

The apparent definitional paradox involved in the juxtaposition of the words *productivity* and *nonconformity* points to the seeming illogicality of human behavior, which has notable illustrations in everyday life, and with which it is exactly the problem of this investigation to deal (Pauline Pepinsky, 1961). How conceptual reconciliation can come about may be clearer, if the central questions with which this research is concerned are restated as follows: given a group's (or an organization's or a society's) definition of what constitutes productive behavior in a special setting, under what circumstances will the group fail to be consistent in applying this general rule to the assessment of the individual case?

How is it possible to predict social accreditation of some nonconforming behaviors? How can we account for the acceptable exceptions that prove—in the sense of "test"—the established rules? It may be clinically and sociologically accurate to say that such questions occur to the student of behavior as a projection of his own part of the autistic dreams of the alienated intellectual, who would have his social cake and eat it too. Even so, there can be little argument that the problems he states also have a general pertinence for this society.

Productive Independence in Three Natural Settings

The major purpose of the initial research was to arrive inductively at a set of experimentally testable hypotheses about the conditions apparently antecedent to productive, independent behavior. The inquiry started with three field studies, in which nonconforming and productive behavior were treated as independent variables and from which a search was made backward in time for the events to which such behaviors seemed to lead historically, the prior events thus being treated as if they were dependent variables. While the inferences so obtained are based on observations, their status is that of the documented—but *post hoc*—hunch, whose predictive value we are now only beginning to test. With deliberate intent, the field studies were undertaken in three quite different natural settings: (1) the campus of a large state university, (2) the main laboratories of a large industrial research organization, and (3) an architecturally planned and privately incorporated suburban neighborhood. Interest was not centered in student behavior, technical research operations, or architectural projects as such. These situations were selected, rather, with several other considerations in mind. First, all three satisfied expedient research demands in that information already available gave us foreknowledge of social norms relevant to the behavior to be observed; second, they appeared to have distinctive characteristics that would make it possible to look for both specific and general antecedents to productive and independent behavior, and later to structure accordingly the properties of the laboratory situation; and third, preliminary indications were that behavior that could be viewed as productive independence did occur with observable frequency in each.

Despite their surface disparity, it may be noted that the situations studied have an underlying continuity. In each case, the behavior examined is linked to attainment of a status-conferring objective in the social progression of American life—whether in its educational, vocational, or domestic aspect: (1) acquisition of a college education, (2) advancement in a technical scientific profession, and (3) acquisition of a "custom built" home in a suburban community. The nature of the data obtained and the observational procedures used varied with the setting. Some of the emergent hypotheses also are limited to the one or another of these settings. There are other hunches, however, that seemed to find recurring support, regardless of differences among situations. Since all three of these studies have just been reported elsewhere (Pauline Pepinsky, 1959, 1960) in overpowering detail, this paper will mercifully confine itself to summarizing what seem to us to be some of the most intriguing results.

PRODUCTIVE NONCONFORMITY ON A UNIVERSITY CAMPUS. The first study was conducted on the campus of a large mid-western university. Two previous studies by Florence (1956a; 1956b) provided an empirical definition of the standards against which undergraduates in that university judged themselves and their peers to be successful students.[2] These data were collected from undergraduate contemporaries of those involved in the present study, and so comprised an appropriate base line from which to view the behavior of our selected sample. This sample was comprised of 19 women students who were members of an organization to be identified here as the Senior Honor Group (SHG). New members are selected

---

[2] The normative information yielded by Florence's work emerged in the process of the development and cross validation of an ingenious forced-choice instrument called the Student Behavior Description (SBD). A detailed description of the construction of the SBD is available elsewhere (Florence, 1956a), as is the report of her validation study (Florence, 1956b), which included separate analyses of data obtained from women students in the same university.

by the unanimous vote of the incumbent membership, and on the basis of superior scholarship, leadership, and service to the university. The members of SHG did not conform in important respects, as individuals and as a group, to the prevailing image of the successful student, and yet they were socially accredited as highly productive members of particular student organizations and of the campus society at large. Data provided by ratings, direct observation, and by ten semistructured interviews have permitted us to arrive at a number of hunches about the special characteristics of people and circumstances that can permit nonconformity to occur and to be assessed as productive. Selected case records of ten other students regarded by staff members as nonconforming and nonproductive provided another basis for comparison with the members of SHG. Despite the fact that our observations were almost exclusively restricted to females, the inferences drawn, with a few exceptions, do seem to have general implications.

It is hardly surprising and clearly evident that individuals —certainly individual women—who conspicuously demonstrate an ability to be both independent and productive are quite remarkable people, whose incidence is extremely rare. In their reported personal histories there is repeated mention of early independence and achievement training (Krebs, 1958), of parental respect for achievement, but supportive encouragement of the child to make her own decisions, to think things through for herself, to permit the child to test the consequences of her own decisions. There was also a pronounced tendency among these women students to identify more strongly with their fathers or older brothers than with the same sex parents or siblings. Both the members of SHG and the selected, nonproductive cases were predominantly either the oldest children or oldest girls in their families, which suggests—as do some other studies (Mussen & Conger, 1956)—that ordinal position among siblings may be a predisposing factor toward deviation from accepted standards. The suggestion is highly tenuous, but seems worth noting, that in the case of the female in our culture, the "oldest sibling effect" may be modified in the direction of achievement orientation, where the variable of ordinal position interacts with identification with a masculine figure.

The single term that most strongly suggests itself as descriptive of these relatively independent and highly productive individuals is "ego strength" (Barron, 1953a; Barron, 1953b; Crutchfield, 1955; Maslow, 1950; Shoben, 1957). Their independence seems to proceed from an internalized, well-integrated set of standards, but these values are not reflected in a negative and self righteous puritanism. They have both spontaneity and self control; they can be alone without discomfort, but they are able to form warm, nonexploitative attachments to others. They accept some limits as inevitable, but their attitude toward authority is one of critical respect, rather than of unquestioning servility. They do conform to the majority view on trivial matters, but when they differ with others on issues they see as important (Jahoda, 1959), they can maintain their positions under pressure. They are, however, willing to listen to and consider alternatives; their typical set is that nearly any situation is capable of constructive restructuring. Because they can "see both sides" they sometimes have trouble in reaching decisions, but they can and do get things done. They regard nonconformity as an end in itself as pointless.

On the other hand, the behavior of the selected nonproductive cases seems to be more accurately definable as "negative conformity" than as independence. Here, *immaturity* is the term that comes first to mind. One of three things seems to be happening: (1) there is a rebellion against authority, against accepted peer or adult standards without the development of an integrated set of personal standards to replace them; (2) there may be a kind of oscillation, a confused wavering between one set of values and another; or (3) in some instances there appears to be an internalization of a set of defensive-repressive standards representing an attempt to deny a need for others—a kind of affiliative reaction formation. The operative standards invoked in all three ways seem not only to be dysfunctional in the achievement of social approval per se, but also irrelevant to the accomplishment of socially valued task objectives. Most of these students have superior measured academic aptitude. Yet they tend either to be withdrawn or in trouble through an uncontrolled acting out of their difficulties. They appear to be both socially hostile and self destructive. They show a typical history of conflict with both parents and close identification with neither. They seem to have unusual difficulties in relating to the opposite sex. They clearly are functioning below capacity both academically and socially, and their self-concern precludes an active involvement with any problems other than their own. They demand special consideration, but unlike the students in SHG, they do not provide admissible grounds upon which they can be regarded as acceptable exceptions (see analagous descriptions of "maturity levels" designated 2 and 5 by Grant and Grant [1959]).

If, by contrast, the description of the members of SHG seems to picture an implausible ideal, it may be interjected that even for that organization, this was generally considered to be an exceptional group. The group as a whole appeared to develop a norm of its own that placed a premium upon constructive individualism. It is a sociological cliché to say that nonconformity in one situation is simply conformity to the norms of some other reference group (e.g., see Homans, 1950; Merton, 1957; Newcomb, 1943; Parsons, 1951; Sherif & Sherif, 1956). The distinctive characteristic of these students, however, was that their own standards seemed more often to have been brought to, than to have been derived from the groups with which they identified most closely. When discrepancies existed or appeared, they were more apt to work toward changing the group, to affiliate with different groups, or to develop new friendships, than they were to change themselves. The actions taken by the group as such were typically directed toward innovation and modification, not only of its own traditions and practices, but also those of other students.

These exceptional students did have to cope with opposition and dissent among their peers. That they were able to persist and often to prevail may be explained in large part by their unusual personal qualities and also by (1) their skill in social strategy, (2) the support of prestigeful patron-sponsors, (3) their previously acquired status or "credit ratings" (H. Pepinsky, 1954),[3] (4) to some extent by the very nature of the tasks they undertook, and (5) the significance to them of the issues at stake. At the crux of the constructive uses of nonconformity are personal standards that incorporate the interests of both individual and group as valued objectives. If people are not often encountered whose actions are consistently governed by such principles, and who, in addition, possess the talents and skills necessary to produce significant effects, the study of special cases does provide specific clues as to how productively independent behavior may be more frequently elicited and reinforced than its present incidence would imply.

PRODUCTIVE NONCONFORMITY IN A RESEARCH INSTITUTE. The second field study also took as a point of departure previous research, a study by Stoltz (1956), which provided in this instance an empirical definition of standards against which productivity was assessed by supervisory personnel in a large nonprofit, contract research organization. The strategy

---

[3] Hollander (1958) has independently discussed the importance of building up "idiosyncrasy credits," and Verba (1959) has similarly spoken of conserved "acceptance capital."

in our own study was to use Stoltz's findings toward the identification of some persons whose behavior could be regarded as visibly independent of, and also as either relatively productive or nonproductive in terms of, the professed standards of the Institute. Then through interviewing such people and their supervisors, the aim was to arrive at inferences about conditions that make productive independence possible or probable in that setting. Preliminary discussion suggested as another useful resource persons in "technical consultant" positions, which seemed to be in part a device to make a legitimate place in the organization for individuals whose special inclinations and abilities were somehow different from those of people oriented toward promotion in the administrative hierarchy (Shepard, undated ms.).

Again, the data consist mainly in the protocols of semistructured interviews, held with 20 persons in all. The following resumé represents a collation of the inferences drawn by two trained observers who independently examined these records. There was a particular interest in this study in trying to see whether, given a highly structured organization, particular situational or task variables could be identified, such that their manipulation might increase the concomitant occurrence of independent and productive behavior.

Without the intervention of certain "mediator" variables conditions that increase productivity and other conditions that facilitate independence may well have contradictory effects upon what people do. In a large and hierarchically structured organization, it is evident that independence and productivity can be increased simultaneously only under restricted circumstances and within certain limits. Thus, the problem of making likely the joint occurrence of these behavioral events becomes one of optimizing—not maximizing—the occurrence of each. The implication is that under favorable conditions the relationship of independence to productivity will be curvilinear.

The personal characteristics that the individual brings to the situation do seem to make a difference in his ability to maintain his identity and to obtain reward within the organizational system. Adherence to independent standards of his own or of his profession, persistence in pursuing his own interests, and a tendency to see himself as more influencing than influenced by the organization all contribute to the individual's autonomy, but are not sufficient to ensure that his contribution will be officially valued. The individual whose performance also is recognized as productive is professionally competent, work oriented, and inventive, but in addition he has resources and skills that enable him to live with, to evade, or to surmount limitations and obstacles with which others find it impossible to cope. He is able to take a depersonalized view of his circumstances, to view them with perspective; he sees the forest as well as the trees. It could be said that making things work *for* him acquires a game-like character, but this should not be construed to mean that he has no stake in the outcome of that game. It is more that he is confident of winning and is skilled in strategy. Regardless of apparent external restrictions, such an individual typically views assigned tasks and bureaucratic requirements as capable of constructive restructuring; he has broad training and interests; he is sensitive to matters of timing; he is able to sell his own ideas and proposals to those in power positions (Hovland, Janis, & Kelley, 1953).

Nevertheless, the nature of the tasks available to the individual and how, or how much, team assignments are structured or allocated may extend or limit the likelihood that nonconformity can occur and can be productive. As important as personnel selection and appropriate job assignment are, however, other critical determinants of productive independence are subsumed in a complex of social situational variables. Having listened to the people concerned, one is tempted to say that in the process of bureaucratization, *the* central problem for the individual is his depersonalization by others.

On the one hand, this is reflected in expressions of frustration by persons who believe themselves to be caught in the system. On the other hand, there is repeated positive emphasis upon treatment that takes into account the constructive uses of individualism. In this connection the following conditions may have special significance: (1) the ability and willingness of the organization to afford risk taking in the individual case; (2) the active reward and recognition by management of the concomitant occurrence of independence and productivity; (3) provision for the assignment of atypical individuals to special roles or positions with acceptable status, but where "standard" requirements are reduced, and unusual abilities and interests can be utilized; and (4) the maintenance of as much simplicity and flexibility of formal structure as practical necessity permits. Finally, and perhaps most important—to judge by the number of specific comments that apply to his behavior—is (5) the practicing role of the immediate supervisor and the subordinate's relationship to him *as a person.*

To the men under him, the supervisor is the critical figure; he epitomizes, but also personalizes the organization. To those supervised, two things are essential: the existence of mutual trust between supervisor and subordinate; and the competence of the superior, if not to perform, then at least to comprehend the subordinate's own task. Without these old fashioned components of mutual trust and respect, the application of human relations techniques is perceived and resented by the supervised as condescending manipulation. Within a hierarchically structured organization, the immediate supervisor can play a key role in eliciting and reinforcing productive independence. He may function as a patron-sponsor of independence; he is in a position to define and structure the tasks of his subordinates; and he may define as well the criteria against which their productivity is assessed.[4]

Where independent behavior occurs and persists, nearly always (as the other two field studies attest)—if you look for it—there is another individual who like a parent similarly *plays the role of "sponsor" or "patron."* The patron-sponsor is a person or agency who is not a member of the peer group, but possesses prestige or authority in the same social system. He has several significant functions: (1) regardless of his own views the sponsor encourages the other to express and to test his ideas, to think things through for himself; (2) he protects the individual from the counter reactions of his peers long enough to permit him to try out his own notions; (3) he at least keeps the structure of the situation open enough so that independence *can* occur. This last may be a highly significant function. It is, indeed, a real question in our hierarchically structured and highly organized society whether productive independence and considered innovation are possible *without* the support of patrons with power.

Perhaps in the face of the seemingly irreversible social facts of organizational bureaucracy and bigness, it would be wise to accept these as given and to try to learn how to select and train individuals for survival under these conditions. The problems presented by extreme *physical* conditions—in submarines, in the Arctic, in space travel—have been confronted with experimental ingenuity. The problems of survival under extreme *social* conditions have been studied to find constructive ways of coping with the effects of social disorganization or emergency—military capture, concentration camp experiences—but the same view has not been taken toward the study of the extreme of social *organization*. In any case, there

---

[4] Relevant here are the characteristics of the "ideal" manager as reported in a study by Godfrey, Fiedler, and Hall (1957), and the findings of The Ohio State University Leadership Studies (e.g., Stogdill & Coons, 1957), which suggest the importance of both "consideration" and "initiation of structure" in leader effectiveness. The negative effect upon team productivity of the subordinates' inability to trust their superior was clearly demonstrated in an experiment by Pepinsky, Pepinsky, Minor, and Robin (1959).

often seems to be more "give" within organized social struc-
tures than has been exploited.

PRODUCTIVE   NONCONFORMITY   IN   AN   ARCHITECTURALLY
PLANNED NEIGHBORHOOD.   The third in this series of preliminary studies was quite different in both setting and
method from the other two. This report is a participant
observer's account of the recent and continuing efforts of a
privately organized group of some 30 families to develop a
tract of land and to build there a neighborhood planned in
keeping with the principles of an organic architecture as ex-
pounded by the late Frank Lloyd Wright. This project,
which will be given here the name "Taliesonia," is located
within the limits of Heritage, a long-established residential
village on the outskirts of Midwest City.[5]

The procedure here was to record a general description and
history of the community, together with certain "critical inci-
dents" selected and modified to avoid embarrassment to
identifiable persons, but without distorting their point and
substance. Another psychologically trained observer, not acquainted with Taliesonia, except through these anecdotal
materials, reviewed them independently and drew his own
inferences. Thus, some measure of objectivity was introduced
at this level, although his speculations were, of course, based
upon information already filtered through the screen of the
original participant-observer's selective reporting.

Despite these limitations it seemed wasteful to ignore this
unusual chance to try to see in a real-life experiment what
some determinants of productive independence may be—to
observe at close range what happens when a few people, as
members of an identifiable minority, embark upon a course
of action that challenges the status quo, counters predomi-
nant community trends, and poses a threat to vested local

[5] These names are, of course, fictitious. Although this informal study of
Taliesonia is an open secret among its members, specific identities have been
camouflaged.

interests. Taliesonia itself is regarded as a nonconformist enterprise both by outsiders in the surrounding territory and by its members themselves. At a number of points the prevailing norms of the village of Heritage and the professed ideals of Taliesonia are incompatible. The consequence is that in many instances conformity to one set of standards constitutes deviation from the other. The special questions of interest in the present context were, first, how has it been possible for Taliesonia to happen—to gain support and to survive? Secondly, *within* Taliesonia itself, to what extent can nonconformity occur and still be productive?

It was possible to consider the behavior of the Taliesonians in two ways—to view these persons either (1) as members of the Taliesonia colony or (2) as citizens of Heritage of Midwest City, with the group project and the parent communities seen as components of a social system. The apparent answers to our central questions, asked separately at the individual-group and group-community levels, are in many instances the same. The importance of special personal qualities and abilities is evident at once. An examination of what were called the "rationalities" of apparent nonconformity led us to the conclusion that nonconformity to the prevailing norms is not apt to occur and persist unless such behavior is compatible with the maintenance of the individual's private system of motive and defense. Not only must he believe that his chosen course of action will help him to get what he wants, but he must be able to maintain against public onslaught a private conviction about the justifiability of his actions. Where ways to give open ratification to private positions were not available, the individual was more apt to seek protection in the safety of the majority view. He was apt to withdraw from Taliesonia, if participation in it either failed to satisfy his wants or placed him in an exposed, but privately indefensible position.

It again appears that independence of prevailing standards

increases as individual actions are governed by reference to highly integrated, internalized value systems that do not depend upon deference to the judgment of others or deep concern for social approval. Such independence may be reinforced and maintained through the individual's affiliation with a compatible clique or minority (Asch, 1952). Very rarely does nonconformity seem to approach complete personal autonomy; more frequently, the individual turns for support to some kindred spirits whose views conform to his own. Given a group task whose accomplishment demands innovation or departure from precedent, its achievement depends in part upon (1) the personal value placed by the individual members upon the successful outcome of that task, and (2) their ability as individuals to forego immediate satisfaction or to withstand hardship in the interest of expected future gain.

Whether independence is viewed as productive in terms of an external assessment also depends partly upon personal characteristics—in particular, the possession of distinctive talents and abilities directly relevant to the accomplishment of the job at hand. In Taliesonia the operation of personal variables has fostered a natural selection in the composition of the group, which, in turn, has markedly affected the course the project has followed over time. By contrast with the highly structured Research Institute in which the preceding study was conducted, however, Taliesonia's characteristics *as an organization* of relative informality, simplicity, flexibility, and youth are social factors that have permitted the characteristics of the individual to have a more immediate and certainly more readily discernible impact upon the group and its tasks.

But a glib conclusion that productive independence is solely a function of the qualities of an elite set of individuals is at once belied, critical though certain characteristics may be in any situation. It is almost as obvious that the very nature of the task that the individual or the group undertakes will in its definition or redefinition extend or restrict the likelihood that independence of precedent may be productive. Certainly, in the case of Taliesonia, the novelty of its major tasks and the diversity of the alternatives they have presented have predisposed both individual members and the group toward independence, and have established the possibility that such behavior could be productive.

However tough, ingenious, determined, and talented the individuals or the minority coalition concerned, the probability that nonconforming behavior will lead to visible task achievement is directly related to the social-situational conditions that operate in their favor. Again, the influence of benign and powerful patron-sponsors is significant. Also important is the appropriate allocation of special roles to otherwise nonconforming individuals, so that others take their idiosyncrasies for granted and find them useful. This policy seems to be more or less possible or constructive in effect at particular phases of complex tasks. Where individualism itself becomes a valued group standard, independence is fostered. And where group members share a belief in some unifying idea, task accomplishment is facilitated. Once more, the complexity of the problem of assessing individual and group productivity is underscored in the confrontation of changing and multiple criteria in the attempt to judge the "success" of Taliesonia in meaningful terms.

The lessons to be learned from Taliesonia's experience are neither easy nor simple. The circumstances are highly restricted under which nonconforming behavior is apt to occur and to be socially productive by contemporary standards, but they seem to be specifiable, and they do appear to happen in everyday life. The given circumstances of Taliesonia's founding made it a "natural" for observing the active struggles of a group and its members with the very problems to which the present research is addressed. With little previous experimentation to profit from, problems were moved to a stage of application in the absence of available data that would have appalled any social scientist. The crises with which the Taliesonians have dealt have found them often daunted, but somehow the group has so far muddled through. It may be, too, that from the trials and errors of Taliesonia can come more systematic tests of possible answers to basic questions about the means to peaceful and positive social change.

A Conceptual Transition to the Laboratory

The next phase of our work, which I shall present in bare outline, was an attempt to erect a conceptual bridge from the field situations to the laboratory. This skeleton structure has been built inductively with materials found on the sites, so to speak, during the preliminary explorations. This framework in its present form does not pretend to the properly dignified status of a "formal model." It is little more than a working outline whose primary usefulness now is to define the scope of the inquiry and to label the classes of variables involved. The point in presenting here in such crude form the tentative beginnings of a theory is to illustrate one means by which research can move from a relatively unstructured phase toward a more precise formulation, potentially capable of working on its own to produce new and experimentally testable predictions.

SOME BASIC RESTRICTIONS. The occurrence of independent and productive behavior (as defined in the introductory section of this paper) appears to be logically dependent upon the presence of certain conditions. These basic assumptions are limiting characteristics of behavior and situations to be transposed into experimental procedure:

1. The formal characteristics of the given task are such that alternative solutions or modes of solution are logically possible.

2. A group fluctuates in its "rationality" over time.

3. Situations can be so constituted that nonconformity and productivity constitute overlapping behavioral categories.

4. Independent behavior on the part of one individual constitutes a stimulus to the task-relevant behavior of others.

5. The social structure of a given situation is such that independent behavior *can* occur within it.

6. A set (or sets) of task-relevant behavioral norms that have functional meaning for the members of a given group can be specified.

7. Task accomplishment in the given situation is susceptible to assessment in terms of specifiable criteria at a given time.

Translation of Basic Concepts into the Terminology of Sets[6]

Through their restatement in the language of the algebra of sets certain fundamental notions have been clarified and condensed. I shall simply indicate here the principal sets of variables with which we are concerned and state the central proposition to which we have come as an inductive generalization from the field studies. Table 11.1 summarizes the major components of what is referred to as an "Actor-Observer-Group-Task System" for the study of productive independence.

The specific inferences yielded by the field studies referred to manipulable antecedents that were initially classified into

[6] See Pauline Pepinsky (1959, pp. 104-111), for the more complete statement from which the material in this section is largely taken. In general, the special notation used follows that of Kershner and Wilcox (1950). For the reader who cares to trace the present abridgment to the cited source, one change should be made explicit. For what seem now to be good reasons, but which are outside the scope of this paper the antecedent conditions referred to in the field studies are pre-experimentally classified into the sets $[A_1]$, $[A_2]$, and $[A_1 . A_2]$. Originally (Pauline Pepinsky, 1959, Table 2, p. 110), a more restricted view was taken in defining the first two categories, and those antecedents were placed in sets defined as the set-theoretic differences, $[A_1 - A_2]$ and $[A_2 - A_1]$.

TABLE 11.1. Outline for the Study of Productive Independence Within an Actor-Observer-Group-Task System [X]ᵃ

Independent Variables [C]		Inferred Mediating Events [M]	Behavioral Consequences [B]
Manipulable Antecedents [A]	Time Loci of Manipulable Antecedents [L]→ Remote [R] Immediate [I]		
[A₁] Reinforcing Stimulus Conditions for Independent Behavior: [A₁] > specific hypotheses $(a_{1,1}, a_{1,2}, \ldots, a_{1,n})$ $\in$[A₁]	[P] Personal Variables	[m₁] *Phenomenal* conditions such that there is correspondence between the actor's behavior and maintenance of his system of motive and defense	[B₁] Independent Behavior
[A₂] Reinforcing Stimulus Conditions for Productive Behavior: [A₂] > specific hypotheses $(a_{2,1}, a_{2,2}, \ldots, a_{2,n})$ $\in$[A₂]	[T] Task Variables	[m₂] *Logical* conditions such that there is correspondence between the actor's behavior and the formal requirements of the task	
[A₁·A₂] Reinforcing Stimulus Conditions under which Independence is assessed as Productive: [A₁·A₂] > specific hypotheses $(a_{(1·2),1}, a_{(1·2),2}, \ldots, a_{(1·2),n})$ $\in$[A₁·A₂]	[S] Social-situational Variables	[m₃] *Social* conditions such that there is correspondence between the actor's behavior and the rules applied in the accreditation of the individual case	[B₂] Productive Behavior

$\supset$ [B₁ B₂] Behavior that is Independent and Productive

SOURCE: Pauline N. Pepinsky. *Originality in group productivity: I. Productive independence in three natural situations.* Columbus: The Ohio State Univer. Research Foundation, 1959.

ᵃ The fact that there are three classifications in each column is *not* intended to represent one-to-one correspondence across rows between columns.

(i.e., could be viewed as elements of) three gross and obvious categories or sets: personal variables, or the set $[P]$; task variables, or the set $[T]$; and social-situational variables, or the set $[S]$. Cutting across these classes are three others: conditions apparently antecedent to independent or nonconforming behavior, or the set $[A_1]$; those apparently antecedent to productive behavior, or the set $[A_2]$; and conditions apparently antecedent to behavior that is both independent and productive, or the set $[A_1 \cdot A_2]$, which includes the elements common to $[A_1]$ and $[A_2]$. The conditions in the third set seemed to be necessary but in themselves, however, *not* sufficient to produce productive independence.

Three subsets of mediating conditions (or intermediate criteria) appear to be relevant: $[m_1]$, a subset of phenomenal conditions, such that there is for the actor correspondence between his behavior and the maintenance of his system of motive and defense; $[m_2]$, a subset of logical conditions, such that in the observer's view there is correspondence between the actor's behavior and formal task requirements; and $[m_3]$, a subset of social conditions such that there is correspondence between the actor's behavior and the rules applied in the accreditation of the individual case. The major classes of dependent variables involved have been designated as subset $[B_1]$, defined as all independent or nonconforming behavior; the subset $[B_2]$, defined as all productive behavior; and the restricted subset $[B_1 \cdot B_2]$, defined as all behavior that is both independent and productive.

The substance of our thinking to date is contained in a central proposition, which has not been formally derived, but which is an inductive generalization from the field studies. It does, however, presuppose certain axiomatic characteristics of and relations among the above sets; for those statements I must refer you elsewhere (Pauline Pepinsky, 1959; Pepinsky, Norton, & Pepinsky, 1960), and for the sake of brevity, ask you now to take those postulates for granted. The general theorem is this:

$$[A_1 + A_2] \; R \; [m_1 \cdot m_2 \cdot m_3] \; \cup \; [B_1 \cdot B_2]$$

A free translation is as follows: If (1) antecedent conditions capable of eliciting and reinforcing independent and productive behaviors are established, such that (2) those behaviors are in turn compatible with the specified phenomenal, logical, and social *intermediate* criteria, then (3) behavior that is *both* independent and productive will occur.

The theorem also may be read as another illustration of the psychologist's well-known ability to make the self-evident abstruse. In other words, if the individual is willing and able to be independent of the relevant social norms; if what he does can, in the nature of his task, lead to its solution; and if others concerned will at least allow and, if need be, support his action—then independence is apt to occur and, furthermore, to be regarded as productive. Now *all* we have to do is to identify the specific circumstances that will converge in time to bring about this happy combination of events. At this point, we turn for help to our observations of natural situations to look for leads about those "specific circumstances." And we move next to attempt to reconstruct them in the laboratory.

In a particular instance it may or may not be possible to draw valid inferences about all three inferred mediating processes. To the extent that such inferences can be drawn, experimental results will have more precision and generality. To the degree that valid inferences cannot be drawn about one or another mediating condition, explanation is limited thereby, and conclusions must be restricted accordingly. The general problem does not become in principle impossible to investigate. It may be necessary, however, to invoke subsets of "all productive, independent behavior" $[B_1 \cdot B_2]$; e.g., behavior so assessed (1) in the view of an observer, (2) in the view of the actor's peers, or (3) in the view of his superiors in a hierarchically structured organization.

It should be noted that provision is made in the conceptual scheme to take account of the location in time, remote or immediate, of events antecedent to the behavior observed. As yet, nothing specific has been made of this possible classification in relation to productive independence. At the moment, schematic inclusion of this dimension of the independent variables serves as a reminder that confining experimental interest to the characteristics of the immediate stimulus situation can lead to predictive error (as by ignoring, for example, the variable of early independence training). The whole concept of temporal relations among manipulable antecedents, mediating events, and consequent behavior is almost certainly of importance to the central problem and will be brought explicitly into the theoretical structure as it is developed further.

Experimental Beginnings

AN ILLUSTRATIVE EXPERIMENT: PRODUCTIVE INDEPENDENCE UNDER TWO REINFORCEMENT CONDITIONS. So far, one experiment has been completed, and another "two-in-one" study is in progress. The first experiment (Pepinsky, Norton, & Pepinsky, 1960) simulated a hierarchically structured organization and tested the effects upon productive independence, within a subordinate team, of favorable executive sanction for such behavior (element of $[A_1 \cdot A_2]$). Operationally, the experimental task consisted in the successive presentation of stimulus cards of varying ambiguity, each of which required visual discriminations among four alternative sets of components as to which comprised a single integrated figure. In its formal properties the task was like many real-life situations in that more than one "good" solution was possible, and "the group" was neither always right nor always wrong, but varied in the correctness of its judgment over time.[7] In each of a series of 24 trials, the four members of a team first made individual decisions, next received feedback of a spurious majority opinion, and then made individual, final decisions. In their initial responses, the decisions of the individual team members, regardless of condition, favored one of the correct alternatives more than 80 percent of the time, whereas the prearranged group average corresponded to one of these on only 50 percent of the trials. Thus, the situation was one in which independence and productivity were, in effect, given as positively correlated; each man was placed in the position of a person whose ability as an individual was above average for his group. Since his first responses corresponded to the feedback only by chance, he also found himself in a minority postion 75 percent of the time.

Two experimental conditions provided consistent reinforcement by an "executive" for either (1) productive independence (i.e., individual behavior that on any trial was invariant from the first decision to the second, and that was also correct), or (2) productive conformity (i.e., individual behavior that was modified from the first to the second decision, and where the latter response also was correct). The experimental prediction was, of course, that productively independent behavior would occur more frequently under the first condition than the second. A control condition under which no special reinforcement was introduced provided an additional basis for comparison. All teams were subjected to a preliminary session during which an attempt was made to arouse their anxiety about possible social retribution from their peers for failure to perform as "good group members" (adapted from Thibaut & Strickland, 1956), and they were

[7] The design of the task and the experimental procedure were influenced and facilitated by reference to the classical experiments of Asch (1952) and Crutchfield (1955). The stimulus cards were similar to the kind of item used in the Minnesota Paper Form Board.

reminded of this possibility twice during the experimental trials.

The results give unequivocal support to the central prediction. Under all conditions there was some decrement in performance from initial to final decisions as a function of the spurious feedback, but this influence was minimized where the superior gave favorable recognition to productive independence. The control subjects were intermediate between the two experimental conditions in both independence and accuracy of judgment. In everyday situations whose formal characteristics are comparable to those established in the laboratory, special sanctions invoked by authority figures —e.g., top management in a business organization, or a teacher in a classroom—can have a significant positive effect, not in producing autonomy of judgment in an absolute sense, but in increasing the ability of an above-average individual to have confidence in his own judgment and to disengage himself from an uncritical dependence upon his peers. On the other hand, when such an authority awards favorable recognition to an able subordinate only when accurate individual performance is visibly associated with group accomplishment, the effects are to reinforce a trend toward mediocrity.

In another experiment Campbell (1961) has demonstrated that in a collective bargaining situation more impartial solutions are reached in conferences where bargaining teams contain a negotiator who is relatively independent psychologically of his own group's standards and who identifies more closely with the opposition. The experiment now underway is attempting (1) to test the effects of the influence of a patron-sponsor (element of $[A_1]$) upon individual independence and (2) given controlled levels of independence and task ability in one team member, to test the effects of varied strategy (element of $[A_1 \cdot A_2]$) upon the assessment of his productivity by his peers. This study is really two, procedurally and conceptually joined like Siamese twins at vital points in order to increase our ability to interpret and to generalize the results from one set of conditions to the other.

Conclusions and Prospects

A central methodological difficulty is the problem of maintaining experimental control over variables of possibly significant effect upon independence and productivity, other than the one, or the few, under test at a given time. If the field studies have demonstrated nothing else, they have made it overwhelmingly clear how many factors may exert demonstrable influence upon such behaviors. To investigate one variable entails an assumption that for the time being all the rest are held in abeyance. The experimenter's only feasible recourse is to control experimentally as many as he can of what appear to be the most likely sources of distortion, and for the rest, to fall back upon the well-worn device of assuming their random variation. This practice is no real escape, of course, and if his predictions fail of support, then any one or more of his assumptions may be in error.

This fact is a powerful reason to keep a theoretical structure as simple as possible and to complicate it only under empirical duress. In the present case, the behavior selected for study at the outset, and the multiplicity of variables that crowded the observer's view in the field situations have combined to forestall elegance and simplicity in this first conceptual try. It does constitute a beginning toward condensation and order.

Among other psychologists who have attempted to account for behavior that is both productive and independent, Hollander (1958) has laid stress upon "idiosyncrasy credits"; Jahoda (1959) has emphasized personal "investment in an issue"; Maslow (1950) has singled out "self-actualizing people." In substance, the subjects of the studies reported here seem to reply, "Yes, what each of you says is so—but there is much more to it than that." If, at the conclusion of the first phase of the present research, one is impressed with the great complexity of the general problem, he must be impressed as well with the very familiarity of many of the specific inferences to which the field studies lead. And despite wide disparities among the three settings, comparisons among them show considerable redundancy in the apparent determinants of the behavior examined. The eventual contribution of this project may be, not as much in the content of isolated observations that are new in themselves, as in progress toward a different kind of configuration and application of old wisdom.

There is surely no shortage of promising hypotheses about the conditions that foster productive nonconformity. A number of the most intriguing seem also to be least susceptible to easy test in the laboratory. Nevertheless, questions of more than trivial interest to the scientist and to the citizen can be asked and answered under experimental conditions, to the extent that the laboratory is made to provide for its subjects not a physical but a formal correspondence to the critical exigencies of "real" life. More explicit attention needs to be given to the properties of the laboratory *as* a field situation. With this recognition, the challenge to the experimenter is not less sharp, but he does have before him a way to proceed.

A pronouncement by Merton is, I think, an appropriate conclusion to this description of a beginning:

Under certain conditions, public nonconformity can have the manifest and latent function of changing standards and values which have become dysfunctional for the group. . . . It is not infrequently the case that the nonconforming minority in a society represents the interests and ultimate values of the group more effectively than the conforming majority. This . . . is not a moral but a functional judgment, not a statement in ethical theory but a statement in sociological theory. It is a statement, finally, which once made, will probably be accepted by the same social observers who, by using an insufficiently differentiated concept of "deviant behavior" deny in their sociological analysis what they affirm in their ethical precepts [Merton, 1957, pp. 366-368].

REFERENCES

Asch, S. E. *Social psychology*. New York: Prentice-Hall, 1952.

Barron, F. An ego-strength scale which predicts response to psychotherapy. *J. consult. Psychol.*, 1953a, **17**, 327–333.

Barron, F. Some personality correlates of independence of judgment. *J. Pers.*, 1953b, **21**, 287–297.

Campbell, R. J. *Originality in group productivity: III. Partisan commitment and productive independence in a collective bargaining situation*. Columbus: The Ohio State Univer. Research Foundation, 1961. (offset)

Crutchfield, R. S. Conformity and character. *Amer. Psychol.*, 1955, **10**, 191–193.

Florence, Edwiges De. G. Construction of a forced-choice technique for the evaluation of college students' goals. Unpublished doctoral dissertation. The Ohio State Univer., 1956a.

Florence, Edwiges De. C. *Motivational factors in individual and group productivity: II. Validation and standardization of the student behavior description*. Columbus: The Ohio State Univer. Research Foundation, 1956b. (offset)

Godfrey, E. P., Fiedler, F. E., & Hall, D. M. *Boards, management and company success*. Danville, Ill.: Interstate Printers & Publishers, 1957.

Grant, J. D., & Grant, Marguerite Q. A group dynamics approach to the treatment of nonconformists in the Navy. *Annals of Amer. Academy of polit. & soc. Sci.*, 1959, **322**, 126–135.

Hollander, E. P. Conformity, status and idiosyncrasy credit. *Psychol. Rev.*, 1958, **65**, 117–127.

Homans, G. C. *The human group*. New York: Harcourt, Brace, 1950.

Hovland, C. I., Janis, I. L., & Kelley, H. H. *Communication and persuasion: Psychological studies of opinion change*. New Haven: Yale Univer. Press, 1953.

Jahoda, Marie. Conformity and independence: A psychological analysis. *Hum. Relat.*, 1959, **12**, 99–120.

Kershner, R. B., & Wilcox, L. R. *The anatomy of mathematics.* New York: Ronald Press, 1950.

Krebs, A. M. Two determinants of conformity: Age of independence training and achievement. *J. abnorm. soc. psychol.*, 1958, **56**, 130–131.

Maslow, A. H. Self-actualizing people: A study of psychological health. In W. Wolff (Ed.), *Personality: Values in personality research.* New York: Grune & Stratton, 1950. Pp. 11–34.

Merton, R. *Social theory and social structure.* Glencoe, Ill.: Free Press, 1957.

Mussen, P. H., & Conger, J. J. *Child development and personality.* New York: Harper, 1956.

Newcomb, T. M. *Personality and social change.* New York: Dryden Press, 1943.

Parsons, T. *The social system.* Glencoe, Ill.: Free Press, 1951.

Pepinsky, H. B. Research on productive behavior. *Personnel Guid. J.*, 1954, **33**, 140–144.

Pepinsky, H. B., Pepinsky, Pauline N., Minor, F. J., & Robin, S. S. Team productivity and contradiction of management policy commitments. *J. appl. Psychol.*, 1959, **43**, 264–268.

Pepinsky, H. B., Pepinsky, Pauline N., & Pavlik, W. B. Task relevant belief and task accomplishment. *J. counsel. Psychol.*, 1958, **5**, 305–311.

Pepinsky, Pauline N. *Originality in group productivity: I. Productive independence in three natural situations.* Columbus: The Ohio State Univer. Research Foundation, 1959.

Pepinsky, Pauline N. A study of productive nonconformity. *Gifted Child Quarterly*, 1960, 4 (4), 81–85.

Pepinsky, Pauline N. The social dialectic of productive nonformity. *Merrill-Palmer Quarterly*, 1961, in press.

Pepinsky, Pauline N., Norton, B. A., & Pepinsky, H. B. *Originality in group productivity: II. The effects of varied executive sanctions upon productive independence in subordinate teams.* Columbus: The Ohio State Univer. Research Foundation, 1960. (offset)

Pepinsky, Pauline N., & Pepinsky, H. B. Originality in group productivity. *Annu. summary Rept.*, Project NR 170–396, Contract NONR 495 (15). The Ohio State Univer. Research Foundation, November 15, 1958. (Mimeographed)

Pepinsky, Pauline N., & Pepinsky, H. B.   Originality in group productivity. *Annu. summary Rep.* Project NR 170–396, Contract NONR 495 (15) The Ohio State Univer. Research Foundation, November 15, 1959. (Mimeographed)

Shepard, H. A.   The dual hierarchy in research. Undated. (Mimeographed)

Sherif, M., & Sherif, Carolyn W.   *An outline of social psychology.* New York: Harper, 1956.

Shoben, E. J.   Toward a concept of the normal personality. *Amer. Psychol.,* 1957, **12**, 183–189.

Stogdill, R. M., & Coons, A. E. (Eds.)   Leader behavior: Its description and measurement. *Ohio studies in personnel,* Research Monograph No. 88. Columbus: Bureau of Business Research, Ohio State Univer., 1957.

Stoltz, R. E.   A study of productivity in a research setting. Unpublished doctoral dissertation, Ohio State Univer., 1956.

Thibaut, J. W., & Strickland, L. H.   Psychological set and social conformity. *J. Pers.,* 1956, **25**, 115–129.

Verba, S.   The experimental study of politics: The contribution of small group experiments in leadership to the understanding of political leadership. Unpublished doctoral dissertation, Princeton Univer., 1959.

CHAPTER 12

Conformity and the
Idea of Being Well Born

DAVID WECHSLER

Bellevue Psychiatric Hospital and New York University

Insistence on compliance with decreed rules of behavior and disapproval of comportment not in accord with expectations has always been one of the core tenets of organized groups. Conformity is demanded so that the group's way of life will not be interfered with, deviancy frowned upon because the ends of the group are threatened by it. In general, the resulting disharmony can be explained in terms of conflicts between the needs and presses of the individual and the interests of the group. Much of the present book has been devoted to a consideration of the problems engendered by these conflicts. In addition, however, there are often historically determined beliefs and ideas which can account for persistent and recurrent attitudes of a group, not only toward the individuals which compose it, but also vis-à-vis other groups by which they feel threatened.

One of these beliefs is the idea of being well born, that is, the belief that some men are so favored by their Maker or so well endowed by nature that they are by right, divine or otherwise, destined to rule over their fellowmen. This is a very important idea, not only because of the mischief and misery which its exploitation has caused throughout history, but because it has been so widely and persistently held by so many different kinds of people, good as well as evil. In the past decades we have seen what heinous crimes have been committed in its name by a group of vicious and obscene men and their misguided or enslaved followers. It would be a mistake, however, to assume that the Nazis and their like have been the only ones who made use of this idea for their own ends. The greatly admired Greeks of the Periclean age likewise believed that some men were born better than others, and for this reason permitted slavery.

THE IDEA OF SUPERIORITY. Even more significant than the ubiquity of the idea of being well born is the large role which this belief has played in the philosophy and codes of those born to power and prerogative, or franchised to it. From the Pharaohs of Egypt to the Hitlers of modern Europe, from the Brahman priests to the Nazi Gauleiters, from the votaries of divine rights to the apologists of modern eugenics, there runs the same theme: master people, master race. Those born to power, those born to wealth, the would-be strong, the would-be rich, the would-be anybodies; their claims are the same: "We are the elite, we are the deserving." How this idea has manifested and maintained itself is a story too long to be detailed in a single paper. It begins with man's earliest effort to exploit his genealogy.

Forebears and Status

Genealogy is the oldest of human "sciences." The first records of literate man are ancestral rosters and social registers. In describing the heroes of the Trojan War, Homer never fails to tell us who their fathers were. Achilles, the Fleet of Foot, is not only the mightiest of Greek warriors but the son of Peleus; Agamemnon and Menelaus are always referred to as the Atridae, that is, the descendants of Atreus; and Odysseus of many devices, peer of Zeus in council, as the son of Laertes.

The modern reader may wonder why Homer has to identify the greatest of Greek warriors by reference to one Peleus, a minor princeling, the king of one of the lesser Thesselian tribes, who participated in the war against Troy. If so, he will also find it hard to understand why the author of the first gospel goes out of his way to prove that the son of God was of the direct line of David. The explanation of both accounts is not hard to find, if one bears in mind the epochs to which the personnae are related. Three thousand years ago man expected all his heroes to be of divine origin. Two thousand years ago, at least his kings and prophets. Homer was reminding his readers that Achilles was of divine origin on his father's as well as on his mother's side. Peleus was not himself a great hero but his father Aeacus was the son of Zeus.

Emphasis on the father's derivation, place of birth and mother's maiden name, so curiously like the information required on applications for country clubs or admission to an Ivy League college, was ancient even in Homer's day. The genealogies of the Iliad, like the "begats" of the Bible, were seemingly an established custom practiced by the scribes of Tutankhamen and the major-domos of the brick-writing Sumerians.

HEROES AND HISTORY. From the beginning of recorded history, men have expected their heroes to be well born. In ancient times men meant that they were either related or descended from the God-heads themselves; at other periods a few select were permitted to claim this kinship. This kinship might be claimed both for the individuals or a clan or a nation as a whole. In any case, the descent was described to unique or a single pair of ancestors. Primitive genealogy always begins with the creation story, the progenitors of the first man.

There are many legends or hypotheses as to how the first

man came to be. The one with which the peoples of the West are most familiar is the story of Adam in Genesis. God created Adam on the sixth day after he had finished with the heavens, the earth and all living creatures. And God said, "Let us make man in our own image after our own likeness and let him have domination over the fish of the sea and the fowl of the air and over the cattle and all over the earth" (Gen. 1:26). "So God created man in his own image, in the image of God created He him" (Gen. 1:27).

The story of creation, as recounted in Genesis, is not unique, nor original with the authors of the Bible. There are many similar related stories in the legends of other peoples. These differ in detail but are generally alike in two important respects. They asseverate man's special creation and represent him as having been fashioned in his Maker's image.

OTHER VIEWS.   In opposition to the theory of special creation there has long existed the contrary hypothesis that man was evolved from a lower form of life. This second theory is at least as old as the first and, according to Frazier, almost as widely distributed among primitive peoples. It is most frequently encountered among Totemic, particularly African tribes, who believe that their ancestors sprang from certain animals or plants. It is also common among certain tribes of American Indians. Thus, the Osages believe that they were descended from the female beaver, the Iroquois from the mud turtle, the Delaware Indians from the rattlesnake, and the Indians of Peru from the puma. These legends indicate that theories of evolution far from beginning with Darwin or even Democritus, go back to the earliest speculations of primitive man. Until recent times they seemed to have relatively little impact on major religions and social mores, particularly those of the Western world. We can only conjecture what might have been man's outlook toward life and attitude toward his destiny if the reverse had been true, but we can follow more definitely some of the consequences of the special creation theory.

BLOODLINES AND STATUS.   One of these is the concept of uniqueness or exclusiveness; another, the view that those who did not share the heritage or origin of the group were in some way deviant or damned. These did not necessarily go together. The descendants of Abraham, for example, considered themselves the chosen people; and the descendants of Romulus and Remus thought of themselves as a noble line of conquering sons. But while they regarded the others as less fortunate, they did not look upon other peoples as inferior or species apart. The latter view seems to have been a later-day addition. Here again time does not permit me to enlarge on the manner in which this view developed, nor to detail the different forms it has taken. I shall skip some two thousand years and examine only one or two of its modern versions.

Modern Versions of Superiority

The most familiar example is the doctrine of Aryan superiority. This doctrine, most extensively espoused by peoples of northern Europe, began about the middle of the last century, following speculations of a number of philologists, particularly Frederick Max-Muller, Professor of Comparative Philology at Oxford, who sought to account for some striking similarities in the root forms of Indo-European languages. The evolved theory, as you will recall, was that the communality or similarity of these root words testified to the probable derivation of these languages from some original tongue. The tongue so identified was the ancient Sanskrit or hypothetical Aryan language. From a reconstructed Aryan language it was only a step to an assumed Aryan race. In fairness to Max-Muller, it should be noted that in his later years he denied there was any connection between blood and language. "If I say Aryans," he wrote, "I mean neither blood, nor bones, nor brain, nor skull. I mean simply those who speak the Aryan language."

The denial was of no avail; a new school of political and social anthropologists had already taken over the seeming implications of Max-Muller's theory and began using them as a base for their own doctrine, namely, that of a unique primordial stock from which this basic Aryan language was derived. The origin of this Aryan stock was variously located, among other places in the high plateaus of Persia, from whence after some wandering it supposedly settled in the hills of the Kush Mountains of India. Here lived a tribe known as the Aryas whom the original stock conquered and with whom it later intermingled. These Aryas or Aryans were pictured as a virile and aggressive people who at some unspecified date left their original mountainous abodes and eventually ended up somewhere along the shores of the Baltic. In their trek from Asia to Europe they left a trail of progeny behind them, which became the ancestors of the Indo-Germanic peoples. These prehistoric Aryas were, for the needs of the doctrine, described as a superbly endowed race whose superlative physical and mental traits determined not only the linguistic but the cultural destinies of the dominant peoples of Europe.

SKULLS AND SUPERIORITY.   A seeming aid to the Aryan doctrine came at about the same time from the new science of anthropometry which attempted, among other things, to classify peoples on the basis of certain measures of body physique. The measurement which seemed to give the most promising basis for classification is the now familiar cephalic index, that is, the ratio between the vertical and horizontal diameters of the skull. The cephalic index offered a simple way of classifying the crania into three main groups, the long heads (dolichocephalics), the short heads (brachycephalics) and the in-betweens (mesocephalics). When some early studies indicated that a large proportion of Swedes, Danes, and inhabitants of certain parts of Germany were predominantly dolichocephalic, the advocates of Nordic supremacy made use of this finding as additional proof that the Nordics were the lineal descendants of the Aryas. Dolichocephaly was then made a criterion for general superiority, and the last quarter of the nineteenth century produced many attempts to prove this theory.

Why the length of a man's head, any more than the length of his foot, should be associated with superior traits may be hard to understand. But, the fact to be borne in mind is that the object of this hypothesis was not to validate a possible correlation between physical and mental traits, but rather to exploit it as a biological argument in support of an already accepted theory. We need not go into these particular claims which have long since been discredited, nor stop to evaluate similar attempts to supplement dolichocephaly with other physical characters like fair skin and blonde hair as evidence for the existence of a picked race of men. Error is a protean monster which cannot be destroyed in one fell swoop. Like the Lydian hydra it may sprout two heads for every one that is cut off. Gobineau was followed by Lapouge and Aman; Chamberlain by a host too long to mention. The Gobineaus and Chamberlains of the late nineteenth century, no less than the Rosenbergs of the present one, were obviously not interested in scientific data, but an evidence, however spurious, that would support their prejudices.

The type of "evidence" exploited by groups claiming superior endowment has varied with the cultural sophistication of the eras at which it was entertained. Divine genealogy, historic philology and cranial measurements have largely given way, though not entirely, and been replaced by the popularized errors of modern genetics. We need not go into the question as to whether the particular traits posited are transmitted by way of heredity, actually very few, if any, have been demonstrated to be so; nor whether the traits in question are possessed to any greater degree by the groups that claim them than by those to whom they are denied. For example, whether the white are in point of fact more intelligent than the colored people, Nordics more adventuresome than Mediterraneans, the English less volatile than the French, and so on. The argument is still the same, except that endowment is no longer traced to divine ancestry but to genetic heredity. This is small gain for those who are excluded by either.

CLUBS, LODGES, AND THE NEW NEED FOR STATUS.   The idea of being well born has generally been a belief entertained by dominant groups which by virtue of and in proportion to their dominance have been able to implant their philosophy on a people or a nation as a whole. But even in places or countries not so affected, one always finds numerous self-constituted groups who harbor the idea and, in one way or another, seek to exploit it. They may not be sufficiently strong to influence national politics significantly but nevertheless affect the cultural patterns of large portions of the population. They may consist of loose associations or well-knit organizations, tied together by religious, political or economic interests, and be inspired by old or new "isms." They may take the form of snob societies, military cliques, professional associations, splinter parties and almost any kind of socio-economic interest group. Sooner or later, they develop views regarding their own superiority and the conviction that those whom they seek to exclude are inferior. In this last respect the Daughters of the American Revolution and the eating clubs of Princeton are no different from various benighted and class prejudiced groups, although in terms of social goals and everyday behavior they may be far apart.

Political Aspects

These examples thus far cited have emphasized primarily the negative consequences of the idea of being well born. These are not inevitable sequellae but the most usual ones encountered. There are occasions, however, when it has been used in a positive way to emphasize obligations and duties as well as prerogatives either to account for a group's claim to unique origin or to justify the continuance of its special status. Such, for example, was the influence of Sparta's claimed descent from a line of demigods whose mighty and adventurous deeds form the first chapters of the nation's history, and served as a model for the mores of its rulers in later days. A similar role may be ascribed to legends pertaining to the origins of other ancient peoples. In other eras, the positive aspects of the idea were reflected in the self-imposed codes of honor among various orders of nobility. Familiar examples are the knight errantry of medieval feudalism, the special obligations assumed at times by royal houses and their followers, the assumed responsibilities of the gentry classes, the ideals expressed in the concept of the gentleman and in the codes of divers groups which include the concept of *noblesse oblige* as part of their ideology.

RESPONSIBILITY AND PRIVILEGE. But whether the idea of being well born has been employed to furnish a glorified account of a nation's early history, as a way of encouraging social responsibility or as a means of perpetuating special privilege, its basic significance for those who appropriate it has been that, by virtue of their origin, they constitute an elite or noble class. The original Greek word *eugenes* for nobility in fact meant being well born, and this has constituted its basic definition the world over. The implementation of the idea has varied from time to time, but while the codes of the Eugenes of Sparta, the Patricians of Rome, the Brahmins of India and the Peers of England have differed in certain details they are all in accord that the members of their class constitute a group apart. In most places this *apartheid* was ascribed to divine ordination, and was generally buttressed by a State religion, the priesthood itself constituted an elite class. But it has taken other forms as well.

The belief in class distinctions, whether considered innate or acquired, is of course, a philosophy not confined to groups imbued with the idea of being well born. It is an essential tenet of all groups who are afraid of being ousted or displaced, and in particular of totalitarian governments. And this obtains whether they are weak or strong. Contemporary communist states are striking examples of the latter. In spite of their egalitarian proclamations and claims to being a classless society, the leaders of these states regard themselves as in some way specially anointed, not by way of hereditary perhaps, but by a dialectic which crowns them as a select group entrusted with all the answers of how to organize a new world. The leaders do not, of course, designate themselves as a class apart, but so far as their treatment of demurring or minority groups is concerned, there is little to distinguish between their dictatorship of the proletariat and the dictatorship of any other sort. Thus, the Russian communist state, with its entrenched bureaucracy, as Milovan Djilas has shown, is just a new exploiting and dominating class with a philosophy vis-à-vis dissenting groups no different from other oligarchies, only more implacable. The commissars and members of the party are an elect, chosen to be sure not by an accepted divinity, but nevertheless tracing their lineage to an equated set of demigods (Lenin and Stalin). They thus constitute an elite class, and like all privileged classes, assert their power by the usual ukase, "conform or else." The communist code differs from historically similar ones in that it seeks to control the individual's thinking as well as his behavior. Thought control, per se, is not an entirely new technique. As practiced by the communists it is closely linked to otherwise widely accepted psychological theory. Brain washing and forced confessions are employed by them not merely for the purpose of intimidating future dissenters but also because, like the exponents of the hidden persuaders, they are firmly convinced that sooner or later thought may lead to action.

Thus far I have spoken more of conformity than nonconformity because it is the aspect of social behavior most often associated with the idea of being well born. Conformity is also easier to define than nonconformity, particularly if we focus our attention on the individuals rather than the terms descriptive of the concepts involved. A conformist is, broadly speaking, a person who does what is expected of him in any given society or subgroup of it, that is, complies with accepted rules of conduct. A nonconformist can be anyone who does not comply with the rules; but the ways in which he may demur from or defy prevailing thought or mores are innumerable. Nonconformists run the entire gamut of dissidents from the religious reformer and political maverick to the beatnik and delinquent. In the latter category they are also called deviants. Deviancy implies not only atypicality in the statistical sense, but abnormality in any one of a variety of meanings. A nonconformist may be disapproved, even thought of as eccentric, but seldom as immoral, antisocial. These distinctions are not mutually exclusive and actually involve considerable overlap. Much depends on the mores of the day, how threatening the views put forth, how ready the majority is for change, and so on. The nonconformist of today may be the conformist of tomorrow. This is particularly true of forerunners of religious thought and political change. I dare say Calvin, Luther, and Fox were considered the arch nonconformists of their day as have nearly all revolutionary figures from the Gracchi to some of the Fathers of the American Revolution in theirs. Some of these figures may have felt divinely inspired but seldom based their claims on the virtue of being well born. This status was generally bestowed or ascribed to them by their followers.

Summary

The idea of being well born is one of the oldest and most pervasive concepts in the history of Western civilization. It can be traced back to the early Greeks and beyond, and is still current today. Some examples have been given to illustrate its impact on societal interactions and in particular, of its mischievous influence on historical attitudes of groups vis-à-vis other groups. The main point made is that it has been used primarily to maintain privilege and special status, however obtained, and that one of the main instruments for doing so has been the insistence of conformity of the group in power to its own ideology. The idea of being well born is not the only concept so employed. In the long run it has not been as relentless as some others, for example, the class distinctions now employed by most of the communist states. Psychological determinants of conformity as related to the idea of being well born are many, but basic to all has been the feeling of insecurity of various groups induced by fear of being ousted or displaced from positions of power and privilege.

CHAPTER 13

A Summary: Deviation in the Study of Conformity

HAROLD B. PEPINSKY

The Ohio State University

In the foregoing chapters we are exposed to theory, to methodology, and to a variety of empirical findings on a socially important topic. Some of the methodological suggestions, in particular, are highly ingenious, even brilliant. The subject matter and general level of excellence of the present symposium have made appropriate the inclusion in it of the two persons who have, through their own important contributions over the past 25 years, given the greatest impetus to research on "conformity and deviation." That these two, Solomon Asch and Muzafer Sherif, are restive over the conceptual and procedural impotence of their many stepchildren is ironic but understandable. To the masters are often given an openness to experience and a depth of understanding rarely accorded their disciples; more often the latter follow blindly and imperfectly. Yet the present volume offers a refreshing contradiction to the pessimism expressed by Asch and Sherif.

Overview chapters on the topic are provided by Asch, Campbell, Bass, and Blake. Because Blake's own research provides the strongest support for his argument, I shall return later to his contribution. Asch is unhappy with current research on conformity and deviation. From the standpoint of the Gestalt social psychology for which he has been a major spokesman, he finds such research still shackled to a deceptively oversimplified behaviorism. Human behavior, Asch maintains, is a manifestation of complex affective-cognitive processes, inadequately accounted for by a stimulus-response psychology. For this reason, what may appear to the naive observer to be conforming behavior may be actually different kinds of behavioral events along varied continua. To interpret accurately what is observed to occur as a response to a proferred stimulus situation, we must attempt to understand the actor's phenomenal view of situation and task, and the motivating influences, again as complex cognitive-emotional processes, that direct the actor's behavior. Asch deplores the fact that these complex phenomena have not yet received serious study. What may seem to be a unitary disposition toward conformity, for example, may be alternatively fear, trust, concern for personal ties—or even a *productive* trend, such as a manifestation of personal independence.

As Campbell implies, however, what Asch rejects seems to be an outmoded kind of behaviorism. Campbell, in his turn, bravely tries to reconcile social Gestalt with behavioral theories. Taking a leaf from the Gestalter's book, Campbell asserts that the perceptual focus of the Gestalter is *isomorphic* to the behaviorist's focus on observed activity. And with a broad conceptual sweep Campbell integrates the two frames of reference into a more general theory of conformity as acquired behavioral disposition on the part of the actor. Allegiance to traditional behaviorism is forsworn; instead the position is taken that such behavioral dispositions may be acquired as much through perception as through "blind" trial and error. Individual modes of "knowing" are often incompatible with social modes—an incompatibility that the actor reconciles for himself through the formation of resolved, dominative, or compromised composites. By reference to an extensive array of research studies, Campbell arrives at a number of primitive assumptions about acquired behavioral dispositions which he, as the observer of other persons, can use to explain their actions without recourse to knowledge about their conscious decision-making processes.

As reviewer, I blush at my inability to summarize Bass's own condensation of much that is discussed more fully in his recent book on leadership referred to in his chapter. Like Campbell, Bass has cited an impressively large sample of direct sources and summary statements of research on conformity. Treating conformity as a corollary of leadership behavior, he defines the former as "behavior reflecting the *successful* influence of other persons," and he lists 38 propostions about conforming behavior, taken from his "general theory of interpersonal behavior." Deviation is included here as what Bass calls "the mirror image of conformity." What is noteworthy, since I cannot hope to reproduce Bass's propositions themselves, is that his generalizations from relevant experimental and descriptive studies sound remarkably similar to many of those arrived at by Campbell, working independently and out of another frame of reference. Bass's propositions have the advantage over more simplified conceptualizations of closely hugging the data from which they derive. His propositions should prove to be highly useful in the derivation of second, third, and even higher order generalizations and in serving as checks upon deductions from other theories.

A refreshing departure from usual discussions of deviation and conformity and a meticulous devotion to clarity of definition are provided by Rokeach in his conception of "open and closed orientations to authority." Like Asch, Rokeach is concerned about the misunderstandings that arise from labeling overt behavior as simply "conforming" or "deviant" and he, too, wants us to investigate complex emotional-cognitive states. But Rokeach rejects Asch's phenomenology as too shallow, on the one hand, and psychoanalytic theories as lacking in parsimony, on the other. So

Rokeach has turned to the cognitively oriented theories of Lewin, Tolman, and Krech and has emerged with a conceptualization of the structure of human belief systems in which, for the actor, a belief system and increasingly dissimilar disbelief subsystems are arranged along a gradient. What the actor does with cognitively related empirical events, then, is to order them preferentially along a particular gradient of belief. With unfilial lack of devotion to others of his ancestors at Berkeley, however, Rokeach tears into the "authoritarian personality" research, pointing out that appeal to authority is necessary to the transmission of human knowledge. In other words, reliance on authority is not all bad, as Adorno *et al.* have implied, nor is fascism necessarily worse than communism for that matter. The key to "open-mindedness" is that here authority is used by the actor as a source of information or substantive knowledge, while "closed-mindedness" is an actor's reliance on authority as a means of coping with rewards and punishments that the authority is expected to mete out to the actor. Rokeach also distinguished (watch your step here) between "conformity" and "compliance," the latter being an overt act of acquiescence which, however, may be a knowing response to coercion. In this view an act becomes a conforming one only when the actor thinks he is behaving of his own accord, when in fact he has been coerced into it by someone else's demands. Conformity is a blind yielding to the demands of a prestigeful other person, but if the yielding is a rationally calculated response to a situational exigency—such as doing what the concentration camp guard says to do because it is the only avenue of survival, then it is *not* conformity. Rokeach thus assumes that an informed other person, e.g., a researcher, can determine what is rational and nonrational in the behavior of one who is being observed.

With ingenuity characteristic of dyed-in-the-Skinnerians, Bachrach, Candland, and Gibson make clear that a simpleminded behaviorism must still be considered as a plausible and parsimonious alternative to more elegant cognitive theories of conformity and deviation. In their chapter on "group reinforcement of individual response" these authors invoke a reinforcement model, in which a designated response class of events is followed by events (inferred reinforcements) that increase or decrease the probability of future responses belonging to the designataed response class. To Bachrach *et al.*, "a group is, simply, a cohesion of three or more individuals whose responses are associated in some activity." Although this definition is not as simple as its creators would have us believe it to be, it does permit a definition of conformity as "as situation in which the group's reinforcement is adequate to produce and maintain behavior by the individual, and in which the behavior is, in turn, reinforcing to the group"; conversely, "deviation" is inferred when these reinforcements "are not adequate" to produce the individual or group behavior. In a series of experimental "for instances" Bachrach and company illustrate the use of a novel "tandem conditioning" method, in which the conversation (verbal behavior) of an unsuspecting subject is followed by the predetermined reinforcements—"positive," "negative," and "neutral"—of a pair of stooges, posing as equally naive participants in a study of symbolic problem-solving. What emerges at this stage is a lot of headache in the control and manipulation of experimental conditions and some highly intriguing individual differences in the amount of talk (frequency of verbal output) by the subjects, under varied antecedent conditions. The author's reinforcement paradigm is appealingly uncluttered, although its group application does seem to offer methodological difficulties at present.

But even if one did not have to equivocate on such laboratory findings, how far could they be generalized? Blake, Sherif, and Pauline Pepinsky have something to say about this. The typical *ad hoc* group, single occasion experiment, in which the subject is given impetus to modify his behavior to conform with that of a group standard, is heatedly attacked by Blake. He thinks that a more correct research procedure in the study of response to conformity pressures is to create a situation in which a subject has a great deal at stake. Over days, weeks, or even longer a strong reference group "anchorage" must be created for the subject. Blake turns to his own work in support of his argument, after failing to be satisfied by what other available conformity research has to offer. For example, he has manipulated situations in which teams of persons live together for two-week training session. Each team spends from four to six hours a day together, for a total of 60–90 hours; there are no externally designated leaders. Data from such research indicate (1) that "natural" groupings are thus induced, and (2) that it is almost impossible for a person to avoid conforming to group pressure, when he understands clearly what the group expects of him and when the group's accomplishments have become highly important to him. As one of the other symposium participants remarked, in contrast to some real life situations, say labor-management negotiations, Blake's subjects were not given reason to think that either they, personally, or their constituents had anything to lose by failure to resolve their differences with representatives of other groups. Nevertheless, Blake's experimental conditions and their consequences for individual susceptibility to group pressures are uncomfortably true-to-life. It appears that closed-mindedness occurs much more frequently than open-mindedness when group representatives attempt to negotiate intergroup conflicts in everyday situations.

Sherif is also vehement in his protest against the usual laboratory experiment as a means of testing hypotheses about important social events, such as those involving conforming or nonconforming behavior. More than a decade ago Sherif turned to evidence from sociological and anthropological research on small group behavior as this occurs in natural settings. Referring to a number of studies, including several under his direction, he pounds away at the problem of situational validity. Sherif's argument has much in common with that of the late Egon Brunswik, who regretted that the "environmental probability" of events studied in most psychological research was very low—in other words, it was improbable that like events would occur in everyday life either as stimuli or responses. Thus Brunswik supported the use of "representative design" in research, to elicit behavior whose occurrence could be expected in the everyday world. And thus Kenneth Burke has argued for the "representative anecdote" or "natural metaphor." Although others have stated his case, Sherif has obviously discovered these things for himself; what he has to say about the situational (Brunswik called it "ecological") validity of conformity research merits careful reading in its own right.

A means of reconciling the findings of field and laboratory research is suggested by Pauline Pepinsky: if laboratory situations can be created whose *formal* properties correspond to those encountered in field settings, then the laboratory research can help to answer questions arising in everyday life. In Pepinsky's research on productive nonconformity ("social exceptions that prove the rule") she has combined the two methods. Beginning with explicit definitions of "productivity" and "nonconformity," she traces for us a search whose objective is to make visible the conditions under which the rare combination of "productivity nonconforming" behavior is likely to occur. "Nonconformity" is defined as individual behavior that is both statistically and psychologically *independent* of prevailing social norms, and "*productive* nonconformity," as independence that contributes to the successful task accomplishment of a group, organization, or society, or to that of an individual in a social setting. Three natural settings in which relevant instances of the behavior were observed are described, and she tells us of the methods by which she then attempted to search for personal and situational antecedents of such behavior. Using a number of hypotheses derived from field studies, Pepinsky has developed a schema of general antecedent and mediating conditions and of their consequences in the form of productive behavior, nonconforming behavior, and behavior that is both nonconforming and productive. Clarification and condensation of certain basic ideas has been achieved through their translation into the language of the algebra of sets. She is now testing selected hypotheses, under laboratory conditions, whose formal properties are related to the formal properties of situations encountered earlier in the field.

Still another methodological tack in the study of conforming and deviant behavior in our society is provided by Matarazzo and Berg, who emphasize the structural, as opposed to the content or phenomenal, properties of such behavioral events. Matarazzo gives a concise, lucid summary of eight years of research on the "interview interaction patterns of normal and deviant groups." With Saslow, a medical colleague, he has developed methods for testing under controlled conditions many of the ideas proposed—a number of them more than 20 years ago—by E. D. Chapple and his associates. Although Chapple has written extensively about his method and discoveries, his major psychological publication was in the *Genetic Psychology Monographs* series. Prior to Matarazzo and Saslow, Chapple's assertions tended to be lightly dismissed by psychologists. Yet Matarazzo and his coworkers, through painstaking effort, have established as valid many of the intuitions that Chapple has described and used in his consultant activities. Not only do there seem to be amazing consistencies in individual interaction patterns, there appear to be clear differences, too, between "normal," "outpatient," and "schizophrenic" persons. Also, there appear to be salient regional differences in the interaction patterns of "normals," which offers support for Chapple's claim that normalcy itself is "situationally bound." Four factors, derived from Chapple's original measurement categories, account for 96 percent of an individual's interaction variance within an interview: *duration of utterance, duration of silence, initiative,* and *adjustment.* The measuring and recording device used up to now has been Chapple's interaction chronograph, and the technique of measuring interaction pattern itself is highly reliable. A more highly automated processing of data is about to become possible, however, with the introduction of the Buros 101 computer. Matarazzo's investigations, in content and method, offer much to the behavioral scientist in the area of social conformity and deviance. Specifically, we are given direct access to the measurement of verbal and other kinds of behavioral interaction.

Berg has 15 years of research on "deviant response sets" to buttress his contention that a structural analysis of behavior is based upon more parsimonious assumptions about the responding organism than alternative content analyses, and it works just as well in accounting for what does occur. Just as Selye has argued that "when you are sick, you are sick all over," so Berg can claim that deviant behavior, when elicited in response to noncritical stimuli, is apt to be accompanied by other manifestations of deviancy in everyday life. This is his "deviation hypothesis." Berg's chapter substantially documents the proposition that "response bias" is likely to occur in a wide variety of stimulus situations, and the research evidence in support of the "deviation hypothesis," collected by Berg and others, is voluminous. As Berg himself points out, however, the difficult conceptual and research task remains of establishing "operationally clean" criteria with which to discriminate deviant groups from each other. Perhaps the "noncritical" area measures themselves will aid in this work—as, for instance, Hathaway and McKinley found their "psychopathic deviate" key on the MMPI to be useful in helping to establish a clearer discrimination of the psychopathic personality syndrome.

Finally, David Wechsler, who is admittedly taking an enjoyable excursion out of his own area of inquiry, presents us with a thoughtful chapter on "nonconformity and the concept of being well born." Even today, as they have throughout history, self-interested groups of persons in every culture exploit the concept of being well born, making those whom such groups seek to exclude seem to be inferior. It is Wechsler's hope that such groups, if they have to exist, can use their influence "positively," as in the creation of useful social models for the regulation of societies.

It is difficult for me to present a concluding, integrative statement about the contents of the present book. The topic of conformity and deviation itself has proved to be a unifying theme because everybody has talked about it. Beyond a common allegiance to the problem of persons thinking and acting alike or dissimilarly in our society, however, the contributors have followed their own scholarly noses. Integrative trends are less visible than the important issues which emerge. For example, the ecological validity of the field situation is countered by the ability to control conditions in the laboratory; a Gestalt social theory, by a modified field theory and several brands of neobehaviorism; conformity as adherence to social norms, by conformity as blind obedience to another person's demands; and the content analysis of a reconstructed phenomenalism, by the structural analysis of directly measured behavorial events. A few of the chapter authors have attempted to reconcile otherwise contradictory events; e.g., we are invited to consider the isomorphism of perceptual and behavioral events as "acquired dispositions" and the formal reconciliation of field and laboratory conditions by means of set terminology. But most authors are content to be partisan. And why not? No doubt some reviewers will be annoyed that the book does not fit their preconceived notions about the scope of the problem, its investigation, and its resolution. Such parochialism, in the face of the idiosyncrasy exhibited here and the innovative outputs that accompany it, seems less than wise at this stage of our knowledge. In sum total, the present book offers diverse evidence that productive inquiry is being directed at a critical social problem.

Index of Names

Abelson, R. P., 116, 126, 130, 131
Adair, J., 321
Adams, H. E., 333, 354, 355, 360, 361, 364, 365, 370, 371
Adelson, J., 246
Adorno, T. W., 231, 246, 330, 427
Alessi, S. L., 333
Allport, F. H., 126, 149, 173
Altus, W. D., 333
Anderson, J. A., 333
Angermeier, W. F., 121, 124
Applezweig, M. H., 19, 43, 69, 117, 131
Archimedes, 344, 368
Arendt, H., 233
Arensberg, C. M., 294
Argyle, M., 45, 54, 128
Asch, S. E., 3, 4, 10, 12, 14, 20, 44, 54, 55, 57, 58, 67, 68, 69, 75, 77, 81, 83, 84, 87, 101, 108, 109, 110, 112, 113, 117, 121, 122, 123, 128, 133, 143, 171, 251, 252, 253, 362, 397, 405, 424, 425, 426
Ash, P., 291

Bachrach, A. J., 258, 427, 428
Back, K. W., 15, 73, 127
Bacon, M. K., 129
Bagby, J. W., 111
Baker, J. M., 44, 120, 125, 130
Ballard, K. B., 88
Barch, A. M., 11, 45
Barnes, E. H., 342, 344, 346, 349, 350, 351, 354, 356, 359, 360, 361, 366, 368, 370, 371
Baron, S. H., 21
Barron, F., 19, 20, 117, 120, 126, 131, 388
Barry, H., 121, 129
Bass, B. M., 38, 40, 41, 42, 44, 48, 56, 59, 60, 64, 69, 72, 73, 78, 329, 330, 424, 426

Bauer, R. W., 332
Behringer, R., 12
Bell, E. G., 131
Bellamy, R. Q., 11
Beloff, H., 19, 43, 44, 116, 130, 131
Benne, K. D., 70
Bennett, E. B., 21
Berenda, R. W., 10, 13, 18, 19, 84, 88
Berg, I. A., 328, 329, 332, 333, 334, 335, 338, 344, 347, 351, 353, 358, 360, 362, 364, 365, 369, 370, 371, 431, 432
Berkowitz, L., 11, 15, 80, 127
Berkowitz, M., 19, 88
Bernheim, H., 145
Bernreuter, R. G., 330
Bettleheim, B., 250
Binet, A., 146
Bird, C., 260
Blake, R. R., 1, 3, 4, 5, 9, 10, 11, 12, 13, 14, 15, 17, 18, 19, 20, 42, 43, 45, 47, 51, 53, 60, 61, 65, 87, 89, 112, 113, 114, 116, 117, 119, 121, 122, 128, 131, 132, 199, 202, 225, 424, 428, 429
Bloch, B. L., 13, 17, 59, 72, 85, 116, 119, 120
Boozer, D. G., 355, 356
Bovard, E. W., Jr., 15, 21
Bray, D. W., 14, 19
Brehm, J., 12, 16
Brodbeck, M., 51
Brown, D. R., 332
Brown, W., 108
Brunswik, E., 261, 427, 430
Bryant, H. A., 60
Bullock, D. H., 363
Burke, K., 430
Buros, O. K., 432
Burt, C., 333
Burtt, H. E., 18

Index of Subjects